THE LADIES' ROOM

Where 115 Famous Women Talk All About Men, Sex, Love
A Playbook for the Female Heart

Edited by Walter Oleksy

waltmax69@gmail.com
www.walteroleksybooks.com
His books are best ordered at CreateSpace eStore

Cover art

"Psyche Revived by Cupid's Kiss"
Antonio Canova (1757-1822)
Louvre Museum, Paris, France

Ladies, start your powder puffs.

Are you ready for love? Is love ready for you? Has love given you heartaches? Do you think you're through with love, or will never love again? How can you find true love? Answers to those and many more questions of the heart are inside *The Ladies' Room*.

While powdering their noses and refreshing their lipstick, 115 famous women – straight, bisexual, or lesbian -- movie, television, rock stars, authors, athletes, psychologists, politicians and others -- tell about the men in their life and men in general. Imagine them not all in the powder room together at the same time, but several at a time, revealing their most intimate feelings to each other about men and women, love, marriage, divorce, relationships, sex and sexual preference, careers and career mothers. Sometimes catty about other women, their wit, wisdom and advice constitute a women's playbook not only for survival, but happiness.

As author and journalist Carol Hymowitz recently wrote in the *Wall Street Journal*, "Ladies' Room banter is an endless source of wisdom and comfort. For many of us, it is a place to bond… You're often going to find your female allies in the john." And dishing the dirt about men, sex, and love lost and found not only can be therapeutic, but lots of fun, since both misery and joy love company.

The editor who assembled the information and quotations from his own library of books and magazines and from outside sources is a former *Chicago Tribune* reporter, feature writer, and author. Most men have forefathers; he had four fathers, which made him marriage-shy, so he remained a bachelor.

Read on, laugh, and maybe even weep in this kind of 2016 Kinsey Report on women, men, and sex in America. You, like the famous women in this book, are a survivor. Love is yours for the taking and for the holding. All the women in *The Ladies' Room* have one thing in common: they just want or wanted love. As Halle Berry says:

"The times may have changed, but people are still the same. We're still looking for love, and that will always be our struggle as human beings."

Men ask what do women do when they go to the Ladies' Room together? Christina Tran replied recently on the web site Psych2Go:

Everyone knows girls do more than the natural necessary in the restroom. We touch up our makeup, fix our hair and do what's necessary for us to leave better looking than we appeared when we entered it. ***The restroom is a very sacred place for a woman.***

Aside from doing the above, we're also talking about our dates and gossip. Regardless of how independent and secure a woman is, she'll always value an opinion of another girlfriend. We like to validate our hair, makeup and outfit decisions, and if necessary touch it up.

Women are well aware that guys theorize about secret bathroom meetings and question what secrets we're sharing in there. ***Women bathroom meetings are like a secret garden that men are forbidden to enter.***

What women say to each other in the Ladies' Room is a big mystery to men, and women like that. Mystery is often a part of loving and being loved.

Cameron Diaz says:

"Any of my guy friends, when I tell them what women really talk about, they just don't want to hear it. But maybe it's time."

As this book was being written, Pope Francis on April 7, 2016 urged Catholic Church priests around the world to be less judgmental and more accepting and tolerant of gay men and lesbians. "By thinking that everything is black and white, we sometimes close off the way of grace and growth."

He emphasized that "unjust discrimination" against gay men, lesbians, the divorced, and nontraditional families is "unacceptable" and downplayed the idea of "living in sin."

When asked about homosexuality, he said, "Who am I to judge?"

A sampling of what you will hear in *The Ladies' Room*:

"I married a German. Every night I dress up as Poland and he invades me."
-- **Bette Midler**

"Love is the hardest habit to break, and the most difficult to satisfy."
-- **Drew Barrymore**

"The best smell in the world is that man that you love."
-- **Jennifer Aniston**

"Husbands are like fires... they go out when they're left unattended."
-- **Cher**

"The only time a woman really succeeds in changing a man is when he is a baby."
-- **Natalie Wood**

"Sex is my favorite sport. I'm always in the mood."
-- **Cameron Diaz**

(On Brad Pitt): "We have both been married before so it's not marriage that necessarily kept some people together." *(But they have since married and are divorcing).*
-- **Angelina Jolie**

"You know it's love when all you want is that person to be happy, even if you're not part of their happiness."
-- **Julia Roberts**

"Marry Prince William? I'd love that. Who wouldn't want to be a princess?"
-- **Britney Spears**

"Being a princess isn't all it's cracked up to be."
-- **Princess Diana**

Women in
THE LADIES' ROOM

Julie Andrews, film and stage actress - 8
Jennifer Aniston, actress - 9
Francesca Annis, British film actress - 12
Jane Austen, British novelist - 13
Lauren Bacall, film and stage actress - 16
Lucille Ball, television and film actress - 18
Tallulah Bankhead, stage and film actress - 22
Brigitte Bardot, French film actress -26
Drew Barrymore, film actress - 29
Ingrid Bergman, film and stage actress -32
Halle Berry, film actress - 36
Juliette Binoche, French film actress - 40
Cate Blanchett, Australian film actress -42
Erma Bombeck, humorist, author - 44
Joyce Brothers, psychologist, author - 46
Sandra Bullock, film actress - 49
Carol Burnett, film, television, stage actress - 52
Barbara Bush, former U.S. First Lady - 55
Laura Bush, former U.S. First Lady - 57
Mariah Carey, singer -59
Coco Chanel, French fashion designer - 62
Cher, film and television actress - 65
Julia Child, television chef, author - 68
Hillary Rodham Clinton, politician - 70
Claudette Colbert, film and stage actress - 74
Joan Collins, film and television actress - 79
Joan Crawford, film actress, businesswoman - 81
Penelope Cruz, film actress - 86
Bette Davis, film actress - 89
Ellen DeGeneres, television personality - 95
Catherine Deneuve, French film actress - 99
Cameron Diaz, film actress - 101
Marlene Dietrich, film actress, singer - 106
Phyllis Diller, film and television actress - 110
Jane Fonda, film actress, author - 114
Zsa Zsa Gabor, film actress - 121
Lady Gaga, actress, singer -125

Greta Garbo, film actress - 127
Ava Gardner, film actress - 131
Judy Garland, actress, singer - 137
Janet Gaynor, actress - 140
Whoopi Goldberg, film actress - 143
Betty Grable, film actress - 145
Jean Harlow, film actress – 147
Rita Hayworth, film actress - 151
Anne Heche, film actress - 155
Audrey Hepburn, film actress - 157
Katharine Hepburn, film and stage actress - 163
Lena Horne, singer, film actress - 168
Whitney Houston, singer, film actress - 172
Caitlyn Jenner, athlete, actress – 176
Scarlett Johansson, actress - 179
Angelina Jolie, film actress - 182
Grace Kelly, film actress - 186
Nicole Kidman, Australian film actress - 190
Billie Jean King, tennis champion - 193
Beyonce Knowles, singer, actress - 196
Hedy Lamarr, film actress, inventor - 198
Ann Landers, gossip and lovelorn columnist - 204
Queen Latifah, actress - 208
Gypsy Rose Lee, film actress, author - 211
Vivien Leigh, British film and stage actress - 213
Lindsay Lohan, actress, singer, songwriter - 219
Gina Lollobrigida, Italian film actress - 221
Jennifer Lopez, film actress - 223
Sophia Loren, Italian film actress - 225
Clare Boothe Luce, author, playwright, diplomat - 229
Shirley MacLaine, film and television actress - 232
Madonna, film and television actress -235
Jayne Mansfield, film actress - 240
Bette Midler, film and television actress - 243
Marilyn Monroe, film actress - 245
Mary Tyler Moore, film and television actress - 256
Rita Moreno, film actress - 258
Lupita Nyong'o, film actress - 260
Michelle Obama, U.S. First Lady, teacher - 262
Merle Oberon, film actress - 265

Rosie O'Donnell, television host - 268
Bree Olson, actress - 270
Jackie Kennedy Onassis, former First Lady, editor - 272
Anna Paquin, film actress - 275
Dorothy Parker, author - 276
Dolly Parton, film and television actress - 279
Princess Diana, first wife of British Prince of Wales - 281
Queen Elizabeth II, British monarch -286
Ayn Rand, author - 289
Nancy Reagan, former First Lady, film actress - 292
Debbie Reynolds, film actress - 296
Joan Rivers, television comedienne - 298
Julia Roberts, film actress - 304
Jane Russell, film actress - 306
George Sand, French poet, author, playwright - 310
Susan Sarandon, film actress - 313
Ann Sheridan, film actress - 315
Britney Spears, singer - 318
Barbara Stanwyck, film actress -321
Gloria Steinem, women's rights activist - 327
Martha Stewart, entrepreneur, television host – 329
Meryl Streep, film actress - 331
Barbra Streisand, film actress, singer - 334
Elizabeth Taylor, film and television actress - 338
Shirley Temple, film actress, ambassador - 344
Mother Teresa, humanitarian, saint - 348
Gene Tierney, film actress - 350
Lily Tomlin, film and television actress - 355
Lana Turner, film actress - 357
Mae West, film and stage actress, writer - 363
Ruth Westheimer, sex advice personality - 369
Serena Williams, tennis champion - 371
Oprah Winfrey, film and television actress, author – 374
Kate Winslet, film actress - 377
Shelley Winters, film actress - 380
Reese Witherspoon, film actress - 384
Natalie Wood, film actress - 385
Catherine Zeta-Jones, film actress - 389

Julie Andrews

"Mary Poppins, practically perfect in every way." (Julie Andrews after measuring herself with a tape measure in "Mary Poppins" 1964).

"The hills are alive with the sound of music... With sounds they have sung for a thousand years... The hills fill my heart with the sound of music.,.. My heart wants to sing every song it hears." (Julie Andrews singing in "The Sound of Music" (1965).

"I'm your equal. I'm going to meet you men on your own terms, cater to your craving for efficiency, learn to talk sports, tell jokes, smoke, drink, and yes, if I have to, I'll kiss you back!" (To men in general, as a 1920s "Flapper" in "Thoroughly Modern Millie" (1967).

Julie Andrews contradicts her film image and dialogue by saying while in the ladies room:

"Singing has never been particularly easy for me."

"I don't want to be thought of as wholesome. I hate the word. Sometimes I'm so sweet even I can't stand it."

"Does Mary Poppins have an orgasm? Does she go to the bathroom? I assure you, she does."

Film, stage, and television actress and singer Julie Andrews was born Julia Elizabeth Wells October 1, 1935 in Walton-on-Thames Surrey, England. Her parents were vaudeville actors and she performed in music halls as a child and teenager. Her stage career began at the age of 20 in London and she rose to fame on the stage or films including "My Fair Lady" and "The Sound of Music," winning a Best Actress Academy Award for "Mary Poppins."

Andrews was married to stage producer Tony Walton in 1959 but they divorced in 1967 after having one child. She then was happily married to film producer Blake Edwards from 1969 until his death in 2010 and they had two children.

She filed a malpractice suit in 1999 against a New York City hospital and two doctors there, saying the destroyed her voice in a botched operation to remove non-cancerous throat nodules in 1997. She said, "Singing has been a cherished gift, and my inability to sing has been a devastating blow." She later regained her voice. She was named a Dame by Britain's Queen Elizabeth II in 1999.

On Love -- "All love shifts and changes. I don't know if you can be wholeheartedly in love all the time."

On Marriage -- "All careers go up and down like friendships, like marriages, like anything else, and you can't bat a thousand all the time." 10,

"Blake [*film producer husband Blake Edwards*] and I have this wonderful arrangement that while one is working hard, the other tries to be at home as much as possible and vice versa."

The Inner Woman – "I am a liberated woman. And I do believe if a woman does equal work she should be paid equal money. But personally I am feminine and I do like male authority to lean on."

"Perseverance is failing 19 times and succeeding the 20th."

[*On being a gay icon*] "I don't know. I'm sort of aware that I am. I've never been able to figure out what makes a gay icon, because there are many different kinds. I don't think I have the image that, say, Judy Garland has, or Bette Davis."

Jennifer Aniston

Jennifer's character in the movie "He's Just Not Into You" (2009) could have spoken for her when she asked her lover: ***"You don't ever feel like we're going against nature or something by not being married?... I just need you to stop being nice to me unless you're gonna marry me."***

Aniston confides in the ladies' room her true feelings on marriage:

"Marriage brings up all the things I pushed to the back burner... the fears, the mistrust, the insecurities. It's like opening Pandora's box."

"Just finding somebody that was your best friend, who you could be with and enjoy the passage of time... and that's what I found."

American movie and television actress, film director, and producer Jennifer Aniston was born Jennifer Joanna Aniston in Sherman Oaks, California on Feb.11, 1969. She and actor Brad Pitt were married in a lavish Malibu wedding on July 29, 2000. The marriage was considered a rare Hollywood success, but they divorced five years later. After her divorce, Aniston reportedly became romantically linked to actor Vince Vaughn, British model Paul Sculfor, and musician John Mayer. Aniston says she is dyslexic and also a control freak.

She began a relationship with actor Justin Theroux in 2011 and they bought a home in the Los Angeles Bel-Air neighbourhood for about $22 million. They secretly married at their Bel Air home in August 2015 with just a few of their friends present, including Ellen DeGeneres and Courtney Cox. Theroux said later, "Married life is fantastic. Something really does shift in a wonderful way and it refocuses things and in a weird way it was a long time coming."

On Love – "If we can say, I loved, and I received a lot of love, then great. That's enough."

"When somebody follows you 20 blocks to the pharmacy, where they watch you buy toilet paper, you know your life has changed."

"The most unconditional love that you can encounter is with a dog. They're excited the minute you come home, and they show the same amount of excitement everyday. They're loyal and they're always, always faithful."

"If you want to make me smile, show me puppy videos. Cute puppy videos!"

On Men – "The best smell in the world is that man that you love."

"I think a good relationship is about collaboration."

"I would say I couldn't be in a relationship without equality, generosity, integrity, spirit, kindness and humor. And awesomeness!"

On Marriage -- "Marriage brings up all the things I pushed to the back burner... the fears, the mistrust, the insecurities. It's like opening Pandora's box."

(On her marriage to Brad Pitt, which she does not regret): "(They were) Seven very intense years together. It was a beautiful, complicated relationship." (*Before their divorce*): "He's the sweetest goofball on the planet."

On Divorce -- "A man divorcing would never be accused of choosing career over children. That really pissed me off. I've never in my life said I don't want to have children. I did and I do and I will! The women who inspire me are the ones who have careers and children; why would I want to limit myself? I've always wanted to have children, and I would never give up that experience for a career. I want to have it all."

[On seeing pictures of Angelina Jolie and her ex-husband Brad Pitt together] "I will not let myself down like that -- I also know what feels good and it doesn't feel good to harbor anger and resentment ... We do have tools to work through stuff. Everybody does."

The Inner Woman -- "I've learned that you can get through things that hurt. Nothing will kill you. Nothing. People are unbelievable. We have such resilience."

"It's impossible to satisfy everyone, and I suggest we all stop trying."

"I always say, don't make plans, make options."

"I don't know what it means to be a sexual symbol. When I look at myself on a magazine cover I don't see it as me, but as someone painted, fluffed, puffed and done up."

Aniston and Theroux separated in September 2016 after five years of marriage.

Francesca Annis

"I don't need a piece of paper to suggest that I can commit myself." (British actress talking in the ladies' room about marriage.)

"I've never been married and I've no more desire to be married now than I ever have. I hate bureaucracy and I am not religious."

Born Francesca Annis in Brazil on May 14, 1944, her mother half Brazilian and French and her actor father French. She was educated in a Catholic convent and had considered becoming a nun, then at the age of 14 chose acting as a career. She has never married but was in a 22-year relationship with British photographer Patrick Wiseman, with whom she had three children. She left him to begin a relationship with British actor Ralph Fiennes, who was almost twenty years younger than she, which lasted eleven years.

On Love -- "You can love more than one person in your life, but things will be different. There'll be a different dynamic. Needs and desires change."

The Inner Woman -- "There is not enough celebration of companionship. Relationships aren't just about eroticism and sexuality."

"However successful you are, there is no substitute for a close relationship. We all need them."

"Truly charismatic people, in my experience, don't come along very often."

"I think you live a fuller life with someone else, you know, you're firing on all cylinders. It can be a nightmare at times, we all know that, but nevertheless in the end I think to have someone else's input on anything… a book, a meal, your children, life, a walk… is fantastic."

"After all my various relationships I find myself now home alone."

"The minute anyone's getting anxious I say, You must eat and you must sleep. They're the two vital elements for a healthy life. That will feed your nervous system and your psyche."

"I don't regret the passing of time. I try to live in the present, which should mean my life's full. I do think it's important to live in the present because in that way you won't be living in a state of regret."

"As you grow older, your whole life becomes very rich, multifaceted."

"Each decade, I've lived in that decade, so I could easily shed the twenties, the thirties, the forties."

"Thank God we're not like America. Everyone wants to look like they're twenty. In Europe we admire grown-up women. I think men revere older women."

"You have to be careful not to let your fear stop you doing things. It's very exciting to test yourself."

"The biggest privilege I've had in my life is being able to make a choice. If you make a choice, it can't be the wrong choice because it seemed like a good idea at the time."

(*On Life*): "It's like a fire. It goes through a journey, and each stage is interesting."

"The funny thing is I'm not bothered or sad about being on my own. After all, I've never had a husband."

Jane Austen

It is unlikely that Jane Austen visited many public ladies' rooms, but while living in Seventon, a small rural English village, she and her sister Cassandra had a private "dressing room" where they lived. It was next to their bedroom where she wrote early versions of her first novels in privacy. She could well have shared her thoughts there on men and other society with her sister, such as:

"The more I know of the world, the more I am convinced that I shall never see a man whom I can truly love."

"Happiness in marriage is entirely a matter of chance."

Jane Austen was born on December 16, 1775 in Stevenson, Hampshire, England, the seventh child born to an Anglican minister and his wife. Austen and her siblings wrote plays they performed and read from their father's extensive library. She never married. Most famous for her comic novels of love and romance among the landed gentry of England in the early 1800s *Pride and Prejudice*, *Sense and Sensibility*, and *Emma*, she died on July 28. 1817. Not widely read in her own time, her works became popular after 1869 and have become classics considered among the best of British literature.

On Marriage -- "Single women have a dreadful propensity for being poor. Which is one very strong argument in favor of matrimony."

"A lady's imagination is very rapid; it jumps from admiration to love, from love to matrimony in a moment."

On Men -- "It is a truth universally acknowledged, that a single man in possession of a good fortune, must be in want of a wife."

"Men have had every advantage of us in telling their own story. Education has been theirs in so much higher a degree; the pen has been in their hands. I will not allow books to prove anything."

"Every man is surrounded by a neighborhood of voluntary spies."

On Love -- "There is no charm equal to tenderness of heart."

"Friendship is certainly the finest balm for the pangs of disappointed love."

On Women -- "A woman, especially, if she has the misfortune of knowing anything, should conceal it as well as she can."

"There are certainly not so many men of large fortune in the world, as there are pretty women to deserve them."

"Woman is fine for her own satisfaction alone. No man will admire her the more, no woman will like her the better for it. Neatness and

fashion are enough for the former, and a something of shabbiness or impropriety will be most endearing to the latter."

"In nine cases out of ten, a woman had better show more affection than she feels."

"Give a girl an education and introduce her properly to the world, and ten to one but she has the means of settling well, without further expense to anybody."

"Good-humored, unaffected girls, will not do for a man who has been used to sensible women. They are two distinct orders of being."

"Where youth and diffidence are united, it requires uncommon steadiness of reason to resist the attraction of being called the most charming girl in the world."

"An engaged woman (*engaged in some pursuit*) is always more agreeable than a disengaged. She is satisfied with herself. Her cares are over, and she feels that she may exert all her powers of pleasing without suspicion. All is safe with a lady engaged; no harm can be done."

"A large income is the best recipe for happiness I ever heard of."

The Inner Woman -- "Vanity and pride are different things, though the words are often used synonymously. A person may be proud without being vain. Pride relates more to our opinion of ourselves; vanity, to what we would have others think of us."

"Selfishness must always be forgiven you know, because there is no hope of a cure."

"Life seems but a quick succession of busy nothings."

"Nobody minds having what is too good for them."

"Surprises are foolish things. The pleasure is not enhanced, and the inconvenience is often considerable."

"We have all a better guide in ourselves, if we would attend to it, than any other person can be."

"My sore throats are always worse than anyone else's."

Lauren Bacall

She had more than Humphrey Bogart in her love life, as she may have revealed in ladies' rooms because she had affairs at least after him and perhaps before, when she was a very alluring model.

Bacall and Bogart scorched the screen in "To Have and Have Not" (1945) when she delivered her famous line, *"You know, you don't have to act with me, Steve. You don't have to say anything, and you don't have to do anything. Not a thing. Oh, maybe just whistle. You know how to whistle, don't you, Steve. You just put your lips together and... blow."* Her sultry delivery of the line in a husky voice made movie history and she and Bogart then married a few months after the film was completed when she was 19 and he 44.

(After Bogie's death): *"A woman isn't complete without a man. But where do you find a man -- a real man -- these days?"*

"They're guys who want to screw around all the time, which interests me not at all. God knows we've done that, been there, and we don't want to do that any more."

"Men need to feel important. They feel better when they're with younger girls or unknown girls."

Lauren Bacall was born Betty Jane Perske on September 16, 1924 in The Bronx, New York to Jewish parents, her father working in sales and her mother a secretary, but they divorced when she was five years old. She never saw her birth father again but formed a close relationship with her mother. She was a model before becoming an actress and was tall, 5 feet 8 ½ inches.

She had two children with Bogart and they remained married until his death in 1957. She said they were always in love during their marriage and she was never jealous of another woman but was jealous of his love for his yacht, the Santana. Bogart said of their marriage, "Making love is the most fun you can have without laughing." It took two years, however, before she had her first child with him. Her doctor said the problem was she needed to relax. Their marriage was considered to be one of Hollywood's greatest romances. He also said of it, "It was too strong, but I liked the taste." Bogart loved the idea of becoming and father and they called their son Steve, after Bogart's name in "To Have and Have Not." They named their second son Leslie, after Bogart's mentor, British actor Leslie Howard. They had appeared together on Broadway in the play "The Petrified Forest" and Howard insisted to Warner Bros. that Bogart be signed to repeat his role of a gangster in the 1936 film which started Bogart on his way to stardom.

Bogart became ill with throat cancer and before he died in 1957 he and Bacall kissed and he said, "Goodbye, kid." John Huston who had directed Bogart in "The Maltese Falcon" (1941) gave the eulogy at Bogart's funeral, saying "Bogie was lucky at love and he was lucky at dice." After Bogart's death, Bacall was briefly engaged to Frank Sinatra and afterwards had an affair with Anthony Franciosa while he was married to Shelley Winters.

Bacall then married actor Jason Robards Jr. and had a child with him. Robards died in 2000. Bacall remained a film star in many movies, then retired. She was awarded an Honorary Academy Award for her lifetime work in films, and died of a stroke in her Manhattan apartment in 2014 at the age of 89.

On Men – "A man's illness is his private territory and, no matter how much he loves you and how close you are, you stay an outsider. You are healthy."

"I don't sit around thinking that I'd like to have another husband; only another man would make me think that way."

"Find me a man who's interesting enough to have dinner with, and I'll be happy."

On Marriage -- (*To Bogart*): " I fairly often thought how lucky I was. I knew everybody because I was married to Bogie, and that 24-year difference was the most fantastic thing to me to have in my life."

"Was he tough? In a word, no. Bogey was truly a gentle soul."

"Young people ask me, 'Were you really married to Humphrey Bogart?' I reply, 'Well, yes, I think I was.' You realize yourself when you start reflecting, because I don't live in the past, although your past is so much a part of what you are, that you can't ignore it. But I don't look at scrapbooks. I could show you some, but I'd have to climb ladders, and I can't climb."

"I never believed marriage was a lasting institution. I thought that to be married for five years was to be married forever."

"I put my career in second place throughout both my marriages and it suffered. I don't regret it. You make choices. If you want a good marriage, you must pay attention to that. If you want to be independent, go ahead. You can't have it all."

"Frank (*Sinatra*) did me a great favor. He saved me from the complete disaster our marriage would have been. But the truth is that he behaved like a complete s---."

"I would hate now (*2005*) to be married. It does occur to me on occasion that, if I fall and hit my head, there will be no one to make the phone call. But who wants to think about that disaster? I'd prefer not to."

On Divorce -- "In Hollywood, an equitable divorce settlement means each party getting fifty percent of publicity."

The Inner Woman -- "I was this flat-chested, big-footed, lanky thing."

"You can't start worrying about what's going to happen. You get spastic enough worrying about what's happening now."

"I am not a has-been. I am a will-be."

"Imagination is the highest kite that one can fly."

"I don't think being the only child of a single parent helped. I was always a little unsteady in my self-belief. Then there was the Jewish thing. I love being Jewish, I have no problem with it at all. But it did become like a scar, with all these people saying you don't look it."

"You learn to cope with whatever you have to cope with. I spent my childhood in New York, riding on subways and buses. And you know what you learn if you're a New Yorker? The world doesn't owe you a damn thing."

(*On filming her famous "whistle scene" with Bogart, in "To Have and Have Not," 1944*): "My hand was shaking, my head was shaking, the cigarette was shaking, I was mortified. The harder I tried to stop, the more I shook. I realized that one way to hold my trembling head still was to keep it down, chin low, almost to my chest, and eyes up at Bogart. It worked and turned out to be the beginning of 'The Look.'" (*The Look was sultry.*)

Lucille Ball

If she was a playgirl, which has never been known, she was a woman who wanted to be loved by and married to a man who was faithful to her. Desi Arnaz loved her, but was not faithful. She tells of their troubled love in the ladies' room:

"Desi was the great love of my life. I will miss him until the day I die. But I don't regret divorcing him. I have tried, so hard, to be fair and solve our problems. But now I find it impossible. I just couldn't take it anymore."

Television and movie actress and comedienne Lucille Ball was born Lucille Desiree Ball on August 6, 1911 in Jamestown, New York. Her father was a telephone company electrician who died before she was four and her mother worked several jobs so she and her younger brother were raised by their grandparents. She worked during high school at an ice cream store but kept forgetting to put bananas in banana splits, so she was fired.

In her twenties, she studied at a drama school in Manhattan but while her classmate Bette Davis got all the raves, Ball was sent home for being "too shy." She became a model at age 22 and then began appearing in films. While filming "Too Many Girls" in 1940 she met Desi Arnaz, a Cuban actor-musician, and they fell in love. They eloped and were married in November of that year. Besides movies, she starred on radio and television, most notably in "I Love Lucy" with Arnaz. Ball became the first woman to own her own television studio as the head of Desilu Productions.

Ball and Arnaz had two children together (Lucie Arnaz and Desi Arnaz Jr.),but personality differences led to their divorce in 1960. She was then married to television producer Gary Morton from 1961 until her death n April 26, 1989 at the age of 77.

Lucille Ball and Desi Arnaz met in 1940 when he was to start in a film version of his Broadway stage show "Too Many Girls." They fell in love almost immediately but as Arnaz later said, "We spent the better part of our courtship telling each other it would hurt our careers."

Lucy recalled: "I threw away all my conservativeness and took the plunge because I loved him. It was the most daring thing I ever did. Hollywood gave our marriage six months. I gave it six weeks!" The marriage was turbulent, but lasted 20 years, from 1940 to 1960. She had several miscarriages but gave birth to their first child after ten years of marriage. The birth was written into the script of their television show and millions watched the "birth" on their television sets.

Carol Channing, a close friend of Lucy and Desi, said, "Putting aside any and all personal problems they might have had, I would defy anyone to deny that they were one of the 20th century's greatest couples." A film is reportedly to be made of their love story with Cate Blanchett as Lucy.

Lucy took a back seat to Desi from the start. Another friend, actress Ruta Lee, said "If he wanted something, she would get it for him. If they were seated and he needed more room, she would slide over. I found it surprising because she was such a strong, independent lady, but when it came to Desi, she was very old-fashioned."

Long absences while he was touring with his band hurt their relationship and Lucy almost divorced him more than once over his infidelity. They remained close friends after the divorce and Channing said, "They spoke so lovingly of each other, you almost forgot they weren't together anymore."

On Love -- "You really have to love yourself, to get anything done in this world."

"It wasn't love at first sight (*with Desi Arnaz*). It took a full five minutes."

On Men -- "Once in his life, every man is entitled to fall madly in love with a gorgeous redhead."

On Divorce -- "I hate failure and that divorce was a Number One failure in my eyes. It was the worst period of my life. Neither Desi nor I have been the same since, physically or mentally."

"Desi is a loser. A gambler, an alcoholic, a skirt-chaser… a financially smart man but self-destructive. He's just a loser."

(*Arnaz on Lucy*): "Lucy isn't a redhead for no reason. She has a big comic talent, but she also has a big, not very funny temper. Not a temperament but a *temper*. Her tongue is a lethal weapon. She can be very cruel when she wants to be."

(*Phyllis Diller*): "Lucille Ball was a control freak. Had to be in charge of everything. Never saw a woman who took her comedy so seriously ."

The Inner Woman -- "In life, all good things come hard, but wisdom is the hardest to come by."

"If you want something done, ask a busy person to do it. The more things you do, the more you can do."

"One of the things I've learned the hard way was that it doesn't pay to get discouraged. Keeping busy and making optimism a way of life can restore your faith in yourself."

"The more things you do, the more you can do."

"I'm not funny. What I am is brave."

"I am a real ham. I love an audience. I work better with an audience. I am dead, in fact, without one."

"I think knowing what you cannot do is more important than knowing what you can."

"I'd rather regret the things I've done than regret the things I haven't done."

"Women's Lib? Oh, I'm afraid it doesn't interest me one bit. I've been so liberated it hurts."

"Not everything that is faced can be changed, but nothing can be changed until it is faced."

"Those so-called love goddesses like Rita Hayworth had beauty and class. They had an unattainable quality; there was a perfection and a mystique that's vanished today. With all these peroxide blondes, there's not only no class, they seem utterly attainable."

Tallulah Bankhead

She was a genuine enigma to most people, probably to herself as well. She had affairs with men but liked having them with women more. The ladies' rooms she told-all in would have to be air-conditioned even in January:

"I've tried several varieties of sex, all of which I hate. The conventional position makes me claustrophobic, the others give me a stiff neck and/or lockjaw."

"The main reason I accepted to be in 'The Devil and the Deep' (1932) *was to* (expletive) *that divine Gary Cooper!"*

"I'm as pure as the driven slush."

Born Tallulah Brockman Bankhead in Huntsville, Alabama on January 31, 1902, her father a leader in the Democratic Party who was Speaker of the U.S. House of Representatives from 1936 to 1940. Named after the Tallulah Falls in Alabama, she began a stage career at the age of 15, then moved to New York City to live with an aunt and look for work as an actress on Broadway.

She turned down a role in the silent film version of "Dr. Jekyll and Mr. Hyde" in 1920 because its star, John Barrymore, wanted her to audition for it on the casting couch. Her best film was Alfred Hitchcock's "Lifeboat" (1944), but, famous for not wearing underwear. the crew complained she showed her naked butt while climbing a ladder to get into the boat. When they objected to Hitchcock he said he did not know if it was a matter for wardrobe or hairdressing. Unlucky as a film star, she did some radio and television work including playing the Black Widow, one of the villainesses in the "Batman" series (1966).

She was known for her famous greeting, "Hello, Dahling!," and said she used it because she could never remember anyone's name. She was married only once, to supporting actor John Emery, from 1937 until their divorce in 1941. She is said to have been the inspiration for Cruella De Vil in Walt Disney's "101 Dalmatians" (1961). Regarding her lesbianism or bisexuality, she had a one-time affair with African-American actress Hattie McDaniel who won a best supporting actress award playing "Mammy" in "Gone With the Wind" (1939). Bankhead also spent several nights in bed with the great Ethel Barrymore.

Tallulah met Joan Crawford and Joan's then-husband Douglas Fairbanks Jr. on a train to California and told Joan, "Dahling, you're divine. I've had an affair with your husband. You'll be next." Crawford replied, "I'm sorry, Miss Bankhead, but I just love men." Tallu loved going to jazz clubs in Manhattan and Los Angeles and is said to have had a long-term relationship with the great African-American jazz and blues singer Billie Holiday. Bankhead died in Manhattan, New York on December 12, 1968 of double pneumonia, influenza, and emphysema at the age of 66; her last words on her deathbed were "Codeine... bourbon."

On Men – (*On seeing a former lover she had not seen in years*): "I thought I told you to wait in the car."

"I'll come and make love to you at five o'clock. If I'm late, start without me."

On Marriage – "No man worth his salt, no man of spirit and spine, no man for whom I could have any respect, could rejoice in the identification of being Tallulah's husband. It's tough enough to be bogged down to be a legend. It would be even tougher to marry one."

(*On John Emery, she was asked why she married him, and she said,* "Because I loved him" *Then asked why she divorced him, she said,* "Because I loved him.")

The Inner Woman – (*Patsy Kelly, comedienne-actress, on Bankhead*) "Tallulah had more girlfriends than Errol Flynn!... (actress) Estelle Winwood is not Tallulah's best friend. I am! And I've got the scars to prove it!... Tallulah never beat around the bush... she'd gossip about you in front of your back!"

(*When gossip columnist Earl Wilson asked if Bankhead had ever been mistaken for a man on the telephone because of her deep and husky voice, she replied*): "No, have you?"

"I read Shakespeare and the *Bible*, and I can shoot dice. That's what I call a liberal education."

(*On not remembering people's names*): "I once introduced a friend of mine as Martini. Her name was Olive."

"It's the good girls who keep diaries; the bad girls never have the time."

"My father warned me about men and booze, but he never mentioned a word about women and cocaine. Cocaine isn't habit-forming. I should know, I've been using it for years."

"I have three phobias which, could I mute them, would make my life as slick as a sonnet, but dull as dish water. I hate to go to bed, I hate to get up, and I hate to be alone."

"Nobody can be exactly like me. Even I have trouble doing it."

(*On Bette Davis*): "Don't think I don't know who's been spreading gossip about me. After all the nice things I've said about that hag. When I get hold of her I'll tear out every hair of her mustache!"

(*On sex researcher Alfred Kinsey when he asked for details about her sex life for his 1948 book The Kinsey Report*): "Of course, Dahling, if you'll tell me yours."

(*When told there was no toilet paper available at a party*): "Well, do you have two fives for a ten?"

"Television could perform a great service in mass education, but there is no indication its sponsors have anything like this on their minds."

"I've been absolutely hag-ridden with ambition. If I could wish to have anything in the world, it would be to be free of ambition."

"There is a rule I recommend. Never practice two vices at once."

"There is less in this than meets the eye."

"The only thing I regret about my past is the length of it. If I had to live my life again, I'd make the same mistakes, only sooner."

Brigitte Bardot

The famous movie "sex symbol" of the 1950s and 1960s was every bit as sexy and had many affairs off-screen, but ultimately traded love and romance for giving her heart not to two-footed animals but to those with four.

"Men are beasts, and even beasts don't behave as they do."

"I'm a girl from a good family who was very well brought up. One day I turned my back on it all and became a bohemian."

"When I love, I do it without counting. I give myself entirely. And each time, it is the grand love of my life."

Brigitte Bardot was born Brigitte Anne-Marie Bardot on September 28, 1934 in Paris and grew up in a middle-class Catholic home. She became a fashion model and then a film actress. She caused a sensation in the French film "…And God Created Woman" in 1956 and became an overnight film sex goddess, remaining a star for nearly the next twenty years.

She retired from films in 1973 when she was 37, to become an animal rights activist. She was married to French film director Roger Vadim from 1952 until their divorce in 1957; to Jacques Charrier from 1958 until their divorce in 1962; to Gunter Sachs from 1966 until their divorce in 1969; and to Bernard d'Ormale from 1992 to the present. She has one child.

"I started out as a lousy actress," she said in 2013, "and I have remained one." Her fans didn't care, they loved her during her career in which she made about 50 films. She said the secret of her success was lucky timing in two waves of social change in the 1950s – the rise of mass media in France, and the emergence of a feminist critique of the conventional roles of women.

While other actresses walked the red carpet in designer gowns, she appeared at film and other events barefoot with messy hair as though she'd just fallen out of bed, or in a bikini as if going to the beach. It was said that her "masculine" attitude towards her own sexuality, and her high-handed approach to her career, was at once subversive, and rooted in the sense of security that comes from a privileged background.

On Love -- "Do you have to have a reason for loving?"

"It is better to be unfaithful than faithful without wanting to be."

"No one has any security in loving me."

"I don't think when I make love."

"I have not always loved wisely, but I was young."

On Men -- "If only every man who sees my films did not get the impression he can make love to me, I would be a lot happier."

On Marriage -- "I am against marriage, and I don't give a fig for society."

"Have you ever heard of a good marriage growing in front of the cameras?"

"Vadim (*husband Roger Vadim, film director*) was both my teacher and my husband. I placed myself entirely in his hands."

(*Vadim on Bardot, 1960 while she was married to Jacques Charrier*): "Brigitte is a very confused girl. She doesn't know what she wants, except that she prefers whatever it is she doesn't have."

(*Her friends have added*): "Brigitte always has to be in love. Above all, she likes *falling* in love. She needs love as others need food and drink. With the other men in her life, she was the businesswoman. With Jacques, perhaps, she can be the little girl… loved and petted and coddled as she likes to be."

On Divorce -- "I leave before being left. I decide."

On Women -- "Women get more unhappy the more they try to liberate themselves."

"I was raised in that generation where it was all 'Women can have it all!', and I don't think you can. I think something falls off the table. The good thing is that the things that stay on the table become so much more important."

The Inner Woman -- "I know what sin is. They may call me a sinner, but I am at peace with myself."

"I was afraid of not living up to what people expected of me."

"If I upset some notions and went against established rules, that wasn't part of what I wanted to do. It wasn't my goal."

"I have been very happy, very rich, very beautiful, much adulated, very famous, and very unhappy. Fame has brought me so much unhappiness."

"I stopped making films to look after animals. No matter whether it's someone from the political left or right, we just have to stand up and defend animal rights."

"I gave my beauty and youth to me. I am going to give my wisdom and experience to animals. Animals have never betrayed me, They are an easy prey, as I have been throughout my career. So we feel the same. I love them."

"Only idiots refuse to change their minds."

"I have understood that the most important things are tenderness and kindness. I can't do without them."

"I regret nothing."

"I wanted to be myself. Only myself."

Drew Barrymore

Few if any actresses in Hollywood ever had a rougher, tougher girlhood, including affairs with men, alcohol, and drugs, but she grew out of it and became a happy housewife and mother. She does, however, have a lot to tell in the ladies' room about her earlier life:

"I come from a hippie mentality where I just think to know someone, you need to look into their eyes. Eyes are so important."

"Love is the hardest habit to break, and the most difficult to satisfy."

"Kissing, and I mean like, yummy, smacking kissing, is the most delicious, most beautiful, and passionate thing that two people can do, bar none. Better than sex, hands down. Kisses, even to the air, are beautiful."

Film actress and producer Drew Barrymore was born Drew Blyth Barrymore on February 22, 1975 in Culver City, California to actors John Drew Barrymore, and Ildiko Jaid Mako. He was the son of famous actors John Barrymore and Dolores Costello, while she was the daughter of Hungarian immigrants.

A daughter of the "Hippie" generation, her turbulent childhood included drug and alcohol abuse and two enrollments in rehabilitation, but she has successfully overcome those abuses. She has been in films since the age of six, and her adult film career began to skyrocket in the 1990s and she has become one of the most bankable leading ladies in films. She also has become a film director and producer as well as an author.

She was married to Jeremy Thomas from March 1994 to their divorce the following February; to Tom Green from July 2001 to their divorce in October 2002; and has been married to Will Kopelman from June 2012 to the present, with whom she has had two children. In a 2003 interview with Contact Music she said, "Do I like women sexually? Yeah, I do. Totally. I have always considered myself bisexual." She as spoken about many relationships she had with women in the past.

On Love -- "I love romance. I'm a sucker for it. I love it so much, it's pathetic."

"I want people to love me, but it's not going to hurt me if they don't."

"Life's too short. We have to love each other."

On Marriage -- "Sometimes I bust out and do things so permanent. Like tattoos and marriage."

The Inner Woman -- "Being a Barrymore didn't help me, other than giving me a great sense of pride and a strange spiritual sense that I felt okay about having a passion to act. It made sense because my whole family had done it and it helped rationalize it for me."

"Going through hell as a kid made me sensitive to what others in this world go through, too."

"The low points I had all helped make up my character, so I probably wouldn't want to do away with them because I like being flawed and I like having them help me grow and change and become better and stronger."

"It's my crusade to help women feel good about themselves."

"I think that being happy makes the biggest impact on your physical appearance. I swear to God, happiness is the best make-up."

"The best kind of parent you can be is to lead by example."

"I think happiness is a choice. If you feel yourself being happy and can settle in to the life choices you make, then it's great. It's really, really great."

"I'm a real stay-at-home mom. I'm really hands-on. Everything else became secondary."

"Whether you're throwing up or breaking up, you want your girlfriend right there! I don't trust women who don't go to their girlfriends."

"I am not someone who is ashamed of my past. I'm actually really proud. I know I made a lot of mistakes, but they, in turn, were my life lessons."

"Life is very interesting. In the end, some of your greatest pains become your greatest strengths… I never regret anything, because every little detail of your life is what made you into who you are in the end."

"I'm so in control of my life, you shouldn't dislike anything I do, because I'm not only in the best place I've ever been, but it keeps getting better and better… Everything I do, I do infinite percent."

"If you're going to be alive and on this planet, you have to, like, suck the marrow out of every day and get the most out of it."

"When things are perfect, that's what you need to worry most."

"I'm just learning who I am and how relationships work and how to make them function; no different from anyone else."

"I have always been fond of recognizing the spiritual side of someone's personality. It's a very lovely concept."

"It's only through listening that you learn, and I never want to stop learning."

"You've just got to do the best that you can."

Ingrid Bergman

Among the most scandalous love affairs in Hollywood, Ingrid Bergman's desertion of her husband and children to live with a married man in Italy ranks as perhaps the greatest. But she learned from it, never regretted it, and went back to being a beloved star with some steamy things to say:

"I've gone from saint to whore and back to saint again, all in one lifetime."

"Happiness is good health and a bad memory."

"Be yourself. The world worships the original."

Humphrey Bogart says to Bergman in "Casablanca": *"We'll always have Paris. We didn't have. We lost it until you came to Casablanca. We got it back last night."*

Film-goers like us always will have "Casablanca," ranked near or at the top of the most romantic films of all time, and we always will have Ingrid Bergman.

Ingrid Bergman was born on August 29, 1915 in Stockholm, Sweden, to a German mother and a Swedish father, an artist and photographer. Her mother died when Ingrid was two years old and her father when she was twelve, and she went to live with an elderly uncle. She trained for the stage but became one of the most beloved and famous film stars of Hollywood's Golden Age of the 1940s, winning three Academy Awards, two for Best Actress ("Gaslight," 1944, and "Anastasia" 1956), and one for Best Supporting Actress, "Murder on the Orient Express," 1974).

She was married three times: to Dr. Peter Lindstrom from 1937 until their divorce in 1950 and they had one child together; to Italian movie director Roberto Rossellini from 1950 until their divorce in 1957 and they had three children; and to Lars Schmidt in 1958 and until their divorce in 1978. Leaving Lindstrom to marry Rossellini caused worldwide scandal but about five years later she was welcomed back to the public's hearts and to the movies. She died August 29, 1982 of breast cancer; her ashes scattered at sea off the coast of Sweden.

On Love -- *(In a 1960 interview while married to Lars Schmidt):* "I could never enter into a frivolous relationship with a man. I am often shocked when I see women flirting outrageously and treating love as a capricious game. To me, love is a sacred feeling. It should not be regarded lightly. I like being married and I am not afraid of it, despite everything. A woman's life is empty without love."

(*On Cary Grant*): "I fell in love with Cary Grant... He did not reciprocate the emotion, and that disappointed me. Then I spoke with one of his ex-wives, who I prefer not to name, and she revealed that he is not prone to fall in love with, let us say, actresses. Cary and I became good friends. Not close friends, because he doesn't let you come too close. If we had gotten married, I doubt he would have let me get too close. It is better to have a crush on Cary Grant than to have him for a husband. A crush allows you to keep your fantasies."

Gary Cooper said that he and Bergman had an affair together while filming "For Whom the Bell Tolls" (1943), and that "Ingrid loved me more than any woman in my life loved me." Years later, she admitted it, but with qualification, saying "Every woman who knew him fell in love with Gary."

"A kiss is a lovely trick designed by nature to stop speech when words become superfluous."

"I have had my different husbands, my families. I am fond of them all and I visit them all. But deep inside me there is the feeling that I belong to show business."

On Marriage -- "Never again! I can see no reason for marriage, ever at all. I've had it. Three times is enough."

(*On her marriage to Roberto Rossellini, in a January 1960 interview*): "I don't regret one minute of it... (*But*) Roberto was so domineering, very Italian. Actresses hated him, but I knew he was brilliant. With time, I liked it less and less, and when he would bark an order at me (*while directing her in a film*), sometimes I would forget we were married and shout back, 'Who do you think you are, my husband?' Naturally, with time, we had to cease both associations; the magic was gone."

(*She was always silent about her marriage to Peter Lindstrom, but it became known that he ruled their home like a dictator and tried to alienate their daughter Pia against her. He kept them apart for six years, until he had remarried. Meeting her again, Ingrid said*: "It's the happiest day of my life!" (*It was the heaviest price she paid for leaving Lindstrom to marry Rossellini*, much *more than the damage it had done to her career and public image.*)

The Inner Woman -- "Success is getting what you want; happiness is wanting what you get."

"Because I also come from Sweden, I am constantly being compared to (*Greta*) Garbo., and there is no more unfair comparison than that!"

"Never marry a director. He'll want to direct you at home, too. It happened to me with Roberto Rossellini, and Paulette Goddard says the same of Charlie Chaplin."

"I've never sought success in order to get fame and money; it's the talent and the passion that counts in success."

"Getting old is like climbing a mountain; you get a little out of breath, but the view is much better."

"Until 45 I can play a woman in love. After 55 I can play grandmothers. But between those ten years, it is difficult for an actress."

"I don't worry about it because we are all growing old. If I were the only one I would worry. But we're all in the same boat, and all of my friends are coming with me. We all go toward old age. How many years left we don't know. We just have to accept it."

"Be yourself. The world worships the original."

"I have grown up alone. I've taken care of myself. I worked, earned money, and was independent at 18."

"People didn't expect me to have emotions like other women."

"I've gone from saint to whore and back to saint again, all in one lifetime."

"I don't think anyone has the right to intrude in your life, but they do. I would like people to separate the actress and the woman."

"I remember one day sitting at the pool and suddenly the tears were streaming down my cheeks. Why was I so unhappy? I had success. I had security. But it wasn't enough. I was exploding inside."

"Having a home, husband, and child ought to be enough for any woman's life. I mean, that's what we are meant for, isn't it? But still I think every day is a lost day. As if only half of me is alive. The other half is pressed down in a bag and suffocated. If you took acting away from me, I'd stop breathing."

"Hollywood was a terribly lonely place for me. I had wonderful associations with Humphrey Bogart, Gregory Peck, and all the others (*Cary Grant*) while I worked with them, but after they left the studios at night, they retired to their own circle of friends.

"I've made so many films which were more important, but the only one people ever want to talk about is that one with Bogart."

"I was the shyest human ever invented, but I had a lion inside me that wouldn't shut up!"

(*On having cancer*) "Time is shortening. But every day that I challenge this cancer and survive is a victory for me. Cancer victims who don't accept their fate, who don't learn to live with it, will only destroy what little time they have left."

"I have no regrets. I wouldn't have lived my life the way I did if I was going to worry about what people were going to say."

Halle Berry

Halle Berry reveals in the ladies' room that her life has been guided by being a romantic:

"The times may have changed, but people are still the same. We're still looking for love, and that will always be our struggle as human beings."

"I'm just going to live my life and be who I am. After all, everybody has secrets and there are some things that nobody knows about you but only you, right?"

"I'm not done with love, but I refuse to settle. I'm a hopeless romantic. And I won't stop till I get it right."

"Let me tell you something... being thought of as a beautiful woman has spared me nothing in life. No heartache, no trouble. Love has been difficult."

Halle Berry was born Maria Halle Berry on August 14, 1966 to Judith and Jerome Berry, in Cleveland, Ohio. Her white mother was then a psychiatric nurse and her black father a hospital attendant in the same ward where her mother worked. They named her after Halle's Department Store, a local landmark in the city of her birth.

Her parents divorced when she was four years old, and she and her older sister were reared by her mother. After high school she worked as a department store sales girl, then studied at Cuyahoga Community College. She won beauty contests and became a model, then moved to New York City in 1989 and while trying out for television roles she lived in a homeless shelter. She then moved to Los Angeles and found work on television, making her film debut in Spike Lee's "Jungle Fever" in 1991, then starred in the television miniseries "Queen." She won the Academy Award as Best Actress for "Monster's Ball" in 2001.

Berry married professional baseball player David Justice in 1993 and they had a daughter together but separated three years later and were

divorced in 1997. She reportedly was so depressed that she considered taking her own life. She married singer-songwriter Eric Benet in 2001 but they separated two years later and divorced in 2005.

She then married French Canadian model Gabriel Aubry in 2005 and had a daughter together but divorced in 2010. She met handsome French actor Olivier Martinez while filming "Dark Tide" in South Africa in 2010, they became engaged two years later, and married in France in 2013. They have a son, born later that year. They divorced in 2015.

Halle made news on March 29, 2016 when she appeared for the first time on Social Networking. She showed herself topless from the back on Twitter and Instagram, standing in a bamboo forest. She said, "I'm looking forward to sharing our world through images that reflect my emotions and perceptions. I hope the images will inspire, promote conversation, and bring you joy."

On Men -- "I once was stupid enough to say, in a previous relationship, 'I'm going to be with this person forever,' and realized, as I grew, that I don't know if forever is possible."

"The man for me is the cherry on the pie. But I'm the pie and my pie is good all by itself. Even if I don't have a cherry."

"I don't think I'm unlike a lot of people. I am just someone who is trying to find that mate, and I think it's a really hard thing to do."

"I wish all men were like dogs." (*Dogs give unconditional love.*)

"The worst thing a man can ever do is to kiss me on the first date."

On Marriage – "I guess you could say I have bad taste in men. But I no longer feel the need to be someone's wife."

(*Before marrying Martinez*) "I'll never get married again, and I always hate to say never to anything, but I will never marry again."

"I won't have a traditional marriage. I don't find the value in that anymore. But I am such a hopeless romantic and I really want love and I want a committed relationship, so I am going to reinvent marriage for myself."

"I know that I will never find my father in any other man who comes into my life, because it is a void in my life that can only be filled by him."

The Inner Woman -- "Beauty is essentially meaningless and it is always transitory."

"I don't think nudity *(in films)* is never necessary."

"I'm a hopeless romantic, and I won't stop until I get it right!"

"Being a mother is probably the most important thing in my life right now. Career is important, but nothing really supersedes my role as a mother."

"You think you know what love is, until you have a child and discover that unconditional mother love."

"The best mother is the mother who adapts, and the best children are the children who adapt as well."

"If you set out to do something and you give it your all and it doesn't work out, be willing to modify your goal slightly. Have the ability to look in another direction. A small shift could guide you to the real purposes of your life."

"Don't take yourself too seriously. Know when to laugh at yourself, and find a way to laugh at obstacles that inevitably present themselves."

"When I was a kid, my mother told me that if you could not be a good loser, then there's no way you could be a good winner."

"My whole life I've had the fear that I was going to be abandoned."

"I was black growing up in an all-white neighborhood, so I felt like I just didn't fit in. Like I wasn't as good as everybody else, or as smart, or whatever."

"I don't see a white woman. I see a black woman, even though my mother is white. Knowing that has made my life easier, I think."

"I want to be the next Spike Lee. I want to help other black folks to get into Hollywood and be successful in Hollywood."

"What is my real purpose here? I've looked at what I do. I make believe and make movies. I entertain people and get paid for it. Sometimes it seems like such a shallow existence. How insignificant in the scheme of life."

"Being biracial is sort of like being in a secret society. Most people I know of that mix have a real ability to be in a room with anyone, black or white."

"Blackness is a state of mind, and I identify with the black community. Mainly, because I realized, early on, when I walk into a room, people see a black woman, they don't see a white woman. So out of that reason alone, I identify more with the black community."

"My favorite actresses are Dorothy Dandridge, Jodie Foster, and Whoopi Goldberg."

"Throughout my career I have been talked out of things I wanted to do, and when I look back I think, I should have followed my instincts. I relied on others to guide me because I thought they knew better. But as I've gotten older, I've learned to trust myself... I think it's always best to be who you are."

Juliette Binoche

A modern woman, she is in love with a scuba diver and does not believe in marriage, and having children without a wedding ring on her finger is okay, as she tells in a ladies' room in Paris:

"Maybe it's because my mother divorced and my grandmother divorced, so maybe I'm frightened deep down. But then I also feel there is no real need. Why do I need to get married? To reassure me? No, I don't need reassurance."

"My only ambition is to be true every moment I am living… I want to know why I'm alive. I want to understand. It's like exploration; it's like someone being interested in a place and its history, digging into the earth and looking for it, searching. It's a passion… I live for the present, always. I accept this risk. I don't deny the past, but it's a page to turn."

French film and stage actress Juliette Binoche was born March 9, 1964 in Paris, her mother an actress and acting teacher, and her father an actor and director. Her parents separated when she was two years old and while they pursued their careers she and a sister were sent to a boarding school. She found purpose and direction in life by becoming an actress.

Binoche was 20 when photographer-director Jean-Luc Goddard saw her photograph as a model and thought she had potential as an actress. She said later, "He became my first boyfriend. He really took care of me when I had no place to live, no money, no nothing, and I was, you know, a cashier in a department store and doing my theater classes in the evening, because my parents couldn't help me financially."

Goddard took some photographs of her and then starred her in his 1985 film, "Hail Mary." Binoche won the Academy Award for best supporting actress in "The English Patient" (1996) and was so surprised, "When I got the Oscar, it was like a big joke to me. I just could laugh inside so much because life is – it never ends, you know? It's always surprising you."

She has never married but has been involved in several relationships, one of the longest with Leos Carax, a film director, and had a daughter by Benoit Magimel, also a film director, as well as a son with professional scuba diver Andre Halle.

On Men -- "Attraction is beyond our will or ideas sometimes."

"What makes a person sexy is when he's not trying to be sexy."

"If you told me tomorrow that I couldn't act anymore, it wouldn't bother me. I have only one wish: to meet the man of my life."

On Marriage -- (*She says she has remained unmarried because she has struggled to find the perfect match*): "You've got to search without searching, and that is what's so difficult."

The Inner Woman -- "I am not obsessed by looks. I think you can become a prisoner of your own image."

"Acting is a tough business, and you need to be in good shape mentally and physically... My ambition is to have beautiful encounters, not to make money."

"The thing is that I never felt beautiful. I really never did. I think I can change my looks and be different things, but I've never thought of myself as this face."

"I was so happy when they cast me in 'Chocolat,' because it's one of my vices."

"It's not a struggle to be on a diet. You feel lighter, and your spirit is lighter, too. But I love chocolate, and I allow myself to have chocolate. That doesn't go against a diet for me."

"You must understand, I don't have to be happy to be happy... I think it's the same simple thing for everyone... to be happy, and have love in your life."

(*On aging*) "It's a little different in Europe, because forty is really the best age for a woman. That's when we hit our peak and become this ripe fruit... Fighting the aging process just doesn't work. I think that actresses, ultimately, are responsible for the faces we give to women."

"Choosing to be in the theatre was a way to put my roots down somewhere with other people. It was a way to choose a new family."

"I love the unknown. I think because it brings fear, and to embrace fear is the best feeling... What I love most about this crazy life is the adventure of it."

Cate Blanchett

Blanchett also is a modern woman, but has a totally different view from Juliette Binoche on marriage and having children, so if they meet in the ladies' room, they might need a referee. However, she does say to enter into marriage with caution:

"I'm not sitting on a soapbox telling women what they should and shouldn't do, but I know what works for me."

"Marriage is a risk. I think it's a great and glorious risk, as long as you embark on the adventure in the same spirit."

Cate Blanchett was born Catherine Elise Blanchett on May 14, 1969 in Melbourne, Victoria, Australia, to an American father and an Australian mother. She has both an older brother and a younger sister. When she was ten years old, her father died of a sudden heart attack at the age of 40. Her mother never remarried and her grandmother lived with them to help.

After college she appeared in stage plays, and television roles. Her film debut was in "Paradise Road" in 1997. She won the Academy Award for Best Supporting Actress for her portrayal of Katharine Hepburn in the film "Aviator" and as Best Actress for "Blue Jasmine" (2013).

Blanchett married playwright and screen writer Andrew Upton in 1997, but they didn't like each other on first meeting on the set of a television show the year before. He thought she was aloof and she thought he was arrogant. They connected over a poker game at a party; three weeks later he proposed and they married. They gave birth to three sons and live in a harbor side suburb of Sydney. She is a strong advocate of women's rights and women in politics.

On Men -- "If you are with somebody, you go through so many roles… you're lovers, friends, enemies, colleagues, strangers; you're brother and sister. That's what intimacy is, if you're with your soul mate."

On Marriage -- "My husband keeps me really honest."

The Inner Woman -- "I've never looked upon myself as being a beauty, per se."

"If you know you are going to fail, then fail gloriously."

"I think it's always good to take on things that at first seem bigger than you. Then you just try and surmount them."

"An actress once advised me, 'Make sure you do your own laundry. It will keep you honest.'"

"I'm always without sleep. I've got two kids. I understand sleep deprivation on a profound level."

"Things present themselves to you, and it's how you choose to deal with them that reveals who you are. We all say a lot of things, don't we, about who we are and how we think. But in the end it's your actions, how you respond to circumstances that reveals your character."

"If I had my way, if I was lucky enough, if I could be on the brink my entire life, that great sense of expectation and excitement without the disappointment, that would be the perfect state."

"I'm not focused on what other people think of me."

"I think that's what I love about my life. There is no maniacal master plan. It's just unfolding before me."

"It's not the normal way to look at things, but I experienced death at a really young age and because of that it's been part of my mental landscape that death is really very possible."

"I don't understand a way to work other than bold-facedly running towards failure."

Erma Bombeck

There are lots of laughs when this lady is in the ladies' room and talks about men and marriage:

"Marriage has no guarantees. If that's what you're looking for, go live with a car battery."

"For years my wedding ring has done its job. It has led me not into temptation. It has reminded my husband numerous times at parties that it's time to go home. It has been a source of relief to a dinner companion. It has been a status symbol in the maternity ward."

"I haven't trusted polls since I read that 62 percent of women had affairs during their lunch hour. I've never met a woman in my life who would give up lunch for sex."

Born Erma Fiste on February 21, 1927 in Bellbrook, Ohio, her father, a crane operator, died when she was five years old. She and her mother moved into her grandmother's home in Dayton. She wrote humorous articles for her high school and college newspapers and worked as a termite control accountant.

In 1944 she married Bill Bombeck, whom she met at the University of Dayton. Doctors said she could not have a child, so they adopted a girl in 1953, but two years later she gave birth to a son. After a few years as a housewife and mother she began writing again and her weekly newspaper columns in the *Dayton Journal Herald* were published in a book in 1967 which led to her becoming a household word for her family-oriented humor. More books and television appearances followed until her death in 1996 at the age of 69 from kidney disease.

On Men -- "If a man watches three football games in a row, he should be declared legally dead."

"Thanksgiving dinners take eighteen hours to prepare. They are consumed in twelve minutes. Half-times take twelve minutes. This is not coincidence."

"What's with you men. Would hair stop growing on your chest if you asked directions somewhere?"

On Marriage -- "People shop for a bathing suit with more care than they do a husband or wife. The rules are the same. Look for something you'll feel comfortable wearing. Allow for room to grow."

The Inner Woman -- "It is not until you become a mother that your judgment slowly turns to compassion and understanding... Children make your life important."

"Do you know what you call those who use towels and never wash them, eat meals and never do the dishes, sit in rooms they never clean, and are entertained until they drop? If you have just answered 'A house guest,' you're wrong because I have just described my kids."

"Who in their infinite wisdom decreed that Little League uniforms be white? Certainly not a mother."

"One thing they never tell you about child raising is that for the rest of your life, at the drop of a hat, you are expected to know your child's name and how old he or she is."

"All of us have moments in our lives that test our courage. Taking children into a house with a white carpet is one of them."

"In general, my children refuse to eat anything that hasn't danced in television."

"My kids always perceived the bathroom as a place where you wait it out until all the groceries are unloaded from the car."

"I take a very practical view of raising children. I put a sign in each of their rooms: Checkout Time is 18 years."

"Never go to a doctor whose office plants have died."

"Never lend your car to anyone to whom you have given birth."

"Guilt: the gift that keeps on giving."

"If you can't make it better, you can laugh at it. When humor goes, there goes civilization. There is a thin line that separates laughter and pain, comedy and tragedy, humor and hurt."

"Some say our national pastime is baseball. Not me. It's gossip."

Joyce Brothers

Joyce Brothers is a psychologist but also talks about men and love with a sense of humor, as does Erma Bombeck. She also gets serious about it all:

"No matter how love-sick a woman is, she shouldn't take the first pill that comes along."

"Marriages, like careers, need constant nurturing."

"Love comes when manipulation stops; when you think more about the other person than about his or her reactions to you. When you dare to reveal yourself fully. When you dare to be vulnerable."

Born Joyce Diane Bauer on October 20, 1927 in Brooklyn, New York, her parents were both lawyers. She became famous in 1955 for winning the top prize on the American television quiz show "The $64,000 Question" answering questions on boxing. In the 1950s, she was the first to use television as a means of offering advice on mental health issues that had earlier been considered socially unacceptable, years before Dr. Phil, Dr. Ruth and Dr. Oz.

She was called "Doctor Joyce Brothers" because she held a doctorate degree in psychology from Columbia University. She also wrote books and a newspaper column, then a magazine column on popular psychology topics offering advice on subjects ranging from sex to divorce for *Good Housekeeping* for forty years. She was married to Milton Brothers from 1949 until his death in 1989 and they had one child together. She died at the age of 85 on May 13, 2013.

On Love -- "The best proof of love is trust."

"The topic of trust is an important factor in all matters of the heart, and here's why. Men lie to women. Women lie to men. And most people agree that some lying is even necessary, to avoid petty squabbles and to grease the wheels of a relationship."

"Virginity is such a personal thing. You can't judge anyone on it. A lot of young women feel they want to save themselves for the man who they think they'll love forever."

"The cynic finds love with the idealist. The rebel with the conformist. The social butterfly with the bookworm. They help each other balance their lives."

"If Shakespeare had to go on an author tour to promote *Romeo and Juliet*, he never would have written *Macbeth*."

On Men -- "Men are not conditioned to be less powerful than a woman. It will be the wise woman who realizes this and is sensitive to that issue."

"For men to be virgins, we think it's negative. We think that there's something wrong with them."

On Marriage -- "Marriage is not just spiritual communion, it is also remembering to take out the trash."

On Divorce -- "My husband and I have never considered divorce... murder sometimes, but never divorce."

The Inner Woman -- "Anger repressed can poison a relationship as surely as the cruelest words."

"When you look at your life, the greatest happiness are family happiness."

"No matter how much pressure you feel at work, if you could find ways to relax for at least five minutes every hour, you'd be more productive."

"A strong, positive self-image is the best possible preparation for success."

"Success is a state of mind. If you want success, start thinking of yourself as a success."

"I have found in work that you only get back what you put into it, but it does come back gift-wrapped."

"The person interested in success has to learn to view failure as a healthy, inevitable part of the process of getting to the top."

"I don't give advice. I can't tell anybody what to do. Instead I say this is what we know about this problem at this time. And here are the consequences of these actions."

"Being taken for granted can be a compliment. It means that you've become a comfortable, trusted element in another person's life."

"Credit buying is much like being drunk. The buzz happens immediately and gives you a lift. The hangover comes the day after."
"Trust your hunches. They're usually based on facts filed away just below the conscious level."

"Never try to negotiate with anyone after he or she has eaten. People are best persuaded on an empty stomach. And forget 'power breakfasts.' There is no convincing anyone of anything before 10 a.m."

"Listening, not imitation, may be the sincerest form of flattery."

"Accept that all of us can be hurt, that all of us can and surely will at times fail. Other vulnerabilities, like being embarrassed or risking love, can be terrifying, too. I think we should follow a simple rule: If we can take the worst, take the risk."

"Real intimacy depends on truth… lovingly told… especially in the bedroom."

"The world at large does not judge us by who we are and what we know; it judges us by what we have."

"I've enjoyed the pleasures of working since I was twelve and earned my own spending money since I was fourteen."

"There's a very positive relationship between people's ability to accomplish any task and the time they're willing to spend on it."

"The secret of having it all is loving it all."

Sandra Bullock

A pragmatist about love and marriage, she was cautious about marrying, but once she really fell in love, she wanted to be married and would work to make it work:

"Relationships that start under intense circumstances, they never last." (Bullock's character says in "Speed" (2015), and she says of herself):
"I've always been skeptical about marriage, because I only want to do it once; I want to do it the right way."

Born Sandra Annette Bullock on July 26, 1964 in Arlington, Virginia, she grew up on the road with her parents and her younger sister, their mother a German opera singer and father an American voice teacher. She often performed in the children's chorus of productions her mother was in. A stage career led to television and then movies.

She has become one of the most popular and bankable film stars and won a Supporting Actress Academy Award for "The Blind Side" in 2009. In 2013 the Guinness Book of World Records listed her as the highest-paid actress in the world, with an income of $56,000,000. She was married to actor-producer Jesse James from 2005 to their divorce in 2010. She left him after discovering he had been unfaithful to her.

Bullock says she hates "selfies" because "the image they project just isn't reality. "We're not representing ourselves truthfully. Like when you're yelling at your child, you're not taking a selfie of you being a horrible parent. No, you're waiting for the perfect selfie. 'Do I look thinner now?' 'Do I look great?' It's this false projection of one's life. Hollywood has now gone global. Everyone's Hollywood now.
I think it's frightening for kids and young people developing who they are to have that false sense of acceptance based on an image. How do you unravel that when it's being pushed so hard?"

She has given birth to a son and adopted a daughter. She does love taking home movies and said her son, when was recently six, said he thought he should get an acting award for his starring role in a home movie.

On Men --"The sexiest man alive? My husband (*before she divorced Jesse James*) and then, Keanu!" (*Reeves*).

On Marriage -- (*Before her marriage*): "The only reason I haven't married yet, is because I take it too seriously."

The Inner Woman – *(Before becoming an actress, she was a bartender):* "I learned a lot of accents as a bartender. A lot of girls came in looking for rich husbands. I learned to imitate them."

"I have no desire to maintain a lifestyle. I am a horrible celebrity. If I am out in public, I dress like a pig."

"I've learned that success comes in a very prickly package. Whether you choose to accept it or not is up to you. It's what you choose to do with it, the people you choose to surround yourself with. Always choose people that are better than you. Always choose people that challenge you and are smarter than you. Always be the student. Once you find yourself to be the teacher, you've lost it."

"My goal now is to remember every place I've been, only do things I love and not say yes when I don't mean it."

"Movie sex scenes are never romantic, and you're never swept off your feet. It's always very technical. I'm counting the beats: Okay, we're supposed to kiss for two beats, then I say my line, then they want another kiss for four beats. I'm going, One Mississippi, two Mississippi, three and break. It's like choreography. Sometimes, you have actors who feel it's their job to get as far down into your throat as possible. You're like, 'Excuse me, I like you, but not that much.'"

(*About films with love interest*): "Why do you need one? I don't understand why there needs to be a love interest to make women go see a film. I think society sort of makes us feel that way... that if you don't have a guy, you're worthless."

"Whoever established the high road, and how high it was going to be, should be fired."

"I'd rather take risks than make something that's cookie cutter."

"I don't like to talk about personal things. And by keeping it private, you have a better shot at a healthy relationship. I learned at a young age that there are certain things you just don't talk about."

"I used to be an optimist, but now I know that nothing is going to turn out as I expect."

Carol Burnett

Twice divorced, Carol is happy in her third marriage and shares her happiness openly in the ladies' room, always the optimist:

"You have to have faith that there is a reason you go through certain things. I can't say I'm glad to go through pain, but in a way one must, in order to gain courage and really feel joy."

Born Carol Creighton Burnett on April 26, 1933 in San Antonio, Texas, to alcoholic parents. While she was a preteen, her parents divorced and left her to be reared by her maternal grandmother who moved with her to Hollywood and they lived together in a one-room apartment. Her grandmother was both a Christian Scientist and a hypochondriac. Carol studied drama at UCLA which eventually led to her breakthrough on Broadway in 1959 starring in "Once Upon a Mattress."

She then appeared for three years on "The Garry Moore Show" on television which led to her starring in her own show," The Carol Burnett Show" on CBS television from 1967 to 1978 and becoming one of the most popular comediennes on television and in the movies.

Carol grew up watching movies in the 1940s and audiences love her parodies of Joan Crawford in "Mildred Pierce," Lana Turner in "The Postman Always Rings Twice," and especially Vivien Leigh as Scarlett O'Hara coming down a long stairway wearing a green gown she had made from velvet curtain drapes, the wide curtain rod sill on them and her shoulders. Rita Hayworth got such a kick out of Carole's satire of her as "Gilda," she sent a telegram asking if she could come on the show, and she did. Carol always believed in a strong supporting cast, and she had it on her show – Harvey Korman, Tim Conway, Vicki Lawrence, and Lyle Waggoner.

Carol was married three times, her first two husbands being Don Saroyan (1955-1962), and television producer Joe Hamilton (1863-1984). She and Hamilton were in an affair while both were married and he had had eight children with his wife, so he was a producer in more ways than one. She divorced him because he was an alcoholic and difficult to live with.

She has been happily married since 2001 to musician Brian Miller who is 23 years younger than she. She won an Emmy, Golden Globe and People's Choice awards and, among many others, the Screen Actors Guild award for lifetime achievement in 2016.

The Inner Woman -- "My childhood was rough, we were poor and my parents were alcoholics, but nobody was mean. I knew I was loved. We were on welfare, but I never felt abandoned or unloved."

"Adolescence is just one big walking pimple."

"Originally, I came from Texas, and we lived on… I guess you'd call it welfare, what we called relief." (*Federal government deliveries of basic food each month… oatmeal, potatoes, prunes.*)

"On the good days, my mother would haul out the ukulele and we'd sit around the kitchen table, a cardboard table with a linoleum top, and sing."

(*Moving to* California *as a child*)**:** "My grandmother and I followed my mother here, to a house a block north of Hollywood Boulevard, but a million miles away from Hollywood, if you know what I mean. We would hang out behind the ropes and look at the movie stars arriving at the premieres."

"My grandmother and I saw an average of eight movies a week, double features, second run."

"My grandmother and I would go see movies, and we'd come back to the apartment, we had a one-room apartment in Hollywood, and I would kind of lock myself in this little dressing room area with a cracked mirror on the door and act out what I had just seen."

"Nobody goes through life without a scar."

"You have to go through the falling down in order to learn to walk. It helps to know that you can survive. That's an education in itself."

"When you have a dream, you've got to grab it and never let it go."

"Only I can change my life. No one can do it for me."

"Everybody I know who is funny, it's in them. You can teach timing, or some people are able to tell a joke, though I don't like to tell jokes. But I think you have to be born with a sense of humor and a sense of timing."

"I love writing. I love the idea of typing and seeing it on the computer and printing it out myself and, you know, moving sentences around. I like that."

"I think the hardest thing to do in the world, show-business-wise, is write comedy."

"Comedy is tragedy, plus time."

(*On helping others*): "It's also selfish because it makes you feel good when you help others. I've been helped by acts of kindness from strangers. That's why we're here, after all, to help others."

"I don't begrudge anybody, because I know how hard it is to have that dream and to make it happen, whether or not it's just to put a roof over your head and food on the table."

"I'm really not that funny in real life! But I am the best audience one could find. I love to laugh."

"Celebrity was a long time in coming; it will go away. Everything goes away."

"I do the *New York Times'* crossword puzzle every morning to keep the old grey matter ticking."

"I was kind of shy as a kid. I was a pretty good student. I was a wallflower, or nerd, if you will."

"I have a good loud voice and I wasn't afraid to be goofy or zany."

"I was once asked to do my Tarzan yell at Bergdorf Goodman, and a guard burst in with a gun! Now I only do it under controlled circumstances."

"It's almost impossible to be funnier than the people in Washington."

"I'm not always optimistic. You wouldn't have all cylinders cooking if you were always like Mary Poppins."

Barbara Bush

She doesn't talk much in the ladies' room, but when she does, it's a doozy:

"I married the first man I ever kissed. When I tell this to my children, they just about throw up."

Born Barbara Pierce on June 8, 1925 in New York City, she became the wife of George H. W. Bush, the 41st President of the United States, and also the mother of George W. Bush, the 43rd President of the United States, and of Jeb Bush, the 43rd governor of Florida.

She was 16 when she met her future husband at a Christmas holiday dance and they were married in 1945 while he was a Naval torpedo bomber pilot in World War II. They moved to Midland, Texas, where her husband entered political life and they had six children together.

She and the former President now live in Houston. As First Lady, she has supported universal literacy. She also has stated that abortion and homosexuality are personal matters and the Republican Party platform should not take stands on them. "I hate abortions," she has said, "but I just could not make that choice for someone else."

On Family, Friends -- "To us, family means putting your arms around each other and being there."

"I think togetherness is a very important ingredient to family life."

"At the end of your life, you will never regret not having passed one more test, not winning one more verdict or not closing one more deal. You will regret time not spent with a husband, a friend, a child, or a parent."

"Cherish your human connections; your relationships with friends and family."

"Family and friends and faith are the most important things in your life and you should be building friendships."

"I'm worried about parents who aren't parenting."

"You have to love your children unselfishly. That's hard. But it's the only way."

"Raising five boys is a handful, trust me."

"You may think the President is all-powerful, but he is not. He needs a lot of guidance from the Lord."

"When you come to a roadblock, take a detour."

"Value your friendship. Value your relationships."

"Never lose sight of the fact that the most important yardstick of your success will be how you treat other people... your family, friends, and co-workers, and even strangers you meet along the way."

"If human beings are perceived as potentials rather than problems, as possessing strengths instead of weaknesses, as unlimited rather than dull and unresponsive, then they thrive and grow to their capabilities."

"Bias has to be taught. If you hear your parents downgrading women or people of different backgrounds, why, you are going to do that."

"You just don't luck into things as much as you'd like to think you do. You build step by step, whether it's friendships or opportunities."

"I'm not a competitive person, and I think women like me because they don't think I'm competitive, just nice… Nancy Reagan was a perfectionist, and I am not."

"I hate the fact that people think 'compromise' is a dirty word."

"My worst expectations never happened."

"Everything I worry about would be better if more people could read, write, and comprehend."

"I do have the most marvelous husband, children, and grandchildren."

"I really built myself up, darn it, to be very strong."

Laura Bush

She talks mainstream about gay marriage and abortion:

(*On same-sex marriage, she views it as a "generational issue"*): **"When couples are committed to each other and love each other, they ought to have the same sort of rights that everyone has."**

(*On abortion, she supports the Roe v. Wade decision*): **"I think it's important that** (abortion) **remain legal. Because I think it's important for people, that for medical reasons and, and other reasons."**

Born Laura Lane Welch on November 4, 1946, in Midland, Texas, she is the wife of George W. (Walker) Bush, the 43rd President of the United States. She was graduated from Southern Methodist University in 1968 with a bachelor's degree in education and became a second grade teacher. After attaining a master's degree in library science art the University of Texas she became a librarian.

She met her future husband at friends' barbecue in 1977 and they were married later that year. They had twin daughters in 1981. She became First Lady when Bush won the 2000 Presidential election and has become a strong advocate of education and reading for children of the world. "I worked as a teacher and librarian," she has said. "and I learned how important reading is in school and in life." Her other campaigns have been those relating to the health and well-being of women.

The Inner Woman -- *(When she was First Lady):* "We always get up about 5:30, and George gets up and goes in and gets the coffee and brings it to me, and that's been our ritual since we got married. And we read the newspapers in bed and drink coffee for about an hour probably."

"Maybe it is the media that has us divided. I think there are a lot of reasons to be critical of the media in America."

"We can overcome evil with greater good."

"I also know that there are a lot of people around the United States who want my husband to win *(a second term as President),* and who are for him and who support our troops in Iraq and Afghanistan. And I feel good about those people, too."

"I have the privilege of traveling around our country and meeting people all over the country who are making a huge difference in the lives of their neighbors and themselves. That's what I'm really fortunate to be able to do."

"I'm not the one who was elected. I would never do anything to undermine my husband's point of view."

"I don't really feel like I have to have a debate with my husband over issues."

"I like politics. I like traveling in the United States."

"Politics is a people business. I like people."

"It's not easy to have the job of President. It's not easy to run for it. And it's not a job for the feint of heart."

"Any First Lady can do whatever they want to do. In this country, people expect them to work on whatever they want or to have a career of their own."

"If I'm in the White House, I have meetings in my office, I sign letters, I plan different things. Late in the afternoon, I'll quit working and wait for my husband to get home."

"No one likes to be criticized. The part no one likes is the criticisms, and the unfair criticisms, of my husband. But that's also just a fact of life in politics."

"We've faced very difficult decisions and challenges in our country, every one of us have, as we, since September 11th, *(the 2001 terrorist attacks in New York and Washington)* as we fought the war on terror, all of those decisions that the President had to make to put young men and women in harm's way."

Mariah Carey

In the ladies' room she is a cautious optimist about love and marriage:

"There is a light at the end of the tunnel... hopefully it's not a freight train!"

Mariah Carey, an American singer, songwriter, record producer, and actress, was born March 27, 1969 in Huntington, New York. Her aeronautical engineer father was of African-American and Venezuelan descent, and her opera singer and vocal coach mother of White Irish descent.

Her parents divorced when she was three years old and she and a brother then lived with her father while her sister lived with her mother. She felt it difficult to grow up as a girl of mixed color. She began writing songs while in high school and worked as a waitress in restaurants. Her singing career began after releasing an album in 1990 which led to her becoming one of the top female popular vocalists.

Fame and fortune came at a price since after her film "Glitter" was released in 2001 she suffered a physical and emotional breakdown and was hospitalized for severe exhaustion. She since recovered to regain her status as a leading pop singer, having throughout her career sold more than 200 million records worldwide.

She is a philanthropist involved in the Fresh Air Fund and a camp that enables inner-city boys and girls to practice the arts and get career opportunities. She was married to record company executive Tommy Mottola from 1993 to 1998 and to singer and actor Nick Cannon from 2008 to their separation in 2014, and has two children.

On Love -- "My heart has never been broken; I've never broken anyone else's."

"You really just want to know that somebody loves you for you. Sometimes you feel like an ATM machine with a wig on it."

The Inner Woman -- "Pregnancy was probably the best and the hardest thing I'll ever go through. I know for a lot of women, it can be wonderful and relatively easy."

"I am very insecure about my looks, and I always have been because of being mixed race.

"My mother is Irish, my father is black and Venezuelan, and me... I'm tan, I guess."

"This is for all of you out there tonight, reaching for a dream... Don't ever give up! Whatever you're going through in your life, don't ever give up."

"Never ever listen to anyone, when they try to discourage you, because they do that, believe me!"

"I always felt like the rug could be pulled out from under me at anytime. And coming from a racially mixed background, I always felt like I didn't really fit in anywhere."

"You really have to look inside yourself and find your own inner strength, and say, 'I'm proud of what I am and who I am, and I'm just going to be myself."

"Butterflies are always following me, everywhere I go."

"If you see me as just the princess then you misunderstand who I am and what I have been through.'"

"I'm not one of those people that goes into details of my personal life on national television to get attention. Some things are better left unsaid."

"I've seen the real extreme diva behavior, and I don't think that's who I am."

"I don't think anyone knows as much about what's right for me as I do."

"In this world, I call the shots and I think I know best."

"If critics have problems with my personal life, it's their problem. Anybody with half a brain would realize that it's the charts that count."

"I'm not vain. I'm insecure."

"I try not to be a jerk. I really do. I try to be nice and cordial."

"Basically, I started singing when I started talking. Music has just been my saving grace my whole life."

"I really rebel against authority."

"It's hard to be someone that people talk about and write about, you know? They don't know me."

Coco Chanel

Ladies get a lot of good advice from her, not only on fashion:

"Great loves too must be endured."

"Men are always seeking from women a little pillow to put their heads down on. They are always longing for the mother who held them as infants."

"As long as you know men are like children, you know everything!"

French fashion designer Coco Chanel was born Gabrielle Bonheur Chanel on August 19, 1883 in Saumur, France, to a peddler and his wife. After her parents died when she was young, she was reared in a Catholic convent where nuns taught her how to sew. During a brief career as a nightclub singer, she acquired the name "Coco" which was short for the French word "coquette" or kept woman. She opened a hat shop in Paris in 1910 and soon afterward added stores where the wealthy vacationed in Deauville and Biarritz.

In the 1920s she introduced her first perfume and the "Chanel ladies suit" and little black dress intended to make clothes more comfortable for women. The suit was a collarless jacket and well-fitted skirt, patterned after men's suits which freed women from corsets and other confining undergarments.

Her fashion designs made her world-famous and wealthy and remain popular today among best-dressed women. She never married but had relationships with several men including classical composer Igor Stravinsky and the British Duke of Westminster. She met him aboard his yacht in 1923 but turned down his marriage proposal saying, "There have been several Duchesses of Westminster, but there is only one Chanel!"

During the Nazi occupation of France in World War II, she shut down her shops and became involved with a German Army officer, Hans Gunther von Dincklage who shared her apartment in the Hotel

Ritz in Paris, which created scandal, but she was never charged as a Nazi collaborator. The scandal resulted in her self-exile in Switzerland. She made a triumphant return to the fashion world at the age of 70 with her feminine yet comfortable designs that appealed to modern women around the world.

Her fashion legacy lives on, partly due to a 1969 Broadway musical, "Coco," starring Katharine Hepburn, and "Coco Chanel," a 2008 television movie of her life starring Shirley MacLaine. Chanel died on January 10, 1972 in her apartment in the Hotel Ritz in Paris.

On Love – "There is no time for cut-and-dried monotony. There is time for work. And time for love. That leaves no other time!"

"Jump out the window if you are the object of passion. Flee it if you feel it. Passion goes, boredom remains."

"I never wanted to weigh more heavily on a man than a bird."

"As soon as you set foot on a yacht you belong to some man, not to yourself, and you die of boredom."

"Women must tell men always that they are the strong ones. In truth, women have always been the strong ones of the world."

"I don't know why women want any of the things men have when one of the things that women have is men."

The Inner Woman -- "A girl should be two things: classy and fabulous."

"Luxury must be comfortable, otherwise it is not luxury."

"Fashion fades, only style remains the same... Fashion is not something that exists in dresses only. Fashion is in the sky, in the street, fashion has to do with ideas, the way we live, what is happening…Fashion is architecture; it is a matter of proportions."

"Fashion is always of the time in which you live. It is not something standing alone. But the grand problem, the most important problem, is to rejuvenate women. To make women look young. Then their outlook changes. They feel more joyous."

"Perfume is the unseen, unforgettable, ultimate accessory of fashion… that heralds your arrival and prolongs your departure… A woman who doesn't wear perfume has no future."

"It is always better to be slightly underdressed."

"Elegance does not consist in putting on a new dress. Look for the woman in the dress. If there is no woman, there is no dress."

"Success is often achieved by those who don't know that failure is inevitable."

"Nature gives you the face you have at twenty; it is up to you to merit the face you have at fifty… A woman has the age she deserves."

"I am not young, but I feel young. The day I feel old, I will go to bed and stay there. *J'aime la vie*! I feel that to live is a wonderful thing."

"In order to be irreplaceable one must always be different."

"Don't spend time beating on a wall, hoping to transform it into a door."

"There are people who have money and people who are rich."

"Guilt is perhaps the most painful companion of death."

"The most courageous act is still to think for yourself. Aloud."

"Since everything is in our heads, we had better not lose them… How many cares one loses when one decides not to be something but to be someone."

Cher

She and her great love parted and divorced, so she jokes about men:

"Men aren't necessities. They're luxuries."

"The trouble with some women is that they get all excited about nothing, and then marry him."

"A girl can wait for the right man to come along, but in the meantime that still doesn't mean she can't have a wonderful time with all the wrong ones."

"Men should be like Kleenex; soft, strong, and disposable."

Born Cherilyn Sarkisian in El Centro, California, on May 20, 1946, she is a film and television actress and singer nicknamed the "Goddess of Pop." Her father was an Armenian-American truck driver with drug and gambling addictions, and her mother was a model and actress of Irish, English, German, French, Dutch, and Cherokee ancestry. Her parents divorced when she was ten months old, but remarried and divorced twice more, for a total of eight marriages and divorces.

Cher worked as a waitress while attempting an acting career on television. She recalls being so poor she used rubber bands to hold her shoes together and had been put in an orphanage for a short time. She dropped out of high school at age 16 and left home to live with a friend in Los Angeles where she took acting lessons and danced in small night clubs.

She met singer Sonny Bono in 1962 and they began performing and singing together. Her fame began in 1965 with recordings with Bono, by then her husband, as "Sonny and Cher." A hit television series followed in which she became known for her outlandish and often sexy costumes,. She and Bono had a daughter together, called Chastity, but their marriage ended in 1975. He died in a skiing accident in 1998.

After her divorce from Bono she began to appear as a solo singer and actress on television and in films. She married Gregg Allman in 1975 and they had a son together, but divorced in 1979. Chastity came out as a lesbian when she was 17, and Cher supported her decision. In 2009 Chaz came out as a transgender individual and his transition from female to male was legalized the following year.

Cher won the Academy Award as Best Actress in 1988 for "Moonstruck." She has six tattoos including one on her buttock. She is a philanthropist in supporting causes including health research, care of AIDS patients, anti-poverty, veterans rights, aiding vulnerable and disfigured children, and has taken part in construction of houses for Habitat for Humanity.

On Men -- "I don't need a man. But I'm happier with one. I like to have someone I can touch and squeeze and kiss. But I don't fold up and die if I don't have a man around."

"I think that the longer I look good, the better gay men feel."

"Anyone who's a great kisser I'm always interested in."

On Marriage -- "Husbands are like fires. They go out when they're left unattended."

On Women -- "Women are the real architects of society."

"Women have to harness their power. It's absolutely true. It's just learning not to take the first no. And if you can't go straight ahead, you go around the corner."

"Yes, it's a man's world, but that's all right because they're making a total mess of it. We're chipping away at their control, taking the parts we want. Some women think it's a difficult task, but it's not."

The Inner Woman -- "I think I am a product of my father's sensibilities and my mother's values. There has been a lot of battling and lots of love, and it's never an easy road for us. But in the deepest recesses, I do have my mother's values."

"I can trust my friends. These people force me to examine myself, encourage me to grow."

"I'm still friends with all my exes, apart from my husbands."

"Don't take your toys inside just because it's raining."

"I'm scared to death of being poor. It's like a fat girl who loses 500 pounds but is always fat inside. I grew up poor and will always feel poor inside. It's my pet paranoia."

"If you really want something, you can figure out how to make it happen."

"Until you're ready to look foolish, you'll never have the possibility of being great."

"Hate crimes are the scariest thing in the world because these people really believe what they're doing is right."

"Words are like weapons; they wound sometimes."

"I've always taken risks, and never worried what the world might really think of me."

"Some years I'm the coolest thing that ever happened, and then the next year everyone's so over me, and I'm just so past my sell date."

"I really don't think of myself as a singer. I think of myself as an entertainer, and the best place I do it is onstage."

"I only answer to two people, myself and God."

"I'm amusing and crazy on Twitter. I talk about important things, stupid things."

(*She was diagnosed with dyslexia when she was 30*): "I can't spell or do grammar, but I'm smarter and more serious than people think. I'm no featherweight when it comes to digging deep and being involved. So many stars I know do so much. It's out duty to give back."

"I'm from a Gypsy background! The road is a nasty place and lonely."

"I wish that I did the things that I really believe in, because when I do, my life goes much smoother."

"My passion lies with whatever I'm doing at the time. I only see what is front of me."

"I'm insecure about everything, because... I'm never going to look in the mirror and see this blonde, blue-eyed girl. That is my idea of what I'd like to look like."

"I'm not like Jane Fonda or any of these other women who say how fabulous they think it is to turn forty. I think it's a crock of (*expletive*). I'm not thrilled with it."

Julia Child

As might be expected, The French Chef says the way to grill, broil, or bake a man's heart is by keeping his stomach happy and full, but you have to want to cook for him:

"The secret of a happy marriage is finding the right person. You know they're right if you love to be with them all the time."

"I wouldn't keep him around long if I didn't feed him well."

Born Julia Carolyn McWillams on August 15, 1912, she was an American chef specializing in French cuisine, an author of many cookbooks, most famously *Mastering the Art of French Cooking*, and became the hostess of the most famous television cooking show which premiered in 1963.

During World War II, she was a top secret researcher for the U.S. Office of Strategic Services (OSS), serving in Sri Lanka and China.

While working for the OSS in Ceylon she met Paul Cushing Child, an artist and poet who was also an OSS employee, and they married in 1946. They had no children. They moved to Paris in 1948 when he was assigned there while with the U.S. Foreign Service and introduced her to fine French cuisine which led to her writing her most famous book and her ground-breaking television shows.

She died of kidney failure on August 13, 2004, two days before her 92nd birthday. Her last meal was French onion soup. She ended her last book, *My Life in France*, with "Thinking back on it now reminds that the pleasures of the table, and of life, are infinite. *Toujours bon appétit!*"

On Love -- "I think careful cooking is love, don't you? The loveliest thing you can cook for someone who's close to you is about as nice a Valentine as you can give."

The Inner Woman -- "Find something you're passionate about and keep tremendously interested in it."

"I hate organized religion. I think you have to love thy neighbor as thyself. I think you have to pick your own God and be true to him., I always say *him* rather than *her*. Maybe it's because of my generation, but I don't like the idea of a female God. I see God as a benevolent male."

"In my generation, except for a few people who'd gone into banking or nursing or something like that, middle-class women didn't have careers. You were to marry and have children and be a nice mother. You didn't go out and do anything. I found that I got restless."

"Life itself is the proper binge."

Hillary Rodham Clinton

Hillary Clinton was not the first wife or First Lady whose husband strayed, but President Bill's straying became worldwide headlines and nightly television news. She demonstrated she was not only a very loyal First Lady, but a very loyal wife. Everyone who meets her in the ladies' room wants to know why she stuck by her husband when he two-timed her.

"You don't walk away if you love someone. You help the person."

"I'm not sitting here like some little woman standing by my man, like Tammy Wynette. I'm sitting here because I love him, and I respect him, and I honor what he's been through and what we've been through together. And you know, if that's not enough for people. Then heck, don't vote for him."

Former United States First Lady and Secretary of State, Hillary Rodham Clinton was born Hillary Diane Rodham on Oct. 26, 1947, in Chicago, Illinois. Her parents were Dorothy and Hugh Rodham, then a prosperous fabric store owner. Hillary and two younger brothers were reared in Park Ridge, a suburb northwest of Chicago. She is a graduate of Wellesley College and Yale Law School.

She and Bill Clinton met in law school and she became the First Lady of Arkansas during his years as governor (1983-1992), and as First Lady of the United States during Clinton's years as President (1993-2001.) The President admitted he had what he called an "inappropriate relationship" with a White House intern, Monika Lewinsky, when she worked there in 1955 and 1956, but she called it much more. The scandal resulted in his impeachment but he remained in the presidency and Hillary stood by him. Lewinsky benefited from the affair by designing a line of handbags and becoming spokesperson for a diet plan, among other ventures.

Hillary served as a U.S. Senator from New York from 2001 to 2009. President Barack Obama appointed her the 67th U.S. Secretary of State and she served from 2009 to 2013. She ran for President of the United States in 2008 and again in 2015.

On Love -- "At the end of the day, you know, love does not happen between too people as much as we would wish."

On Marriage -- "I never thought that the long-haired, bearded guy I married in law school would end up being President."

"I think in a marriage you have to be honest and ask yourself, you know, what is my role? What is my responsibility?"

The Inner Woman -- "When I am talking about 'It Takes a Village,' I'm obviously not talking just about or even primarily about geographical villages any longer, but about the network of relationships and values that do connect and bind us together."

"You show people what you're willing to fight for, when you fight your friends."

"Women are the largest untapped reservoir of talent in the world."

"I don't think feminism, as I understand the definition, implies the rejection of maternal values, nurturing children, caring about the men in your life. That is just nonsense to me."

"It is past time for women to take their rightful place, side by side with men, in the rooms where the fates of peoples, where their children's and grandchildren's fates, are decided."

"I fought all my life for women to make their own choices, in their personal and professional lives. I made mine."

"In too many instances, the march to globalization has also meant the marginalization of women and girls. And that must change."

"Human rights are women's rights, and women's rights are human rights."

"Women have always been the primary victims of war. Women lose their husbands, their fathers, their sons in combat. Women often have to flee from the only homes they have ever known. Women are often the refugees from conflict and sometimes, more frequently in today's warfare, victims. Women are often left with the responsibility, alone, of raising the children."

"There cannot be true democracy unless women's voices are heard. There cannot be true democracy unless women are given the opportunity to take responsibility for their own lives. There cannot be true democracy unless all citizens are able to participate in the lives of their country."

"Parents are the most important people in a child's life… I just think that giving a child a chance and sharing what you have with a child is one of the greatest gifts you can give yourself, as well as a child… All of us have to recognize that we owe our children more than we have been giving them."

"My wish for the new millennium is for all children to grow up wiser, and stronger and more prosperous for the future than ever before."

"We don't have enough support for maternal leave and the kinds of things that some of the European countries do. So we still make it hard on women to go into the work force and feel that they can be good at work but then doing the most important job, which is raising your children in a responsible and positive way."

(Asked in 1996 if she keeps a diary): "Heaven's no! It could get subpoenaed. I can't write anything."

"Always aim high, work hard, and care deeply about what you believe in. When you stumble, keep faith. When you're knocked down, get right back up. And never listen to anyone who says you can't or shouldn't go on. Life is too short, time too precious, and the stakes are too high to dwell on what might have been. We have to work together for what still can be."

"You know, everybody has setbacks in their life, and everybody falls short of the goals they might set for themselves. That's part of living and coming to terms with who you are as a person."

"I believe that the rights of women and girls is the unfinished business of the 21st century."

"You have to be true to yourself."

"Our lives are a mixture of different roles. Most of us are doing the best we can to find whatever the right balance is. For me, that balance is family, work, and service."

"Possibly my worst quality is that I get very passionate about what I think is right."

"We used to say in the White House that if a place is too dangerous, too small or too poor, send the First Lady."

"Being gay is not a Western invention. It is a human reality. It should never be a crime to be gay."

"It is often when night looks darkest, it is often before the fever breaks that one senses the gathering momentum for change, when one feels that resurrection of hope in the midst of despair and apathy."

"The worst thing that can happen in a democracy, as well as in an individual's life, is to become cynical about the future and lose hope… I am someone who hopes for the best and prepares for the worst….There is a sense of things, if you keep positive and optimistic about what can be done, they do work out."

"I feel like every day, every minute, I have to make the most of."

"I have met thousands and thousands of pro-choice men and women. I have never met anyone who is pro-abortion. Being pro-choice is not being pro-abortion. Being pro-choice is trusting the individual to make the right decision for herself and her family, and not entrusting that decision to anyone wearing the authority of government in any regard."

"There hasn't been anybody whose life has been picked apart and distorted as much as mine. The truth is that sometimes it is hard even for me to recognize the Hillary Clinton that other people see."

Claudette Colbert

Most older women visiting the ladies' room know Claudette Colbert as being one of the screen's most charming, beautiful, and feminine actresses from the 1930s to the 1950s. Only when she truly lets her hair down do they know the real woman, who was more lesbian than heterosexual or bisexual.

She was, after all, a great actress, perhaps even more in her private life than on the silver screen. She was so discreet and secretive about her affairs with women that her fans never knew about her sexual preference.

"I know what's best for me. After all, I have been in the Claudette Colbert business longer than anybody."

Born Emilie Claudette Chauchoin in Saint-Mande, France on September 13, 1903, her parents owners of a bakery. When she was three years old, the family moved to the United States, settling in New York City where she attended high school. She wanted to become a Broadway stage actress and studied drama, paying for her lessons by working in a dress shop. She made her Broadway debut in 1923 and changed her name to Claudette Colbert. She went to Hollywood and made her film debut in 1927.

Her breakthrough into stardom came in 1932 when Cecil B. DeMille cast her as a sultry woman in "The Sign of the Cross," opposite Fredric March. She and the film were bit hits and two years later she starred as Cleopatra in the DeMille epic of that name in which she was seen taking a beauty bath in donkey's milk. That same year she reluctantly agreed to star in a romantic comedy about an heiress who deserts her fiancé at the altar and winds up on a road trip with a newspaper reporter played by Clark Gable, who also took his role reluctantly. The film, directed by Frank Capra was a surprise sensation winning multiple Academy Awards for both stars, Capra, and winning best picture of the year.

Colbert remained a major star in films into the 1940s, racking up two more Oscar nominations over the years. She began playing matronly roles into the 1950s, then retired from the screen, but made a brief comeback in 1961 as Troy Donahue's mother in "Parrish," which became her final film. She made a television movie, then returned to the stage.

Colbert married twice, first to handsome film actor and later director Norman Foster in 1928, but they never lived together and divorced in 1935 after seven years. During her marriage to Foster she lived with her domineering mother. Soon after the divorce from Foster, Colbert married a surgeon, Dr. Joel Pressman but they barely lived together and maintained separate residences until his death in 1968.

In a biography, *Claudette Colbert: She Walked in Beauty*, Bernard F. Dick tries to discern her enigmatic private life having been married to two men for years but never living with either of them. Other sources are more specific, that the marriages were studio-arranged to mask her alleged lesbianism. It was a typical studio ploy practiced from the silent film days of Rudolph Valentino to Rock Hudson and other stars today. Colbert is said to have really loved Foster and had a child with him, but her domineering mother persuaded her to have an abortion.

Colbert and Foster were married from 1928 to 1935, and a few months after their divorce he married actress Sally Blane, a sister of Loretta Young. He and Blane reminded married until his death in 1976, having had two children together.

Dick also writes that Colbert had a relationship in her late fifties with a lesbian artist, Verna Hull, and had lived for some time in the same Manhattan apartment building and later had houses next door to each other in Barbados. Dick also wrote that Colbert's final 20 years were spent with a companion, Helen O'Hagan, but she has stated that Colbert never had a sexual relationship with any woman and called the rumors of Colbert's alleged lesbianism "the stigma."

Colbert had an obsession that her left profile looked better than her right and so she insisted she be filmed that way in close-ups. After her acting career, Colbert retired to Barbados where she died in Speightstown after a series of strokes on July 30, 1996 at the age of 93.

On Marriage -- (*Colbert, early in her arrival in Hollywood in 1929 eschewed marriage*): "No man ought ever to marry an actress. A man can be ideally happy only if he is married to a woman who is completely interested in him. An actress never is." (*She said that while already married, to Norman Foster, although they never lived together, but the interviewer did not know any of it. She later said she might have loved Foster, but did not like him, and she lived with her mother because her mother needed her more.*)

(*Colbert on marriage to Norman Foster*): "We do not like the same people. My friends would be unbearable to him. I am not one bit domestic. I don't know anything about housework and don't want to." (*He said*): "We go where we please and with whom we please."

(*Colbert on marriage to Joel Pressman, in a 1953 interview*): :"Now write this down word for word, so there is absolutely no mistake about it… Perhaps once and for all it'll be understood, even by those who for some peculiar reason don't want to understand. I have been Mrs. Joel Pressman for 18 years. If I live that long, I will be for 80.

"If those vicious harpies had as wonderful a husband as I have, they'd stop writing such bilge about my marriage. There is no basis whatsoever, no rhyme, reason, nor accuracy in the gossip the rumormongers are spreading. They have been, they are, they always will be wasting their time."(*Then her demeanor lightened*) "Most of the time I never take these things so seriously. It's our friends who do. "

(*Colbert in the same interview, about why she and Pressman were apart so much*): "You see, my husband does important work – more important work than I do. He teaches medicine at the University of California and that keeps him busy continuously from September to June. In addition, he is a specialist of prominence, he is always being consulted by patients and doctors everywhere. Then there are medical conventions, research papers, special research papers, special reports. I admire Joel and respect his remarkable ability and his uncompromising concentration on his work. If you want to put it that way, he's a star too, a brilliant star who is making a great contribution to people's welfare."

(*More from that 1953 interview in Paris*): "We have a marvelous life together. I adore medicine, and half our friends are from the film world, half from the medical profession. It's a good and stimulating combination. But because we both take our work seriously, we sometimes can't avoid situations which are difficult to bear. I saw Joel here (*in Paris*) at Christmas. (*The previous year.*) I can't tell you what it meant to be together. I'll see him again before I go home. Each visit is a short one, but it has to be, and I'm not going to complain. People need Joel. I need him too, of course, but I have always made an effort to avoid making unnecessary demands on him. Joel is a scientist, through and through, dedicated to his profession. I seem to be his Achilles heel, his one weakness. And I'm grateful; and glad!"

(*Writer Robert Shaw, on Colbert's many-year relationship with writer Helen O'Hagan*): "I know she (*Colbert*) cared about Jack Pressman (*her second husband*) a great deal. But after he was gone (*he died in 1968*), she told all her friends they should treat Helen the way they had treated Jack -- as her spouse."

Colbert and Marlene Dietrich were frequent guests at the parties film director George Cukor, a homosexual, gave for his Hollywood friends. They included gays such as British playwright Noel Coward, composer Cole Porter, director James Whale, actors William Haines and Richard Cromwell, and actress Lili Damita who was courted by Gary Cooper but married Errol Flynn. Other guests often included Judy Garland, Joan Crawford, Spencer Tracy, Humphrey Bogart and Lauren Bacall, Laurence Olivier and Vivien Leigh.

According to author William J. Mann in *Behind the Scenes* (2001), Colbert "moved with great ease in gay circles (*never shocked at the carrying-on at Cukor's parties and*) it was a world she was comfortable in. It was taken for granted that she was gay, or at least not conventionally straight. Mann wrote that the Colbert-Dietrich relationship was brief.

(*Dietrich on Colbert, as quoted by Mann in his book*): "Dietrich described her as 'that ugly Claudette Colbert, so shop girl French.'"

Some said the two stars did not even like each other, while writer Robert Shaw, who knew her in the 1950s, said, "Maybe they became unfriendly later, but I'm quite sure they were lovers for a time before (*Claudette*) married Jack Pressman (*her second husband*). I knew Claudette adored Dietrich."

On Marriage -- "This I know for sure. Of all the marriages I've seen where the husband has love for his wife after fifteen years, the wife has the ability to make him laugh. She is gay (*pleasant*) when he comes home. She doesn't bore him with her petty ills."

The Inner Woman -- "Most of us don't know about happiness until it's over."

"Why do grandparents and grandchildren get along so well? They have the same enemy – the mother."

(*On Clark Gable, in "It Happened One Night"*): "I was so happy to be within two feet of him."

"Some women think if you don't expect too much, you won't be let down. I always expect miracles. Sure, I'm let down. But they're near-miracles."

(*During the 1960s):* "I think there was more sex in those old films than in all the thrashing around today. I'm tired of sex scenes."

"In the old days, the romantic symbols had individuality. Gable, (*Tyrone*) Power, even George Brent at Warner Bros. They were handsome, but they had personalities. Nowadays, the so-called sex symbols are made with cookie-cutters, they're all alike."

Joan Collins

The girl's been around, and isn't shy talking about it in the ladies' room. Her boyfriends read like the Who's Who of handsome young, and not-so-young Hollywood men and "Pretty Boys."

"Having had five husbands, I guess I should know a thing or two about marriage. The sad truth is that most of my husbands turned out to be convincing liars. I've never yet met a man who could look after me. I don't need a husband. What I need is a wife."

One of her most handsome young actor lovers was, as she says below, *"insatiable."*

"The compartment that's easy to put me in is 'freethinking, sexy broad with a dirty mouth, who pretty much does what she wants.' But there's more to me than that."

Born Joan Henrietta Collins in London, England on May 23, 1933, her younger sister was the women's novelist Jackie Collins. Joan's career as an actress began when she was in a London play at the age of nine. She studied acting at the Royal Academy of Dramatic Art, then began appearing in British films and then went to Hollywood to make many films there. Joan is best known for starring in the television series "Dynasty" (1981-1989), earning $120,000 per episode and winning a Golden Globe for best actress in 1982.

She was just 16 when she was courted by Larry Hagman, who was 19 at the time and dutifully checked in with her father on each date. The son of singer-actress Mary Martin, Hagman later became famous as nasty J.R. Ewing on the television series "Dallas" (1978-2013).

Collins has had an affair with Warren Beatty, became pregnant and had an abortion. Other relationships were with Ryan O'Neal, Dennis Hopper, Sydney Chaplin, Arthur M. Lowe Jr., and George England, and she lived with art dealer Robin Hurleston for 13 years. Married five times, her husbands being: actor Maxwell Reed (1952-1957); actor Anthony Newley (1963-1971) with whom she had two children; Ronald S. Kass (1972-1984), with whom she had a child; Peter Holm (1985-1987); Percy Gibson (2002 to the present.) Maxwell Reed is said to have tried to sell her to an Arab Sheik seven months after their wedding.

On Men -- (*On actor George Peppard*): "He's arrogant, the sort of man who expects women to fall at his feet at the slightest command, who throws his weight around. He gives the impression that he's the star, what he says goes, and that nobody else is very important."

(*On actor John Forsythe, her friend and co-star on "Dynasty"*): "He was one of the last of the true gentlemen of the acting profession. I enjoyed our nine years of feuding, fussing, and fighting as the Carrington's."

(*On James Dean*): "Intense, moody, incredible charisma. He was short, myopic, not good-looking in life really. I drove with Jimmy in his new red Porsche once. We were pissed (*drunk*) and went down Sunset (*Boulevard*) and I was scared. He had the windows open, the music up, driving really fast. He died in that same Porsche two or three months later. You know who he was like? A young, better-looking Woody Allen, in a way. He had those same qualities of shyness, uncertainty, and insecurity."

(*In a 1960 interview about her plans to marry Warren Beatty*): "Nothing matters when you're in love. Warren has given me strength. But then, all lovers give each other strength don't they? Our plans? Marriage, yes. But I don't think we should rush into it. If we take time now to get to know each other well, then I think we can face the ups and downs of marriage. Like every woman, I needed love to bring me back to life. Do you know that line by the poet Rilke? (Rainer Maria Rilke, 1875-1926). It sums up my feelings about love and life: 'Love consists in this, that two solitudes protect and touch and greet each other.' That's what I believe."

(*On Warren Beatty*): "He was insatiable. Three, four, five times a day, every day was not unusual for him, and he was also able to accept phone calls at the same time."

"It is unseemly to undress on stage. I won't do that."

"The problem with beauty is that it's like being born rich and getting poorer."

"Even when you win the rat race, you're still a rat."

"Show me a person who has never made a mistake and I'll show you somebody who has never achieved much."

Joan Crawford

Joan had been around the block even more than Joan Collins, and not to walk a dog. She married into Hollywood nobility to get noticed and, among others and just for fun, slept with a Hollywood cowboy who was not very tall in the saddle. She was frequently shown in fan magazines with her husbands or lovers. Gays adored her and many still do, considering her to be one of them, but that has never been substantiated, although rumored a lot, and she once said about Greta Garbo:

"Garbo and I starred in 'Grand Hotel' (1932), but we had no scenes together. Alas. For her, and her alone, I could have been a lesbian."

"Love is a fire. But whether it's going to warm your heart or burn down your house, you can never tell."

"When it comes to husbands, there really are no guarantees, except headaches along the way. Brother!"

"I need sex for a clear complexion, but I'd rather do it for love."

Born Lucille Fay LeSeur on March 23, 1904 in San Antonio, Texas, she aspired to become a movie star but before her film career she became a stripper in Chicago. Burlesque theater owners said she was very good at it, knowing how to entice the men in the audience. She also understood that strippers were expected to accept invitations of men to spend a night after the show. One night she contracted a venereal disease and under went a series of abortions.

She gradually graduated from stripper to chorus girl and finally movie actress. After a decade of top stardom she was considered to be "box office poison in the early 1940s, She made a big comeback by winning the Academy Award as Best Actress for "Mildred Pierce" in 1945, She continued as a top star in films and in 1955 she became a spokeswoman for the Pepsi-Cola company through her marriage to company chairman Alfred Steele.

Crawford was married to actor Douglas Fairbanks, Jr. from 1929 to 1933). Charles "Buddy" Rogers, actor-husband of Mary Pickford, was blunt about why Crawford married Douglas Fairbanks, Jr., saying, "Joan Crawford's first marriage was very shrewd on her part. She married for social position in Hollywood. It didn't matter a bit that it was Douglas Fairbanks, Jr. Joan had set her sights on Mary Pickford as an in-law; she married into Pickfair). It just happened that Junior was the son of Douglas Fairbanks Sr. (*the silent film superstar*) and the stepson of Mary Pickford. That put Joan on the map, and she more than took it from there!" (*After* Fairbanks, Sr. died, Rogers *became Pickford's last husband.*)

Crawford's next husbands were actor Franchot Tone, from 1935 to 1939; and actor Philip Terry from 1942 to 1946. After Terry, she had an affair with cowboy actor Don "Red" Barry, telling technicians that supporting men were sexier than leading men: "They may not get top billing, but they get the highest marks in the bedroom." Her final husband was Alfred Steele, chief executive of Pepsi-Cola, from 1955 until his death in 1959. Both strong-willed people, they fought a lot, but the marriage was happy. During her marriages, she adopted three girls and a boy. Joan Crawford died May 10, 1977 at the age of 73 from cancer and a heart attack.

On Love -- (*On sex in the movies*): "I find suggestion a hell of a lot more provocative than explicit detail. You didn't see Clark (*Gable*) and Vivien (*Leigh*) rolling around in bed in 'Gone With The Wind,' but you saw that shit-eating grin on her face the next morning and you knew damned well she'd gotten properly laid."

On Men – (*On Clark Gable*): "I was closer to Clark Gable than any of his wives, except Carole Lombard, and we were a twosome longer than any of them. I would have married Clark if he'd asked me, but he thought we would over-power each other. He needed, frankly, a wife who wasn't as big a star as he was, though we did love each other dearly." (*Joan said of* Lombard, cattily, "Carole required some artificial help with her (*bosoms*). Before she would go before the cameras, she was famous for yelling out to her costumers, 'Bring me my breasts!'"

"Recently I heard a 'wise guy' story that I had a party at my home for twenty-five men. It's an interesting story, but I don't know twenty-five men I'd want to invite to a party."

On Marriage -- "Sensitive husbands don't like second billing."

(*In 1935, on Franchot Tone*): "I am deeply grateful to Franchot Tone. He has the educational and cultural background that I would give anything to own... He has guided my reading, has been my teacher in many things. I am swayed too much by my emotion." (*They remained friends the rest of their lives.*)

(*On marriage to Alfred Steele*): "It's heaven to find love and be loved. There are things you learn in a good marriage. I learned that you don't use sex. You give it."

The Inner Woman -- (*Crawford had her whole life and career ahead of her when she wrote in a 1928 fan magazine*): "How can I write my life story? A woman's life is not a matter of 'I was born here' or "I was educated there.' It is a matter of thoughts, longings, temptations succumbed to, or temptations repudiated. It is a series of sorrows which have carried her to the depths of woeful despair.; it is a series of joys which have wafted her to such heights that the vary clouds in their mystic, colorful glories have seemed to flood in the heavens *beneath* her!

"And to any woman, if she be honest with herself and her Creator, Life is a series of men – men who have influenced her growth, her career, her ambitions. Men! We may hate them; we may love them. But whatever we feel toward the man of the moment, it is *he* who is the very life and soul of a woman during that period when he dwells in her thoughts with her... There are certain memories buried deep within that she cannot drag out even though she wills it. The innermost corner of a woman's soul is a dark, dark secret prison."

"I like to think that every director I've worked with has fallen a little in love with me. I know Dorothy Arzner did." (*Arzner, who was open with being a lesbian, was one of the first female directors of Hollywood films and one of the most successful regardless of sex,*
"I like to think that every director I've worked with has fallen a little in love with me. I know Dorothy Arzner did." (*Arzner, who was open with being a lesbian, was one of the first female directors of Hollywood films and one of the most successful regardless of sex, her career spanning from the 1920s to the 1940s. She directed silent stars Rudolph Valentino and Clara Bow, and in talking pictures Katharine Hepburn, Claudette Colbert with whom she had a brief affair, and Joan Crawford with whom she had a "fiery affair."*)

(*In a 1935 interview*): "Off-screen, an actor must be himself...Sincerity is the most precious thing in life. Without it, there's nothing but shallowness, sham, and pretence... I hate flattery and flatterers."

(*In concluding her 1935 interview*): "A life well-lived is a life well-balanced. To get the most out of living, there must be a certain amount of so many things... work and play, strenuous effort and complete relaxation, friendships and solitudes, joys and sorrows... Old age is merely a stagnation of the mind. When the desire passes to earn something new each day, each hour, then you have grown old. There are so many things I want to know and so little time in which to learn about them!... I have experienced a great deal of unhappiness, even bitter tragedy. I cannot help but believe that the future will be much kinder. Nearly everything is equalized, in the long run. I have hopes of finding that calm, philosophical happiness that leads to permanent contentment. I don't believe I ask too much of life to hope for this."

(*In a 1940 interview, when asked if she was a "home girl"*): "Why, I've always been one. I can't remember when I haven't washed dishes or made my bed or worked around the house." When she was nervous or upset about something, she would relax by scrubbing a floor at home. (*She said she liked being active*): "To settle down is to die a little."

"I think that the most important thing a woman can have, next to talent, of course, is her hairdresser."

"Any actress who appears in public without being well-groomed is digging her own grave. I never go outside unless I look like Joan Crawford the movie star. If you want to see the girl next door, go next door."

"I have always known what I wanted, and that was beauty… in every form."

"Find your own style and have the courage to stick to it. Choose your clothes for your way of life. Make your wardrobe as versatile as an actress. It should be able to play many roles. Find your happiest colors… the ones that make you feel good. Care for your clothes, like the good friends they are!"

"It has been said that on screen I personified the American woman."

"Women's Lib? Poor little things. They always look so unhappy. Have you noticed how bitter their faces are?"

"If you have an ounce of common sense and one good friend you don't need an analyst."

"I believe in the dollar. Everything I earn, I spend!"

"Don't (*expletive*) with me, fellas. This cowgirl has been to the rodeo before."

"I love playing bitches. There's a lot of bitch in every woman; a lot in every man."

"If you've earned a position, be proud of it. Don't hide it. I want to be recognized. When I hear people say, 'There's Joan Crawford!' I turn around and say, 'Hi! How are you?'"

"You have to be self-reliant and strong to survive in this town (Hollywood). Otherwise you will be destroyed."

"Hollywood is like life. You face it with the sum total of your equipment."

"Nobody can imitate me. You can always see impersonations of Katharine Hepburn and Marilyn Monroe. But not me. Because I've always drawn on myself only.'"

"I think it's sad that today's actresses feel they have to resort to advertising (*products*) to make extra money. Esther Williams is selling swimwear and Marilyn Monroe sells everything under the sun. I don't mean that unkindly, but in my day, actresses had more class than that." (*Crawford later became a spokesperson for Peps-Cola while her husband Alfred Steele was chairman of its board of directors and chief executive officer.*)

Penelope Cruz

"I don't know why, but women in a hair salon share their deepest George Cukor secrets." (And for many, in the ladies' room).

(Before her marriage to Javier Barden): *"I don't know if I believe in marriage. I believe in family, love, and children."*

Born Penelope Cruz Sanchez in Madrid, Spain, on April 28, 1974, her father was a retailer and mother a hairdresser. Her flair for performing began when she was a toddler, reenacting television commercials for her parents and siblings. She studied to become a classical ballet dancer but switched to acting at the age of 15.

Television commercials and music videos followed and she made her film debut in Madrid in 1993. Within a few more years she began her Hollywood movie career and she is among the most sought-after actresses. She married popular actor Javier Barden, also of Spanish descent, in 2010 and they are parents of two children. Barden won a best supporting Academy Award for "No Country for Old Men" in 2007.

When Cruz first came to Hollywood, she was so lonely she picked up stray cats and brought them to her small apartment to keep her company. Since her stardom and marriage, she has an elegant home and entertains Hollywood elite such as directors Woody Allen and Pedro Almodovar and her costar on the "Pirates of the Caribbean" films, Johnny Depp. She calls him "The Man with the Hat," and he calls her "This Curious Spanish Creature." He also calls her a "One-of," "magnificent," and "magical."

Cruz was the first Spanish-born actress to be nominated for an Academy Award and the first to win, as best supporting actress in Woody Allen's "Vicky Cristina Barcelona" (2009). Allen said, "She has a wild kind of animal quality that was perfect for the unstable character I had written. A lot of actresses would not have been able to go that deeply."

She loves being the mother of a baby: "Some nights you sleep more, some nights less, but you don't care… From the first second (of birthing), you feel so much love. It is a revolutionary experience. It transforms you completely, in a second. Nature is very wise and gives you nine months to prepare, but in that moment – when you see that face, you are transformed forever.

"All those clichés, those things you hear about having a baby and motherhood… all of them are true. And all of them are the most beautiful things you will ever experience.

"I breastfed my son for thirteen months, and I plan to do at least the same with my daughter. That's an amazing thing for babies, but it's also really good for the mother because it regulates your body again after pregnancy."

Cruz has had other life-changing experiences. When she was 22, she worked at one of Mother Teresa's orphanages in Calcutta, India, and met the future saint. She also is active in humanitarian causes such as the Red project to benefit AIDS research and cure.

On Men -- "Johnny Depp *(her co-star in the Pirates of the Caribbean films)* is so special that he's like a Martian. In fact, that's what I call him, Martian."

On Marriage -- "I always knew I wanted a family because of the way I grew up. Family has always been the most important thing."

"I want my son, and my kids if I have more, *(by 2014 she had two children)* to grow up in a way that is as anonymous as possible. The fact that his father *(Barden)* and I have chosen to do the work that we do doesn't give anybody the right to invade our privacy."

The Inner woman -- "I am amazed about how everyone wants to know about my love life. They whisper to me, *Tell me the truth? Is it true?* Who cares? Because we have this job, we are to say to everybody what we do, or with whom we sleep? It's a bit absurd, but that's why everybody lies so much."

"My ambition is to be happy."

"Ever since I was a little girl, I've worried too much. It always bothers me because sometimes you end up worrying more about the worry and you are not resolving things that are right there in front of you. I have been like that all my life, and it's hard to change."

"I love the Italian culture. It's a beautiful culture. I love the language, the Italian people, their music, their attitudes. I just love it! Sometimes I think I'm an Italian trapped in a Spanish woman's body."

"The most difficult thing in the world is to start a career known only for your looks, and then try to become a serious actress. No one will take you seriously once you are known as the pretty woman."

"You cannot live your life looking at yourself from someone else's point of view."

"One thing that I am proud of: I am really capable of laughing at myself."

"I have a strong personality, and I say what I think. I'm strong and opinionated. Those qualities brought me a lot of problems since I was a little girl in school, saying *I don't agree* and fighting with the children. It's part of my curiosity for life."

"My favorite actress is Meryl Streep. Oh, and Anna Magnani."

"I always feel scared and insecure on a film set. I don't know any other way."

"I try not to label myself in any way. I just have an allergy to labels in general. I can tell you that I am surrounded by very strong women and that I really appreciate that, but I'd rather not label myself."

"I am living for every day and trying to have less fear, less worry. But I have always worried about everything; it's my nature. It's the thing that makes me suffer the most."

"I was raised Catholic, but then I discovered Buddhism, and I used to have a boyfriend who was a Scientologist, and they are all good religions that help people. As far as I'm concerned, you can have all three religions at once and it's okay!"

"I am just too much."

Bette Davis

Bette plays a Plain Jane until love transforms her into being beautiful in "Now, Voyager" (1942). On a shipboard ocean crossing, she meets a lover (Paul Henreid), with whom she has a child. He returns her love but is locked in a loveless but unbreakable marriage, and their love affair is doomed. He asks if she will be happy, they being just ships that pass in the night? He lights two cigarettes, one for her, one for him, and she replies, **"Oh, Jerry, don't let's us ask for the moon. We have the stars."**

In real life, Bette Davis asked for the moon four times, but clouds always passed over it..

There was never a doubt that Bette Davis liked men, and only men, and let everyone know it.

"I've always liked men better than women."

"Brought up to respect the conventions, love had to end in marriage. I'm afraid it did."

"An affair now and then is good for a marriage. It adds spice, stops it from getting boring. I ought to know."

Born Ruth Elizabeth Davis in Lowell, Massachusetts on April 5, 1908, her father was a patent attorney, and he and her mother divorced when she was 10 years old. She and her sister were then reared by their mother. At first she thought she would become a professional dancer, but soon fell in love with stage acting. She attended an acting school in Manhattan and made her Broadway debut in 1929. This led to her first Hollywood film in 1931 and a seven-year contract with Warner Brothers the following year.

Her performance in "Of Human Bondage" in 1934 began her ascent to starring roles and she won the first of two Academy Awards in 1935 for "Dangerous," and her second for "Jezebel" in 1938, but may be best remembered for "All About Eve" in 1950 as a stage actress who warns guests at a party, "Fasten your seatbelts, it's going to be a bumpy night!" Despite that film's huge success, her career fell into decline and in 1961 she placed a Job Wanted ad in the movie trade papers. This led to a new career in horror films starting with "What Ever Happened to Baby Jane" in 1962 and she continued making movies almost until her death of breast cancer in France on October 6, 1989.

Davis was married four times, the longest lasting ten years (1950-1960), to actor Gary Merrill, with whom she had a daughter and a son. Her earlier marriages were to musician Harmon Nelson (1932-1938); airline pilot Arthur Farnsworth from 1940 until his death in 1943 from an accidental fall; and artist William Grant Sherry (1945-1950) with whom she had a daughter. She is remembered as being one of the top movie stars from the 1930s to the 1960s.

She delivered more famous lines than any other film actor. Besides the seatbelt and voyager lines, were these: "What a dump!" (In "Beyond the Forest" 1949 and reprised in "Dead Ringer" (1964); and "I'd love to kiss ya, but I just washed my hair" (To Richard Barthlemess in "Cabin in the Cotton" (1932). There was only one Bette Davis, a true original.

On Men -- "Strong women only marry weak men."

"Men become much more attractive when they start looking older. But it doesn't do much for women, though we do have an advantage: make-up."

"Nowadays, the women are sexually aggressive, to an extreme, like Madonna, and the men are sexually passive, or not at all, like Michael Jackson. Worst of all, the biggest stars in Hollywood now aren't even actors; they're singers whose voices are undistinguished and merely serviceable. Whatever happened to class?"

(*On Laurence Olivier*): "Larry Olivier is not an actor. He's a chameleon. He wears all that makeup and all those costumes and just disguises himself. Half the time you don't even know it's him."

On Marriage -- "I'd marry again if I found a man who had fifteen million dollars, would sign over half to me, and guarantee that he'd be dead within a year."

"My fourth husband was an actor [*Gary Merrill*]. We had tremendous fights. He used his fists more than his mouth... It was a hell of a marriage, even the making up. They ought to rewrite the ceremony.. 'in sickness and in hell...'"

The Inner Woman -- "This has always been a motto of mine: Attempt the impossible in order to improve your work."

"To fulfil a dream, to be allowed to sweat over lonely labor, to be given a chance to create, is the meat and potatoes of life. The money is the gravy."

"Basically, I believe the world is a jungle, and if it's not a bit of a jungle in the home, a child cannot possibly be fit to enter the outside world."

"The best time I ever had with Joan Crawford was when I pushed her down the stairs in 'Whatever Happened to Baby Jane?'"

(Davis *had more fun with Crawford before Joan became ill and had to drop out of co-starring with her in* "Hush, Hush Sweet Charlotte" *in 1964 and was replaced by Olivia de Havilland. Davis knew that at the time, Crawford was promoting Pepsi-Cola, so she had a Coca-Cola vending machine installed on the set. When Joan left the film,* Davis *held up a bottle of Coca-Cola and saluted her.*)
"Everybody has a heart. Except some people."

(Davis *also gave Olivia de Havilland a morsel of praise for her performance in* "Charlotte," *telling her that when they were not in a scene together, she thought that Olivia managed to hold the audience's attention.*)

"A sure way to lose happiness, I found, is to want it at the expense of everything else."

"If you've never been hated by your child, you've never been a parent."

(*On Joan Crawford*): "One area of life Joan should never have gotten into was children. She *bought* them. Joan was the perfect mother in front of the public, but not behind the front door. She wanted this image that wasn't meant for her. I've never behaved like... well, I doubt my children will ever write a book." (*Referring to Christina Crawford's 1978 tell-all book* Mommie Dearest *in which she wrote that her mother was a cruel, abusive alcoholic.*)

"I survived because I was tougher than anybody else."

"I am doomed to an eternity of compulsive work. No set goal satisfies. Success only breeds a new goal. The golden apple devoured has seeds. It is endless."

"The key to life is accepting challenges. Once someone stops doing this, he's dead."

"I often think that a slightly exposed shoulder emerging from a long satin nightgown packs more sex than two naked bodies in bed."

"Sex is God's joke on human beings."

"I am just too much."

Perhaps her most famous line was not in a film but what she said in her senior years: "Old age is no place for sissies."

(*Joan Blondell, a fellow actress at Warner Bros., said about Bette Davis*): "Hedda Hopper (*the Hollywood gossip columnist*) inquired,

'If you hadn't been an actress, what would you have wanted to be?' Bette said, "A man.'"

The Inner Woman -- (*When asked by Elizabeth Taylor about it being rumored that Davis was in an affair with actress Mary Astor (who was not a lesbian but was man-crazy)*): "I love men! I had four husband, for C's sake!"

(*Ava Gardner on Bette Davis*): "I saw Bette Davis in a hotel in Madrid once and went up to her and said, 'Miss Davis, I'm Ava Gardner and I'm a great fan of yours.' And she behaved exactly as I wanted her to behave. 'Of course you are, my dear,' she said, 'of course you are.' And then she swept on."

(*Bette Davis on Miriam Hopkins, her co-star in two films*): "Hopkins? She was a swine!"

"Faye Dunaway is the most unprofessional actress I ever worked with. And that includes Miriam Hopkins, even!" (*Davis and Dunaway appeared together in "The Disappearance of Aimee" (1976), a television movie based on evangelist Aimie Semple McPherson in which Dunaway was the star, playing McPherson.*)

(*Davis on actress Constance Bennett*): "In Hollywood, after 'The Wizard of Oz' (1939), Constance Bennett was known as the Wicked Witch of the West. A witch on wheels, if you want to be polite. And although she was very highly paid at one time, she represented the sort of actress for whom I had contempt... the type that cared more about makeup than motivation. Her face was her talent, and when it dropped, so did her career, right out of sight!"

(*Actress Estelle Winwood on Joan Crawford*): "I saw her once at her very worst. I do not condone sadism."

(*Bette Davis on Joan Crawford*): "I wouldn't sit on her toilet. Joan Crawford... Hollywood's first case of syphilis."

(*Davis on Errol Flynn*): "At Warner Brothers, I acted with Errol Flynn. *I* acted... At one point, Jack Warner wanted to loan me out to play Scarlett O'Hara in 'Gone With the Wind,' with Flynn as Rhett Butler. I was torn, because I wanted to play her, naturally, but not with *him*. He couldn't have carried it off, so regretfully I declined. Then they went and cast Clark Gable, and *he* wasn't much more of an actor, so it finally dawned on me that unlike Scarlett, Rhett was an actor-proof part!" (*Davis later changed her mind about Flynn and said that besides being the most handsome actor in Hollywood, he was really a fine actor.*)

(*Davis on Cary Grant*): "He needed willowy or boyish girls like Katharine Hepburn to make him look what they now call 'macho.' If I'd co-starred with Grant, or if (*Joan*) Crawford had, we'd have eaten him for breakfast!"

(*Davis on director Ron Howard*): "He was good... And he was respectful, which is almost as important as being good."

(*Actor John Mills on Bette Davis*): "I was never so scared in my life. And I was in the war!" (*World War II.*) Mills and Davis were among the stars in "Murder with Mirrors" (1985), a television movie based on an Agatha Christie "Miss Marple" stor

(*Joan Crawford on Bette Davis*): "I don't see how she built a career out of a set of mannerisms instead of real acting ability. Take away the pop eyes, the cigarette, and those funny clipped words and what have you got? She's phony, but I g guess the public likes that."

(*Bette Davis on Bette Davis*): "I'm the nicest goddamn dame that ever lived."

Ellen DeGeneres

Openly lesbian and proud of it, she advises other women and girls who are of her sexual preference:

"Find out who you are and figure out what you believe in. Even if it's different from what your neighbors believe in and different from what your parents believe in. Stay true to yourself. Have your own opinion. Don't worry about what people say about you or think about you. Let the naysayers nay. They will eventually grow tired of naying."

"The thing everyone should realize is that the key to happiness is being happy for yourself and yourself."

"Who's to say what's better or worse anyway? Who's to even say what's normal or average? We're all different people and we're allowed to be different from on another. If someone ever says you're weird, say thank you. And then curtsy. No, don't curtsy. That might be too weird. Bow. And tip your imaginary hat. That'll show them."

Born Ellen Lee DeGeneres on January 26, 1958 in Metaire, Louisiana, her father was an insurance agent and mother a speech therapist. Her parents divorced n 1973 and when her mother remarried she and her sister lived with them, while a brother lived with his birth father. Before being discovered for her comedy abilities, she was a clothing clerk in a department store and was a waitress, a house painter, and a bartender.

Her success as a stand-up comedienne in small clubs and coffee houses led to starring in a television sitcom, "Ellen," from 1994-1998, and she has been hosting the syndicated television talk show "The Ellen DeGeneres Show" since 2003. She "outed" herself in an article and appearing on the cover of *Time* magazine April 14, 1997. She and actress Anne Heche were partners from 1997 to 2000, then she partnered with actress-photographer Alexandra Hedison from 2001 to 2004, and married actress Portia de Rossi in 2008.

On Sexual Preference -- "I think one of the turning points in my life came a few years ago. I started going to sleep at night just talking to myself, saying, "You're perfect just the way you are,' because I used to beat myself up about weight and working out, and no matter what I did I never felt good about myself. I decided to accept myself and know that I am good. Just those affirmations every night changed my belief I who I was, because I had been told for so long, over and over, that I was something else."

"I personally like being unique. I like being my own person with my own style and my own opinions and my own toothbrush."

"I knew if I came out, there was a possibility I would lose my career. But I didn't do it for my career, I did it for me to live my truth. I thought, 'I don't want to live and have any shame whatsoever.' I should be proud of who I am, and I don't care if people approve or not. It is who I am."

"But I do believe that's when you do your soul-searching. I think when you have these trials that life gives you, it is an opportunity to find out who you are. Not just who you are when everything's great, but who you are when everything is taken away from you and you have nothing."

"So, be who you really are. Embrace who you are. Literally. Hug yourself. Accept who you are. Unless you're a serial killer. Do things that make you happy within the confines of the legal system."

"I wish that I wasn't seen differently. I wish that people looked at me and just saw that I was a good person with a good heart. And that wants to make people laugh. And that's who I am. I also am happy to be gay. And I would love to have the same rights as everybody else. I would love, I don't care if it's called marriage. I don't care if it's called, you know, domestic partnership. I don't care what it's called, I wish that I wasn't seen differently.... And it's like, I can't convince them that I'm not sick or wrong, that there's nothing wrong with me. You know, I can live my life and hope that things change, and hope that we're protected as any other couples."

"My name is Ellen and I'm a vegetarian. Just to add another label to me: I am a lesbian, Aquarian, and vegetarian. I've said it…"

The Inner Woman -- "Beauty is about being comfortable in your own skin. It's about knowing and accepting who you are."

"True beauty is not related to what color your hair is or what color your eyes are. True beauty is about who you are as a human being, your principles, your moral compass."

"Laugh. Laugh as much as you can. Laugh until you cry. Cry until you laugh. Keep doing it even if people are passing you on the street saying, "I can't tell if that person is laughing or crying, but either way they seem crazy, let's walk faster." Emote. It's okay. It shows you are thinking and feeling."

"Now, I'm no scientist, but I know what endorphins are. They're tiny little magical elves that swim through your blood stream and tell funny jokes to each other. When they reach your brain, you hear what they're saying and that boosts your health and happiness. "Knock Knock... Who's There?.. Little endorphin... Little endorphin who?... Little Endorphin Annie." And then the endorphins laugh and then you laugh. See? Its Science."

"When you take risks you learn that there will be times when you succeed and there will be times when you fail, and both are equally important."

"My point is, life is about balance. The good and the bad. The highs and the lows. The pina and the colada."

"What's not so great is that all this technology is destroying our social skills. Not only have we given up on writing letters to each other, we barely even talk to each other."

"If your Birthday is on Christmas day and you're not Jesus, you should start telling people your birthday is on June 9 or something."

"People have become so accustomed to texting that they're actually startled when the phone rings. It's like we suddenly all have Bat phones. If it rings, there must be danger. Now we answer, "What happened? Is someone tied up in the old sawmill?" "No, it's Becky. I just called to say hi." "Well you scared me half to death. You can't just pick up the phone and try to talk to me like that. Don't the tips of your fingers work?"

"Way, way back in the day, like in the 1990s, if you wanted to tell everyone you ate waffles for breakfast, you couldn't just go on the Internet and tweet it out. There was only one way to do it. You had to go outside and scream at the top of your lungs, 'I ate waffles for breakfast!' That's why so many people ended up in institutions. They seemed crazy, but when you think about it, they were just ahead of their time."

"It's failure that gives you the proper perspective on success."

"Our flaws are what makes us human. If we can accept them as part of who we are, they really don't even have to be an issue."

"Contribute to the world. Help people. Help one person. Help someone cross the street today. Help someone with directions unless you have a terrible sense of direction. Help someone who is trying to help you. Just help. Make an impact. Show someone you care. Say yes instead of no. Say something nice. Smile. Make eye contact. Hug. Kiss."

"It always helps to think about other people instead of ourselves."

"Above all things physical, it is more important to be beautiful on the inside -- to have a big heart and an open mind and a spectacular spleen."

"You just have to keep driving down the road. It's going to bend and curve and you'll speed up and slow down, but the road keeps going."

Catherine Deneuve

Another modern-thinking French actress, she was married and divorced and has had affairs with men and had children with them.

"Marriage is obsolete and a trap."

"I don't see any reason for marriage when there is divorce."

Born Catherine Fabienne Dorleac in Paris, France, on October 22, 1943, her parents were actors. She made her first film in 1957 when she was still just thirteen and continued to have small parts until she gained international success in the musical "The Umbrellas of Cherbourg" in 1964.

Her fame as an actress and beauty was enhanced by starring in films made by Roman Polanski, Luis Brunel, and Francois Truffant. She continues to star in movies, mainly in Europe. In 1995 a British magazine named her No. 36 in its list of the 100 sexiest stars in film history.

She was married once, to David Bailey from 1965 until their divorce in 1972, but had a son with director Roger Vadim in 1963 when she was 19, and a daughter from actor Marcello Mastroianni in 1972 when she was 28. In 2013 she received the European Film Academy's lifetime achievement award. Besides acting and being grandmother to five children, she designs eyeglasses, shoes, jewelry, and greeting cards.

On Love -- "Love is suffering. One side always loves more."

On Sex -- "Sex is a big question mark. It is something people will talk about forever."

On Men -- "I like men who have a light spirit. It's okay to be serious about your work, but in everyday life it's difficult to find men who are very alive and positive. In life, I like people who are cheerful."

"There are relatively few role models for young people (*women*). We are in a society that is ruled by men."
"A woman has to be intelligent, have charm, a sense of humor, and be kind. It's the same qualities I admire from a man."

"I wouldn't say no to being in a film with Jude Law. I love English actors."

"Prostitution happens to you because of troubles you had. In reality, no woman would choose to do that. All women who kill or have sexual obsessions or who are prostitutes have trouble with their fathers."

The Inner Woman -- "People who know me know I'm strong, but I'm vulnerable."

"Directors have to push me because I never start high, and then need to be pushed down. I have to be pushed up. Not all the time, but often."

"I am shocked when people talk about me and sum me up as: blonde, cold, and solemn. People will cling to whatever reinforces their own assumptions about a person."

"I am a feminist through experience, not choice. I was a feminist from a very early age because I am from a family of women, so it comes naturally to me. Over the years I have been involved with various causes for women."

"I get irritated, nervous, very tense or stressed, but never bored."

"I have no fear of aging. I am still working. When you are young you suffer and worry so much more – everything is so important and serious, but with time things get better."

"I was never a dangerous woman. I'm not the prissy blonde woman that could take your husband away."

"Lesbians and gays… they still have to fight, even inside. It's not that simple, even if they seem to be accepted."

"I love to not work. I like to travel. I work maybe half the year, no more."

"People don't know very much about me. They do not know what really goes on in my private life."

"I don't enjoy. I suffer from enjoying. It's very Christian."

"It has been very erotic and provocative for people to wonder about my feelings for women. I cannot imagine having a physical relationship with a woman. I have not done that. But I really love women."

Cameron Diaz

After being in affairs with some of Hollywood's new handsome young actors, she has since married.

"Any of my guy friends, when I tell them what women really talk about, they just don't want to hear it. But maybe it's time."

The time is now, guys.

"I'm primal on an animalistic level, kind of like, 'Boink me over the head, throw me over your shoulder. You man, me woman.' Not everybody has the right kind of primal thing for me...I love physical contact. I have to be touching my lover, like, always. It's not optional."

"Sex is my favorite sport. I'm always in the mood."

"I believe that when you're in love, you have to pour your heart and soul out to your partner... or why bother? So in that sense I'm an incurable romantic when it comes to men."

"I'd rather have my heart broken a thousand times than never to love at all."

Born Cameron Michelle Diaz of Cuban descent in San Diego, California, on August 30, 1972, her father was an import-export agent for an oil company. She became a member of the dance-drill team at Long Beach Polytechnic High School in Long Beach,

California. An independent girl, she left home at 16 and traveled all over the globe for the next five years before returning to California at the age of 21 when she began working as a fashion model.

With no acting experience, she was cast opposite Jim Carrey in "The Mask" in 1944 and become an overnight star. She became one of Hollywood's sexiest actresses and earns as high as $20 million per picture. She was in relationships with Alex Rodriguez, Jared Leto, Justin Timberland, and lived with video producer Carlos De La Torre from 1990 to 1995, then after a year of dating rock guitarist Benji Madden, married him early in 2015 when she was 42 and he 35.

Four years before her marriage, Diaz had different thoughts on the subject, saying marriage is a dying institution. "I think we have to make our own rules. I don't think we should live our lives in relationships based off old traditions that don't suit our world any longer."

But she still believed in love, saying "I love men more than anything. I want all men to be happy and have rad women in their lives. But guys need women who challenge them and don't let them get away with their s—t. Women, conversely, need to not be crazy bitches who blow up when their guys tell them something that scares them."

On Love -- "Oh gosh, I can't even count how many times I've gotten on a plane for love. It's not unusual in this business; my lifestyle demands it. I'm always traveling for [*whispers expletive*]. You've got to go where it is."

On Men -- (*In 2015 on what makes a good relationship):* "You have to find someone in the same place as you are. Timing is everything. If you get into a relationship where you want something the guy doesn't want, it's never gonna work. You're never going to get him to be in that place. No matter how old you are, finding the guy who's in the same places you are and wants to show up is the only way a relationship works, period."

"Men are wonderful. I don't think my feeling about that is ever going to change. I'm never going to feel differently about men. I'm not a man-hater. It's just not in my nature. I think guys are amazing. I love the dichotomy, the differences in men and women. I think it's wonderful. It keeps things interesting. We can't walk in each other's shoes. We don't know what it's really like, but we certainly can make an effort to know each other a little bit better."

"Here's the thing… You make the same mistake over and over again until you learn your lesson. We girls sometimes do the thing where we pick the same person over and over again… they look and seem different, but deep down, they're the same. And that's on us."

"My father's death will be a part of me forever, and I'm sure it's going to be a part of all of the roles that I play now. It's been a year since he died, and it's been an incredibly transformative year. It's just something that's going to be with me forever. We all fall in love with our parents."

"What's changed from 10 years ago is that now I want a man who knows who he is. Someone who understands himself, has already dealt with his issues and who can say: 'I see where I've been foolish before and I'm not going to be like that again.'"

"I just love the fact that a man possesses something that a woman can never understand because we don't have the experiences of it, and that a woman possesses something that the man doesn't understand because only she possesses it."

"I don't want to go to work (*in a film*) and get into bed with someone else, not even Tom Cruise. It's not like I enjoy it."

"I love the feeling that you get when you can really laugh with a man and be natural and not always think that there's a sexual element going on. For me, flirting with a man means making fun of myself and trying to open myself and be very unpretentious."

"You haven't partied until you've partied at dawn in complete silence with Buddhist monks."

"I love older men."

(*On what she would do if she could be a man for a day*): "I would have sex. I would love to know how it operates! Like what the real mechanics feel like! It would be fun to feel the other side, wouldn't it?"

On Sex -- "The fountain of youth [for me], let's see...I guess it's exercise, healthy diet, lots of water, lots of laughter, lots of sex. Yes, we all need that as human beings. Its healthy, it's natural, it's what we are here to do."

On Women -- "We have a voice now and we're not using it. Women have so much to lose. I mean, we could lose the right to our bodies. If you think rape should be legal, then don't vote. But if you think you have a right to your body and you have a right to say what happens to you and fight off that danger of losing that, then you should vote."

"I'm like every other woman: a closet full of clothes, but nothing to wear: So I wear jeans."

"I'm not comfortable with the idea of cutting myself up. I hope I never become that vain. I will never get breast implants. I think in LA, a lot of girls are doing it to please other people. So, having big boobs may be in now, but in the future the flat-chested look will probably be back. I'm happy with the way I look."

"I think that all women have been sexually attracted to another woman at some point. It's natural to have connectivity and an appreciation for the beauty of other women."

"I love Shirley MacLaine. Love that woman."

"I've always been a huge fan of Julia Roberts. Without her, what would the world be like?"

(Diaz served as maid of honor at her best friend Drew Barrymore's wedding to Will Kopelman on June 12, 2012).

"Women have always behaved badly. I think probably worse than men. Maybe men just don't have the stomach for it. They don't want to see it on film because they just can't take it." Any of my guy friends, when I tell them what women really talk about, they just don't want to hear it. But maybe it's time."

"Women are capable of doing so many things these days, physically, emotionally, within relationships and career. There are so many things that women have evolved into, and I feel really proud about where women are right now."

"What we women need to do, instead of worrying about what we don't have, is just love what we do have."

"Your regrets aren't what you did, but what you didn't do. So I take every opportunity. I grew up with a lot of boys. I probably have a lot of testosterone for a woman."

Cameron made news in 2014 when she cut short a radio interview with talk show hosts Kyle Sandilands and Jackie O in Australia when Kyle made a derogatory remark about Diaz's best friend, Drew Barrymore's years of taking drugs when she was a preteen and a teenager. Diaz hung up and Jackie later scolded Kyle, saying, "You ruined that interview. We all know how protective Cameron is about her private life."

The Inner Woman -- "Fame does not define me. If you are looking for fame to define you, then you will never be happy and you'll always be searching for happiness, and you will never find it in fame."

"Fulfillment comes from within you, by being authentic to yourself, not chasing fame."

Marlene Dietrich

While in a ladies' room crowded with women eager to hear her wit and wisdom, she has a lot to say about men and women, including bisexuals and lesbians, of which she was both at one time or another.

"To be completely a woman you need a master, and in him a compass for your life. You need a man you can look up to and respect. If you dethrone him, it's no wonder that you are discontented, and discontented women are not loved for long."

"A country without bordellos is like a house without bathrooms."

"I am at heart, a gentleman."

Born Marie Magdalene Dietrich in Berlin, Germany, on December 27, 1901, her father was a police lieutenant. She became a cabaret singer in Germany in the 1920s and married handsome actor Rudolf Sieber in 1924, and while they lived together only five years, and had a daughter together (Maria Riva), they remained married until his death in 1976.

Dietrich appeared in silent films in Germany until she was discovered by German film director and producer Josef von Sternbeg. He cast her as the sultry cabaret singer Lola in "The Blue Angel" in 1930, and she became an overnight star. She and r became lovers and came to America where he began directing her in films co-starring Gary Cooper and other Hollywood leading men and she became the highest paid actress in the 1930s.

Besides her sultry singing voice, Dietrich became famous for her beautiful legs and often wearing men's tuxedoes, hats, and tailored suits. She was more feminine in "Destry Rides Again" (1939), and her co-star, James Stewart, later said, "After a week's work on the picture, I fell in love with her. She was beautiful, friendly, enchanting. (*Everyone on the picture*) fell in love with her."

Both Dietrich and Greta Garbo were attracted to French film star Jean Gabin. Dietrich said about him, "He has the most beautiful loins in the world." At the same time, Dietrich was in a lesbian affair with French songbird Edith Piaf.

While making dozens of movies, in later years as Dietrich aged and film roles declined, she took to the stage and became one of the most sought-after songstresses in Las Vegas and other night clubs. She became a U.S. citizen in 1937 and was an outspoken critic of Adolph Hitler, calling him an idiot. Hitler, however, was a great admirer of hers and had her films shown at his retreat in Berschtesgaden. Dietrich was awarded the U.S. War Department's Medal of Freedom in 1947 for entertaining American troops during World War II and her strong stand against Nazism.

Dietrich was voted the 43rd Greatest Movie Star of all time by *Entertainment Weekly*. In 1999, The American Film Institute named Dietrich the ninth greatest female star of classic Hollywood cinema. Several falls left her bedridden in a Paris apartment for the last dozen years of her life and she died of renal failure on May 6, 1992 at the age of 90.

On Love -- "In Europe, it doesn't matter if you're a man or a woman -- we make love with anyone we find attractive."

On Sex -- "Sex is much better with a woman, but then one can't live with a woman!"

"In America, sex is an obsession. In other parts of the world it's a fact."

On Men -- (*Dietrich reportedly prided herself in having slept with three men of the Kennedy family: Joseph P. Kennedy and his sons Joseph P. Kennedy Jr., and John F. Kennedy.*)

"Most women set out to change a man, and when they have changed him they do not like him."

"Gary Cooper was neither intelligent nor cultured. Just like the other actors, he was chosen for his physique, which, after all, was more important than an active brain."

(*On Cary Grant*): "The champion."

"Ernest Hemingway is the most positive life force I have ever encountered. I hate anything negative, and I hate waste. In Hemingway, nothing is wasted… Hemingway and I were never lovers. It was too special for that."

(*On Orson Welles):* "You should cross yourself when you say his name. When I talk with him, I feel like a tree that has been watered… He is a perpetual motion machine."

(*On Rock Hudson*): "He was one of the gentlest, kindest men in Hollywood – and all those journalists should burn in Hell for the bile they printed about him when he died."

(*On Ray Milland*): "When we did 'Golden Earrings' (1947), I played a gypsy. (*She was mad because he got billing over her.*) He was not careful about his personal hygiene. He stank! I decided to out-do him. I didn't take any baths during filming, and he had to do love scenes with me, and sometimes I flubbed a line, and the director (*Mitchell Leisen, who was gay and had a thing for Milland and also for Fred MacMurray*) made Ray Milland more nervous and agitated (*by making passes at him*). By the time we finished the picture, I left my top-billed co-star a nervous wreck!… Now I see that Ray Milland has lost all his hair. So there!"

On Women -- "Once a woman has forgiven a man, she must not reheat his sins for breakfast."

(*On actress Jane Wyman*): "I did one film with Alfred Hitchcock (*"Stage Fright," 1950*). Jane Wyman was in it. I heard she'd only wanted to do it if she were billed above me, and she got her wish. Hitchcock didn't think much of her, saying "She looks too much like a victim to play the heroine, and God knows she couldn't play a woman of mystery. Miss Wyman looks like a mystery nobody has bothered to solve."

(*On Elsa Lanchester and Charles Laughton, with whom she appeared in "Witness for the Prosecution," 1957*): "Poor Elsa. She left England because it already had a queen. And she wanted to be queen of the Charles Laughton household, once he became a star, but he already had the role."

The Inner Woman -- (*On filming "The Blue Angel"*): "I thought everything we were doing was awful. They kept a camera pointed here [at my groin]. I was so young and dumb."

"Who is this Miss Madonna? The idea that she would make a film from my 'Blue Angel' is outrageous! She's no angel... on the contrary!"

"I'm not an actress – I'm a personality. I never ever took my career seriously."

"I never enjoyed working in a film. I had no desire to be a film actress, to always play somebody else, to be beautiful with somebody constantly straightening out your every eyelash. It was always a big bother to me."

"Think twice before burdening a friend with a secret."

"The legs aren't so beautiful. I just know what to do with them."

(*On her preference for wearing trousers*): "They are so comfortable. It takes too much time to be a well-dressed woman. I have watched others. Bags, shoes, hats. They must think of them all the time. I cannot waste that time."

"I have a child and I have made a few people happy. That is all."

Phyllis Diller

The comedienne's marriage was not happy, but a later partnership was. She was plagued with family tragedy, but was a survivor into her mid-90s. If comedy is born from tragedy, she was a living example of it. Through it all, she kept her sense of humor and got many laughs in the ladies' room:

"Burt Reynolds once asked me out. I was in his room."

"I admit, I have a tremendous sex drive. My boyfriend lives forty miles away."

Born Phyllis Ada Driver in Lima, Ohio, o July 17, 1947, she was the only child of an insurance agent and his wife. She met Sherwood Anderson Diller in college and they eloped to Kentucky in November, 1939 while she was pregnant with their first child. During World War II, Diller worked at the Willow Run Bomber Plant in Ypsilanti, Michigan, where they lived and had five more children together. Her husband was sex-driven, could not keep a job very long, and spent his time inventing products that never got produced, so she divorced him in 1965.

She married actor Warde Donovan that same year but divorced him after three months when discovering he was bisexual and an alcoholic. They reconciled the day before their divorce was to become final and remained married until she divorced him in 1995. She was the partner of Robert P. Hastings from 1985 until his death in 1996. She said that "Fang," her fictional husband in her comic routines, was not like any of her husbands.

Her career began on radio, moved to television and then films and Broadway. In 2003 she was awarded the Women in Film Lucy Award, named after Lucille Ball, honoring Diller for her work enhancing the perception of women through the medium of television. A better pianist than she credited herself, she appeared as a piano soloist in classical concerts with about 100 symphony orchestras in the 1970's and received glowing reviews from critics.

Life was not full of laughs for Diller. She suffered heartaches as a mother, when her first child, a boy, died of cancer when he was 58 years old, and her second child, a girl, was a schizophrenic most of her life. A third child, a son, lived only two weeks in an incubator, and a daughter born in 1948 died of a stroke in 2002, but another son and daughter survived Diller.

Diller began suffering from various ailments when she was 80 and in 1999 suffered a heart attack and was fitted with a pacemaker. She retired from stand-up comedy as she approached 90. She continued as a performer until her death on August 20, 2012. She died at the age of 95 with what family members said was a smile on her face.

On Sex -- "Sex can be a great burden for men, because their role is still more important than women's. Men still have to act, while all women have to do is react."

On Men – "His finest hour lasted a minute and a half."

"I'm a sucker for beauty… be it in a man, a woman, a child, a house, or a car. Both my husbands were very attractive. If there is ever a choice in anything, I'll always choose beauty."

"A bachelor is a guy who never made the same mistake once."

"The thing that gets me is an attractive man who treats me like a lady. I'm a candlelight-and-romance lady, and I can't compromise in anything because I know that you can get romance if you wait long enough for that man to come along."

"Women's liberation is never going to change relationships between men and women. I'm a third-generation career girl, so I've always been liberated and I take it for granted. And I like being a woman."

"The ideal man is sensitive and cares about how the other person feels. Really, men should stop being so uptight about being good lovers and just do what comes naturally. But if a man is worrying about sex and making love, he should listen to instruction from a female. It's often unfortunate being a woman to teach a young man because experienced men are much better than beginners. They have been taught by many women."

"Men don't approach me. I'm not an approachable woman and I never have been. I wasn't even an approachable child. I was bright, and boys don't approach bright girls."

"The male ego is the most delicate thing in the world. It is nurtured in such a way that it is supposed to be solid rock, and isn't allowed to be human. So men assume the role of being completely impervious to any ego threats. That's why you get men who go to single bars wanting sex but no marriage responsibility."

On Marriage – "I've been asked to say a couple of words about my husband, Fang. How about short and cheap?"

"Whatever you may look like, marry a man your own age. As your beauty fades, so will his eyesight."

"Our dog died from licking our wedding picture."

"It's a good thing that beauty is only skin deep, or I'd be rotten to the core."

"My photographs don't do me justice. They just look like me."

"It costs a lot of money to look this cheap."

"I'm not offended by all the dumb-blonde jokes because I know that I'm not dumb. I also know I'm not blonde."

"Old age is when the liver spots show through your gloves."

"You know you're old if your walker has an airbag."

"The reason women don't play football is because eleven of them would never wear the same outfit in public."

"Women want men, careers, money, children, friends, luxury, comfort, independence, freedom, respect, love, and a three-dollar pantyhose that won't run."

"My cooking is so bad, my kids thought Thanksgiving was to commemorate Pearl Harbor."

"Housework can't kill you, but why take a chance?"

"Cleaning your house while your kids are still growing up is like shoveling the walk before it stops snowing."

"The best way to get rid of kitchen odors: Eat out."

"I'm eighteen years behind in my ironing. The only time I ever enjoyed ironing was the day I accidentally got gin in the steam iron."

"I buried a lot of my ironing in the back yard."

The Inner Woman – "I wanted to become me, totally me. The more me, the better. I instinctively knew this and I was right."

"Beautiful women are not funny. Can you feature Grace Kelly as a comedienne?"

Composer Leonard Bernstein said of Diller: "She used to be hilarious. Then she had all those face-lifts, so now she looks good… and she's dull."

"My recipe for dealing with anger and frustration: set the kitchen timer for twenty minutes, cry, rant, and rave, and at the sound of the bell, simmer down and go about business as usual."

"Aim high, and you won't shoot your foot off."

"Never go to bed mad. Stay up and fight."

"A smile is a curve that sets everything straight."

"If it weren't for baseball, many kids wouldn't know what a millionaire looked like."

"Tranquilizers work only if you follow the advice on the bottle – Keep away from children."

"Most children threaten at times to run away from home. This is the only thing that keeps some parents going."

"We spend the first twelve months of our children's lives teaching them to walk and talk and the next twelve telling them to sit down and shut up."

"Always be nice to your children because they are the ones who will choose your rest home."

Jane Fonda

Most of her life a human punching bag, Fonda has survived heartaches and emerged a mature and content woman, apparently even happy. The walls of her homes could not talk, but she could, in the ladies' room.

"I always had a penchant for falling in love. Every time I found myself without a mate, I fell into a state of low-sizzling panic."

"I was a chameleon, the woman men wanted me to be."

"The only thing I have never known is true intimacy with a man. I absolutely wanted to discover that before dying."

Born Lady Jane Seymour Fonda on December 21, 1937 in New York City, her father was the famous film and stage actor Henry Fonda and her mother a socialite, Frances Brokaw. Her mother committed suicide when Jane was 12. Jane Fonda attended Vassar College in Poughkeepsie, New York, then followed in her father's footsteps into becoming a film actress, winning two Academy Awards for best actress, for "Kulte" in 1971 and "Coming Home" in 1978.

After her appearances in several sexy films including "Barbarella" in 1968 for her then-husband Roger Vadim (*married 1965-1973*), she made headlines by championing anti-establishment causes, especially opposing America's involvement in the Vietnam War when many criticized her for being anti-American. Her anti-war activities continued with her next husband, Tom Hayden (*married 1973-1990*), from the late 1970s and into the early 1980s.

"I was so devastated by my second divorce (*to Tom Hayden in 1990*) that I had a nervous breakdown... When Tom and I split up, I wanted to kill him. But a wise woman said, "It will take two years, and you'll be friends." "I said, "No way!" But then we became friends. I (also) was at Vadim's bedside when he died. No matter how angry I get, I try to stay friends with the men I've been close to."

During her marriage to Roger Vadim, who earlier had affairs with Brigitte Bardot and Catherine Deneuve, he was not faithful, claiming that jealousy was "so bourgeois." To be a good wife, she embraced his passions, including sometimes threesomes in bed. "Sometimes it was even I who did the soliciting," she wrote in her autobiography. "So adept was I at burying my real feelings, that I eventually had myself convinced I enjoyed it."

"My interest in what men think about me started with my father," she wrote in a 2005 autobiography. "I saw myself in him, and I wanted his approval." (*Her father had told her that she would not be loved unless she was perfect.*)

She was 12 when her mother committed suicide and she said she shut down emotionally afterward. "I would become whatever I felt people whose love and attention I needed wanted me to be. I would try to be perfect."

Although her father was apprehensive about her becoming an actress, she made a screen test in 1959 with Warren Beatty for a film that was never made. It was his first screen test, too, and they were both very passionate. He said, "We were thrown together like two lions in a cage and kissed until we had practically eaten each other's heads off." Fonda said, "I thought Warren was gay. He played piano, and all his friends were gay." In later films, she was attracted to Robert Redford, her co-star in "Barefoot in the Park" (1967) and other films. "I was so in love with Bob. Nothing ever happened between us, but he certainly was fabulous to kiss."

Fonda's career in exercise videos began in 1978 when her stepmother suggested she try an exercise class that included ballet. Fonda loved it and she and her teacher began a business with *Jane Fonda's Workout* which sold 17 million copies. "I had a vision. I wanted to give a cultural face to older women." She had her own need of physical rehabilitation because she had both hip and knee replacements.

She had one child with Vadim and two with Hayden. In 1995 she was chosen 21st of the 100 sexiest stars in films. A very rich woman, her wealth in 1984 was estimated at $50 million, but it keeps increasing as she releases more exercise videos.

Fonda says about the greatest thing of her life: "It's called resilience. And it's a very mysterious thing. (*When she went to auditions as a young actress*), "Half of the other actresses were far more beautiful than I, and the other half were far more talented, but none of those women made it. I'd wonder, Why did it happen for me and not for them? Now I think it had to do with that core resilience. I was born that way, and they just weren't. On my bad days, I say to myself, 'Fonda, you're resilient, and you've never stopped trying to get better.' That's my mantra, and it's saved me many, many times."

On Love -- "All my life I had believed that unless I was perfect, I would not be loved."

"Real love and intimacy can be much more possible when you're older."

On Men -- "When you have, like I did, a father incapable of showing emotion (*in life*), who spends his life telling you that no one will love you if you aren't perfect, it leaves scars. We're not meant to be perfect. It took me a long time to learn that."

"I've been accused of being too flexible, too willing to mold myself to men, and that's something I'm constantly working on."

"I'm a very brave person. I can go to North Vietnam, I can challenge my government, but I can't challenge the man I'm with, if it means I'm going to end up alone."

"A man has every season, while a woman only has the right to spring."

"Acting with Laurence Harvey (*reportedly gay or bisexual*) is like acting by yourself, only worse." (*The film was "Walk on the Wild Side," 1962.*)

"I see many more men who are feminist, or at least who have learned about life in the context of feminism."
"I think feminism is about the spirit. Feminism is not just about women; it's about letting all people lead fuller lives."

(O*n her marriage to Ted Turner*): "Ted Turner needs someone to be there 100 percent of the time. He thinks that's love. It's not love. It's babysitting."

(**On Marriage to Ted Turner**): "I hadn't dated in 17 years. Turner was smitten. He devoured me with his eyes. It had been a very long time since someone had that reaction to me. I was a very different person I had been with Hayden or Vadim. I felt great with Ted. Very liberated." She also said, "For his own reasons, Ted moves laterally through life, very fast. Across his millions of acres, I wanted to go vertically. I knew if I stayed with him, I'd be safe, I wouldn't need to work, and it would be interesting. But I would never be a whole person, and I wanted to be a whole person."

On Women -- "I am blessed beyond reason with women friends."

"Seek women mentors. If you're a businesswoman, look at the TEDx conferences. There's a lot of businesswomen that speak on there. I find them extremely inspiring."

(*In her senior years*): "I am able to talk about my life in a way that helps other women – and men, but mostly women – understand their own life. I feel real proud of that. And then the fact that my children are okay. You know, you're only as happy as your least happy child. So if your kids aren't okay, you're not (*feeling*) good."

The Inner Woman -- "My childhood was influenced by the roles my father played in the movies. Whether Abraham Lincoln (*"Young Mr. Lincoln, 1939*) or Tom Joad in' The Grapes of Wrath' (*1940*), his characters communicated certain values which I try to carry to me to this day."

"I was never a hippie! I went to India because so many friends like Mia Farrow and The Beatles were going there to discover truth. And so I went and trekked through India by myself, but instead of discovering truth, I wanted to join the Peace Corps."

"You don't learn from successes; you don't learn from awards; you don't learn from celebrity; you only learn from wounds and scars and mistakes and failures. And that's the truth."

(*In 1970, speaking to students at the University of Michigan on her Vietnam War position*): "It hurt so many soldiers (*her support for the Viet Cong*). It galvanized such hostility. It was the most horrible thing I could possibly have done. It was just thoughtless. I, a Socialist, think we should strive toward a Socialist society, all the way to Communism. If you understood what Communism was, you would hope, you would pray on your knees that one day we would become Communist."

"It's hard to imagine a happy ending for the U.S.-led war in Iraq. What it's going to mean for stability as a nation, for terrorism, for the economy I can't imagine."

(*In her later years*): "Dating's not something I spend a lot of time thinking about. Nor do I miss it, frankly. I feel 71 years old. I'm really aware of the miles that have been logged and of the life that has gone under the bridge and how it has made me grow. I'm someone who has always tried to think about what it has all meant. I'm a quester. So I feel my age. I feel grown up."

"I try to live my third act in such a way that I won't have regrets. You never get there entirely, but you can spend your life working at it."

"I took (*the 1971 role in*) 'Klute' because, in it, I expose a great deal of the oppression of women in this country – the system which makes women sell themselves for possessions."

"Aging is not what we used to think it was, where you peak at middle age. It's ascending a staircase into growth, wisdom, well-being and happiness."

"The people who did you wrong or who didn't quite know how to show up, you forgive them. And forgiving them allows you to forgive yourself, too."

"I feel like my honesty gives people the freedom to talk about things they wouldn't otherwise."

"Instead of drifting along like a leaf in a river, understand who you are and how you come across to people and what kind of impact you have on the people around you and the community around you and the world, so that when you go out, you can feel you have made a positive difference."

"We cannot always control our thoughts, but we can control our words, and repetition impresses the subconscious, and we are then master of the situation."

"While not impossible, it is essentially challenging for teenage parents to develop bonds with their children. A high percent of them were themselves children of teenage parents and have never experienced appropriate parenting."

"The reality is sobering: in the United States, one in three girls will become pregnant before age 20, totaling more than 750,000 girls per year."

"If we as a nation are to break the cycle of poverty, crime and the growing underclass of young people ill-equipped to be productive citizens, we need to not only implement effective programs to prevent teen pregnancy, but we must also help those (*teenagers*) who have already given birth so that they become effective, nurturing, bonding parents."

"The bond between a parent and child is the primary bond, the foundation for the rest of the child's life. The presence or absence of this bond determines much about the child's resiliency and what kind of adult they will grow up to be."

"I don't think there's anything more important than making peace (*with your children*) before it's too late. And it almost always falls to the child to try to move toward the parent."

"A mother who is obsessing about being thin and dieting and exercising is not going to be a very good mother."
"I was in my mid-40s. I was a bulimic (*compulsive eating while emotionally stressed and then throwing up, so you do not gain weight, a malady from which Princess Diana also suffered*), and I realized if I continue with this addiction of mine, I will not be able to continue doing my life. The older you get, the more damage it does; it takes longer to recover from a binge (*eating*). And it was very hard."

"When you can't remember why you're hurt, that's when you're healed."

"One part of wisdom is knowing what you don't need anymore and letting it go."

"The most important thing to do as you age is to stay physically active. Lots of people just throw in the towel if they can't do what they used to do, and that's terrible."

"As I started getting older, I realized, I'm so happy! I didn't expect this! I wasn't happy when I was young."

"It's never too late – never too late to start over, never too late to be happy."

Zsa Zsa Gabor

An Hungarian Cinderella, she had nine Prince Charmings for husbands who all turned out to be frogs in disguise. No wonder she laughs at men and love:

"A man in love is incomplete until he has married. Then he's finished."

"A girl must marry for love, and keep on marrying until she finds it."

"Personally, I know nothing about sex because I've always been married."

Born Sari Gabor on February 6, 1917 in Budapest, Hungary, she was known less as an actress than as an international personality who was often married. Her sisters were actress Eva Gabor and socialite Magda Gabor. Their Jewish mother escaped Nazi-occupied Hungary in World War II and took her daughters to California. Zsa Zsa's beauty as a young woman landed her in television series and movies from the 1950s into the 1970s.

She was married nine times: Berhan Belge (1937-1941); hotel magnat Conrad Hilton (1942-1947, with who she had a child); actor George Sanders (1949-1954); Herbert Hunter (1962-1966); Joshua S. Cosden Jr. (1966-1967); Jack Ryan (1975-1976); Michael O'Hara (1976-1982); Felipe de Alba (1983-1983), and German Prince Frederic von Anhalt to whom she was married in 1986 and they remain married to the present. Her sister Magda also was married to Sanders from 1970 to 1971. Zsa Zsa turned 100 in 2016, following rumors she had died the year before.

Gabor made news in 1989 when she slapped the face of a 6 foot, 4 inches tall police officer who stopped her while she was driving in Beverly Hills, California. He found that she was driving without a license and there was an open flask containing Jack Daniels in her $215,000 Rolls-Royce. She took a possible 18-month jail sentence lightly by saying, "That would be wonderful. I'd have time to write my book." She did not go to jail but was fined for the misdemeanors. She had earlier been convicted in England of hitting a police officer with her purse and fined $5,000.

Gabor made headlines again, in 1995, when actress Elke Sommer won a law suit alleging that Gabor libeled her in two German magazine articles calling her a "bald-headed Hollywood has-been who needed to sell hand-knitted pullover sweaters to eke out a living. And hung out in seedy bars." Sommer had said Gabor was a "fat pig who needed three or four men to lift her onto the saddle of a horse." A Santa Monica Superior Court jury ended their feud by awarding Sommer $3.3 million from Gabor and her husband, the largest personal libel judgment in history. Gabor and her husband were worth more than $8 million and had to sell their mansion to pay the bill. One juror afterward said, "Both ladies looked fine."

On Love -- "To be loved is a strength. To love is a weakness."

(*After fighting with boyfriend Porfirio Rubirosa in which he gave her a black eye*): "Rubi loves me. Rubirosa in Spanish means red rose. For me it means black eye. A man only hits a woman if he loves her deeply."

"I only cook when I'm in love."

On Sex -- "The women's movement hasn't changed my sex life. It wouldn't dare."

On Men -- "I have never hated a man enough to give his diamonds back."

"To a smart girl men are no problem -- they're the answer."

"I pay all my own bills."

"I want to choose a man. I do not permit men to choose me."

"Macho does not prove mucho."

"I like a mannish man: a man who knows how to talk to and treat a woman, not just a man with muscles."

"The only place men want depth in a woman is in her décolletage."

(*On Cary Grant*): "They are trying to show he's a great lover, but they'll never prove it to me."

"The only way to learn a language properly, in fact, is to marry a man of that nationality. You get what they call in Europe a "sleeping dictionary". Of course, I have only been married five times and I speak seven languages. I'm still trying to remember where I picked up the other two."

"The best way to attract a man immediately is to have a magnificent bosom and a half-size brain and let both of them show."

On Marriage -- "I believe in large families: every woman should have at least three husbands."

"The feather in your cap is to get a man you love who'll marry you."

"When you are married to an actor, you feel you are nothing but an understudy to him. He only has eyes for himself. It is really the one situation I know of where, with just two people you have a triangle."

(*On George Sanders, the favorite of her husbands before her present one, and while she was married to Conrad Hilton*): "I thought he (*Sanders*) hated women, and that was a marvelous challenge. When I met him I said, 'Mr. Sanders, I'm madly in love with you.' And he said, 'Mrs. Hilton, how well I understand that.'"

(*When asked how many husbands she had*): "You mean other than my own?"

"It's never as easy to keep your own spouse happy as it is to make someone else's spouse happy."

On Divorce -- "Getting divorced just because you don't love a man is almost as silly as getting married just because you do."

"Conrad Hilton was very generous to me in the divorce settlement. He gave me 5,000 *Gideon Bibles.*"

"I am a marvelous housekeeper. Every time I leave a man, I keep his house."

"You never really know a man until you have divorced him."

"Getting divorced just because you don't love a man is almost as silly as getting married just because you do."

The Inner Woman -- "I don't remember anybody's name. How do you think the 'dahling' thing got started?"

"Being jealous of a beautiful woman is not going to make you more beautiful."

"If they had as much adultery going on in New York as they said in the divorce courts, they wouldn't have had enough time left over to run the subways or mow the grass in Central Park and they would never have a chance to make the beds at the Plaza."

"I want a man who's kind and understanding. Is that too much to ask of a millionaire?"

Lady Gaga

The outlandishly sexy dresser both on-stage and off is candid about her views on love and marriage. There is no one quite like her in the ladies' room:

"Love is like a brick. You can build a house, or you can sink a dead body."

"Be yourself and love who you are and be proud. Because you were born this way, baby."

Born Stefani Joanne Angelina Geremanotta in New York City on March 26, 1986, her father was an Internet entrepreneur. She is of Italian, French-Canadian, English, German, and Scottish ancestry. Her parents were Roman Catholics and she attended a Catholic school from the age 11 where she was bullied for being smaller and more plump than the other girls. Three years later she was singing in clubs and bars and at the age of 17 enrolled in New York University's Tisch School of the Arts.

She moved out of her parents' home and began a career as a professional singer. A talent scout, Rob Fusari, gave her stage name which is a reference to the song "Radio Ga-Ga" by Queen (*the British rock group whose lead singer Freddie Mercury died in 1991 from bronchopneumonia resulting from AIDS.*) She then began singing in go-go dance bars wearing a bikini and experimenting with drugs. Besides singing she wrote songs for other performers including Britney Spears.

She began recording and touring Europe and gay bars in the United States to promote her first album in 2008 but was not much of a success. Her first hit was "Just Dance" the following year and she was on her way to becoming famous. Her 2009 singing tour grossed more than $227 million, one of the highest-grossing pop concert tours of all time.

During her shows, she encourages fans to be self-confident and "be whoever you want to be." She performs in various colored wigs, dances wildly in suggestive clothes, wears high heel and elaborate sunglasses, and lovingly calls her fans "Monsters." She has 14 tattoos, a peace sign on her left wrist. "Little Monsters" and a Rainer Rilke quote both on her left inner bicep, the death date of her aunt Joanne and daisies on her left shoulder blade, a treble clef on her center lower back, flowers up her left side, a unicorn with "Born This Way," the word "ARTPOP" on her left forearm, an anchor on the left side of her ribcage, a cherub and "Rio" on the back of her head.

She quit drinking liquor and smoking marijuana, becoming addicted after a hip injury in 2013. She is very generous with donations to charities including the Red Cross for disaster relief, and causes such as AIDS and Alzheimer's cures and needy children. She has won two Grammy awards for her singing.

Lady Gaga was in a relationship with musician and bartender Luc Carl, but since 2011 has been in one with actor Taylor Kinney and they became engaged in 2015. Kinney is a handsome hunk who starred in the "Chicago Fire" television series and the film "Vampire Diaries." They were expected to marry in 2016.

On Men -- "You must never let a guy know how much you like him, because then he'll run in the other direction. When you don't play hard to get, if you're too easy or you come off too eager, they run away, so you gotta keep your poker face on."

(*On Freddie Mercury*): "Freddie was unique – one of the biggest personalities in the whole of pop music."

"Some women choose to follow men, and some women choose to follow their dreams."

On Sex and Sexuality – *(In a 2009 interview she said her interest in women is purely physical, but it makes the men in her life "uncomfortable."*

(*Sex*): "It's always been important to me, as it's for my generation, a most relevant consideration when you're growing up. Sex doesn't mean nothing; sex means so much. I hope that young women know that sex is still a biological deal, and they don't have to put out soon.

If they want someone to court them for a while before they give it up, that's wonderful and beautiful, and a man will only respect you more for honoring your body. I am that way."

The Inner Woman -- "The truth is, the psychotic woman that I truly am comes out when I'm not working. When I'm not working, I go crazy."

"First thing in the morning, try to think compassionate thoughts about yourself for five minutes. I don't always do it, but I try to."

"Acceptance, tolerance, bravery, compassion. These are the things my mom taught me!"

"My mother and I have initiated a passion project. Together we hope to establish a standard of Bravery and Kindness, as well as a community worldwide that protects and nurtures others in the face of bullying and abandonment."

"Don't you ever let a soul in the world tell you that you can't be exactly who you are."

"The performer ages and the music ages and so do the things that we create. But at the end of the day, I will still always live for the applause -- even when I'm an old lady and no one knows who I am anymore."

Greta Garbo

Garbo, one of the most beautiful actresses desired by worlds of men, among them the handsomest and wealthiest, was a lesbian. She kept it secret, like the Sphinx. You would never hear her talk about it in the ladies' room, but she had others things to say there, about both men and women:

"There are some who want to get married and others who don't. I have never had an impulse to go to the altar. I am a difficult person to lead."

"You don't have to be married to have a good friend as your partner for life."

Born Greta Lovisa Gustanfsson on September 18, 1905 in Stockholm, Sweden to a laborer father and a factory working mother. Her father died when Greta was 14 and she had to leave school. She worked in a department store and modeled for the store's newspaper ads. While still a teenager she appeared in a short advertising film for the store and was given a small part in a film in 1922.

She then won a scholarship to study at a Swedish drama school where she was noticed by Swedish director Mauritz Stiller who cast her as the lead in his film "The Saga of Gosta Berlings" in 1924 when she was 18 and she quickly rose to stardom in Sweden.

Her first film in America, the silent "Torrent," in 1928 launched her to stardom in America. She remained in silent films until "Anna Christie" in 1930, and became one of the top female stars of that decade, often co-starred with John Gilbert, one of the leading matinee idols of the silent films. He loved her but it was unrequited. It was reported in newspapers in 1938 that she and Leopold Stokowsky, conductor of the Philadelphia Symphony Orchestra, were to be married, but she denied it saying they were only friends.

Garbo's private life was bisexual and perhaps more lesbian, having been in affairs with silent screen lesbian Lilyan Tashman and another lesbian, Mercedes de Acosta, the daughter of a butcher who masqueraded as a duchess. De Costa once asked, "Who of us are only one sex? I, myself, am sometimes androgynous."

Movie legend Louise Brooks said about Garbo: "She was a completely masculine dyke, which makes her films even more wonderful." To cover rumors about her lesbian affairs, her studio, MGM, had its publicity department spread the story that she and her co-star in several top films, John Gilbert, were in love with each other off-screen. It was only half-true because while he loved her, she just acted the part of being in love with him. Brooks said Garbo "went out with him and gave him a casual lay from time to time for the sake of her career."

Garbo later admitted she loved Gilbert but backed out of plans to marry him because he was "overbearing." Said Garbo, "I was afraid he would tell me what to do and boss me. I always wanted to be the boss." Garbo lost interest in Gilbert and entered an affair with her next co-star, Nils Asher who was gay and even more handsome than Gilbert.

Garbo then became the main focus of celebrity photographer Cecil Beaton. He and de Costa had been in an affair and when she heard Garbo call him "Darling," she went into a rage, telling Garbo,
Garbo then became the main focus of celebrity photographer Cecil Beaton. He and de Costa had been in an affair and when she heard Garbo call him "Darling," she went into a rage, telling Garbo, "Don't you dare call anyone darling but me!" Garbo then became enraged at Beaton for publishing his diaries which went into detail about their affair together and ended their relationship.

Nominated for the Academy Award three times, she received an honorary one in 1954 for her "luminous and unforgettable screen performances." In 1999, the American Film Institute named her fifth on their list of the greatest female stars of Classic Hollywood Cinema, after Katharine Hepburn, Bette Davis, Audrey Hepburn, and Ingrid Bergman.

Garbo retired from movies at the age of 35 after acting in 28 films. She wanted and got a private life then, neither marrying nor having children, living a reclusive life in a Manhattan apartment. She

survived breast cancer in 1984 but died of pneumonia and renal failure on April 15, 1990 at the age of 84. She died a very wealthy woman, investing in the Stock Market and paintings, her estate valued at $57 million by 2013 rates, the fortune left to a niece.

On Marriage -- "There is no one who would have me . . . I can't cook."

The Inner Woman – *(In a 1926 fan magazine interview shortly after arriving in Hollywood and not speaking English very well):* "I don't want to be bad woman on the screen. That is my only trouble in

America. People say I am what you call 'vamp type.' I know what they mean, but do not think I am. I do not want to play 'bad woman.'"

"The story of my life is about back entrances, side doors, secret elevators and other ways of getting in and out of places so that people won't bother me."

"Being a movie star, and this applies to all of them, means being looked at from every possible direction. You are never left at peace, you're just fair game."

"I never said, 'I want to be alone.' I only said, 'I want to be left alone.' There is a whole world of difference."

"If only those who dream about Hollywood knew how difficult it all is."

"There are many things in your heart you can never tell another person. They are you, your private joys and sorrows, and you can never tell them. You cheapen yourself, the inside of yourself, when you tell them."

"I wish I were supernaturally strong so I could put right everything that is wrong."

"Every one of us lives his life just once; if we are honest, to live once is enough."

(*In 1932, about her recreational preferences*): "If I needed recreation, I liked to be out of doors: to trudge about in a boy's coat and boy's shoes; to ride horseback, or shoot craps with the stable boys, or watch the sun set in a blaze of glory over the Pacific Ocean. You see, I am still a bit of a tomboy. Most hostesses disapprove of this trousered attitude to life, so I do not inflict it upon them."

(*In 1932, about her desire for privacy*): "I am still a little nervous, a little self-conscious about my English. I cannot express myself well at parties. I speak haltingly. I feel awkward, shy, afraid. In

Hollywood, where every teat table bristles with gossip-writers, what I say might be misunderstood. So I am silent as the grave about my private affairs. Rumors fly about. I am mum. My private affairs are strictly private."

(*On director Mauritz Stiller and her relationship with him*): "Stiller's death was a great blow to me. For so long I had been his satellite. All Europe regarded Stiller as the most significant figure in the film world (*in the late 1920s*). Stiller had found me, an obscure artist in Sweden, and brought me to America. I worshiped him. There are some, of course, who say it was a love story. It was more. It was utter devotion which only the very young can know -- the adoration of a student for her teacher, of a timid girl for a mastermind.

"In his studio, Stiller taught me how to do everything: how to eat; how to turn my head; how to express love--and hate. Off the screen I studied his every whim, wish and demand. I lived my life according to the plans he laid down. He told what to say and what to do.

"When Stiller died I found myself like a ship without a rudder. I was bewildered – lost -- and very lonely. I resolutely refused to talk to reporters because I didn't know what to say. By degrees I dropped out of the social whirl of Hollywood. I retired into my shell. I built a wall of repression around my real self, and I lived -- and still live -- behind it."

"Life would be so wonderful if we only knew what to do with it."

Ava Gardner

Her three husbands had a total of 19 wives between them at one time or another. Three times a bride, the love of Ava's life was her third husband, Frank Sinatra. They adored each other but were just incompatible as a married couple. Even a partnership didn't work for them. It could make one cry, hearing about it in the ladies' room.

"I think the main reason my marriages failed is that I always loved too well, but never wisely."

"I suffered, I really suffered, with all three of my husbands. And I tried damn hard with all three, starting each marriage certain that it was going to last until the end of my life, Yet none of them lasted more than a year or two."

"Maybe, in the final analysis, they saw me as something I wasn't, and I tried to turn them into something they could never be. I loved them all, but maybe I never understood any of them. I don't think they understood me."

"Because I was promoted as a sort of siren and played all those sexy broads, people made the mistake of thinking I was like that off the screen. They couldn't have been more wrong. I was just a country girl with a country girl's values."

Ava Gardner was born by Caesarean section on Christmas Eve, on December 24, 1922 in Grabtown, North Carolina, to Mary Baker Gardner and Jonas Gardner and had six siblings. She was born on a tobacco farm where she got her lifelong love of earthy language and going barefoot, and grew up in the rural South. A photograph of her at age 18 was seen by a talent scout for MGM Studios and when the head of the studio, Louis B. Mayer, saw her screen test, he said, "She can't talk, she can't act, she's terrific." Like fans worldwide, he had fallen for her beauty and some sense of chemistry in her.

She appeared in small roles in 17 films at MGM and then was "discovered" when she was loaned out to Universal for "The Killers" in 1946. Because MGM kept her in minor roles in mostly mediocre films while under contract from 1941 to 1958, she never believed in her acting ability. Despite that, she was nominated for a Best Actress Oscar for her role in "Mogambo," a 1953 John Ford jungle dramatic romance co-starring Clark Gable.

Gardner was married three times, first to actor Mickey Rooney (14 months: 1942-1943). He bragged that she lost her virginity to hi. The marriage got off to a lonely start. The day after they married, Rooney went off to play golf with some pals, and Ava said later that she saw little of him on their honeymoon and she never forgave him for that.

Next, she married band leader Artie Shaw (7 months: 1945-1946); and then singer-actor Frank Sinatra (1951-1957), who called her "Angel" and who she considered to be the love of her life, but they just couldn't get along.

Ava became pregnant twice by Sinatra but on both occasions had an abortion. Ava filed for divorce from Sinatra on the grounds of desertion but in fact is was out of jealousy because he was having an a affair with Lauren Bacall. Ava's three husbands had 19 wives between them, Rooney with eight, Shaw with seven, and Sinatra with four. After her failed marriage to Sinatra she moved to Spain in 1955. There she met and became a good friend of author Ernest Hemingway, sharing his love of bullfighting, and later starred in three films based on his novels.

Tax problems in Spain led to her move to London where she spent her last 22 years in reasonable comfort as a recluse in an apartment. She suffered from a severe case of emphysema in her later life and could not travel far without an oxygen tank for breathing. Two strokes in 1986 left her partially paralyzed and bedridden and she contemplated suicide. She died of bronchial pneumonia at the age of 67 on January 25, 1990. None of her three former husbands was present at her funeral and she was buried in her native North Carolina.

The American Film Institute named her as one of the greatest American female screen legends. She left a considerable sum of money in her will for care of her dog, a Welsh Corgi, who was taken in by her friend, actor Gregory Peck, her co-star in "On the Beach:" (1959). A statue of Gardner from "The Barefoot Contessa" (1954), was given to Sinatra as a gift. He kept it in his backyard garden long after their divorce, but when he married Barbara Marx, widow of Zeppo Marx of the Marx Brothers comedians, she forced him to get rid of it.

On Sex -- "Sex isn't all that important, but it is when you love someone very much."

On Love and Marriage -- "I'm frequently asked what I saw in Mickey Rooney. In retrospect, I think one reason I married him was what he saw in me… Don't forget, he was one of the biggest movie stars at the time, and I was fresh from the cotton and tobacco fields of North Carolina."

(*They had met on the set of one of his films while she was 18 and he 21, he was immediately struck by her beauty, began dating her and within a few months they were married, in a simple ceremony in Ballard, California on January 10, 1942. Soon friction came between them as he began seeing some of his earlier girlfriends. They separated and reconciled several times until in September she said*, "Things weren't happy around the house and we decided to call it quits." They reconciled again but divorced in February 1943. She then fell in love with Artie Shaw and Rooney married a 17-year-old girl 16 days after meeting her but they divorced a few years later.

Summing up her marriage to Rooney, Ava said, "He was a little boy and I was a little girl. We were immature in entirely different ways."

(*On her wedding to Frank Sinatra*): "Most of all, I want a marriage that's happy. That should be the most important thing in any woman's life, and I know it is in mine. Everything else should be secondary. Let me choose between a happy marriage and a successful career and I'd choose the first every time." (*Yet, that was a main reason their marriage failed, their careers often keeping them apart and neither of them believed the other respected their career enough.*)

(*On Frank Sinatra; Gossip columnist Louella Parsons wrote in February 1954, about hearing him singing at his shows in Las Vegas*): "He sang his heart out. Never had he sung such love songs

with such feeling. He was singing right to Ava (*whether she was in the audience or not*). This we all knew. (*He told me*): 'I can't eat. I can't sleep. I love her. (*But*) She doesn't love me anymore." (*What kept them apart, she wrote, was pride, stubbornness, and jealousy. He said:* "Ava's wrong this time. I've been wrong other times, but this time it's all her fault. She'll have to call me."

Sinatra told Parsons that he needed sympathy and understanding from Ava but didn't get it, and their careers separated them. "My career didn't seem important to her." *(One of them finally did call the other and they made up, but the arguments continued until their stormy marriage finally ended.)* Parsons wrote: "They both say that they love each other. Well, this is a curious kind of love, but I suppose when two people are so madly in love, anything can happen."

(*Ava on Sinatra, to Parsons in 1954*): "If he really loves me and thinks my career interferes, I'd give it up, and anything else, just to be with him. He means more to me than anything else in the world." *Among other things, Parsons wrote, Ava was jealous and thought he was having an affair with Deborah Kerr, with whom he starred in "From Here to Eternity" (1953). Parsons said Kerr denied it, saying "We were never anything more than friends. I tried to comfort Frank about Ava." Then, too, Sinatra was jealous of men who fell in love with her, such as the handsome young Spanish bullfighter Mario Cabre.*

(*Parsons on Ava*): "As beautiful as Ava is, I've never known her to look twice at any other man since she married Frank. He seems to think she does, but he's wrong. Ava's whole heart has belonged to Frankie from the time they discovered they were in love. She has told me again and again of her love for him. She told me, 'Careers had nothing to do with their troubles, but they are all too personal to tell you. Our problems are our own affair.'"

On Men -- "I hate cheating. I won't put up with it. I don't do it myself."

"I must have seen more sunrises than any other actress in the history of Hollywood."

(*On Clark Gable*): "He will always be my Sir Galahad."

(*On writer Rex Reed*): "He's either at your feet or at your throat."

(*On Paul Newman*): "I'd rather leave the directing to the directors. I'd find it distracting to be directed by a Paul Newman. Co-starring with him is fine, but I like my directors to be father figures. If Paul directed me, I'd be committing mental incest."

On Marriage and Divorce: -- "Our phone bills (*with Sinatra*) were astronomical, and when I found the letters Frank wrote me the other day, the total could fill a suitcase. Every single day during our relationship, no matter where in the world I was, I'd get a telegram from Frank saying he loved me and missed me. He was a man who was desperate for companionship and love. Can you wonder that he always had mine!"

"All I ever got out of any of my marriages was the two years Artie Shaw financed on an analyst's couch."

"When you have to face up to the fact that marriage to the man you love is really over, that's very tough, sheer agony. In that kind of harrowing situation, I always go away and cut myself off from the world. Also, I sober up immediately when there is genuine bad news in my life. I never face it with alcohol in my brain. I just rented a house in Palm Springs and sat there and just suffered for a couple of weeks. I suffered there until I was strong enough to face it."

The Inner Woman -- "When I lose my temper, honey, you can't find it any place."

"God knows I've got so many frailties myself, I ought to be able to understand and forgive them in others. But I don't."

"I haven't taken an overdose of sleeping pills and called my agent. I haven't been in jail, and I don't go running to the psychiatrist every two minutes. That's something of an accomplishment these days."

"Deep down, I'm pretty superficial."

"Everybody kisses everybody else in this crummy business all the time. It's the kissiest business in the world."

"What I'd really like to say about stardom is that it gave me everything I never wanted."

"Don't think for a minute that bad publicity and endless criticism don't leave their claw marks on everyone concerned. Your friends try to cheer you up by saying lightly, "I suppose you get used to it, and ignore it." You try. You try damned hard. But you never get used to it. It always wounds and hurts."

"I want to remember it all, the good times and the bad times, the late nights, the boozing, the dancing into dawns, and all the great and not-so-great people I met and loved in those years."

(*She always felt cheated and angry that her birthday was on Christmas Eve*): It appeared that there was this whole other person, Jesus Christ, whose birthday a lot of people tended to confuse with mine. I was personally outraged. It was a long time before I forgave the Lord for that."

"When I'm old and gray, I want to have a house by the sea. And paint. With a lot of wonderful chums, good music, and booze around. And a damn good kitchen to cook in."

"I wish to live until 150 years old but the day I die, I wish it to be with a cigarette in one hand and a glass of whiskey in the other."

(*On her friend Lana Turner*): "We don't see each other anymore. Lana's become a recluse. No one sees her. She thinks absence will make the public's heart grow fonder. All absence does is make people think you're dead."

"If I had my life to live over again, I'd live it the same way. Maybe a few changes here or there, but nothing special. The truth is, honey, I've enjoyed my life. I've had a hell of a good time."

Judy Garland

One of the greatest and most multi-talented of movie stars, Judy's personal life was a bad dream over the rainbow. She always fell in love with the wrong men, most of them secret homosexuals. The man she loved most but never married, Tyrone Power, was bisexual but preferred men.

"In the silence of night I have often wished for just a few words of love from one man, rather than the applause of thousands of people."

"Twas not my lips you kissed, but my soul."

"I have the unfortunate habit of not being able to have an affair with a man without being in love with him."

"I can live without money, but I cannot live without love."

"Somewhere over the rainbow bluebirds fly. Birds fly over the rainbow. Why then, oh, why can't I?"

Born Frances Ethel Gumm on June 10, 1922 in Grand Rapids, Michigan, her parents were vaudeville performers and at an early age she joined them on the travelling show circuit. Her mother was the quintessential stage mother who pushed Judy into becoming what she became, a major star. Judy was in her mid teens when she began making movies at the age of 13 as Judy Garland and zoomed to stardom in "The Wizard of Oz" in 1939, singing her signature song, "Over the Rainbow."

The rainbow was elusive for her in life and she fell under the influence of drugs, initiated by her bosses at MGM studios, amphetamines to stay awake and barbiturates to take before going to bed so she could sleep. In between bouts of depression and a nervous breakdown, she starred in a series of teenage musical comedies with Mickey Rooney, then as an adult with Gene Kelly and Fred Astaire.

After a few fallow years in films, she made a sensational comeback in the musical version of "A Star Is Born," 1954, getting a much-deserved Academy Award nomination as best actress but losing to Grace Kelly for "The Country Wife." Groucho Marx said of the snub to Garland, "The biggest robbery since Brinks." Rejection from the Academy nearly broke her heart. But she came back again in for a supporting actress Oscar nomination for "Judgment at Nuremberg," 1961.

She became a brilliant star in the movie sky, one of the greatest American popular singers, married five times, had three children, but failed to find what she wanted so very much: to be loved. She had affairs with bandleader Artie Shaw, actors Frank Sinatra, Orson Welles, Yul Brynner and others, but the great love of her heart was said to be Tyrone Power, of whom she might well have envisioned when in "A Star is Born" she sang "The Man Who Got Away."

Her marriages were to bandleader David Rose (1941-1944), with whom she gave birth to a child, but at his and her mother's and her MGM boss Louis B. Mayer's insistence, she had an abortion; director Vincente Minnelli (1945-1951) with whom she had a daughter, Liza Minnelli; producer Sidney Luft (1952-1965), with whom she had two children; Mark Herron (1965-1967), who she divorced because he was a homosexual; and disk jockey Mickey Deans whom she married in 1969 but she died three months later at the age of 47 on June 22, 1969 in London, England, of an accidental barbiturate overdose.

None of her husbands attended her funeral, and her lifelong friend Mickey Rooney was too distraught to speak, so James Mason, her co-star in "A Song Is Born," delivered a touching eulogy. The American Film ranked her as No. 8 on its list of the top 50 Greatest Screen Legends.

Judy's daughter Liza Minnelli said about her mother in 2012, "We celebrate the privilege of having had Mama touch all of our lives. She left us with so many feelings we never would have discovered until she exquisitely translated them to us with her voice... Mama gave each and every one of us the gift of hope, laughter and love."

When her film career waned at various times, Judy Garland became a one-woman show singing at concerts all over the country including Carnegie Hall. When this editor saw her perform in Chicago, and she was about to end her concert with her signature song, "Over the Rainbow," a man sitting in front him, obviously inebriated, said perhaps through his tears because of a troubled life, "Sing it, Judy. Sing it!"

The Inner Woman -- "MGM had us working days and nights on end. They'd give us pep-pills to keep us on out feet long after we were exhausted. Then they'd take us to the studio hospital and knock us cold with sleeping pills. Then after four hours they'd wake us up and give us the pep-up pills again so we could work another 72 hours in a row. I started to feel like a wind-up toy from FAO Schwarz."

"From the time I was thirteen, there was a constant struggle between MGM and me – whether or not to eat, how much to eat, what to eat. I remember this more vividly than anything else about my childhood."

"Always be a first-rate version of yourself, instead of a second-rate version of someone else."

"I'm a woman who wants to reach out and take forty million people in her arms."

"If I am a legend, then why am I so lonely?"

"Behind every cloud is another cloud."

"I've always taken 'The Wizard of Oz' very seriously. I believe in the idea of the rainbow. And I've spent my entire life trying to get over it."

"As for my feelings toward 'Over the Rainbow,' it's become part of my life. It is so symbolic of all my dreams and wishes that I'm sure that's why people sometimes get tears in their eyes when they hear it."

"We cast away priceless time in dreams, born of imagination, fed upon illusion, and put to death by reality."

Janet Gaynor

Movies are magic, and they seldom were more magical than in the silent film era when love was expressed without a word being spoken. The greatest romantic couple of the silent screen, and into the early talkies, was petite and lovely Janet Gaynor and handsome, stalwart Charles Farrell. Millions of male movie fans wished they were holding her, while female fans dreamed of being in his arms and receiving his kisses. The sad truth was, they were only acting. He was in real life virile and straight, but she was a secret lesbian.

Born Laura Augusta Gainor in Philadelphia, Pennsylvania on October 6, 1906, her father was a paper hanger. Her parents divorced when she was 8 years old and her mother married an electrician.

Small in stature at just 5 feet, Janet Gaynor became a queen of the screen in 11 films with Charles Farrell, winning the first best actress Academy Award for performances in three films, "7th Heaven and "Sunrise" (both 1927), and "Street Angel" (1928) the first and third both with Farrell.

Gaynor was in relationships with actresses Jean Arthur and lesbian Margaret Lindsay, but as actor Robert Cummings said, "Janet was married to Mary Martin." Martin, Broadway star famous for her show-stopping song, "My Heart Belongs to Daddy," may well have meant it belonged to Gaynor. They travelled a lot together, often with their husbands, as decoys. Martin was bisexual, marrying Benjamin Hagman; their son Larry Hagman grew up to star in the television soap opera "Dallas."

Gaynor married three times, first to attorney Jesse Lydell Peck (1929-1933), then costume designer Adrian (Adrian Greenberg) who was openly gay while she was more discreet as a lesbian. Such Hollywood marriages were called "Lavender marriages." Adrian designed the costumes for more than 800 films including "The Wizard of Oz" and the dresses of Joan Crawford that gave her the broad shoulder pads that became her trademark and a nationwide fashion craze.

After divorcing Adrian, Gaynor was married to stage and film producer Paul Gregory from 1964 until her death in 1984), having given birth to a son with him. Gaynor and Martin were with their husbands in a taxi in San Francisco in 1982 when the intoxicated driver of a van plowed it into their cab, killing Martin's manager and injuring both women. Gaynor underwent several operations for her injuries which resulted in pneumonia and she died on September 14, 1984 at the age of 77.

Gaynor was a very private person who seldom gave interviews, so little is known of her thoughts on men, sex, and other personal matters. She did, however, give an interview in a 1935 fan magazine, offering advice to young women in which there were hints as to her inner woman:

"Beauty is a help (in a film career), *but it isn't a requisite. Feminine charm is applied by many girls to attain a goal, but when personality is used in this way, it soon fades.*

"The most valuable asset for one who is starting out (in any career) *is not a tangible thing, but a philosophical viewpoint. I would say that the most valuable asset would be a determination to go through life being real, loyal, and sincere. Early in life, I decided I would try to live up to this platform. If you want your work to ring true, you must crowd it with reality.* (As an actress) *You must live the parts you play, you must become the characters you portray, you must put feeling and reality into every line... into every move.*

"This isn't true alone in motion picture work. It is true in every walk of life. Girls who want to succeed in commercial life can do so if they pack reality into their work – if they refuse to let anything become routine and tackle every task, no matter how small, with vigor and determination. Any girl or woman who permits herself to fall into a rut – to be typed, as it were – is destined for a very dull routine life that will bring very little material gain."

(Gaynor said the next requirement for happiness and success is loyalty): *"That word covers a lot of territory. If you are loyal to yourself and your ideals, that is the most difficult of all. A man or woman who hasn't the quality of loyalty doesn't deserve any consideration, because he or she has no consideration for others. Any girl who starts out in life without this prime asset can follow only one other path – that of the hypocrite."*

Gaynor's third requisite was sincerity: *"If properly applied, sincerity will be your guide through life...* (Sincerity) *Is to your inner self what gasoline is to your automobile."*

"Some will say, 'Oh, it's easy for her to say those things.' But I can truthfully say that the way has not always been easy. There have been many disappointments, many heartaches. There were many times when it would have been easier to quit, but I always had before me that little creed: Be real, be loyal, be sincere."

Whoopi Goldberg

Multi-talented Whoopi has been married three times, but unlucky in love, yet she keeps a realistic outlook on marriage, if it is her own:.

"I wish I had known sooner that I like being on my own. If I'd figured that out earlier, I probably wouldn't have gotten married three times."

Born Caryn Elaine Johnson in the Chelsea district of Manhattan, New York on November 1, 1955, her father was a clergyman and her mother a teacher and nurse. Her nickname was "Da Woop," and she worked as a bricklayer, a dishwasher in a San Diego restaurant, and applied makeup to corpses in a funeral home before appearing in Broadway shows in small parts.

She appeared on television and became a film star in "The Color Purple" (1985), winning a supporting actress Academy Award nomination. She won the Oscar as best supporting actress for "Ghost" (1990), and then became a regular in the "Star Trek" television series. She was once addicted to heroin, and hates flying because she once witnessed an airliner crash, so she travels by bus. She is an active pro-choice advocate, having had an abortion at the age of 14. As she continues in films, she earns as much as $7 million a picture.

Her boyfriends were actors Ted Danson and Frank Langella, with whom she had a five-year relationship, and she was married three times. Her first husband was her drug counsellor, Alvin Martin (1973-1979, when she had been addicted to heroin, and with whom she had a child; David Claessen (1986-1988); and Lyle Trachtenberg (1994-1995).

In her book, *Is It Just Me? Or Is It Nuts Out There?*, she wrote about her pet peeves, that she hated bullying, disrespect for the elderly, the "N" word, and domestic violence. Also, loud cell phone talkers, people who don't turn off their noisy digital devices when travelling, passengers who drink too much, loud kids on airplanes, standing beside someone smelling of too much perfume, "smart-mouthed" children, and mandatory air fresheners in airplane bathrooms.

On Men -- "In my opinion, Mel Gibson isn't a racist... I know him... I'd have noticed if he was a racist... I've met real racists and he isn't one of them. He's a bonehead."

(*On receiving her Oscar for "Ghost"*): "I've said it before and I'll say it again: because of Patrick Swayze, I have an Oscar. (*About his death from pancreatic cancer in 2009*): "This was a well-fought battle. Patrick fought like the dickens to survive it, or to get through it. He never thought of himself as someone who was dying. He said, 'You know, we're all dying.' And so his attitude was 'Until it kills me, I'm going to keep doing what I'm doing.' He worked, he did his show, he just was a cat that never gave up. I would like to be able to be like that."

The Inner Woman -- "I'm a big old egotistical lady, and that's okay. I can accept it."

"You can say whatever you want about me, but talk about my daughter and I'll beat your ass up."

"Actors have no color. That's the art form."

(*On African-Americans actors, in 1994*): "I am black. But I didn't become black yesterday. I'm black and I'm getting the work and I'm doing some good things, but I realize many black actors and actresses are not being given the opportunities. The industry has got to stop thinking in terms of black and white and has to start thinking in terms of who is right, regardless of color, for the role."

(On smoking marijuana): "Just because I do it doesn't mean you should do it."

"There's only one alternative to getting older, so suck it up."

Betty Grable

Just about every GI's Pin-Up Girl during World War II was married to the same man, trumpeter and bandleader Harry James, for more than 20 years. But she spent more than a few nights home alone with the children because he was not always faithful. Maybe every GI would have been, but not Harry. He was often away, blowing his horn for some other woman.

Said Betty: *"You're better off betting on a horse than betting on a man. A horse may not be able to hold you tight, but he doesn't wanna wander from the stable at night."*

"The woman's vision is deep-reaching, the man's far-reaching. With a man the world is his heart, with the woman the heart is her world."

Born Elizabeth Ruth Grable in St. Louis, Missouri on December 18, 1916, her father a stockbroker and his wife who was determined that her daughter would grow up to become a movie star. Her mother enrolled her in a dancing school at the age of 3 and ten years later took her to Hollywood. Betty made her first screen appearance in musicals in 1930 when she was 13, but her mother lied about her age and said she was 15. Her first major role was in "College Swing" (1938). She married actor and former child star Jackie Coogan in 1937 but they divorced in 1940. She achieved stardom that same year and went on to become 20th Century-Fox studio's replacement for Alice Faye who had been their biggest attraction until she retired.

Betty Grable became GI's favorite beauty in World War II and her photo in a white one-piece bathing suit was pinned up on their barracks walls, thus she became known as "The Pin-Up Girl." She posed for the photo with her back to the camera, looking over her right shoulder and smiling, taken that way to show her legs but not the front of her because she was pregnant at the time. She also was known as "The Girl with the Million Dollar Legs" when her studio insured them with Lloyds of London, but only for a quarter of a million dollars.

Her legions of male fans were saddened when she married trumpeter and bandleader Harry James in 1943. Their marriage lasted 22 years Her legions of male fans were saddened when she married trumpeter and bandleader Harry James in 1943. Their marriage lasted 22 years until their divorce in 1965, having had two daughters together. In 1947 she was the highest-paid movie star in America.

When the public tired of musicals in the mid-1950s, she appeared on Broadway and in night clubs, making her final film, "How to Be Very, Very Popular" in 1955. Despite her movie star fame, she led a quiet private life and said her family always came first. She was afraid of crowds and was a sleepwalker. She died of lung cancer on July 2, 1973 in Santa Monica, California.

On Men -- "They say the two best-hung men in Hollywood are (*actor*) Forrest Tucker and (*comedian*) Milton Berle. What a shame... it's never the handsome ones. The bigger they are, the homelier.) (*She was wrong about Tucker, who was good-looking and had a big female following.*)

On Marriage -- "I wanted to be Mrs. Jackie Coogan for life. (*They married on November 19. 1937 but divorced after three months.*)

The Inner Woman -- "I never had a real drive so far as career is concerned. The drive was my mother's."

"There are two reasons why I am successful in show business, and I am standing on both of them. My legs made me."

"I'm strictly an enlisted man's girl."

"I'm a song-and-dance girl. But that's the limit of my talents. I can act enough to get by."

"The practice of putting women on pedestals began to die out when it was discovered that they could give orders better from there."

"There's nothing mysterious about me."

(*On her being a Pin-Up Girl*): "A lot of these kids (*young servicemen in World War II*) don't have any women in their life to fight for. I guess what you would call us girls is kind of their inspiration. It's a grave responsibility."

(*Asked whether her role as a new mother was bad for her image):* "I never thought of it. If they didn't like it, the devil with 'em. Fact is, I've more fan mail since, especially from servicemen telling me about their wives and babies. Maybe it's a wholesome quality or an American girl quality. People write to me as if I were a sister or friend."

Jean Harlow

One of the screen's greatest beauties of the 1930s, Jean was another star who was unlucky in love and had married a man who kept his homosexual secret from her before marrying her. Her second husband preferred reading in bed rather than make love to "The Blonde Bombshell" of the movies.

Jean said: **"When you lie down with dogs, you get up with fleas."**

Born Harlean Harlow Carpenter in Kansas City, Missouri on March 3, 1911, her father was a dentist. She ran away from home when she was 16 in 1927 to marry a businessman, Charles McGrew, who was 23. They settled in Los Angeles where in 1928 at the age of 17 she began working as an extra in silent films, her fleeting roles ranging from a woman passing on the street to a winged ballerina. She appeared in two Stan Laurel and Oliver Hardy short comedies, in one of which her dress was torn off as she exited a taxi, and showed her undies and legs. Her marriage to McGraw lasted less than two years.

Millionaire aviation magnet Howard Hughes became attracted to her beauty and in 1930 when she was 21 but still an unsuccessful actress, signed her as the female lead in his World War I flying epic "Hell's Angels." The film was a huge box-office hit and she was an overnight sensation. Hughes sold her contract to MGM, the top studio in Hollywood.

MGM saw her star potential and cast her opposite their leading male actor Clark Gable in "Platinum Blonde" (1931) and she became America's new sex goddess. She and Gable followed that the next year with "Red Dust" and they made four more films together. By then she had married MGM producer Paul Bern on July 2, 1932, and while on the set filming "Red Dust" she got news that he had committed suicide, after they had been married only two months. He had not told her that he was a homosexual and was unable to make love to her.

Harlow became one of the superstars in "Dinner at Eight" (1933) in which she told older actress Marie Dressler, "I was reading a book the other day," and Dressler, astonished, asked "Reading a book?" Harlow replied. "Yes, it's all about civilization or something. A nutty kind of book. Do you know that the guy said that machinery is going to take the place of *every* profession?" Dressler then delivered one of the most famous lines in film history by assuring her, "Oh my dear, that's something *you* never need worry about."

Harlow next married cinematographer Harold Rosson in 1933, but they divorced after only eight months. She said he read in bed and that kept her awake; she was not rested enough for work the next morning.

That same year, she turned down the leading lady role in "King Kong" and it went to Fay Wray. Following her divorce from Rosson, she had an affair with another top leading actor William Powell, and they became engaged for two years, but she died before they could marry.

While filming "Saratoga" with Gable, she was hospitalized with kidney failure and died of uremic poisoning on June 7, 1937. She was only 27 years old at the time of her unexpected death which shocked her fans all over the world. A double was a stand-in for her in order to complete filming "Saratoga."

It was widely believed that her mother caused Harlow's death because she was a Christian Scientist and refused to let doctors operate on Harlow after she became ill, and preferred prayer to medication or surgery. That later has been proven to be untrue and she played no part in Harlow's illness or death.

Harlow had two superstitions. She always wore a lucky charm, on the ankle of her left leg, and had a lucky mirror in her dressing room; she never left without first looking in it. She never wore any undergarments and always slept in the nude. To maintain a slender figure, she ate mostly vegetables and salads. Before appearing in a scene in a film, she put ice on her nipples, to appear sexier. Icing nipples makes them harder, so they stand out more.

Short but beautiful, she was only 5 feet 1 and a half inches tall. Harlow was everyone's symbol of blonde bombshell beauty until Marilyn Monroe came along. Monroe turned down an offer to play Harlow in a biographical movie. Harlow was the first film star to appear on the cover of *Life* magazine (May 1937), a month before her death. Harlow was ranked No. 22 on the American Film Institute's "100 Years, 100 Legends" list. Two movies have been made about her, both called "Harlow," with Carol Lynley and Carroll Baker portraying her.

On Men -- "I like to wake up each morning felling a new man."

(*In a 1933 interview on what is her ideal man*): "I think honesty, kindliness, a sense of humor, courage and intelligence are the most important qualities. The first thing I notice about a man is his personality." *(She was attracted to men who were "forceful and magnetic.")*

"Men like me because I don't wear a brassiere. Women like me because I don't look like a girl who would steal a husband. At least not for long."

(*On Clark Gable, in a 1933 interview*): "Perhaps Clark can be described best as 'a man's man.' He is very sincere and unaffected, and he has a grand sense of humor. I number Clark among my good friends, but our screen emotions were all in the line of work." *Two years later she wrote:* "I can't imaging having a better friend than Clark Gable. He embodies all the qualities which are necessary for true friendship."

(*Gable said about Harlow, in a 1935 fan magazine*): "To me, Jean always seems to have a man's attitude toward life. You can talk to her so naturally. She understands and appreciates the things men are interested in. Of course this appeals to any man. She never uses her femininity in conversations, to win arguments, for instance, or to put over a point. So many women suddenly 'go feminine' when they think it will turn the tide their way, but I don't think Jean even thinks of her sex in such circumstances. She has, too, a complete sense of fairness. I don't know anyone, man or woman, who is more of a straight-shooter."

On Love -- "If I loved a man, I would give up any man to make him happy."

"To me, love has always meant friendship."

(*When asked in 1933 if 15-year-old girls can fall in love*): "It all depends on what you mean by love. Love at fifteen is certainly not the same as love at twenty-five."

The Inner Woman -- "I was not a born actress. No one knows it better than I. Events made me one. If I had any latent talent, I have had to work hard, listen carefully, do things over and over and then over again in order to bring it out."

"I'm not a great actress, and I never thought I was. But I happen to have something the public likes."

"Underwear makes me feel uncomfortable, and besides my parts have to breathe."

(*In 1933*): "The 'wildness' of Hollywood parties is greatly exaggerated. However, since childhood I've not cared for large parties or crowds. It's my nature to prefer a few close friends."

"There is a God, even in Hollywood."

(*When asked, in 1933, if she was happy*): "Is anyone completely happy? I have my work, my family, my home, and many friends."

"Don't give me books for Christmas. I already have a book."

"No one ever expects a great lay to pay all the bills., so why do they expect it of me? Is it because I am not a great lay?" (*She said this after her gay husband Paul Bern died penniless and owing a lot of money she was expected to have to pay.*)

(*In concluding her 1935 interview*): "A life well-lived is a life well-balanced. To get the most out of living, there must be a certain amount of so many things... work and play, strenuous effort and complete relaxation, friendships and solitudes, joys and sorrows... Old age is merely a stagnation of the mind. When the desire passes to learn something new each day, each hour, then you have grown old."

"There are so many things I want to know and so little time in which to learn about them!... I have experienced a great deal of unhappiness, even bitter tragedy. I cannot help but believe that the future will be much kinder."

Rita Hayworth

Another favorite Pin-Up Girl of GI's during World War II, Rita married and divorced a prince years before the idea ever occurred to Grace Kelly. If the two beauties powder their noses in the same ladies' room they might compare emotional scars.

Hayworth became every man's sex goddess when she starred in "Gilda" (1946), but said, **"Every man I have ever known has fallen in love with Gilda and awakened with me. No one can be Gilda 24 hours a day."**

"What surprises me in life are not the marriages that fail, but the marriages that succeed."

Born Margarita Carmen Cansino in Brooklyn, New York on October 17, 1918, her father was Spanish-American and mother Irish-English, both professional dancers. She performed with them and, at the age of 15, was given a movie contract with Columbia Pictures where she became famous as "Gilda" in the 1946 steamy drama. She appeared five times on the cover of *Life* magazine and the photo by Bob Landry of her in a negligee for the August 11, 1941 cover made her the number two soldier pin-up of World War II, the first being actress Betty Grable.

Hayworth was not a strawberry blonde, which was the title of one of her early films; her natural hair color was black. She was the producer's first choice for the feminine lead in "Casablanca" (1942), but was unavailable so Ingrid Bergman got the part. The Maria Vargas character, played by Ava Gardner in the 1954 film "The Barefoot Contessa" was based on Hayworth.

Her five husbands were promoter Edward Judson (1937-1942); actor-director Orson Welles (1943-1948), with whom she had a child); Prince Aly Khan (1949-1953), a socialite, racehorse owner, and jockey who was the son of the leader of a Muslim sect of Shia Islam, with whom she had a child; singer-actor Dick Haymes (1953-1955); and film producer James Hill (1958-1961), who died of Alzheimer's disease.

While in the process of divorcing Prince Khan in the spring of 1954, while he was seeing other women including beautiful actress Gene Tierney, Rita was in an affair with one of Khan's best friends. He was another royal blueblood, a handsome 40-year old widower, Spanish Count Jose Maria Padierna de Villapadierna, or "Pepe" for short. Unlike Kahn, Pepe was very wealthy, while Rita was down to her last $50,000 and that had to pay for her lawyer, housekeeper, a French maid, two gardeners, a secretary, and her two young daughters.

She had never asked for alimony from her previous husbands, but asked $250,000 from Prince Khan. In an interview at the time of her relationship with Pepe, Rita told an interviewer that in him she had found "a man of character, understanding, wealth, reputation, and stability."

Rita's psychologist said that in Rita's previous husbands, she had sought a man who was a combination of father figure, teacher, and lover. An associate of Rita's said she loved Pepe because he treated her like an equal, as royal as he was. He also was known for his faithfulness. The affair never got to the altar, but no one knows for certain why.

At the age of 42 in 1960 she was diagnosed with Alzheimer's and almost helpless by 1981 she was cared for by her daughter Yasmin Khan until her death from the disease on May 13, 1987 at the age of 68. The American Film Institute lists her as No. 19 of the 50 Greatest Screen Legends

On Marriage and Divorce -- "I owe everything to Ed (*film producer Edward Judson, her first husband*). I could never have made the grade in Hollywood without him. I was just too backward My whole career was his idea. I married him for love; he married me for an investment."

(*On why she was divorcing Orson Welles*): "I can't take his genius any more. (*He*) Sometimes gave me cause to think that he married me so he could direct me. Off the set and, in particular, on it. If the five we did (*"The Lady from Shanghai,"* 1947) had been more successful with the public, our marriage might have lasted longer."

(*Welles said about their marriage*): "I loved Rita. She was my lover, the mother of my daughter, and my wife, in that order. We never quite settled into a groove; we were too busy in those years. If we'd met sooner or if we'd met later in life, it might have worked out."

(*Rita in 1952, on Aly Khan*): "Aly is a European brought up in that way of life. More than that, he is a Prince, brought up to rule millions of people, both as a head of state and as a religious leader. He cannot be judged by the same standards of, say, an American husband, and yet he is a very sweet person, completely charming. It was easy to love him. It is very hard to get him out of my heart."

(*On divorcing Aly Khan*): "He's a playboy who spends his time and my money at race tracks and (*gambling*) casinos while I slave making pictures." *She said he liked to go out every night on the town, but she preferred quiet evenings at home in her robe and slippers before the fireplace.*

The Inner Woman -- "I never really thought of myself as a sex goddess. I felt I was more a comedian who could dance."

"I was certainly a well-trained dancer. *(She starred with Fred Astaire in two musicals)*. I'm a good actress: I have depth. I have feeling. But they *(film producers)* don't care. All they want is the image."

(*When asked what she thought when she looks at herself after waking up in the morning*): "Darling, I don't wake up 'til the afternoon."

(About nudity in movies): "I think all women have a certain elegance about them which is destroyed when they take off their clothes."

"The fun of acting is to become someone else."

"Basically, I am a good, gentle person, but I'm attracted to mean personalities."

(On women's liberation): "We are all tied to our destiny and there is no way we can liberate ourselves. After all, a girl is... well, a girl. It's nice to be told you're successful at it."

"I haven't had everything from life. I've had too much."

"All I wanted was just what everybody else wants, you know, to be loved."

Anne Heche

Being a lesbian and married to a man works for Anne, which may raise some eyebrows in the ladies' room. She lives by different lyrics to the old Frank Sinatra song, "All, or Nothing at All":

"We do not fall in love with the package of the person, we fall in love with the inside of a person."

"I would never limit myself to saying I would be with a man or a woman. I have been very clear to everybody that just because I'm getting married (to actor James Tupper) *does not mean I call myself a straight."*

Born Anne Celeste Heche in Aurora, Ohio on May 25, 1969, her father was an itinerant Baptist minister and choir director who sexually abused her and led a double life as a bisexual businessman. Feeling that her childhood was loveless, at the age of 12 she began appearing in dinner theatre stage shows to help her financially destitute mother and younger sisters and brother. Her father died from AIDS and her brother was killed weeks later in an automobile accident.

Heche and her mother and sisters moved to Chicago and when she was 17 was cast as a twin in the soap opera "Another World," winning awards for her performances. Memories of her sexually abused childhood haunted her as she began appearing in television films.

Her acting success became overshadowed by news in 1997 that she and comedienne Ellen DeGeneres, who had come out as a lesbian, were lovers. Until then, Heche had had boyfriends and a two-year relationship with actor Steve Martin. She and DeGeneres shared a house together. Their relationship ended when she married photographer Coleman Laffoon in 2001, who filed for divorce in 2009 claiming she was having an affair with James Tupper. After her divorce from Laffoon, Heche and Tupper were married and she gave birth to their son. She continues to appear both in movies and on television.

On Love -- "I've always kind of gone with my heart."

"It is important to talk about loving yourself and looking at your tragedies and the stuff that makes you grow."

The Inner Woman -- "I put a very high premium on honesty. What I learned from my father's death is that if you don't accept your sexuality (*he was bisexual*), it will kill you."

"I had another personality. I had a fantasy world. I called my other personality Celestia. I called the other world that I created for myself the Fourth Dimension. I believed I was from that world. I believed I was from another planet. I think I was insane."

(Celestial relates to or suggests other-worldly, heavenly beings, or to the sky and planets such as the Sun, Moon, and stars, all celestial bodies.)

"I told my mother about the seven years of therapy that I had been abused sexually by my father, and she hung up the phone on me. To have gone through so much work to heal myself, and have my mother not acknowledge in any way that she was sorry for what had happened to me, broke my heart. And in that moment, I think I split off from myself. So Anne, this girl who had just confronted her mother, shrunk, and out came Calestia, where I was literally thrown to the ground, and I'm not kidding, in New York City, thrown to the ground and heard the voice of God, and thought I was absolutely insane, I had no idea what to do. I was existing as two people."

"What could I do when I was Celestia? I spoke a different language. I spoke a different language that God and I spoke together. I could,

you name it, I could do it, I could see into the future. I could heal people."

"I was raised to hide. I was raised to pretend. I was raised to always tell everybody that everything was fine, and even though I was in therapy for years I never told anybody that I had another personality. I never told anybody that I heard voices and spoke to God. I never told anybody any of it. I thought it would have to be something I would have to keep secret forever."

(*To escape her childhood traumas*): "I drank. I smoked. I did drugs. I had sex with people. I did anything I could to get the shame out of my life."

"I think everything I've done in all my insanity was to try to get my parents to love me. My father loved movie stars. I decided I needed to become famous to get his love. My mother loved Jesus. That was her thing. So I wanted to become Jesus Christ."

"I've always wanted to heal my life. I always wanted to see the good side of life. I've always wanted to see the good in everything that happened to me."

(On her memoir, *Call Me Crazy*): "I wrote this book to say goodbye, once and for all to my story of shame, and embrace my life choice of love. The fact that there are people hearing my story is the icing on the most beautiful cake in the world, that I imagine says, 'Happy freedom, Anne. You have made it to the other side.'"

Audrey Hepburn

Married and divorced twice was enough for Audrey. Despite heartaches and unrequited love, she remained cheerful and positive, a delight to listen to in the ladies' room. She would love to have married William Holden. He loved her, but the bottle more.

"Good things aren't supposed to just fall into your lap. God is very generous, but He expects you to do your part first."

"The most important thing is to enjoy your life… to be happy. It's all that matters."

"The best thing to hold on to in life is each other."

Born Audrey Kathleen Hepburn-Ruston in Ixelles, near Brussels, Belgium on May 4, 1929, she was the only child of an Anglo-Irish banker and a Dutch baroness descended from French and English kings. Her father left the family when she was very young and she felt the abandonment as the most traumatic event of her life. Her parents divorced in 1935 when she was six and she went to live with her mother in London, where she went to a private girls' school.

Later, she and her mother returned to the Netherlands but fell on hard times when Nazi Germany occupied the country early in World War II. Audrey suffered from malnutrition and depression, living off tulip bulbs and trying to bake grass into bread. When she was 13, she became a carrier of messages for the Belgium Underground's anti-Nazi movement, carrying messages and illegal leaflets stuffed into her socks and shoes. Three years later she became a volunteer nurse in a Dutch hospital in Arnheim, nursing soldiers back to health. Ironically, one of them was a young British paratrooper, Terence Young, who more than 20 years later directed her in one of her films, "Wait Until Dark," in 1967.

After the war, Audrey took ballet lessons in London and began a modeling career. She made her first screen appearance in 1948, a bit part in a European film. In 1951 she moved to America and became an overnight star in "Roman Holiday" three years later and she won the Academy Award as best actress. Her co-star was Gregory Peck, but William Holden also was in Rome at the time and fell in love with her. "She was the love of my life," Holden said later, although After the war, Audrey took ballet lessons in London and began a modeling career. She made her first screen appearance in 1948, a bit part in a European film.

In 1951 she moved to America and became an overnight star in "Roman Holiday" three years later and she won the Academy Award as best actress. Her co-star was Gregory Peck, but William Holden also was in Rome at the time and fell in love with her. "She was the love of my life," Holden said later, although he was married at the time to actress Brenda Marshall who was at home in California with their children. Hepburn broke off their relationship because she wanted to have children, and Holden had a vasectomy "because of her constant talk about babies."

Audrey made many memorable films in the following years but may be best remembered as Holly Golightly, a free-spirited girl in "Breakfast at Tiffany's" (1961), and as Liza Doolittle in the film version of the Broadway musical "My Fair Lady" (1964).

She married actor Mel Ferrer in 1954 and they had a son together, but they divorced in 1968. Publicist Henry Rogers said, "It seemed to me that she loved him more than he loved her, and it was frustrating for her not to have her love returned in kind." Rogers said Ferrer was more interested in his career than hers and it drove them apart, besides him being in an affair with a 15-year-old Spanish dancer. He was 50 at the time. She then married a psychiatrist, Dr. Andrea Dotti, in 1969, and they also had a son together, but they divorced in 1982.

Audrey left films to become a special ambassador to the United Nations UNICEF fund in 1988, helping children in Latin America and Africa, which she continued until her death from appendicle cancer on January 20, 1993. From 1980 until her death, she lived in Switzerland with her partner, Dutch actor Robert Wolders. Some speculated that the emotional stress from trying to help impoverished and sick children took a toll on her both mentally and physically.

Her closest friends were American actresses Elizabeth Taylor, Eva Gabor, Julie Andrews, Shirley MacLaine, French actress Capuchine, actors Gregory Peck and Ben Gazzara, and directors Peter Bogdanovich and Blake Edwards. She was ranked the third greatest female star of all time by the American Film Institute, after Katharine Hepburn and Bette Davis and before Ingrid Bergman and Greta Garbo.

On Men -- "You can always tell what kind of a person a man really thinks you are by the earrings he gives you."

"I loved William Holden, but I could not have knowingly married an alcoholic."

On Love -- "I was born with an enormous need for affection, and a terrible need to give it."

"We all want to be loved, don't we? Everyone looks for a way of finding love. It's a constant search for affection in every walk of life."

"Actually, you have to be a little bit in love with your leading man and vice versa. If you're going to portray love, you have to feel it. You can't do it any other way. But you don't carry it beyond the set."

"For me, the only things of interest are those linked to the heart."

On Sex -- "I think sex is overrated. I don't have sex appeal, and I know it. As a matter of fact, I think I'm rather funny looking. My teeth are funny, for one thing, and I have none of the (*physical*) attributes normally required for a movie queen, including the shapeliness."

On Marriage – *"If I get married, I want to be very married."*

On Divorce: -- "Your heart just breaks, that's all. But you can't judge or point fingers. You just have to be lucky enough to find someone who appreciates you."

The Inner Woman -- "I believe in kissing, kissing a lot. I believe in being strong when everything seems to be going wrong."

(*She was flat-chested and very conscious about it*): "I was too thin and had no bosom to speak of."

"I probably hold the distinction of being one movie star who, by all laws of logic, should never have made it. At each stage of my career, I lacked the experience."

"I was asked to act when I couldn't act. I was asked to sing in 'Funny Face' when I couldn't sing, and dance with Fred Astaire when I couldn't dance, and do all kinds of things I wasn't prepared for. Then I tried like mad to cope with it." (*Yet she and the film were a big success.*)

"I never thought I'd land in pictures with a face like mine."

"You can even say that I hated myself at certain periods. I was too fat, or maybe too tall, or maybe just plain too ugly… You can say my definiteness stems from underlying feelings of insecurity and inferiority. I couldn't conquer these feelings by acting indecisive. I found the only way to get the better of that was by adopting a forceful, concentrated drive."

"I never thought of myself as an icon. What is in other people's minds is not in my mind. I just do my thing."

"My look is attainable. Women can look like Audrey Hepburn by flipping out their hair, buying the large sunglasses and the little sleeveless dresses."

"My own life has been much more than a fairy tale. I've had my share of difficult moments, but whatever difficulties I've gone through I've always gotten a prize at the end."

"Remember, if you ever need a helping hand, it's at the end of your arm. As you get older, remember you have another hand: the first is to help yourself, the second is to help others."

(*About her "comeback" in 1976 after leaving films to raise her two sons):* "Whatever happens, the most important thing is growing old gracefully. And you can't do that on the cover of a fan magazine."

"I understood the dismay of people who had seen Julie on Broadway (*Julie Andrews in "My Fair Lady"*). She made that role her own, and for that reason I didn't want to do the film when it was first offered. But Jack Warner never wanted to put Julie in the (1964) film. He was totally opposed to it, for whatever reason. Then I learned that if I turned it down, they would offer it to still another movie actress. So I felt I should have the same opportunity to play it as any other film actress."

"The beauty of a woman is not in the clothes she wears, the figure she carries, or the way she combs her hair. The beauty of a woman must be seen from in her eyes, because that is the doorway to her heart, the place where love resides. The beauty of a woman is not in a facial mode but the true beauty in a woman is reflected in her soul. It is the caring that she lovingly gives the passion that she shows. The beauty of a woman grows with the passing years."

"I love people who make me laugh. I honestly think it's the thing I like most, to laugh. It cures a multitude of ills. I believe that laughing is the best calorie burner. It's probably the most important thing in a person."

"True friends are families which you can select."

"I'm an introvert. I love being by myself, love being outdoors, love taking a long walk with my dogs and looking at the trees, flowers, the sky."

"It's that wonderful old-fashioned idea that others come first and you come second. This was the whole ethic by which I was brought up. Others matter more than you do, so don't fuss, dear, get on with it."

"I don't want to be alone, I want to be left alone." *(Greta Garbo said the same thing, not "I want to be alone.")*

"I have to be alone very often. I'd be quite happy if I spent from Saturday night until Monday morning alone in my apartment. That's how I refuel."

"When you have nobody you can make a cup of tea for, when nobody needs you, that's when I think life is over."

"If my world were to cave in tomorrow, I would look back on all the pleasures, excitements and worthwhilenesses I have been lucky enough to have had. Not the sadness, not my miscarriages, or my father leaving home, but the joy of everything else. It will have been enough."

"Paris is always a good idea."

"Nothing is impossible, the word itself says *I'm possible!*"

"I heard a definition once: 'Happiness is health and a short memory!' I wish I'd invented it, because it is very true." *(Ingrid Bergman said it.)*

Katharine Hepburn

Was she a lesbian or bisexual is still an open question. Hepburn's love life and her views on love, men, and marriage are not widely known, but she has opened the lid on the privacy box on occasion:

"Love has nothing to do with what you are expecting to get -- only with what you are expecting to give -- which is everything."

"I have loved and been in love. There's a big difference."

"I wouldn't give you ten men for any one woman. All men are poops."

Born Katharine Houghton Hepburn in Hartford, Conn., on May 12, 1907, her father was a doctor and mother a suffragette, who both encouraged her to speak her mind and to develop it fully. She was devastated when her beloved brother died at the age of 14 while practicing a hanging trick. She was mostly home-schooled but was graduated from Bryn Mawr College where she decided to become an actress.

She began appearing in plays on Broadway and made her film debut in "A Bill of Divorcement" in 1932 opposite John Barrymore. An overnight star, her third film, "Morning Glory," in 1933, earned her the first of four Academy Awards as best actress, and of this writing no other actress has won as many. She snubbed the Hollywood glamour scene by wearing slacks and no makeup, refusing to pose or be photographed or give interviews.

Her career descended in the mid-1930s into her becoming called "box office poison," then she returned to Broadway in 1938 and starred in the hit play *The Philadelphia Story*. She bought the screen rights and starred in the film which revived her career in 1940.

She then began teaming in a series of films with Spencer Tracy and they were romantically involved for 25 years, from 1943 until his death in 1967. Tracy was married and his Catholic wife refused to give him a divorce. Hepburn and Tracy never shared the same house.

She lived with a succession of girls, while he lived with his wife or alone, or had several house visitors, especially a handsome and straight Hollywood gas station attendant, Scotty Bowers. His book. *Full Service,* reports that Tracy was a frequent customer who asked him to tend bar at his house parties, then when the guests left, they spent the nights together.

Out of respect for Tracy and his estranged wife and their two children, Hepburn did not attend his funeral service. But she followed the hearse in her car on a six-mile journey through the streets of Los Angeles, driving away just as it arrived at the church, she whispered, "Goodbye, friend. Here is where I leave you."

Some biographers claim that Hepburn was a lesbian, bisexual or even asexual, and that Tracy was bisexual. They also say that of all the men in her life, the only man she really loved in a romantic and sexual way was director John Ford, who was married but reportedly was bisexual and attracted to some of the leading men in his films who included straight men John Wayne, Jeffrey Hunter, and John Agar. His male stars had to audition for him privately and shirtless, and Maureen O'Hara said she once caught Ford and Tyrone Power locked in each other's lips.

Sexual preference ran in Hepburn's family. Her brother Tom killed himself reportedly because of his sexual confusion after coming out of the closet as a homosexual, according to a biography by William J. Mann. He says that while Hepburn was attending Bryn Mawr college, an all-girl school near Philadelphia, she had an affair with a girl named Alice, then had a long-term romance with another girl named Laura. Then there was Nancy, Frances, and actresses Constance Collier and Elissa Landi and others. The fan magazines did not call her "lesbian" but described her as "a very butch woman."

Hepburn was married to Philadelphia industrialist Ludlow Ogden Smith from 1928 until their divorce in 1941, but he was homosexual and they rarely lived together. Mann writes that all of her boyfriends were bisexual including Howard Hughes, John Ford, and Spencer Tracy. Her few close friends were gay, including director George Cukor, says Mann, who says he is, too.

After Tracy's death, Hepburn continued as perhaps the top female film star of the next several decades, earning a total of four Academy Awards as best actress, her last one in "On Golden Pond" in 1981, in which her co-star Henry Fonda won as best actor. Hepburn was hospitalized with pneumonia on 1996 and a tumor was discovered in her neck.

She died at the Hepburn family home in Fenwick, Connecticut on June 29, 2003 at the age of 96. Since she had starred in plays on Broadway, theatres there dimmed their lights in her honor. Her belongings were auctioned and sold for $5.8 million which she willed to her surviving relatives. Called "The First Lady of Cinema," the American Film Institute ranked her No. 1 in its 1999 list of 50 Greatest Movie Legends.

On Men -- "I often wonder whether men and women really suit each other. Perhaps they should live next door and just visit now and then."

"Plain women know more about men than beautiful ones do."

"I find a woman's point of view much grander and finer than a man's."

(*On director George Cukor)*: "He has the ability to make me trust myself."

(*On Humphrey Bogart, her costar in The African Queen" (1951)*: "Bogart was like Henry Fonda – proud and happy to be an actor. He (*Bogart*) was a real man – nothing feminine about him. He knew he was a natural aristocrat – better than anybody."

(*On Peter O'Toole, her co-star in The Lion in Winter (1968)*. "He can do anything. A bit cuckoo, but sweet and terribly funny."

(*On Ginger Rogers and Fred Astaire)*: "She gave him sex. He gave her class."

"Only when a woman decides not to have children, can a woman live like a man. That's what I've done."

On Marriage and Divorce -- (*On why she divorced Ludlow Ogden Smith*): "I didn't want to be known as Kate Smith." (*She was referring to who could be called a heavyweight popular singer in the 1930s and 1940s.*)

"It's bloody impractical. 'To love, honor, and obey.' If it weren't, you wouldn't have to sign a contract."

"If you want to sacrifice the admiration of many men for the criticism of one, go ahead, get married."

On Sex -- "My father, a surgeon and urologist, studied sex professionally all his life. Before he died at 82, he told me he hadn't come to any conclusions about it at all."

The Inner Woman – (*When she was aged 70*): "I put pants on 50 years ago and declared a sort of middle road."

(*Cary Grant on Hepburn in a December 1940 interview*): "If anyone is entitled to say anything about Katharine Hepburn, I am. I know what she's like, for I've made three pictures with her ("Bringing Up Baby" and "Holiday" (both 1938), and "The Philadelphia Story" (1940), and I say she's the most maligned woman in Hollywood history!... As an actress, she's a joy to work with... And as a person, she's real. There's no pretense about her. She's the most completely honest woman I've ever met. The trouble is, the stories about her are all written by people who don't have the faintest idea what the girl's like; people who have never even met her."

(*When asked in that 1940 interview if she was "painfully shy," as it was rumored*): "Call me anything but 'a shy actress.' Shyness has been used to excuse too many sins. It has become the popular explanation for every kind of conduct. I'm not leery of other people. The explanation for me is I'm leery of myself. I get frightened and nervous indigestion. Practically everything or anything can give it to me. But especially throngs of people. At parties, I'm in agony... All this isn't something new to me. I've been cursed with it all my life... Acting, I can get out of myself. No other profession offers me such an exciting way of escape."

"People have grown fond of me, like some old building."

"Sharon Stone... It's a new low for actresses when you have to wonder what's between her ears instead of her legs."

"I don't regret anything I've ever done; As long as I enjoyed it at the time."

"Not everyone is lucky enough to understand how delicious it is to suffer."

"There are no laurels in life . . . just new challenges."

"Afraid of death? Not at all. Be a great relief. Then I wouldn't have to give interviews."

(*On fashion*): "I wear my sort of clothes to save me the trouble of deciding which clothes to wear."

"Life can be wildly tragic at times, and I've had my share. But whatever happens to you, you have to keep a slightly comic attitude. In the final analysis, you have got not to forget to laugh."

(*In 1993*): "In some ways I've lived my life like a man, made my own decisions, etc. I've been as terrified as the next person, but you've got to keep going."

"I'm an atheist, and that's it. I believe there's nothing we can know except that we should be kind to each other and do what we can for people.

"Now to squash a rumor. No, I don't have Parkinson's. I inherited my shaking head from my grandfather Hepburn. I discovered that whiskey helps stop the shaking. Problem is, if you're not careful, it stops the rest of you, too. My head just shakes, but I promise you, it ain't gonna fall off!"

"Who is Katharine Hepburn? It took me a long time to create that creature."

"Life is hard. After all, it kills you... Listen to the song of life."

Lena Horne

Lena was not promiscuous and led a monogamous personal life, happily married to a white man who loved her. Her struggle was with racial prejudice until the end of the Civil Rights Movement.

"You have to be taught to be second class; you're not born that way. But the slanting process is so subtle that you frequently don't realize how you're being slanted until very late in the game."

"I was unique in that I was a kind of black that white people could accept. I had the worst kind of acceptance because it was never for how great I was or what I contributed. It was because of the way I looked."

"I don't have to be an imitation of a white woman that Hollywood sort of hoped I'd become. I'm me, and I'm like nobody else."

Born Lena Mary Calhoun Horne in Brooklyn New York City, on June 30, 1917 while her father was a professional gambler who was playing cards trying to get money to pay the hospital bill. Her mother was an actress with an African American theater troupe who traveled a lot. Her parents divorced while she was a toddler, and her mother left her to find work as an actress, leaving her in the care of her grandparents. Her mother returned when Lena was seven and they traveled to George, Florida, and Ohio as her mother found work acting.

Lena quit school when she was 14 and got her first stage job two years later, dancing and later singing at the famed Cotton Club in Harlem which was one of the few places in the nation where black performers played before white audiences. Cab Calloway and Duke Ellington helped her over what she called "the rough spots." She began singing before packed audiences and then sang on Broadway.

Lena married Louis Jones, a minor politician, in 1937 and gave birth to a daughter and a son with him. They separated on 1940 and divorced in 1944. Three years later she married white bandleader Lennie Hayton but it was kept secret because of inter-racial pressures. He was her manger and pianist until his death in 1971. During the 1960s Lena was active in the U.S. Civil Rights movement and worked on behalf of the National Council for Negro Women. She became a leader in the movement to improve the status of African Americans in the arts and in general.

She made her first film appearance in 1938 but was almost always only a singer and not an actress in the movies. Her scenes were shot so they could be cut out when the films were shown in the South, where theater owners refused to show movies that portrayed blacks in anything other than subservient roles to white, such as maids or waiters.

In her screen test at MGM her skin was photographed as light, and the studio feared audiences would mistake her for a white woman, so they had make-up applied called "Dark Egyptian" to make her appear as a Negro. She eventually appeared in two films with all-black actors, "Storm Weather" and "Cabin in the Sky," both in 1943. They were both successful with audiences and praised by critics, but Horne's movie career then returned to singing in other actors' films.

Her night club singing career soared, but she was often denied rooms at the hotels where she performed because blacks were not allowed to stay there. During World War II, she refused to sing before racially-segregated GI audiences. Government policy was to have separate shows, one for white troops and one for blacks. During the Civil Rights Movement of the 1960s, she worked with Eleanor Roosevelt on anti-lynching laws, and was a frequent White House guest of President John F. Kennedy.

She lost out to Ava Gardner in playing a mulotto in "Show Boat" in 1951 because MGM did not think audiences would accept a black woman playing the part. She and Gardner were close friends and Gardner practiced her songs by singing to Horne's recordings of

She lost out to Ava Gardner in playing a mulotto in "Show Boat" in 1951 because MGM did not think audiences would accept a black woman playing the part. She and Gardner were close friends and Gardner practiced her songs by singing to Horne's recordings of them. However, Gardner's singing in the film was dubbed by someone else and not her or Horne. Lena's final screen appearance was playing Glinda the Good Witch in the 1978 all-black musical, "The Wiz," based on the film "The Wizard of Oz" (1939).

She was married to black jazz musician Louis Jordan Jones from 1937 to 1944 with whom she had two children, and then to Lennie Hayton from 1947 until his death in 1971. Hayton was white, a music conductor and arranger at MGM.

Horne died at age 92 of heart failure in Manhattan on May 9, 2010, and is considered to be one of the most talented and beautiful performers, regardless of color.

On Love and Sex -- "Don't be afraid to feel as angry or as loving as you can."

"It's ill-becoming for an old broad to sing about how bad she wants it. But occasionally we do."

On Men -- (*On MGM studio head Louis B. Mayer*): "He was the most clever, ruthless, smart character that you would never want to know. All those guys were – Harry Cohn (*Columbia Pictures chief*)… Jack L. Warner (*Warner Bros. chief*) – believe me, they weren't dumb. They were the czars of the (*film*) industry – and they had no mercy."

(*On Malcolm X, born Malcolm Little [1925-1965], an American Muslim minister and civil rights leader for blacks, considered to be one of the greatest and most influential African Americans in history*): "I knew him before he became Malcolm X. He made me very strong at a time I needed to understand what I was angry about. He had peace in his heart. He exerted a big influence on me. He raised my consciousness about myself and my people and other people more than any person I know."

(*On William James "Count" Basie [1904-1984], American jazz pianist, bandleader, and composer*): "Count Basie isn't just a man, or even just a band. He's a way of life."

(On Marriage to Lennie Hayton) – "It was cold-blooded and deliberate (*of me*). I married him because he could get me into places a black man couldn't. But I really learned to love him. He was beautiful, just so damned good. I had never met a man like him."

The Inner Woman – "My own people (*her family*) didn't see me as a performer because they were busy trying to make a living and feed themselves. Until I got to café society in the 1940s, I didn't even have a black audience, and then it was mixed. I was always battling the system to try to get to be with my people. Finally, I wouldn't work for places that kept us out… It was a damn fight everywhere I was, every place I worked, in New York, in Hollywood, all over the world."

"I never considered myself a movie star. Mostly, I just sang songs in other people's movies."

"The naked female body is treated so weirdly in society. It's like people are constantly begging to see it."

"Every color I can think of and nationality, we were all touched by Dr. King (*Martin Luther King*) because he made us like each other and respect each other."

"I was lucky, as many of my generation was, in having a man like Dr. King in our lives. He came at a time that we needed to take a long look at each other and see how similar we were."

"As much as I try, when I open my mouth, Lena comes out. And I get so mad."

"I made a promise to myself to be kinder to other people."

"It's so nice to get flowers while you can still smell the fragrance."

"Always be smarter than the people who hire you."

"I really do hate to sing."

"It's not the load that breaks you down, it's the way you carry it. Carry it by the comfortable handles of gratitude for what's positive and that it is not worse, rather than the uncomfortable edges of bitterness for the negatives and that it is not better."

"My identity is very clear to me now, I am a black woman, I'm not alone, I'm free. I say I'm free because I no longer have to be a credit, I don't have to be a symbol to anybody; I don't have to be a first to anybody. I don't have to be an imitation of a white woman that Hollywood sort of hoped I'd become. I'm me, and I'm like nobody else."

"I found out along the way that they like you a little imperfect."

"I'm still learning, you know. At eighty, I feel there is a lot I don't know."

"The best thing about living… Is the chance to keep on doing it!"

Whitney Houston

Whitney gained the heights of stardom only to sink to the depths of despair with drugs, blaming her husband for sneaking them into her drinks. Like Lena Horne, but even after the Civil Rights Movement, she felt the stigma of being an African American performer.

"I don't have to be an imitation of a white woman that Hollywood sort of hoped I'd become. I'm me, and I'm like nobody else."

Born Whitney Elizabeth Houston on August 9, 1963 in Newark, New Jersey, her father an Army serviceman and her mother gospel singer Emily "Cissy" Houston, both African Americans. When she was four, after the 1967 Newark race riots, she and her parents and siblings moved to East Orange, New Jersey. She began singing as a soloist at the age of 11 in the junior gospel choir at the New Hope Baptist Church in Newark.

As a teenager, she attended a Catholic girls' high school where she met her future best friend, Robyn Crawford whom she said was the "sister she never had." In her teen years, she sang at night clubs where her mother performed, and before long became one of the top female vocalists, an actress, producer, and model.

She co-starred with Kevin Costner in "The Bodyguard" in 1992 and its soundtrack won the 1994 Grammy Award for album of the year. Her singing of "I Will Always Love You" became the best-selling single record by a woman in music history. Other films followed including "The Preacher's Wife" in 1996 for which her salary was $10 million. The film's soundtrack became the best-selling gospel album of all time. She became a supporter of Nelson Mandel (1918-2013, South African anti-apartheid crusader), and one of her concerts contributed a quarter of a million dollars to the United Negro College Fund.

She had affairs with American football star Randall Cunningham and actor Eddie Murphy in the 1980s, then fell in love with rhythm-and-blues singer Bobby Brown and three years later they married in 1993 and they had a daughter together. Brown had run-ins with the law and served some jail time. While her career was on a high note, her private life was far less successful, falling victim to depression and drugs.

She had a perfect image as a good girl until the late 1990's when her behavior changed and she began missing performances and losing weight. It became rumored that she and Brown were using drugs. She discovered that he had been unfaithful to her and was having affairs with other women. They divorced in 2007 and two years later she admitted that Brown had laced their marijuana with rock cocaine.

She died on February 11, 2012 in her guest room at the Beverly Hilton Hotel in Beverly Hills, California, having accidentally drowned in the bathtub, with heart disease and cocaine use listed as contributing factors. She was cited in the 2009 Guinness World Records as the most awarded female act of all time. One of pop music's best selling artists of all time with an estimated 170 to 200 million records sold worldwide.

On Men -- (*On her relationship with music executive Clive Davis*): "Critics would say that Clive told me what to do and how to do it. That's all (*b.s.*). I don't like it when they see me as this little person who doesn't know what to do with herself, like I have no idea what I want, like I'm just a puppet and Clive's got the strings. That's (*b.s.*). That's demeaning to me, because that ain't how it is, and it never was. And never will be. I wouldn't be with anybody who didn't respect my opinion. Nobody makes me do anything I don't want to do. Clive and I work well together. We get on each other's nerves sometimes, but we've been (*working*) together ten years now. Anybody can get on anybody's nerves over that long a time."

(*On criticism of her marrying Bobby Brown*): "I'm like an American princess. White America wanted me to marry someone white. They don't understand why I'd want a strong black man."

(*In 1993, on Brown's alleged womanizing*): "I don't think that my husband womanized anybody, because I know that if he wanted them, they definitely wanted him, you know. I don't think, you know, it was about womanizing. I think boys will be boys, and they have their fun and they play (*around*). When they really become smart and they find a good woman, they marry her. And that's what he did."

(*In 2009, on the death of Michael Jackson [1958-2009], American pop singer, dancer, actor, song writer, called the "King of Pop," who died of cardiac arrest induced by propofol and benzodiazepine intoxication*): "I have so many good memories of spending time with him. I've known his family for so many years. For at least twenty. (*On hearing of his death, she thought*): 'This can't be true. This can't be true.' I knew he was on painkillers at one time. I didn't know how far and deep it was (*that he was on drugs*). I just remember doing the anniversary special, the 30th anniversary, and I remember looking at Michael... and then looking at myself going, 'No, I don't want this to be like this. This can't happen. Not both of us.'"

The Inner Woman -- (*In 1993, on frequent rumors of being in a lesbian relationship with Robyn Crawford, her best friend since they* were teenagers at a girls' school and who she called "the sister I never had."): "I am so tired of this. I'm really sick of it. You mean to tell me that if I have a woman friend, I have to have a lesbian relationship with her? That's (b.s.). There are so many, many female artists who have women as their confidants, and nobody questions that. I have denied it over and over again, and nobody's accepted it. Or the media hasn't."

"I had a miscarriage during the filming of 'The Bodyguard.' It was very painful, emotionally and physically. I was back on the set the next day. And it's over."

(*On the media in 1996*): "They're devils to me… and they're out to eat my flesh."

(*In 2002, on her rebellious nature*): "My business is sex, drugs, rock 'n roll. You know? I mean, my friends, we have a good time. But as you get older, you get wiser. You know? You stop a lot of the kid stuff. I had no time to grow up, had no time to party. I didn't even date in my twenties. It was rough. I think I kind of reverted back as I got older, and said 'I'm just gonna party.' It was kind of a rebel in me."

(*In 2009 on drug use during her marriage*): "There were some times we'd laugh our tails off. (*She and Brown*). We had a ball. Sometimes you do have a good time. But when it gets to the point where you're sitting in your home and you're just trying to cover what you don't want people to know, it's painful. And then you want more, just so that you don't let anybody see you cry. Or anybody to see we're not happy."

(*In 2002*): "I can tell you that I am not self-destructive. I'm not a person who wants to die. I'm a person who has life, who wants to live. And I always have."

"I wanted to be a teacher. I love children, so I wanted to deal with children. Then I wanted to be a veterinarian. But by the age of 10 or 12, when I opened my mouth and said, 'Oh God, what's this?' I kind of knew teaching and being a veterinarian were going to have to wait. What's in your soul is in your soul."

"In grammar school, some of the girls had problems with me. My face was too light. My hair was too long. It was the black-consciousness period, and I felt really bad. I finally faced the fact that it isn't a crime not having friends. Being alone means you have fewer problems. When I decided to be a singer, my mother warned me I'd be alone a lot. Basically, we all are. Loneliness comes with life."

(*On her relationship with her mother*): "You learn, you grow up, and you become your own woman."

(*On her first solo singing in church when she was 11*): "I was scared to death… I was aware of people staring at me. No one moved. They seemed almost in a trance. I stared at the clock in the center of the church. When I finished, everyone clapped and started crying. From then on I knew God had blessed me."

(*In 2002*): "Nobody makes me do anything I don't want to do. It's my decision. So the biggest devil is me. I'm either my best friend or my worst enemy. And that's how I have to deal with it."

Caitlyn Jenner

Former Olympic decathlon champion Bruce Jenner made international headlines by becoming the world's most sensational transgender, choosing to put his image as a male behind him and going forward into being the person he/she really is, not a man but a woman. Everyone in the ladies' room is eager to hear her story.

(*In 2015*): *"I've always been very confused with my gender identity… For all intents and purposes, I'm a woman… My brain is much more female than it is male. It is hard for people to understand that, but that is what my soul is."*

"*Life as a woman is primarily a matter of mental state and lifestyle.*"

"I'm saying goodbye to people's perception of me and who I am. But I'm not saying goodbye to me. This has always been me. Please be open-minded (when you think of me). *I am not this bad person. I'm just doing what I have to do."*

Caitlyn Jenner was born Bruce Jenner on October 28, 1949 in Mount Kisco, New York, but became a transgender at the age of 66 in 2015. Jenner's father was an arborist and mother a housewife. She has two sisters but a younger brother was killed in a car accident in 1976 shortly after Jenner won the decathlon at the Olympic Games.

Diagnosed with dyslexia as a child, Jenner nonetheless graduated from Graceland University in Lamoni, Iowa with a degree in physical education. Encouraged by the track coach there, Jenner began training and won the decathlon title at the 1976 Montreal Summer Olympics.

Being called an "an all-American hero" and the "world's greatest athlete," Jenner began a career in films and television. Jenner became spokesperson for several firms and became the box cover athlete for Wheaties, "The breakfast cereal of champions," and continues to be spokesperson for the company after becoming a transgender. Jenner appeared in television shows but the one venture into films, "Can't Stop the Music" in 1980 was a box office flop. Jenner later formed a company selling aircraft supplies.

Prior to her gender transition, as Bruce Jenner she had been married three times and the father of six children. Jenner came out as a trans woman in an April 2015 television interview with Diane Sawyer, saying she had dealt with gender dysphasia since her youth and had for years cross-dressed and took hormone breast replacement therapy. Jenner's 23-year marriage to Kris Kardashian formally ended in 2015. Jenner's name then was legally changed to Caitlyn Marie Jenner and gender to female.

Caitlyn Jenner received the Arthur Ashe Courage Award in July, 2015, with ESPN executive producer Maura Mandt saying Jenner was given the award because "she has shown the courage to embrace the truth that had been hidden for years, and to embark on a journey that may not only give comfort to those facing similar circumstances but can also help to educate people on the challenges that the transgender community faces."

On sex -- *Jenner has said that she has never been sexually attracted to men, but always to women, and that she will identify for now as asexual.*

The Inner woman – (*On pain from hormone injections to enhance breasts and electrolysis to remove facial hair*): "Pain is kind of, for me, part of the pain for being me. This is what you get for being who you are. Just take the pain."

"If I was lying on my deathbed and I had kept this secret and never did anything about it, I would be lying there saying, 'You just blew your entire life. You never dealt with yourself." (*She said she did not want to look back at the end of her life and feel regret.*) "I don't want that to happen."

(*Before coming out as a transgender*): "Underneath my suit I have a bra and pantyhose and this and that and thinking to myself, 'They know nothing about me.'"

(*Upon winning the Olympic decathlon):* "Living with gender dysphasia in the public spotlight was as difficult as anyone can imagine. (*Jenner said he walked off the stage and felt like a liar and thought, 'Fuck, I can't tell my story. There's so much more to me than those 59 hours in the stadium, and I can't talk about it.' It was really frustrating. You get mad at yourself... Little did they know I was totally empty inside.*")

"Caitlyn just wants to enjoy a 'girls' night' out. Where everyone is treating you the same way, you can talk about anything you want to talk about. You can talk about outfits. You can talk about hair and makeup, anything you want. It becomes not a big deal."

Scarlett Johansson

After being in a relationship with one of the handsomest leading actors of recent years and divorcing another, she has found happiness in a current marriage. She has heart-felt things to say about love and men.

"The most precious moment in life is when you're about to fall in love. You're lying in bed together and he's gazing at you and you're gazing at him and there's a sense that something truly wondrous is about to happen. It's a nervous moment... but it's exhilarating."

"I am very independent. I can look after myself, but I still need a lot of love and care."

"I believe in finding a soul mate."

Born Scarlett Ingrid Johansson in New York City on November 22, 1984, her father is from a Jewish family and mother is Danish. Her siblings are a sister, Vanessa, who also is an actress, two brothers, one of whom is her twin, born three minutes after her, and a paternal half-brother. Her parents divorced when she was in her early teens. She showed a flair for acting as a school girl and acted in plays. Her film debut was in 1994 in the comedy "North," but made a bigger impression in "The Horse Whisperer" in 1998.

She was in a relationship with actor Josh Hartnett from 2004 to 2006, then she and Ryan Reynolds, a young Canadian actor, became engaged in May 2008 and married that September, but divorced in 2013 when he cited irreconcilable differences. That same year she became engaged to French journalist Romain Dauriac, they married in 2014, and had a daughter together. A beautiful, curvaceous young woman, she frequently appears in Woody Allen films. She has been ranked as ninth among the 100 sexiest women in the world and the "Sexiest Woman Alive" by *Esquire* magazine in 2013.

On Sex and Sexiness -- " I don't need to be skinny to be sexy."

"I feel comfortable as a young woman – a young, modern, liberal person. I feel comfortable with my sexuality. However, I am protective of my private life. I don't think that if you are in the public eye your life is public. I am an actor. But you can't take things too seriously.'"

"One of the best things for a woman to hear is that she is sexy."

On Men -- "It's nice to have a crush on someone. It feels like you're alive, you know?"

On David Hasselhoff, after working together in the 2004 film "The SpongeBob Square Pants Movie"): "I so fancied him when I was young, that to see my name on the credits next to his makes me go all girly. He was a hunk back in those days."

(*On Woody Allen*): "I just adore Woody, We have a lot in common, We're New Yorkers, Jewish. We have a very easygoing relationship."

On Marriage -- (*On her marriage to Ryan Reynolds):* "I never really thought about getting married. It just kind of happened. It seemed natural, the right thing to do. It was kind of a celebration of the time… I'm kind of making my own little family now, which is funny. It's like a little bit of a tribe. You hope that a relationship makes you better, that you learn things about yourself."

On Divorce -- (*On her divorce from Ryan Reynolds*): "At first I was quite depressed. After about a week or so I pulled myself together and started to go to the gym all the time. Luckily, I've got a few very close girlfriends who have been on my side for 15 years now, whom I can talk to about everything and confide in."

The Inner Woman – "I don't really aspire to being rational. I'm attracted more to the irrational. There is no such thing as total rationality… Like, it's okay to be jealous, for example, which people think is irrational To let yourself care that much that the emotion might hurt you a little."

"Look, I'm (*at heart*) a Frenchwoman. I think jealousy comes with the territory. But I'd rather be with someone who's a little jealous than someone who's never jealous. There's something a little dead fish about them. A little bit depressing. It may not make sense, but you need to *feel* it a little. I know, irrational, right?"

"I didn't think I was a jealous person, until I started dating my current, my one-and-only (*her husband Dauriac*). I think maybe in the past I didn't have the same kind of investment. Not that I liked my partner less, I just wasn't capable of it or caring that much."

"What I respect most in people is naturalness and authenticity. I like to be able to see into their soul. I aspire to be a truthful person."

"I always check in the mirror to make sure nothing is see-through."

"The wonderful thing about my mom (*who also is her manager*), is that she completely respects my creative weirdness and supports any decision I make."

"I don't talk about my personal relationships; it always ends up kicking you in the face. But I've read a lot of things about myself and think, 'Wow! That girl sounds really saucy.'"

"I don't think human beings are monogamous by nature. It's difficult… you have to put a lot of effort into a relationship."

(*On her trip to Rwanda to help fight against AIDS in Africa*): "It was important for me to come here and see the issues we're up against firsthand. I came here with an open mind, wanting to listen, understand and learn. I leave with the overwhelming understanding that the small action of mankind a RED choice in your purchases has an enormous impact on the lives of people in countries like Rwanda." (*Product RED is a brand raising awareness and funds to help eliminate HIV/AIDS in Africa, licensed to partner companies including Nike, American Express, Apple Inc., the Coca-Cola Company, Starbucks, and others. Each company creates a product with the Product RED logo and 50 percent of the purchase is donated to the Global RED Fund.*)

(*On entertaining GIs in the Persian Gulf in 2008*): "This USO tour to the Gulf region truly means a lot (*to me*). I've wanted to go over and visit for some time, and now my moment has arrived. It's one thing to reply to a letter or extend your thanks to service members in a speech, but it's another thing to visit them and spend time with those that do so much for us back home."

"There's no such thing as an aura of mystery anymore. It doesn't exist. That's a thing of the past."

Angelina Jolie

While married to Brad Pitt, one of the handsomest and hottest men in or out of Hollywood, Angelina is outspoken about her liberal views on sex and love, including loving other women:

"Love one person, take care of them until you die. You know, raise kids. Have a good life. Be a good friend. And try to be completely who you are. And figure out what you personally love. And like go after it with everything you've got no matter how much it takes."

"We come to love not by finding the perfect person, but by learning to see an imperfect person perfectly."

"I'm the person most likely to sleep with my female fans. I genuinely love other women, and I think they know that."

Born Angelina Jolie Voight in Los Angeles, California on June 4, 1975, the daughter of actress Marcheline Bertrand and Academy Award best actor Jon Voight. She began acting at 11 and modeling at 16, winning the Oscar for best supporting actress in 2000 for her role in "Girl, Interrupted." She gave the statuette to her mother whom she called "Great Lady." Her mother died of ovarian cancer in 2007 after more than a seven year battle with it. Her name "Jolie" is French for "pretty." She is often named among the most beautiful women in the world, and earns up to $10 million a movie.

While filming a "Lara Croft" movie in Cambodia, her concern for poverty led her to begin humanitarian work and she became a Goodwill Ambassador for the United Nations High Commissioner for Refugees. She adopted a Cambodia refugee boy in 2002 and three years later an Ethiopian refugee girl.

She was married to actor Johnny Lee Miller (1996-1999) and then to actor Billy Bob Thornton (2000-2003). Actor Brad Pitt became her partner after his divorce from actress Jennifer Aniston in 2005. Jolie and Pitt have had three children together, and adopted four others.

It was little known, but Jolie and Pitt were officially wife and husband long before their public marriage in 2014. "Before the wedding in France with the kids, Brad and I were already married in California," she said in interview. "As Americans, we couldn't marry legally in France… One day I said to Brad, 'Let's meet up at 4:30 pm?' I called a justice of the peace and we signed the documents." *(They had previously obtained a marriage license from a California judge before exchanging vows at a chateau. The same judge also conducted their nondenominational civil ceremony. For the sake of their children, they wanted to hold a formal ceremony with them taking part, as ring bearers and throwing flower petals from their garden.)*

On Love -- "Everyone got kind of crazy with me mentioning I was in love with a woman."

"Honestly, I like everything, boyish girls, girlish boys, the heavy and the skinny."

On Men -- (*On Jon Voight*): "You're a great actor, but you're a better father."

(*On Brad Pitt*) "He made me a better person. I've learned so much from him, as you do when you come together with another person. You both make each other better. You both learn about the best of each other, and recognize the things where you're failing, or where you need to step up. When it's a great partnership, you really are patient with each other."

"I grew up in front of everybody, really. The big years of exploration. There was a certain madness I was going through. I learned a lot about myself. People tend to sum up times in your life and simplify."

"To be intimate with a married man, when my own father cheated on my mother, is not something I could forgive. I could not look at myself in the morning, if I did that."

On Marriage, Partnership -- *(On her partnership with Brad Pitt):* "We have both been married before so it's not marriage that necessarily kept some people together."

The Inner Woman -- "I made a strong choice (*to have a double mastectomy in 2013*) that in no way diminishes my femininity."

"I do wear tattoos, and I do wear leather, but there are other sides of me."

"Therapy? I don't need that. The roles that I choose are my therapy."

"I think to be a parent is one of the scariest, boldest things to do, as opposed to, um, getting a tattoo."

"I'm drawn to kids that are already born. I think some people are meant to do certain things, and I believe I'm meant to find my children in the world somewhere and not necessarily have them genetically."

"I think I'm going to have to give up the acting as the kids hit the teenage years. Anyway, too much to manage at home. I have enjoyed being an actress. I am so grateful to the job and I have had great experiences and I have even been able to tell stories and be a part of stories that mattered and I have done things for fun, but... I will do some films and I am so fortunate to have the job, it's a really lucky profession to be a part of and I enjoy it. But if it went away tomorrow I would be very happy to be home with the children. I wake up in the morning as a mum and I turn on the news like everybody else and I see what's happening and I want to be a part of the world in a positive way."

"I have a few girlfriends, I just… I stay at home a lot. I'm just not very social. I don't do a lot with them, and I'm very homebound. I'll talk to my family, I talk to Brad… But I don't know, I don't have a lot of friends I talk to. He is really the only person I talk to."

"The only way to have a life is to commit to it like crazy."

"You want to meet other people that challenge you with ideas or with power or with passion."

"If you don't get out of the box you've been raised in, you won't understand how much bigger the world is."

"I don't believe in guilt. I believe in living on impulse as long as you never intentionally hurt another person, and don't judge people in your life. I think you should live completely free."

"I've been reckless, but I'm not a rebel without a cause."

"Without pain, there would be no suffering; without suffering we would never learn from our mistakes. To make it right, pain and suffering is the key to all windows. Without it, there is no way of life."

"Everyone of us needs to show how much we care for each other and, in the process, care for ourselves."

(On her humanitarian work): "One of the first camps I went to *(in Cambodia)* had 400,000 people. It was a sea of human misery. In Sierra Leone, I saw tens of thousands with their arms and legs cut off *(by rebels)*, orphaned children. I felt guilty for everything that I had. Then I realized I wasn't doing these people any favors by crying. I kept getting angry at the injustices until I couldn't think straight. I took a deep breath and focused on how I could help. I discovered that I was useful as a person. When I met suffering people, it put my life into perspective. It slammed me into a bigger picture of the world."

"Because I am a bad girl *(in some movies)*, people always automatically think that I am a bad girl. Or that I carry a dark secret with me, or that I'm obsessed with death. The truth is that I am probably the least morbid person one can meet. If I think about more about death than some other people, it is probably because I love life more than they do."

Jolie surprised everyone by filing for divorce from Pitt in September 2016 citing "irreconcilable differences." They had lived together for some ten years but had been married only two.

Grace Kelly

While she left the movies as a top star and became a princess, under the crown she was not a virgin Cinderella. Far from it, it has become known since her tragic death in a road accident on the Riviera.

"Fairy tales tell imaginary stories. Me, I'm a living person. I exist. If the story of my life as a real woman were to be told one day, people would at last discover the real being that I am."

"When I married Prince Rainier, I married the man and not what he represented or what he was. I fell in love with him without giving a thought to anything else."

Born Grace Patricia Kelly in Philadelphia, Pennsylvania on November 12, 1929, her mother was a physical education instructor and her father a businessman. She worked as a model before debuting on Broadway in 1949 and her first film was two years later in a small part in "Fourteen Hours."

Her career took off when she was cast as Gary Cooper's wife in "High Noon" in 1952, then the following year with Clark Gable and Ava Gardner in "Mogambo." Star roles followed in the Alfred Hitchcock drama "Dial M for Murder" and "Rear Window," both in 1954. That same year she starred with Bing Crosby in "The Country Girl" and won the Academy Award as best actress. Teamed with Cary Grant in Hitchcock's "To Catch a Thief" in 1955, she then starred with Crosby and Frank Sinatra in the 1956 musical remake of "The Philadelphia Story" called "High Society" which became her final film.

While on the Riviera for the Cannes film festival in 1955 she met Prince Rainier of Monaco. They married the following year and she became Princess Grace and they had three children together. Some speculated that Rainier married her for her fame and money and to give him a son and heir, and that she married him so she could become a princess.

If the prince had read the movie fan magazines he may have known that Grace was not quite so royal or virginal. While in an affair with actor Alexandre D'Arcy, he said about her first night with him in his apartment: "She was a very, very sexual girl. Very warm indeed as far as sex was concerned. You would touch her once, and she would go through the ceiling. It was very obvious she was not a virgin. She was certainly experienced."

Another lover, while she was in her young twenties, her acting teacher in New York, Don Richardson, who was twice her age, took her to his apartment and when he returned to her from making a fire in the fireplace, he found her in his bed, having taken off all her clothes and was waiting for him.. "I never saw anything so splendid," he said later. "Her body was something stunning. She was like something sculptured by Rodin. She had the most beautiful, delicate figure.. small breasts, small lips, and her skin was almost translucent. She was the most beautiful girl I had ever seen naked… She seemed to be madly in love with me. So that night was sheer ecstasy." Richardson said Grace liked to dance naked in the firelight to Hawaiian music. "She was a very sexy girl."

She soon became a movie star and fell in love with her leading men, Clark Gable in "Mogambo" (1953) and William Holden in "The Bridges of Toko-Ri' (1954) and they fell in love with her, but their affairs did not lead to marriage. During filming of "Mogambo," an African jungle romance, Grace learned some Swahili, and came on to Gable saying, "Would you like a nibble of my *ndizi*? (it meant "banana"). Gable replied, "I'd never turn down an offer like that," although she was 24 and he thought he was old enough to be her father. She and Cary Grant began a six-year relationship while co-starring in "To Catch a Thief" (1955). She was engaged to fashion designer Oleg Cassini, ex-husband of actress Gene Tierney, but broke it off when she decided to become a princess.

Grace's marriage to Rainier made worldwide news and she and the prince appeared to be happy together, but she became disillusioned with him and began to drink. After the first two years they began sleeping in separate bedrooms and then lived in separate countries as she moved to Paris. On a return visit to Monaco she was driving alone on a cliff road and had a stroke, the car crashed and she died of injuries on September 14, 1982 at the age of 52. She was mourned the world over. Her favorite flowers were roses, and after her death, Rainier opened a public rose garden in Monaco in her memory.

She was chosen by *Esquire* magazine as No. 5 among the 100 sexiest stars in film history and No. 13 among actresses on The American Film Institute's 50 Greatest Screen Legends." She was the first actress to appear on a U.S. postage stamp, in 1993.

On Men -- "My father had a very simple view of life: you don't get anything for nothing. Everything has to be earned, through work, persistence and honesty. My father also had a deep charm, the gift of winning our trust. He was the kind of man with whom many people dream of spending an evening."

On Marriage -- (*Before marrying Prince Rainier*): "Of course, I think about marriage, but my career is still the most important thing for me. If I interrupt it now to get married, because I don't believe in a part-time family life, I would risk passing the rest of my existence wondering whether or not I would have been able to become a great actress."

"Before my marriage, I didn't think about all the obligations there were awaiting me. My experience has proved useful and I think that I have a natural propensity to feel compassion for people and their problems."

The Inner Woman -- "I hated Hollywood. It's a town without pity. I know of no other place in the world where so many people suffer from nervous breakdowns, where there are so many alcoholics, neurotics, and so much unhappiness. I have many acquaintances there, but few friends."

"It would be very sad if children had no memories before those of school. What they need most is the love and attention of their mother."

"I came to success very quickly. Perhaps too quickly to value its importance."

(*After her marriage*): "My real difficulty was to become a normal person again, after having been a movie actress for so long. For me, at the time I was living in New York and Hollywood, a normal person was someone who made movies."

"My love of flowers opened a lot of doors for me. I've made many friends because of their passion of flowers and their vast knowledge in this field."

"I avoid looking back. I prefer good memories to regrets."

"I'm basically a feminist. I think that women can do anything they decide to do."

"I would like to be remembered as someone who accomplished useful deeds, and who was a kind and loving person. I would like to leave the memory of a human being with a correct attitude and who did her best to help others."

Nicole Kidman

Did she and Tom Cruise marry for mutual career benefit and to mask rumors he was gay? We may never know the answer, even from Nicole, although she says she married him because she loved him, and he says he married her because he loved her.

(*In a 2006 interview she said she still loved Tom Cruise*): *"He was huge; still is. To me, he was just Tom, but to everybody else, he is huge. But he was lovely to me and I loved him. I still love him."*

"It's a very brave thing to fall in love. You have to be willing to trust somebody else with your whole being, and that's very difficult and very brave."

"I think that the most difficult thing is allowing yourself to be loved, so receiving the love and feeling like you deserve it is a pretty big struggle. I suppose that's what I've learnt recently, to allow myself to be loved."

Born Nicole Mary Kidman in Honolulu, Hawaii on June 20, 1967 while her Australian parents were on educational visas to the United States. Her father was a chemist and mother a nursing instructor. She studied acting in Australia and began appearing in films there when she was 16 in 1983. After more films in Australia she made her American film debut co-starred with Tom Cruise in "Days of Thunder" in 1990.

She and Cruise married on Christmas Eve 1990 in Telluride, Colorado and adopted a daughter and a son. They separated in 2001 and Cruise filed for divorce citing irreconcilable differences. Kidman, a Roman Catholic, said she did not want her children to be reared as Scientologists, as Cruise is, and it was speculated that their religious differences were responsible for their divorce. Kidman reportedly expressed shock over her divorce from Tom Cruise. Before marrying Cruise, she lived with Australian actor Tom Burlinson ("The Man from Snowy River" 1982) on and off for three years and also lived with Australian stage actor Marcus Graham in the late 1980s.

Kidman met New Zealand-Australian country singer Keith Urban in 2005 and they married the following year. They have had two daughters together. Kidman has become very wealthy through her films and product endorsements, her 2015 net worth in excess of $330 million. A philanthropist, she has donated and raised money for various causes including disadvantaged children around the world. She became a goodwill ambassador for UNICEF and in 2004 was honored as a "Citizen of the World" by the United Nations. She also has become a donor and fundraiser for the fight against breast cancer, of which her mother died in 1984.

On Sex and Sexiness -- (*On nudity in the movies*): "You don't have to be naked to be sexy."

On Men -- "You just got to have a sense of respect for the person you have children with. Anger doesn't help anybody. Ultimately, you have to say forgiveness is important, and honoring what you had together is important. But it's easy to say and harder to do."

On Love – "It's very easy to fall in love when things are great, but the way to really fall in love is when things aren't great."

"I'm a person that carries everything that happened to me in my past, with me into the future. I refuse to let it make me bitter. I still completely believe in love and I remain open to anything that will happen to me."

On Marriage -- (*On her marriage to Tom Cruise*): "I got married really fast and really young." (*She was 28, so she may have meant she was emotionally young.*)

(*In 2015, on her marriage to Keith Urban*): "We didn't really know each other – we got to know each other during our marriage."

"When you relinquish the desire to control your future, you can have more happiness."

"Every day there is a compromise. Living with somebody requires a lot of understanding. But I love being married (*to Keith Urban*). I really love it."

"I always wanted to get married with just candles! I think candlelight is the most beautiful light there is, and there's something very spiritual about it."

"If you're going to be with someone, you're with them, you're committed to them. I'm not sort of flirting around."

The Inner Woman -- "I'll put it out there: I love getting hugs."

"I am very shy… really shy. I even had a stutter as a kid, which I slowly got over, but I still regress into that shyness. So I don't like walking into a crowded restaurant by myself; I don't like going to a party by myself."

"I love acting, but it's much more fun taking the kids to the zoo."

"Life has got all those twists and turns. You've got to hold on tight and off you go… I don't really make decisions. I go with the flow."

"I would describe myself as emotional and highly strung. If something upsets me, it really upsets me. If something makes me angry, I get really angry. But it's all very upfront. I can't hide it. I'm also loyal and I hope I'm fun."

"I have a boy's body. I would prefer to have more curves because I think that's more beautiful. I would much rather have J. Lo's (*Jennifer Lopez*) body than mine."

"They've said I'm gay, they've said everyone is gay. I personally don't believe in doing huge law suits about that stuff. Tom (*Cruise*) does. That's what he wants to do, that's what he's going to do. You do not tell Tom what to do. He is a force to be reckoned with."

"I'm not sure what the future holds, but I do know that I'm going to be positive and not wake up feeling desperate. As my dad said, 'Nic, it is what it is, it's not what it should have been, not what it could have been; it is what it is."

Billie Jean King

She became known not only for being the best female tennis champion of the world, she became known as being the best lesbian tennis champion of the world. The title crown sat easily on her head.

"I used to be told if I talked about my sexuality in any way that we wouldn't have a tennis tour."

"Everyone has people in their lives that are gay, lesbian or transgender or bisexual. They may not want to admit it, but I guarantee they know somebody."

"When I was outed, it was like, That's done."

"If your partner wants to be private, you have to respect that."

Born Billie Jean Moffitt in Long Beach, California on November 22, 1943, her father was a fire department engineer and her mother an Avon sales representative. She became interested in tennis when she was 11 and saved money to buy her first tennis racket, then played on free public courts in Long Beach. When she was 14 she won her first championship, in a southern California tournament, and soon began getting coaching from Alice Marble, a famous tennis star in the 1930s. Tennis had always been a country club sport for men, but Billie Jean challenged that as she became a champion so women could be admitted.

She is a former World No. 1 professional tennis player, winning 39 Grand Slam titles including 12 singles, 16 women's doubles, and 11 mixed doubles titles. She was a member of the victorious U.S. team in seven Federation Cups and 20 titles at Wimbledon. Her professional tennis winnings were close to two million dollars.

An advocate for sexual equality, in 1973 at the age of 29, she won the legendary Battle of the Sexes tennis match against 55-year-old Bobby Riggs, and was the founder of the Women's Tennis Association and the Women's Sports Federation.

She met attorney Lawrence King when he was a law student and member of the student tennis team at what is now California State University and they married in 1965. He later organized the first professional tennis tour for women and helped found World Team Tennis. They had a child together in 1971 but she had an abortion, and they divorced in 1987. Her partner is Ilana Kloss, also a former professional tennis champion.

On Gender Equality -- "My whole life has been about equal rights and opportunities. For me it really goes back to the health of mind, body, and soul."

"I wanted to use sports for social change."

"A girl didn't get an athletic scholarship until the fall of 1972 for the very first time."

"In 1973, a woman could not get a credit card without her husband or father or a male signing off on it."

"Any therapist will tell you that when you're ready, you will come out. To be outed means you weren't ready. I would just never out anybody. I think everyone has to find it in their own way and their own time."

"Don't worry about what people say. Don't let anyone define you. You define yourself."

"Sports are a microcosm of society. It's just really important that we start celebrating our differences. Let's start tolerating first, but then we need to celebrate our differences."

"I hate being called a homosexual because I don't feel that way. It really upsets me... Being gay can happen in any walk of life, in any world. If you have one gay experience, does that mean you're gay? If you have one heterosexual experience, does that mean you're straight? Life doesn't work quite so cut and dried."

"Reputation is what others think about you. What's far more important is character, because that is what you think of yourself."

"We have, or have had women presidents or prime ministers in Liberia, Chile, Germany, Great Britain.. and yet the U.S. of A. still hasn't had a woman President. It's beyond my thinking. Look at Congress (*where there are women Senators and member of the House of Representatives*)."

On Men -- "The 'old boy network' is still very strong and very true. Just look at the Stock Exchange and how many men and women are there. It is still very much run by men."

"Men still get a lot more opportunity. They have more companies they can get money from."

"It is very hard to be a female leader. While it is assumed that any man, no matter how tough, has a soft side… and a female leader is assumed to be one-dimensional."

On Marriage -- "Marriage isn't a 50-50 proposition very often. It's more like 100-0 one moment and 0-100 the next."

The Inner Woman -- "I think self-awareness is probably the most important thing towards being a champion."

"Champions keep playing until they get it right."

"For me, losing a tennis match isn't failure, it's research."

"Each point I play is in the now moment. The last point means nothing, the next point means nothing."

"Natural talent only determines the limits of your athletic potential. It's dedication and a willingness to discipline your life that makes you great."

"I always listen, I ask children, I even ask adults in tennis, 'What are your children playing?' And most of the time it's not tennis. It's pathetic."

"Tennis taught me so many lessons in life. One of the things it taught me is that every ball that comes to me, I have to make a decision. Champions take responsibility. I have to accept responsibility for the consequences every time I hit a ball.

"The main thing is to care. Care very hard, even if it is only a game you are playing."

"Victory is fleeting. Losing is forever."

"Be bold. If you're going to make an error, make a doozy, and don't be afraid to hit the ball."

"It's really impossible for athletes to grow up. On the one hand, you're still a child, still playing a game. But on the other hand, you're a superhuman hero that everyone dreams of being. No wonder we have such a hard time understanding who we are."

"When people tell you not to believe in your dreams, and they say 'Why,' say 'Why not?'"

"Ladies, here's a (*tennis*) hint. If you're up against a girl with big boobs, bring her to the net and make her hit backhand volleys. That's the hardest shot for the well-endowed."

Beyonce Knowles

Beyonce is a very public African American figure but also a very private person, happily married and a mother, with a strong religious belief in God that is very important to her. Like her big hit song, she is "Crazy in Love."

"My life is a journey... I had to go through my miscarriage, I believe I had to go through owning my company and managing myself...Ultimately, your independence comes from knowing who you are and you being happy with yourself."

"Who I am on stage is very, very different to who I am in real life. But I don't see that having a sexy image when you are on stage means that you don't love God. No one knows what I'm really like from that."

"I like to walk around with bare feet and I don't like to comb my hair. I'm always so glammed up and so diva on stage and that's what they see. People don't understand that... No one knows my personal relationship with God and it's not up to me to prove that to anyone."

Like her big hit song, she is "Crazy in Love."

Born Beyonce Giselle Knowles in Houston, Texas on September 4, 1981, of African-American and Creole descent, her father manages her career and her mother designs her glittering costumes. Her sister, Solange Knowles, also is a singer and dancer. Beyonace and her singing group were discovered by actress-singer Whitney Houston.

In 2008 Knowles married Shawn Corey Carter, known professionally as rapper Jay-Z, and they have had a child together. His net worth reportedly is $520 million, while her's is $450 million, so they can be considered almost a billionaire couple. She is known for performing in revealing clothing and wearing stiletto heels.

In 2001 she became the first African-American woman to win the ASCAP Pop Songwriter of the Year award. Her biggest song hit is "Crazy in Love," from 2003. That same year she performed at a South African AIDS benefit show to combat the epidemic in sub-Saharan Africa. She won five Grammy awards in 2004 and six in 2010.

The Inner Woman – "For me, it's about the way I carry myself and the way I treat other people. My relationship and how I feel about God and what He does for me, is something deeply personal. It's where I came from, my family, I was brought up in a religious household and that's very important to me. But I understand the mentality of people. I know that people judge others based on certain things."

"We all have our imperfections. But I'm human and you know, it's important to concentrate on other qualities besides outer beauty."

(*On her religious faith and gay people:*) "Well, you know, I grew up going to church, but I was raised by my uncle who passed away with AIDS a couple of years ago. He was my mother's best friend. And my mother's cousin. He brought me to school every day. He helped me buy my prom dress. He made my clothes with my mother. He was like my nanny. He was my favorite person in the world. And you know, I never really mixed Christianity with how I felt about him. I am about faith and spirituality more so than religion. Doing right by others and not judging."

"I'm like everyone else. I have days when I look in the mirror and I'm like 'Oh my gosh, I wish I could change this or that.' The more you mature, you realize that imperfections make you more beautiful."

"I don't like to gamble, but if there's one thing I'm willing to bet on, it's myself."

"If you live your life with kindness and give other people great energy, that beauty and great energy come back to you… Not everyone is supposed to be the same. Be healthy and take care of yourself - and be happy with the beautiful things that made you."

Hedy Lamarr

Considered by many to have been the most beautiful woman ever on the screen or off, she was unlucky in love, having married and divorced six times; not a Hollywood record, but close to it. Some of her husbands were very rich men, and she made a lot of money as a film goddess, but died alone and broke. Beauty and sex appeal were not her best friends, nor were the men she married.

"The ladder of success in Hollywood is usually agent, actor, director, producer, leading man. And you are a star if you sleep with them in that order. Crude but true."

"My problem is, I'm a hell of a nice dame. The most horrible whores are famous. I did what I did for love. The others did it for money."

Born Hedwig Eva Maria Kiesler in Vienna, Austria on November 9, 1914, her banker father and pianist mother both were Jewish. She dropped out of high school to become an actress and became a student of theater director Max Reinhardt in Berlin. Her film debut was a bit part in a German movie in 1930, and she became a star three years later in her fourth movie, "Ecstasy." She swam nude and ran naked through the woods which shocked audiences but catapulted her to fame. About this time she married Fritz Mandl, an Austrian munitions manufacturer. He tried to buy up all copies of "Ecstasy," but some prints of it survived. Even Nazi Germany leader Adolph Hitler and Italian dictator Benito Mussolini had copies they watched in private.

Mandl, a Jew, was a fascist who opposed Hitler and Nazi Germany. He transferred most of his money to Switzerland but his remaining wealth and property was seized by the Nazis following Germany's occupation of Austria on March 12, 1938. A few months earlier, Hedy had disguised herself as a maid and fled to Paris where she obtained a divorce. Mandl, meanwhile, trying to save himself from Nazi imprisonment or death, tried to deal with Hermann Goring to supply Germany with iron. When this failed, he fled to South America where he lived out the war.

From Paris, Hedy obtained passage to America aboard the *Normandie,* a ship she knew carried among its passengers Louis B. Mayer, head of MGM Studios in Hollywood. He knew of her success in "Ecstasy," appreciated her beauty as a potential American film star, and by the end of the voyage, agreed to a contract for her, for $600 a week, which would be $3,000 today, providing she learn to speak English, which she quickly did. Mayer also changed her name to Hedy Lamarr, the surname after a silent film beauty Barbara La Marr.

Mayer had no immediate film for Hedy in 1938, so he loaned her to Walter Wanger for his film "Algiers," in which Charles Boyer fell in love with her. She became an overnight star from her performance and women all over the world let their hair grow long and dyed it black to imitate her. The following year she made her MGM debut in "Lady of the Tropics" opposite Robert Taylor. Soon she was among the top stars of the top studio in the world. In "White Cargo" in 1942 she played an African native beauty and in a clinging sarong delivered one of the most sexy opening lines in films: "I am Tondelayo."

Hedy was not too busy in films to forget the horror of war she had left behind in Europe. She put in as few appearances at Hollywood social gatherings as she could, and worked at home as an amateur inventor hoping to make something to help the Allies. In the 1940s, the Nazis had been torpedoing Allied ships in the Atlantic, killing scores of civilian men, women, and children as well as servicemen.

One night at a party in 1940, she met composer George Anthiel whose musical compositions explored modernist sounds. They talked about the tragedy of American and other Allied ships becoming targets of Nazi submarines in the Atlantic because Allied defensive torpedoes were being detected by the enemy. Anthiel shared his thoughts on the need for top-secret weapons systems, and the idea for one such an invention came to Hedy from watching a player piano go around with different holes in the paper.

Hedy set aside one room in her house to work on the invention, had a drafting table installed with proper lighting and drawing tools, and an entire wall stacked with engineering reference books she studied.

Her idea was for a secret communications system, specifically one that could guide an Allied torpedo using a technology so that the signal could not be intercepted or jammed by the enemy. It became the earliest method of telecommunications known as "frequency hopping." Together, she and Anthiel parented their invention in 1941 under the name "Secret Communications System." However, the enormous significance of their invention was ignored by the U.S. Navy during the war. Women inventors were commonly ignored at the time. Countless thousands of lives and ships could have been saved if Hedy's invention had been used. Nazi ships sank, among others, 3,500 Allied merchant ships and 175 warships.

Hedy's invention was first used twenty years later, on U.S. Naval ships during the Cuban Missile Crisis of 1962. It was a 13-day confrontation between the U.S. and the Soviet Union concerning Soviet ballistic missiles being stationed in Cuba that could strike the U.S.

More recently, the "spread spectrum" technology that Lamarr invented helped to generate the digital communications age, forming the technical backbone that makes cellular phones, fax machines, and wireless (Wi-Fi) operations possible.

Neither Hedy nor Anthiel made a dime off of their invention, because the patent was allowed to expire. Anthiel died in 1959, but she, however, received an award from the Electronic Frontier Foundation in 1997 for her pioneering work in spread-spectrum technology. That same year, she became the first female recipient of the BULBIE Gnass Spirit of Achievement Award, a prestigious lifetime accomplishment prize for inventors that is considered to be "The Oscar of Inventing."

On receiving her 1997 award for her 1941 invention of frequency hopping, she said, "It's about time."

Lamarr proved that she was much more than just another pretty face, shattering stereotypes and earning a place among the 20th century's most important women inventors. She truly was a visionary whose technological acumen was far ahead of its time.

Hedy then returned to the movies. Her best performance as an actress may have been playing a woman who chose career over marriage to socialite Robert Young in "H.M. Pulham, Esq." in 1941. She looked more beautiful and alluring in a modest gown than any actress ever looked in a bikini or nothing at all. She was again memorable in "Ziegfeld Girl" 1941) and as the temptress in the Cecil B. DeMille epic "Samson and Delilah" (1949). She made six more films, her last being "The Female Animal" in 1958.

Hedy, who became a naturalized U.S. citizen in 1953, was married and divorced six times. Her husbands were Fritz Mandl (1933-1937); screen writer Gene Markey (1939-1941) with whom she had one child; actor John Loder (1943-1947), with whom she had two children; Swiss band leader Teddy Stauffer (1951-1952); Texas oil tycoon W. Howard Lee (1953-1960); and attorney Lewis J. Boies (1963-1965) who she divorced saying he threatened her with a baseball bat.

The love of her life was handsome actor George Montgomery, perhaps the man who got away. They became engaged in 1942 but instead she married John Loder and he married singer Dinah Shore. Montgomery said he loved Hedy since he first saw her in "Algiers."

(1938). They remained good friends and Montgomery admitted, "Hedy is the only girl I've ever asked to marry me. (*Maybe Dinah proposed to him.*) Hedy later said George Montgomery was a man she "should have married."

Although she earned big money as a movie star, she lost her fortune when her movie production company failed. She retired to Florida being almost broke and was arrested twice for shoplifting, the first in 1966 but was found not guilty, and again in 1991 for which she was put on one year probation. A reporter found her living in a one-room studio apartment, too poor to have her television set repaired. She died of natural causes in Casselberry, near Orlando, on January 19, 2000 at the age of 85. A natural brunette with pale skin, green eyes, and a voluptuous figure, she has been considered by many to have been the most beautiful woman in films and some say even in the world.

On Love -- (*In the 1960s*): "It would be wrong of me to say so, but in this country (*America*) money is more important than love. Most people here betray you, and that's why there is so much chaos. I want to get away from here. I am homesick for Vienna... because my home is Vienna and Austria, not America... never!"

On Marriage -- "I must quit marrying men who feel inferior to me. Somewhere, there must be a man who could be my husband and not feel inferior. I need a superior inferior man."

"Every girl would like to marry a rich husband. I did twice. But what divides girls into two groups is this question… Do you first think of money and then love, or vice versa?"

"You couldn't live with a person, in those days (*the 1940s*), without being married."

"Men are fine, love is fine. It's marriage I'm a little disappointed in."

On Divorce – "Lawyers know how to take isolated complains in a divorce case and build them into one big one."

"Let any pretty girl announce a divorce in Hollywood and the wolves come running. Fresh meat for the beast, and they are always hungry."

On Men – "Men are most virile and attractive between the ages of 35 and 55. Under 35, a man has much to learn, and I don't have time to teach him."

"I am not ashamed to say that no man I ever met was my father's equal, and I never loved any other man as much."

"American men, as a group, seem to be interested in only two things, money and breasts. It seems a very narrow outlook."

"I enjoy countless hundreds of men pursuing me. I love those who love me the most. I am sort of flattered by men showing attention to me."

"I find very often that very ugly women have really handsome men and vice versa because they don't have any competition. Sometimes handsome men have avoided me."

"I have never seen a wrestling match or prize fight, and I don't want to. When I find out a man is interested in those sports, I drop him."

The Inner Woman – (*In her declining poverty years, a reporter said he remembered she sang in one of her films in the 1940s and thought she had quite a good singing voice*): "Honey, if they paid you what MGM paid me in those years, you could sing, too."

Hedy rarely sang in her films, so the reporter must have been referring to her singing the 1922 plaintiff ballad "Three O'clock in the Morning" while dancing in a farewell with Robert Young in "H.M. Pulham, Esq." (1941). It was one of 1920's Jazz Age" author F. Scott Fitzgerald's favorite songs. He wrote in his later memoir, *The Crack-up:* "In a real dark night of the soul it is always three o'clock in the morning, day after day," paraphrasing the 16th century Spanish priest and poet, St. John of the Cross.

(*On nudity in films*): "If you use your imagination, you can look at any actress and see her nude. I hope to make you use your imagination."

"Any girl can be glamorous. All you have to do is stand still and look stupid."

"I find very often that very ugly women have really handsome men and vice versa because they don't have any competition. Sometimes handsome men have avoided me."

"It's funny about men and women. Men pay in cash to get them and pay in cash to get rid of them. Women pay emotionally coming and going. Neither has it easy."

Ann Landers

Ann was one of the most famous and successful advise to the lovelorn newspaper columnists. She often, but not always, took her own advice, since she was married twice.

"Love is friendship that has caught fire. It is quiet understanding, mutual confidence, sharing, and forgiving. It is loyalty through good and bad times. It settles for less than perfection and makes allowances for human weaknesses."

"Sensual pleasures have the fleeting brilliance of a comet. A happy marriage has the tranquility of a lovely sunset."

"All married couples should learn the art of battle as they would learn the art of making love. Good battle is objective and honest, never vicious or cruel. Good battle is healthy and constructive, and brings to a marriage the principle of equal partnership."

Born Esther Pauline Lederer in Sioux City, Iowa on July 4, 1918, to Russian Jewish immigrants, to family and friends she was known as "Eppie," and her identical twin sister born Pauline Esther Lederer was called "Popo." They both attended Morningside College where together they wrote a gossip column for the school newspaper. Afterward, Eppie began writing the "Ask Ann Landers" daily column for the *Chicago Sun-Times* newspaper in 1955 that had been created by the paper's earlier advice columnist, Ruth Crowley in 1943.

Eppie's advice was often controversial since she advocated legalization of prostitution, was pro-choice regarding abortion, and supported legalization of homosexual acts between adults. The Ann Landers column continued for 47 years until Eppie's death in 2002. In her declining years, she wrote it while taking a bath in her tub at home. Her readership was as high as 90 million readers in worldwide syndication. The 1978 *World Almanac* named her the most influential woman in the world.

Eppie also was a fundraiser for several medical charities and served on President Jimmy Carter's cancer advisory board. The sisters became estranged because Popo wrote a competing advice column, "Dear Abby," as Abigail Van Buren while living in San Francisco which was syndicated by what is now Universal Press Syndicate. Popo died on January 16, 2013 at the age of 94, and her daughter Jeanne Phillips took over writing "Dear Abby" which continues to today. Before becoming columnists, the sisters were married on their birthday in 1939 in a double-wedding ceremony.

Eppie was married to Julius Lederer who became a business executive, and Popo married attorney Morton Phillips of Minneapolis. With Lederer, Eppie gave birth to a daughter, Margo, who later also wrote an advice column, and Popo had a son and daughter with Phillips. In her mature years, Eppie said she exercised by walking the length of her apartment in Chicago several times a day. Eppie died in Chicago on June 22, 2002 at the age of 83 and Popo died January 16, 2013 at the age of 94.

On Sexuality -- (*On homosexuality*): "It is my firm conviction that homosexuality is not learned behavior, and that while being gay could be suppressed, it could not be altered." (*She did not, however, support same-sex marriage.*)

On Men -- "The true measure of a man is how he treats someone who can do him absolutely no good."

On Marriage -- "At every party there are two kinds of people... those who want to go home and those who don't. The trouble is, they are usually married to each other."

(*In 1996*): "I cannot support same-sex marriage, because it flies in the face of cultural and traditional family life as we have known it for centuries."

On Sex -- "Women complain about sex more often than men. Their gripes fall into two major categories: (1) Not enough. (2) Too much."

On Love -- "If you have love in your life, it can make up for a great many things that are missing. If you don't have love in y our life, no matter what else there is, it's not enough."

The Inner Woman -- "Opportunities are usually disguised as hard work, so most people don't recognize them."

(*On hard work*): "Nobody ever drowned in his own sweat."

"If I were asked to give what I consider to be the single most useful bit of advice for all humanity it would be this: Expect trouble as an inevitable part of life, and when it comes, hold your head high, look it squarely in the eye and say, 'I will be bigger than you. You cannot defeat me.' And repeat to yourself the most comforting words of all: 'This, too, shall pass.'"

"Trouble is the common denominator of living. It is the great equalizer. One trouble with trouble is that it usually starts out like fun."

"The Lord gave us two ends... one to sit on and the other to think with. Success depends on which one we use the most."

(*On maturity*): "Be able to stick with a job until it is finished. Be able to bear an injustice without having to get even. Be able to carry money without spending it. Do your duty without being supervised."

"What the vast majority of American children need is to stop being pampered, stop being indulged, stop being chauffeured, stop being catered to. In the final analysis, it is not what you do for your children but what you have taught them to do for themselves that will make them successful human beings."

"Don't accept your dog's admiration as conclusive evidence that you are wonderful."

"Some people believe that holding on and hanging in there are signs of great strength. However, there are times when it takes much more strength to know when to let go… and then do it."

"Make somebody happy today. Mind your own business."

"People who drink to drown their sorrow should know that sorrow knows how to swim."

(*On having class*): "Class is an aura of confidence that is being sure without being cocky. Class has nothing to do with money. Class never runs scared. It is self-discipline and self-knowledge. It's the sure-footedness that comes with having proved you can meet life."

"One of the secrets of a long and fruitful life is to forgive everybody everything every night before you go to bed."

"Nobody gets to live life backward. Look ahead; that is where your future lies."

"We need not fear life, because God is the Ruler of all, and we need not fear death, because He shares immortality with us."

Queen Latifah

A self-proclaimed queen of entertainment, she is in a lesbian relationship and does not hide it. After all, a queen can do as she pleases.

"Every woman is a queen, and we all have different things to offer, and we should be treated as such, and we should, you know, sort of request that sort of treatment from others."

"I made decisions that I regret, and I took them as learning experiences... I'm human, not perfect, like anybody else."

"Be bold enough to be your true self."

Born Dana Elaine Owens in Newark, New Jersey on March 18, 1970, her father was a police officer and her mother a high school teacher. Raised in the Baptist faith, she attended a Catholic high school in Newark. Her stage name of Latifah means "delicate" and "very kind' in Arabic.

She became a soul, gospel, jazz, and hip hop singer, songwriter, rapper, actress, model, comedian, and television talk show host. She played a waitress in her first film, "Jungle Fever" in 1991, and steadily rose to become a star in future films and was nominated for an Academy Award as best supporting actress in the musical "Chicago" in 2002 but lost to her co-star Catherine Zeta-Jones. She starred in "Bessie" as the legendary 1920's and 1930's bisexual singer Bessie Smith in the 2015 television film.

Despite her professional successes, her personal life has not been without its sadness and tragedy. Her older brother Lancelot Jr., was killed in a 1992 accident involving a motorcycle she had bought him. His death led to her depression and drug abuse, from which she later recovered. She was charged with possession of marijuana and a loaded handgun in 1996 and convicted in 2002 of driving under the influence and placed on three years' probation.

She has never married and her sexuality is considered to be an "open secret" because she is in a partnership with beautiful choreographer

Eboni Nichols and they are often seen in public holding hands and kissing.

On Love -- "You do silly things for love sometimes, and not-so-smart things for love."

On Men -- "I'm a sucker for a man who cries. That just gets to me."

On Marriage -- "I got a few marriage proposals in my twenties. I just wasn't ready. I just new if I committed, I would've wound up doing something wrong, messing it up. I still felt like that I had some living to do."

On Sexiness -- "I often find it's just the confidence that makes you sexy, not what your body looks like. It's how you feel about yourself that makes you sexy."

"A confident woman is a sexy woman, in my opinion. And I thick guys find that to be the same way."

The Inner Woman -- "Look at people for an example, but then make sure to do things your way. Surround yourself with positive people."

"When I was around 18, I looked in the mirror and said, 'You're either going to love yourself or hate yourself.' And I decided to love myself. That changed a lot of things."

"I don't have to take a trip around the world or be on a yacht in the Mediterranean to have happiness. I can find it in the little things, like looking out into my backyard and seeing deer in the fields."

"I am a strong woman with or without this other person, with or without this job, and with or without these tight pants."

"I lost relatives to AIDS. A couple of my closest cousins, favorite cousins. I lost friends to AIDS, high school friends who never even made it to their 21st birthdays in the '80s. When it's that close to you, you can't – you know, you can't really deny it, and you can't run from it."

"There are times you can't really see or even feel how sweet life can be. Hopefully its mountains will be higher than its valleys are deep. I know things that are broken can be fixed. Take the punch if you have to, hit the canvas, and then get up again. Life is worth it."

"Beauty is not just a white girl. It's so many different flavors and shades."

"I've been giving back since I was a teen, handing out turkeys at Thanksgiving and handing out toys at toy drives for Christmas. It's very important to give back as a youth. It's as simple as helping an old lady across the street or giving up your seat on the bus for someone who is pregnant."

"Racism is ignorant. And it's stupid. And it's old. And it's played out. So beat it already with that, you know what I mean. 'Let's all get along.' I'm so tired of that damn sentence, but it's true."

"Anyone who knows me knows that I'm way more of a joker than I am a serious person."

"I often go to bed in my birthday suit. But I like teddies and cute little undies that match. I like a sexy bra and panty set, or little shorts."

"If we focus on our health, including our inner health, our self-esteem, and how we look at ourselves and our confidence level, we'll tend to be healthier people anyway, we'll tend to make better choices for our lives, for our bodies. We'll always be trying to learn more, and get better as time goes on."

"Dreams become reality when we put our minds to it."

"I have always felt strongly about empowering women. I'm living proof that, with confidence and by believing in yourself, you can accomplish any goal."

"If there are kids who want to follow in my footsteps, I'd say that my shoes are too big for them to fill! But their shoe size is just perfect."

"Always follow your own path."

"Sometimes I pray when I really feel like I need God to help me with something, and sometimes we just have conversations. We just kick it. I do feel like I have a direct connection with God for some reason; always have since I was a little kid – I would talk to God, talk to the sky."

"God is my homeboy. Jesus is my homeboy."

"You can't let fear paralyze you. The worse that can happen is you fail, but guess what: You get up and try again. Feel that pain, get over it, get up, dust yourself off, and keep it moving."

"I enjoy just being me. I don't need to be Queen Latifah, the brand, 24 hours a day."

"I want every day to be life for the living, not just traipsing through it existing. I'm just interested in life and the world and exploring."

Gypsy Rose Lee

The most famous professional stripper who ever took it off never actually took it all off; she was just a master, or rather a mistress, of tease. She believed in show little but tell all.

"It's not what you do. It's the way you do it – stripping, or writing, or talking… or just breathing. Do it with an air, and never admit you're scared."

"I wasn't naked, I was completely covered by a blue spotlight."

"You don't have to be naked to look naked. You just have to think naked."

Born Rose Louise Hovick in Seattle, Washington on January 8, 1911, her father was a newspaper reporter and advertising salesman, and her mother had high show business ambitions for herself and them. Rose was 7 and her sister June, born a year after her, was 6, when their mother put them into her song-and-dance act in vaudeville theaters. Their father objected to this, so their mother divorced him. June resented her mother calling her "Baby June" in the act so she rebelled by marrying a chorus boy when she was only 13 and ran away with him.

When a strip tease artist failed to show up for a performance in a burlesque house when Rose was 15 and performing solo, her mother virtually pushed her on-stage wearing little more than a grass skirt, assuring her the act was more "tease" than "strip." Rose liked it as male audiences cheered as she removed some of her costume and she became a professional stripper, calling herself Gypsy Rose Lee. Although she was a "stripper," she never actually got totally undressed. She became rich and famous teasing audiences in burlesque theaters and made her movie debut in 1937.

By the 1940s her career waned and she began a new one as an author. Her burlesque mystery novel *The G-String Murders* became a best-seller in 1941 and was filmed as "Lady of Burlesque' starring Barbara Stanwyck two years later.

Rose had affairs with showman Michael Todd and director Otto Preminger who became the father of her only child, a boy. She married three times, her husbands all actors: Robert Mizzy (1937-1941), Alexander Kirkland (1942-1944), and Julio De Dieo (1948-1955).

June, meanwhile, changed her name to June Havoc and became a singer-dancer and film star. The sisters were estranged for years but reconciled when Rose was diagnosed with terminal lung cancer in 1969 and died a year later at the age of 59. Books have been written about the sisters and their mother, and Broadway musicals and films and television movies were made as their places in show business history goes on.

On Sex and Sexiness -- "If a thing is worth doing, it is worth doing slowly… very slowly."

On Love -- "God is love. But get it in writing."

On Men -- "Men aren't attracted to me by my mind. They're attracted by what I don't mind."

The Inner Woman -- (*On aging*): "I have everything I had twenty years ago, except now it's all over."

"God will protect us, but to make sure, carry a heavy club."

Vivien Leigh

"Sir, you are no gentleman."

"And you, Miss, are no lady."

"Rhett, Rhett... Rhett, if you go, where shall I go? What shall I do?"

"Frankly, my dear, I don't give a damn."

"I can't think about that right now. If I do, I'll go crazy. I'll think about that tomorrow."

(Famous quotations from Vivien Leigh as Scarlett O'Hara to Clark Gable as Rhett Butler in "Gone With the Wind," 1939.)

(Vivien said, on playing Scarlett): *"I am not Scarlett."*

(Vivien said about playing demented Blanche DuBois in "A Streetcar in Desire," 1951):

"Blanche is a woman with everything stripped away. She is a tragic figure, and I understand her. But playing her tipped me into madness."

Somewhere between the two volatile and enigmatic women was the real Vivien Leigh, as we can imagine her powdering her nose in the ladies' room at the Ritz hotel in London, in spirit if not flesh, talking about herself and men to Joan Fontaine. She envied her for being in the arms of and kissing her lover, Laurence Olivier, in "Rebecca" (1940), a part Vivien wanted desperately after playing Scarlett O'Hara but lost.

Vivien said, after their divorce, **"I will always feel married to Mr. Olivier, in one way or another."**

Born Vivian Mary Hartley in Darjeeling, West Bengal, India on November 5, 1913. Her parents wanted to return to England but because of World War I (1914-1917) they remained in India until after the war. Her mother wanted Vivien to be educated at a Catholic convent but she was unhappy there. After completing her education she decided to become an actress. She married English barrister Herbert Leigh Holman in 1932 and gave birth to a daughter the following year. She changed her first name to be spelled Vivien because it sounded more romantic, and appeared in her first film in 1935.

She divorced Holman in 1937 and then met and fell in love with actor Laurence Olivier. They married on a ranch in Santa Barbara,

California on August 31, 1940 with Katharine Hepburn as matron of honor, and spent their honeymoon on actor Ronald Colman's yacht.

The story of how Vivien Leigh became cast as Scarlett O'Hara in "Gone With the Wind" (1939) is legendary. The role had yet to be cast, after more than 1,400 actresses had been tested for the role, among them some of the screen's top actresses including Bette Davis, Katharine Hepburn, Joan Crawford, and Tallulah Bankhead. Young Paulette Goddard was considered to be closest to getting the much-coveted role.

As chance or luck had it, Vivien met Myron Selznick, brother of the film's producer, David O. Selznick, and he immediately saw her as Scarlett. He took her to where the burning of Atlanta was being shot on an MGM lot in Hollywood where filming had started before an actress had yet been found to play the film's tempestuous heroine. He introduced her to his brother, saying, "Hey, genius! Meet your Scarlett!" David thought he was right, but Leigh had to take a screen test. She passed it brilliantly.

The film swept the Academy Awards, winning Leigh a best actress award, Hattie McDaniel best supporting actress for playing Scarlett's irrepressible Mammy, and Best Picture, among others, but lark Gable lost the best actor award to British actor Robert Donat in "Goodbye, Mr. Chips." Leigh must have been under a lot of pressure and nervous for one reason or another because she was a heavy smoker, smoking four packs a day while filming "Gone With the Wind." The role exhausted her and she worked long hours six days a week. Her salary was $25,000 while Gable, who worked far fewer days, was paid $120,000. Leigh said Gable had bad breath and she disliked him kissing her.

Vivien and Olivier were in competition with each other for who was the best actor, and her winning the Oscar began several years of his jealousy of her success in films, although he thought he was by far the superior actor on stage.

Olivier wrote in his autobiography that sometime after World War II, Vivien told him she was no longer in love with him, but loved him like a brother. She wanted to remain his wife, but was no longer interested in him romantically. He said it devastated him, but did not know that she was diagnosed with manic depression which today is called bipolar disorder and can be manifested in a woman being a nymphomania.

She remained a major star for two more decades, but her health began to fail in 1945 as she had two miscarriages in her marriage to Olivier. The Olivier's' sex life was complicated. She sought sexual fulfillment with other men, including an affair with actor Peter Finch that nearly ended her marriage. Also, Olivier is said to have been homosexual or bisexual, in a relationship for several years with actor Danny Kaye who worshipped him.

Despite her illnesses and fragility, Leigh kept working and won another best actress Oscar as the demented Blanche DuBois in "A Streetcar Named Desire" (1951) opposite Marlon Brando, ironically playing a woman who might have been Scarlett O'Hara in later life. Leigh later blamed the role for spiraling her mental health. Playing a woman so near to being insane unnerved her, while she took in Blanche's mental condition so strongly so she could play her accurately, it was hard for her to let go of it when off the set.

Her marriage to Olivier ended in 1960 and he married actress Joan Plowright. Plowright was a younger actress and Vivien taunted Olivier saying she was not very good-looking. Plowright, however, became a fine actress, especially in her senior years. After the Olivier's divorced, Vivien kept his photograph on her bedside or on her dressing table and until her death, she was called "Lady Olivier." Vivien lived with British stage and screen actor John Merivale from 1959 until her death. Leigh's final film was "Ship of Fools" in 1965.

Vivien Leigh, one of the most accomplished and beautiful film stars ever, died of chronic tuberculosis in London, England, on July 8, 1967 at the age of 54. The American Film Institute named her No. 16 on its list of the 50 Greatest Screen Legends, and her performance as Scarlett O'Hara is ranked No. 3 on *Premiere* magazine's 100 Greatest Movie Characters of All Time. When a stage star dies, Broadway theaters turn off their lights for one minute. In London, West End theatre marquee lights were dark for an hour in Vivien Leigh's honor, as if to say, paraphrasing Rhett Butler's parting words to Scarlett O'Hara, "Frankly, my dears, we *do* give a damn!"

(*In 1940, Charles Laughton praised Vivien Leigh, his co-star earlier that year in "Sidewalks of London"*): "She is one of those very rare extremely beautiful creatures who are ambitious enough to become great actresses. I admire her because (*with her beauty*) she need not be a great actress."

(*Olivia de Havilland on Vivien Leigh*): "I'm sure she was very sensual. She must have been passionate and was surely erotic. On the set of 'Gone With the Wind,' I saw one thing that surprised me. Someone had an engraved antique cameo ring of an erotic subject... She was told about the ring and said, 'Let me look at it! Let me look at it!' It was quite surprising that she looked at this rather explicit carving and took a strange lascivious, and very obvious pleasure in looking at it... (*It was*) A frank, spontaneous 'low-down' reaction in front of the crew, when normally, her attitude was one of ladylike, exquisite discipline."

On Men -- "Who could quarrel with Clark Gable? We got on well. Whenever anyone on the set was tired or depressed, it was Gable who cheered that person up. Then the newspapers began printing the story that Gable and I were not getting on. This was so ridiculous it served only as a joke. From that time on, the standard greeting between Clark and myself became 'How are you getting on today?'"

"Doing love scenes with Clark Gable in 'Gone With the Wind' was not that romantic. His dentures smelled something awful."

(*On Warren Beatty, her co-star in "The Roman Spring of Mrs. Stone" (1961)*): "He has the kind of magnetic sensuality you could light torches with."

The Inner Woman -- "My birth sign is Scorpio, and they burn themselves out and eat themselves up, and they are careless about themselves, like me. I swing between happiness and misery and cry easily (*symptoms of bipolar disorder*). I am a mixture of my mother's determination and my father's optimism. I am part prude and part non-conformist, and I say what I think and don't pretend, and I am prepared to accept the consequences of my actions."

"I've always been mad about cats." (*Olivia de Havilland said Vivien reminded her of a delicate porcelain Siamese cat.*)

"I'm not a film star. I am an actress. Being a film star is such a false life, lived for fake values and for publicity."

She discovered she was pregnant with Olivier's child during filming "Caesar and Cleopatra" (1945). During a scene in which she had to run across a polished floor, she slipped and fell, causing a miscarriage. This is said to have been a trauma that led to becoming depressed and having a nervous breakdown, showing signs of what later would be diagnosed as bipolar disorder.

(*In a March 1940 interview, she said she thought she was perfect to play Scarlett O'Hara*): "It's the most dramatic part I ever read. I'd love to get my teeth into it. It's got everything... lightness and gaiety and great emotional depths. What a woman that Scarlett is!"

(*In a May 1940 interview*): "I am not Scarlett. I don't see any relation between the actress and the part she plays. Reality is so intensified on the screen because of the close-up, that the separation of the player from the role is even more difficult than on the stage...

"I'm not altogether complimented to be compared so intimately with her. She was very spoiled, very selfish, high-tempered, headstrong... I don't think I'm like that. A temper, perhaps, but I attempt to keep it an emotion, and an emotion is necessary for an actress, but there's no good in wasting it. It's best to reserve it for one's work, and try to transform it into something else... fire or intensity, let's say.

"Scarlett had beautiful courage, and I admire that in her tremendously. I'd like to have her courage! But she was ruthless and destructive in getting what she wanted. She stopped at nothing, and in that ruthlessness she also showed dishonesty. She was something of a cheat, and that's not admirable.

"But with all of her bad qualities, she had exceedingly good ones, redeeming ones. Her courage, her strength, her capacity for love, even though it was never fulfilled. And then another great love she had, love for the land, her home, and her willingness to fight desperately to hold onto it. Also, I admire her ability to readjust her life, quickly to adapt herself to new conditions and environment.

"In this sense, perhaps I am like Scarlett. I, too, believe in the importance of living completely today as possible. Scarlett's philosophy, owing to the exigencies of life, became a working design for living... today, always today. Her credo was: Live fully now, today, and then perhaps tomorrow will be taken care of, providing there is a tomorrow. But anyway tomorrow is another day, and I'll be ready to meet it in due time. I can understand all this."

"I cannot let well enough alone. I get restless. I have to be doing different things. I am a very impatient person and headstrong. If I've made up my mind to do something, I can't be persuaded out of it."

"I hope I've one thing that Scarlett never had. A sense of humor. I want some joy out of life. And she had one thing I hope I never have. Selfish egotism."

"People think that if you look fairly reasonable, you can't possibly act, and as I only care about acting, I think beauty can be a great handicap."

"Most of us have compromised with life. Those who fight for what they want will always thrill us."

"People who are very beautiful make their own laws."

"Life is too short to work so hard. I am not afraid of dying. Things are simple when you're going to die. I have just made out my will and given all the things I have and many that I haven't."

"Dear Lord, I'm so grateful I'm still loved."

Lindsay Lohan

Few actresses have had as much bad happen to them as this young lady in so few years on this planet which some call a vale of tears. She ranks up there with a teenage Drew Barrymore or Jane Fonda. But they came through their travails and if Lindsay perseveres she can, too. Meanwhile she has a lot to unload in the ladies' room.

"I'm a sexual person, definitely. I think I'm more sexual than my friends. More comfortable in my skin."

"Sex and sexuality are a part of nature, and I go along with nature. I think Marilyn Monroe said that. I certainly agree with her." (Yes, Marilyn did say that.)

"Life is full of risks anyway; why not take them?"

(In 2004): *"I just try to live my life; I'm not doing stuff like that to get noticed."*

Born Lindsay Dee Lohan in New York City on July 2, 1986, her father is a multi-million-dollar businessman and her mother a Wall Street financial analyst who now manages her career. Lindsay became a model at the age of three and appeared in more than 60 television commercials, some opposite Bill Cosby promoting Jell-O.

Her acting debut was on television in 1996 in the soap opera "Another World." She got excellent critic reviews in her first feature film, "The Parent Trap" in 1998 and steadily progressed to stardom while at the same time becoming a recording star and launching her own fashion line.

She has briefly dated pop star Aaron Carter and was in a relationship with Samantha Ronson (2008-2009), but has not married. *People* magazine named her one of the most beautiful people in the world in 2004, and she was ranked the next year as No. 10 among the 100 sexiest women in the world. Her idols are Marilyn Monroe and Ann-Margret.

She was arrested several times for DUI and served short jail sentences for violating probation involving not attending weekly alcohol education, despite going to the Betty Ford Center. She also was arrested for grand theft involving a $250,000 necklace but was released and ordered to perform more community service. As her career continues, she has earned as much as $2 million a film, and is still working to get her personal life under control.

On Men -- (*On actor Wilmer Valderrama*): "(*He*) was my first love. But the timing was bad. And there were all these girls around; he would flirt with them. And I couldn't handle that. I really didn't trust him. So that was hard, too."

"I understand that I'm a role model, though, and I have to look out for that. I have a 10-year-old sister, too. But you also want to be appealing to guys and stuff, that's just something girls feel. It's hard. You want to be that girl that's unattainable to all the guys because there are so many other girls out there that are like that."

On sex and sexuality -- (*On being a redhead*): "I have this Playboy book called *Redheads*, and I was reading all these things about how redheads are more passionate and apparently they're much more sexual than girls with other hair colors."

"It's so weird that I went to rehab. I always said I would die before I went to rehab."

"It's hard in LA. not to go out; it gets lonely. Being an actress is lonely, and I never want to be alone. I hate sleeping alone."

"I'm Irish-Italian, so I've got a really bad temper."

"I say too much sometimes, but I'm honest, that's the important thing."

"Say no more than yes, and just make sure you surround yourself with good people."

Gina Lollobrigida

This editor was on a train in Italy in the 1960's and a mother and teenage daughter were in the compartment with him. The mother asked him, with a smile, "Gina or Sophia?' Without hesitation he enthusiastically replied, "Gina!"

Millions of men agree with him, although Sophia gets her fair share of votes as the sexiest Italian female stallion. (There is no such animal, but if any did exist, Gina would be it.) She positively sizzles in the ladies' room:

"Sophia Loren plays peasants. I play ladies. She has a noticeable bosom. Whose is bigger, I have no idea and could care less. I became a star without a husband producing my pictures (Carlo Ponti) *and I became a star in respectable pictures!"*

(In 2000): *"I've had many lovers and still have romances. I am very spoiled. All my life, I've had too many admirers."*

"A woman at twenty is like ice, at thirty she is warm, and at forty she is hot."

Born Luigina Lollobrigida in Subiaco, Lazio, Italy on July 4, 1927, her father was a furniture manufacturer and she grew up in a mountain village. She became a fashion model as a teenager which led to winning beauty contests in her twenties. She appeared in films in Italy before going to Hollywood to make movies there, and true stardom came from appearing in "Beat the Devil" with Humphrey Bogart in 1953.

In 1949, she married Milko Skofic, a Yugoslavian doctor, and gave birth to a son. They divorced in 1971 after 22 years together. In 2006, at the age of 79, she announced her engagement to Javier Rigan y Rafols a Spanish businessman half her age, but called it off after discovering that he staged a secret ceremony allegedly marrying her, using a stand-in. She sued him for the charade in which he had intended to lay claim to her estate after her death. Her 1961 performance opposite Rock Hudson in "Come September" won her the Golden Globe as the World's Film Favorite.

In the 1970s she gave up being an international movie star, and took up her two other great interests, sculpture and photography. She became a successful photojournalist and scooped the world's press by photographing Fidel Castro during an interview with the Cuban dictator. During her film career she became known as "The Mona Lisa of the 20th Century" and "The most beautiful woman in the world."

On Men -- "Glamour is when a man knows a woman is a woman."

"I knew right away that Rock Hudson was gay when he did not fall in love with me."

On Love -- "Love… the best cosmetics."

The Inner Woman -- (*On the film "Solomon and Sheba" opposite Yul Brynner in* 1959): "There is only one trouble with having played the most famous courtesan of all times and that is, after Sheba, all other roles will certainly seem tame and anticlimactic."

"We are all born to die – the difference is the intensity with which we choose to live."

Jennifer Lopez

Married and divorced three times and now a single mother of twins, Jennifer may not be a happily married woman, but she is one of the most beautiful and sexiest film stars. Like many other women, she is hopeful that Mr. Right will still come along. Meanwhile, she has already had a lifetime of experience with men to share with others:

"If you kiss on the first date and it's not right then there will be no second date. Sometimes it's better to hold out and not kiss for a long time. I am a strong believer in kissing being very intimate, and the minute you kiss, the floodgates open for everything else."

"We've all had a love of our life and failed love affairs. I'm just the biggest romantic – it's really sad. I tell people that, but nobody listens."

"I throw myself into love because I believe in it, but when things don't work, you have to take responsibility."

Born Jennifer Lynn Lopez in the Castle Hill section of The Bronx, New York on July 24, 1969, her parents were both born in Puerto Rico. Her father is a computer specialist with an insurance company, and her mother is a school teacher. As a young girl, Jennifer had ambitions of being in show business. She started taking singing and dancing lessons when she was five, and left home at age eighteen to work in a law firm, while at nights taking dancing jobs.

Her film debut was in "My Family" in 1995 but she became more noticed two years later for playing Selena Quintanilla Perez in "Selena." Selena (1971-1995, an American actress, singer, and song writer, was murdered at the age of 24 by the founder of her fan club.)

Lopez had been engaged to actor Ben Affleck in 2004 but they never married. She was married and divorced three times, to Cuban waiter Ojani Noa (February 1997-January 1998), Cris Judd (2001-2003), and actor-singer-record producer Marc Anthony (2004-2014) with whom she had twins, a son and daughter. After a nine-month separation, Anthony filed for divorce from her in 2012.

She has often been named to lists of the most beautiful women and became very wealthy from films and endorsements and her lines of J. Lo perfumes, her net worth in 2004 was estimated at $255 million and doubtless is much more since then.

(*In a 2016 interview*): "I was sleeping on a cot at a dance studio before I made it big. My life was about pounding the pavement, breaking away from under my mom and dad's wings and going off and flying on my own... I am happy to be one of the people who are breaking the mold. We can't keep acting like we are in the 1950s. Women are strong. Women are bold. Now it is reflected in our art."

Lopez talked about her love life in a March 2016 television interview on "The Late Late Show with James Corden. He asked about it and she revealed that she is **"so monogamous, it's stupid."**

She said that although she has been married three times, she has been proposed to five times. She refused to say which was the best proposal., then added:

"I don't want to compare one to the others. They were all pretty spectacular. The were nice. And there were some that asked to marry me that were good, but I said no."

The Inner Woman -- (*In 1999 after Jennifer read tabloid stories criticizing her tough love advice from her mother* who told her): "Don't you ever call me crying again! You wanted to be in this business, so you better toughen up!" (*Jennifer said*), "And I did. You laugh it off, you get upset for a little while; you're human and you let it go."

"I've always had a huge fear of dying or becoming ill. The thing I'm most afraid of, though, is being alone, which I think a lot of performers fear. It's why we seek the limelight – so we're not alone, we're adored. We're loved, so people want to be around us. The fear of being alone drives my life."

"I only do what my gut tells me to. I think it's smart to listen to other people's advice, but at the end of the day, you're the only one who can tell you what's right for you.

"If you focus on the money, you're not going to get anywhere. You can want to be successful, but at the end of the day, if money is your motivation, if that's how shallow your outlook is on life, then you're going to be such an empty person. Because there's nothing driving you from the inside -- there's no passion."

"My mom always told me that if you work hard, you can achieve anything. And it's true. It's one of the truest things ever."

"Beauty is only skin deep. I think what's really important is finding a balance of mind,. body, and spirit."

"I've made a ton of mistakes, but you need the messy stuff; you learn from it."

Sophia Loren

Luckier in love than Gina Lollobrigida, Sophia was married only once and it lasted 41 years until her husband's death. Sex appeal could be her two middle names. Because she has walked in beauty so much and so long, she has a lot to say about it in the ladies' room:

"Sex appeal is fifty percent what you've got and fifty percent what people think you've got."

"Beauty is how you feel inside, and it reflects in your eyes. It is not something physical."

"You must all, somewhere deep in your hearts, believe that you have a special beauty that is like no other, and that it is so valuable that you must not abandon it. Indeed, you must learn to cherish it."

Born Sofia Villani Scicolone in Rome, Italy on September 20, 1934, her father was married to another woman and refused to divorce her and marry the woman who gave birth to both Sophia and her sister, who had been born the year before. Sophia grew up in the slums of Rome during World War II without any financial or other support from her father.

She entered a beauty contest when she was 14 and attracted the attention of Italian film producer Carlo Ponti who then guided her film career. They married in 1957, but it was annulled in 1962 to save him from bigamy charges since he had a wife in Mexico. He and Sophia remarried in 1966 and remained married until his death in 2007. She loved him and gave him two sons, both by Caesarean section, but he also became a father figure to her, being 22 years older than she.

Her American film career began in "Boy on a Dolphin" opposite Alan Ladd in 1957 and she steadily rose to becoming a major international film star some called "The Italian Marilyn Monroe." Her leading men in American films included Clark Gable, Paul Newman, Marlon Brando, and Cary Grant. She co-starred with Italian actor Marcello Mastroianni in 11 Italian films but they were only friends in real life and not lovers. She is the godmother of actress Drew Barrymore.

Sophia Loren met Cary Grant during the filming of "The Pride and the Passion" (1957), but a giant-sized cannon came between them. They did not feel the pangs of love together until the following year while filming "Houseboat." She was said to be "enthralled" with him, and he "besotted" with her. He was 30 years older than she. Sophia said that Grant proposed to her but she didn't accept.

"Cary belonged to another world, in America," she said later. "I felt that I would never fit in there. I would never have a future there because of my nationality. I was scared to change completely in life without knowing if this relationship or quasi relationship was going on. The picture ("Houseboat") finished, we exchanged numbers and he said he would call. In fact he did come on the set of 'Two Women' (1960), (*but*) I was together with Carlo and already had my son."

Loren's performance in "Two Women" (1960) about a woman in Italy during the war who is raped while trying to protect her young daughter, earned her an Academy Award for Best Actress. During her film career she received a second Oscar nomination and won five Golden Globe Awards. She received an Honorary Academy Award in 1991 for her body of film work and was declared, "One of the world cinema's greatest treasures."

On Marriage -- (*On her first marriage to Ponti, testifying in court to save him from bigamy charges, for which, if convicted, he could be sentenced to as long as five years in prison*): "I was carrying a child (*his*), but they took me to court, charged me with immorality, threatened me with jail, and forced me in tears, to say I am not married. Those words were the most difficult I've ever had to speak. I could not deny any love for Carlo, but on that day in the Roman court, I knew I must deny the validity of our marriage, the wedding for which I fought so hard and so long."

On Love -- "Hate is unfulfilled love."

"Cooking is an act of love, a gift, a way or sharing with others the little secrets that are simmering on the burners."

On Men -- (*On adultery*): "It's a game I never play."

"Tyrone Power was my ideal man." (*They began filming "Solomon and Sheba" in 1959 but he had a fatal heart attack during a strenuous sword fighting scene and was replaced by Yul Brynner*).

"Marcello (*Mastroianni*) is a man who thinks like a man, talks like a man – is a man! He has so much magnetism, he brings out the very soul in a woman."

(*On Gregory Peck*): "One of the most charming men I've ever met."

(On Cary Grant): "I learned many things working with Cary Grant. He has such tremendous concentration. Many actors do not have the courage to stand still. Cary Grant knows how to concentrate, how to look directly at you, but always with great concentration."

The Inner Woman -- "The two big advantages I had at birth were to have been born wise and to have been born in poverty."

"Oh, how I loved the movies as a little girl. Particularly I loved Yvonne De Carlo. She was my favorite. Others, too, like Rita Hayworth, but I used to dream that I was Yvonne De Carlo. For me there was only one Yvonne De Carlo." *(She said that watching De Carlo in films inspired her to become an actress.)*

"Getting ahead in a difficult profession requires avid faith in yourself. That is why some people with mediocre talent, but with great inner drive, go so much further than people with vastly superior talent." *(Jane Fonda said virtually the same thing.)*

"A woman's dress should be like a barbed wire fence: serving its purpose without obstructing the view."

"The facts of life are that a child who has seen war cannot be compared with a child who doesn't know what war is except from television."

"I've never tried to block out the memories of the past, even though some are painful. I don't understand people who hide from their past. Everything you live through helps to make you the person you are now."

"I hated my father all my life but in his final days I forgave him for all the suffering he caused us. As you grow older, marry, and have children of your own, you learn and forgive. I do not forget easily, but I do forgive."

"There is a Fountain of Youth. It is your mind, your talents, the creativity you bring to your life and the lives of the people you love. When you learn to tap this source, you will truly have defeated age."

"I've never tried to block out memories of the past, even though some are painful. I don't understand people who hide from their past. Everything you live through helps to make you the person you are now."

"Nothing makes a woman more beautiful than the belief that she is beautiful."

"If you haven't cried, your eyes cannot be beautiful."

"After all these years, I am still involved in the process of self-discovery. It's better to explore life and make mistakes than to play it safe. Mistakes are part of the dues one pays for a full life."

Clare Boothe Luce

"Male supremacy has kept woman down. It has not knocked her out."

"A man's home may seem to be his castle on the outside; inside, it is more often his nursery."

"If God had wanted us to think with our wombs, why did he give us a brain?"

"I wish I were a virgin again. The only fun I ever had was holding out."

Born Ann Clare Boothe on March 10, 1903 in New York City, her parents were not married and separated when she was nine years old. She was married twice, first to George Tuttle Brokaw, millionaire clothing fortune heir, when she was 20 in 1923, with whom she had a daughter. They divorced six years later.

In 1935 she married then as Clare Boothe Luce, she became a U.S. Congress representative from Connecticut from 1942 to 1946, during which Henry R. Luce, publisher of *Time, Vanity Fair, Fortune, and Sports Illustrated* magazines. It was she who encouraged Luce to publish the weekly news magazine, *Life*. Known then as Clare

Boothe Luce, she became a U.S. Congress representative from Connecticut from 1942 to 1946, during which she was instrumental in the creation of the Atomic Energy Commission. During World War II she was a war correspondent reporting for *Life* magazine from Africa, India, China, and Burma, often under enemy fire and bombings.

After the war she became the first American woman appointed to be a foreign ambassador, serving in Brazil and Italy. She also was a novelist and playwright, her most famous play being "The Women" (1936) which became a hit movie three years later. She became famous for her witty comments on life, especially on men.

Her daughter died in an automobile accident and the trauma led to her joining the Roman Catholic Church, an influence that led her to write and lecture on her faith and to write the Christmas film classic "Come to the Stable" (1949).

Her marriage to Luce was difficult because of their differing personalities such as he had little or no sense of humor which she had, but they stayed together until his death in 1967. She lived her final years in Washington, D.C. where she died at home of a brain tumor on October 9, 1987 at the age of 84.

Luce is considered to be one of the heroines of the feminist movement in America., among other things co-sponsoring the Equal Rights Amendment to the U.S. Constitution in 1943. President Ronald Reagan awarded her the Presidential Medal of Freedom in 1983, the first female member of Congress to receive the award, saying, "She has been a persistent and effective advocate of freedom, both at home and abroad."

She willed $50 million to establish the Clare Boothe Luce Program which encourages women to compete in technological fields such as science, engineering and mathematics traditionally dominated by men. She also, however, strongly encouraged women to marry and provide supportive homes for their husbands.

On Men – "A man has only one escape from his old self: to see a different self in the mirror of some woman's eyes."

"I refuse the compliment that I think like a man. Thought has no sex. One either thinks, or one does not."

"There are no hopeless situations; there are only men who have grown hopeless about them."

On Women – "Women know what men have long forgotten. The ultimate economic and spiritual unit of any civilization is still the family,

"Because I am a woman, I must make unusual efforts to succeed. If I fail, no one will say, 'She doesn't have what it takes;' They will say, 'Women don't have what it takes.'"

"They say women talk too much. If you have worked in Congress, you know that the filibuster was invented by men."

"In politics, women type the letters, lick the stamps, distribute the pamphlets and get out the vote. Men get elected."

"The politicians were talking themselves red, white, and blue in the face."

"A woman's best protection is a little money of her own."

"A woman can produce what no man can: a child."

On Marriage – "There is nothing like a good dose of another woman to make a man appreciate his wife."

"Widowhood is a fringe benefit of marriage."

The Inner Woman –

(When a war correspondent for Life magazine during World War II): "(War) is a world where men have decided to die together because they are unable to find a way to live together."

"If old age means a crown of thorns, the trick is to wear it jauntily."

"Courage is the ladder on which all the other virtues mount."

"Money can't buy happiness, but it can make you awfully comfortable while you're being miserable."

"The main thing is to get what little happiness there is out of life in this war torn world because 'these are the good old days' now."

Shirley MacLaine

Another one-of-a-kind, MacLaine has been a motion picture treasure since her first film in 1955, and made her presence known and felt 60 years later in a rollicking guest appearance in "Downton Abbey" in 2015. If she ever gets reincarnated (she believes in coming back in another life), her fans will never forgive her if she comes back as anyone other than Shirley MacLaine. They are still talking in the ladies' room about what she said in her 2011 memoirs when she was 76, about men, marriage, sex, and love. She admitted that although she now prefers her pet dog to men, she once slept with three men in one day.

"I have had many love affairs, but I have not had many sexual affairs. I was not sophisticated enough for that. I had to have the emotional component."

"I have found that since sex and I have got over each other in my advancing years, it is such a relief."

"When I look back over my life, I wonder what I was doing with all my hormones and attraction and longings, when I always felt such a strong need for freedom."

"Most of the men I was with wanted to get married. I was already married and stayed that way, so it wouldn't become an issue." (She was in an open marriage to businessman Steve Parker for 30 years until their divorce in 1982.)

"My husband and I had a liberal arrangement when it came to each other's lovers. We were friends. We stayed married so we wouldn't be tempted to marry again."

"I don't understand the need for the institution of marriage, and I could never live a life where I felt tied down to a promise just because my love hormones were raging at the time I made it."

Born Shirley MacLean Beatty in Richmond, Virginia on April 24, 1934, her mother was a drama teacher and father a psychology professor and real estate agent. Reportedly, she was named after actress Shirley Temple. Her brother, actor Warren Beatty, was born three years later. After high school graduation she went to New York with dreams of being a dancer in Broadway shows.

Her dream soon came true and she joined the chorus lines in some hit shows. While performing as an understudy when star Carol Chaney broke her ankle, MacLaine filled in for her in "The Pajama Game" and was spotted by Paramount Pictures' producer and director Hal B. Wallis. Three months later she made her film debut in Alfred Hitchcock's "The Trouble with Harry" in 1955. Audiences loved her quirky personality and her zoom to stardom soon followed. She was nominated for an Academy Award for Best Actress four times, winning for the 1983 film "Terms of Endearment."

She married American businessman Steve Parker in 1954 and said that it was an open marriage and both had had numerous affairs during their marriage. They had a daughter together and divorced in 1982.

Her most recent acting triumph was in the worldwide popular British television series "Downton Abbey," scoring a hit in a cameo role as Lady Crawley's outspoken mother from America in which she nearly stole scenes from the beloved Maggie Smith, which would be very hard to do. She told Dame Maggie that they could have been lovers in another life. She said she had a "cougar crush" on Brendon Doyle, 50, the actor who played Lord Grandham's valet Bates.

Rob James-Collier, who played gay footman Thomas Barrows said, "Spending two weeks (*on the set*) with Shirley MacLaine should be a series in itself. She's absolutely bonkers, but delightful. I had some great chats -- I'll never forget half of them, and the other half I can't repeat."

Now in her eighties, after authoring half a dozen books, MacLaine continues to appear in films and on television and to astound everyone with her uniqueness. Visits to India had profound spiritual effects on her and she is a devoted practitioner of yoga and meditation. MacLaine believes in there being life in outer space and in reincarnation and that she has lived before.

When she took Olaf Palme, the prime minister of Sweden, as a lover in the 1970s, she knew she had seen him somewhere before, then recalled that they had sex together 1,200 years earlier when he had been Charlemagne the Great, ruler of the Holy Roman Empire, and she had been a Moorish peasant girl with an ability for curing impotence in men. She also claims to have been a medieval warrior, an orphan raised by elephants, a Japanese geisha girl, and a model for the post-impressionist Moulin Rouge painter, Toulouse Lautrec. She believes that her rat terrier dog was once an Egyptian god.

On Men -- "It is useless to hold a person to anything he says while he's in love, drunk, or running for office."

(*On her marriage to Parker, whose work often took him away from home*): "I love my husband and we're very happy together... when we are together. That's the secret... If you never see your husband, you're bound to get along together. Seriously, Steve and I have the original excitement of being married because we're separated so much. When we do see each other, it's like falling in love all over again."

(*About her brother*): "Think what Warren Beatty could have achieved if he'd been celibate!"

On Sex and sexuality -- "I was always a character actress and never a sex symbol. Even when I was the leading lady, I was a character actor."

"I think in my forties, right around the time of 'The Turning Point' (1977), that I began to address myself more to the future. See, I wasn't afraid of getting old, because I never had the problems the other actresses my age had. I was never a great beauty. I was never a sex symbol."

"I don't know what the norm is. The latest evaluations on human sexuality say that we are one-third monogamous, one-third serially monogamous, and one-third polygamous. I would say there should be some kind of form to fill out before you promise monogamy."

"The difference between us (*her brother Warren Beatty*) is sex. I can take it or leave it. But my kid brother… well, now, he enjoys his reputation. Sex is the most important thing in his life. It's his hobby, you could say." (*After years of relationships with other women, Beatty married actress Annette Bening in 1992 and they have had four children together.*)

The Inner Woman -- "An actor has many lives and many people within him. I know there are lots of people inside me. No one ever said I'm dull."

"I've made so many movies playing a hooker that they don't pay me in the regular way anymore. They leave it on the dresser."

(*On her female rat terrier dog, Terry*): "I have never known friendship and companionship like it. We sleep cuddled up together every night, so it's a good thing I don't have a man in my life."

"I would rather have a good, loyal dog than a man. It's taken a few years to come to that conclusion, and I'm happier for it. My love for Terry brings me to tears."

"Once the soul of India gets into you, it sits on your shoulder all the time."

Madonna

Madonna has dated or been in relationships with a gaggle of men, but has of this writing in 2016 sworn off marriage, although not men. You would have to be powdering your nose a long time in the ladies' room to hear about her love lives.

(About getting married): ***"I think I'd rather get run over by a train."***

"I think that everyone should get married at least once, so you can see what a silly, outdated institution it is."

"I've never really lived a conventional life. So I think it's quite foolish for me or anyone else to start thinking that I am going to start making conventional choices."

Born Madonna Louise Ciccone in Bay City, Michigan on August 16, 1958, to Roman Catholic parents; her father an automobile design engineer. She began a music career when she moved to New York in 1978 when she was twenty and quickly became a top singer, becoming known as "The Queen of Pop" music. A seven-time Grammy music award winner, she has sold more than 100 million records and compact discs worldwide.

For her stage appearances she has worn rosaries and crosses which started a fashion trend among young women in 1984. Her film career has so far not been as successful although she gets big money from making movies. Her best movie success so far is as Eva Peron in "Evita" in 1996, about the wife of Argentine President Juan Peron from 1945 until her death in 1952.

The men in Madonna's life may not have begun with singer Dan Gilroy from her first band (1979-1981) but most of her biographies start with him. Following him was graffiti artist Jean-Michael Basquait in 1982, but their relationship was brief and he died in 1988 from a heroin overdose. Musician and song producer John Benitez followed from 1983 to 1985 and he helped her work on her 1983 debut album which made her an overnight singing sensation.

She then married actor Sean Penn in 1985 and they starred together in the film "Shanghai Surprise" in 1986. The movie was a colossal flop, as was their marriage which ended in divorce four years later in 1989. Penn said of their marriage: "Loud. That's how I remember it. I don't recall having a single conservation in four years of marriage."

Actor Warren Beatty came next, in 1990. They met when she had a small role in his film "Dick Tracy," but he soon left to have other affairs. Another brief relationship followed with model Tony Ward in 1991, and that same year she was with baseball player Jose

Canseco. He said she wanted them to marry and have children together, but he was trying to reconcile with his wife. Next came dates with singer Vanilla Ice in 1992, then basketball star Dennis Rodman entered her life in 1994, as did Carlos Leon, her physical training instructor.

Madonna went to the altar for the first time when she and British singer and director Guy Ritchie married in 2000 and she had a son by him, then they adopted a Malawian boy. They divorced in 2008 after he was rumored to have been having a gay affair with baseball player Alex Rodriguez who was married. In 2009, when she was 50 years old, she began a relationship with Jesus Luz, a 22-year-old Brazilian model, but it ended the following year.

Madonna thought she finally had found true love in 2011 when dancer Brahim Zaibat became her constant companion and love, but they went their separate ways in 2013. Stay tuned for the further adventures of Madonna's love life. She has since given up acting to direct films, write children's books, and merchandise a line of dolls, apparel, and home décor.

She has been ranked No. 6 on the list of 100 Greatest Women of Rock 'n Roll. Her favorite actresses were Carole Lombard, Betty Grable, and Katharine Hepburn. She posed nude at least three times in her film career, and some nude photos of her were published in *Penthouse* magazine and in a 1992 interview book *Sex* which became a worldwide best seller. Her net work in 2015 was $520 million and she was ranked No. 1 on cable television's VI1's list of 100 Sexiest Artists.

On Men -- "Kevin Costner has personality-minus."

(*On Edward, British Duke of Windsor*): "I couldn't get my mind off the fact that a man gave up the throne for a woman. From my perspective, men since the beginning of time have fought to get on the throne. Men are power-seeking animals, so why would this man run away from power?"

"I want to be like Gandhi and Martin Luther King and John Lennon, but I want to stay alive!"

(*On her marriage to Sean Penn*): "Sean tried to be a good husband. He just tried too hard."

On Sex and Sexuality -- "Being blonde is definitely a different state of mind. I really can't put my finger on it, but the artifice of being blonde has some incredible sort of sexual connotation. Men really respond to it."

(*From her book* Sex): "A lot of people are afraid to say what they want. That's why they don't get what they want."

On Marriage and Divorce (*In 2008 about her divorce from Guy Ritchie, after eight years of marriage): (She said her marital breakup is tough, but is grateful that her heavy workload* "provides a distraction that keeps me going."

"I think when you get married, you have to be willing to make a lot of compromises, and that's fair enough. I think that's the way it goes in relationships. However, you know, I did find myself sometimes in a state of conflict. There were many times when I wanted to express myself as an artist in ways that I don't think my ex-husband (*Sean Penn*) felt comfortable with."

"There were times when I felt incarcerated. I wasn't really allowed to be myself. It doesn't mean that marriage is a bad thing. But if you're an artist, you've got to find someone who accepts who you are and are comfortable with that."

She said she would consider marrying again: "Maybe. Never say never. I don't have any limitations for myself in terms of relationships. I'm single, but I'd like to have a man around the house. That would be nice. My children like that and enjoy that."

The Inner Woman -- "Whether I'm gay or not is irrelevant. Whether I slept with (*Sandra Bernhard*) or not is irrelevant. I'm perfectly willing to have people think that I did."

"k. d. Lang, who's gorgeous... She looks like Sean. I met her, and I thought, Oh, my God, she's the female version of Sean. I could fall in love with her."

"I wouldn't mind having an affair with Marlene Dietrich when she was young. Like, who wouldn't?"

"I'm not the new Marilyn (*Monroe*), I'm me! Do I look like Marilyn?"

"When I'm hungry, I eat. When I'm thirsty, I drink. When I feel like saying something, I say it."

"Better to live one year as a tiger than a hundred as a sheep."

"I sometimes think I was born to live up to my name. How could I be anything else but what I am, having been named Madonna? I would either have ended up a nun or this."

"I am my own experiment. I am my own work of art."

"I'm a gay man trapped in a woman's body!"

"Without the heart, there can be no understanding between the hand the mind."

"I'm tough, ambitious, and I know exactly what I want. If that makes me a bitch, okay."

"I know I'm not the best singer, and I know I'm not the best dancer, but I'm not interested in that. I'm interested in pushing people's buttons, in being provocative, and in being political."

"I have two beautiful children and a brilliant, gorgeous husband. I have my work and I have my faith. None of that means I've lost my sense of humor or my sense of fun. If that's boring to some people, I can't tell you how much I don't care."

"I want to conquer the world."

"You have to be patient… I'm not!"

"I hate people who hate women. Actually, I hate people who hate!"

"I've learned from studying Kabbalah that if your happiness is based on people approving of everything you do, you're doomed to fail. Kabbalah helped me stand up and take responsibility for everything to do with me." (*Kabbalah is a discipline and school of thought that originated centuries ago in Judaism and literally means receiving/tradition*).

Jayne Mansfield

So you've gone to the ladies room at a Hollywood night club to learn how to become a movie sex symbol. Be sure to wait around until this Jayne is there. She can tell you all about it, from bitter experience with the men in her life..

"Men are those creatures with two legs and eight hands."

"What can a girl receive dating a dozen different men, but ten dozen mixed-up situations and men who expect a girl to go to bed after a first date.. Men who go with you because you are a sex symbol get draggy."

"I've been actually miserable when I was fantastically happy. Now I feel clean, wholesome and poised with just one man who loves me." (She was married to muscleman Mickey Hargitay at the time.)

"My father was the only man I ever knew who really loved me unselfishly, who never used me for personal gain."

Born Vera Jayne Palmer in Bryn Mawr, Pennsylvania on April 19, 1933, her father was a attorney and her mother a housewife. Her father died of a heart attack, her mother remarried, and the family moved to Dallas, Texas where as a child she was a talented classical pianist and violinist. When she was 16, she married Paul Mansfield and they had a daughter together the following year. Jayne acted in plays while at the University of Dallas and claimed to have had a high I.Q. of 163 and spoke five languages fluently.

She went to Hollywood and made her first film in 1955 as a cigarette girl in "Pete Kelly's Blues." She had more acting ability than studio bosses gave her a chance to show, casting her repeatedly as a beautiful dumb blonde. She is perhaps best remembered for "The Girl Can't Help It" (1956) in which a gangster hires a press agent to make his girlfriend a singing star. It was a fun film, a spin-off of "Born Yesterday" (1950) in which a gangster hires a writer to teach his dumb blonde etiquette.

She was married three times: Paul Mansfield (1950-1958), with whom she had a daughter; Mickey Hargitay (1958-1964), with whom she had three children; and Matt Cimber (1964-1966), with whom she had a child.

Mansfield became one of the leading film sex symbols of the 1950s and 1960s, but a victim of the type-cast system, called "The Blonde Bombshell" and "Broadway's Smartest Dumb Blonde." She said she wanted to marry a prince, like Grace Kelly had, but her wish list also included Tyrone Power, Clark Gable, Marlon Brando, Robert Wagner, Robert Stack and, oddly enough, Liberace, the gay pianist and king of candelabra.

Her career waned in the mid-1960s and she appeared in television game shows. While enroute to a television show in New Orleans on the morning of June 29, 1967, the car in which she was riding with her boyfriend struck the back of a semi-tractor trailer that had stopped behind a truck spraying for bugs. Jayne Mansfield was killed instantly at the age of 34. Although she had multiple injuries that caused her death, she was not, as initially rumored, decapitated.

On Sex and Sexuality – "Sex appeal is a wonderful, warm, womanly, healthy feeling. If you're a woman, it's womanly; if you're not, it's manly.. it comes only from inside… it's an effervescent desire to enjoy life."

"I love sex. It should be animalistic, it should be sadistic, It should at times be masochistic… There are few rules and moral conventions."

"I love sex. Since it is one of God's gifts to everyone, there should be no shame in saying so. It gives me a glow of happiness all day… When it is honest, it enchants, it captivates, it amuses, it fascinates. It arouses within you the desire to protect and shelter."

On Men -- "Once a man's happy in the bedroom, the kitchen and living room are a cinch."

"Intelligence in a man is the keynote, and no girl in her right mind is going to go shopping for a man who's handsome and husky alone."

"My father was the only man I ever knew who really loved me unselfishly, who never used me for personal gain."

On Love -- "To function as an actress, I have to be in love. I have to have that incentive to work."

(*On her marriage to Mickey Hargitay*): "Mickey's so much in love with me. He's so physically exciting (*Hargitay was a manly-looking hunk*). I am so turned on by him. I wouldn't trade him for all the millionaires or titled men in London… (*Besides*) Mickey is not only powerful and gentle, he's deep. I wish all girls could be movie stars and all men could look like Mickey!"

The Inner Woman -- (*Her ambition was*): "To feel satisfied with myself, to know that I have arrived. To be liked. To be a big personality. The real stars are not actors or actresses. They're personalities. The quality of making everyone stop in their tracks is what I work at."

"Stars were made to suffer, and I am a star." (*She had a drinking problem most of her life.*)

"If you're going to do something wrong, do it big, because the punishment is the same either way."

"I will never be satisfied. Life is one constant search for betterment for me."

"I like being a pin-u p girl. There's nothing wrong with it.... I enjoy being a sex symbol and making people happy."

"I've got the strangest build. It's big in the hips, small in the waist, and I've got these enormous… shoulders."

"I didn't come to Hollywood to be the girl next door. I came to be a movie star."

"Nothing risqué, nothing gained."

"I guess a lot of people think that a girl who shows her bosom and wears tight dresses can't be close to God. God has always been close to me. Only He knew what was in my heart." *(She said she was a good Catholic, but admitted)*: "I am a sexy entertainer."

"I have always considered my career self and my personal self as two different and separate people. There's the Jayne Mansfield at home, a wife and devoted mother, and there's Jayne the sex symbol, which is my career, I have always kept them completely apart and separate."

"It is the most wonderful thing in the world, knowing you are loved and wanted."

"You know which title I like best? I like to be called mother….
Carrying a baby is the most rewarding experience a woman can enjoy."

Bette Midler

Bette is an example of a famous woman who has been happily married for more than 30 years. She is a breath of fresh air to listen to on how to be a successful wife and mother. Bring you sense of humor because she knows you'll need it in love and marriage.

"I married a German. Every night I dress up as Poland and he invades me."

"You can keep the pretty party boys. They're just for show. I like a man who can make me laugh. Looks fade, but a sense of humor is for keeps. I'll take a Woody Allen over a Warren Beauty (meaning Beatty) *any day."*

"Total contentment is only for cows."

"Thank God for the gays. I don't know what would have happened, but I know what did happen. Good for them, and good for me."

Born Bette Davis Midler in Honolulu, Hawaii on December 1, 1945, her mother was a seamstress and her father a house painter. Her parents named her after the actress Bette Davis. After studying drama at the University of Hawaii she began her musical career singing in gay bathhouses with Barry Manilow at the piano.

Her first album was "The Divine Miss M" in 1972, and that name stuck to her. Her successful movie career includes an Academy Award nomination for best actress portraying singer Janis Joplin in "The Rose" (1979). She also has won four Golden Globes, one Tony Award for her work on Broadway, and three Emmy Awards for her television work.

While playing on Broadway in "Fiddler on the Roof," her sister Judy visited New York City to see her perform, and was struck by a taxi and killed. She also mourns the death of her beloved mother. During the 1970s, she had a relationship with actor Peter Riegert and they lived together. Midler married artist Martin von Haselberg six weeks after they met in 1984, had a daughter with him, and they are still married.

On Sex -- "I've never been to a sex orgy in my entire life. Studio 54 (*a Manhattan night club popular especially with gays and lesbians from 1977 to 1981*) was way worse than the (*gay*) baths."

"If sex is such a natural phenomenon, how come there are so many books on how to do it?

On Men – "Men's brains are smaller than those of women so they can fit into their penises."

The Inner Woman – (*On growing up in Hawaii*): "We were very poor. It was a hardscrabble childhood, not particularly happy. The best part was nature, which is so intense there. The sky is bright blue, the clouds are puffy, the grass is lush. I feels like you can touch the stars. But the people were not very nice. I was a white kid in a mostly Asian neighborhood."

"If somebody makes me laugh, I'm his slave for life."

"If you want something done, you'd better do it yourself, or ask another woman to do it."

"My idea of superwoman is someone who scrubs her own floors."

"The only dream that mattered had come true… In this life I was loved by you."

"I have standards. They're low, but I have them."

"I want it all – and I want it delivered."

"The outside world doesn't have a lot to offer. You have to make your own heaven in your own home."

Marilyn Monroe

There is a real long line outside the ladies' room, already full inside, to hear what MM has to say about men and marriage and other tragedies of her life. Some like it hot; some like it hotter. Her life was about as hot as it comes.

"A sex symbol becomes a thing, I just hate to be a thing. Being a sex symbol is a heavy load to carry, especially when one is tired hurt, and bewildered."

"Sex is a part of nature. I go along with nature."

"I think that sexuality is only attractive when it's natural and spontaneous."

"A woman can bring a new love to each man she loves, providing there are not too many."

"A man makes you feel important, makes you glad you are a woman."

Born Norma Jean Mortenson in Los Angeles County Hospital on June 1, 1926, her mother was Gladys Pearl Baker and, according to her birth certificate, her father was Edward Mortenson, but she never really knew who her birth father was. Mortenson deserted them almost immediately after Norma Jean was born. Her mother was institutionalized for mental illness for most of Norma Jean's girl years and she went from foster homes to orphanages, nearly raped by a friend of the family when she was six.

As a child, she stuttered, heard noises in her head, and thought of ending her life, but escaped to the movies where blonde bombshell Jean Harlow became her favorite and she imitated her. To escape further, when she was 16 she married a neighbor's son, James Dougherty, who was four years older than she. He soon went off to the Merchant Marines in World War II and while he was away, she worked in an airplane factory, first as a parachute inspector, then a paint sprayer.

A photo of her at work, taken by an Army photographer, appeared in *Yank*, the Army magazine, and it led to her work as a model. When Dougherty returned from the war he found that his wife as a different person, with ambitions of becoming an actress. After they divorced in 1946, Dougherty bragged, "Never had I encountered a girl who so thoroughly enjoyed a sexual union. It made our lovemaking pure joy." On the other hand, Martin Evans, a friend of Dougherty, said, "She was scared. She even asked if it were possible for her to never have sex with Jim." She wondered if they could just be friends.

A talent scout for 20th Century Fox spotted her and she was signed to a short six-month contract for $125 a month. The studio changed her name to Marilyn and she chose Monroe after her grandmother's maiden name. A cameraman said, "Her natural beauty plus her inferiority complex gave her a look of mystery." She posed nude in 1950 and the photographs were used in a calendar that spread her beauty all over the world. She languished in comedies and musicals but yearned to become a serious actress, leading her to becoming depressed and seeing psychiatrists as she began depending on alcohol, drugs, and sleeping pills.

She married New York Yankees baseball star Joe DiMaggio in 1954, but the marriage lasted only nine months. She cited a conflict of careers, but later testified that he was "indifferent" and "moody."

Marilyn next surprised the world by marrying playwright Arthur Miller in 1956 because he was an intellectual. She insisted to him that she was more than a "dumb blonde." During their five-year marriage she suffered two miscarriages and became more depressed and dependent on drugs. She divorced him in 1961 claiming he left her for a photographer he met on the set of the movie he wrote for her, "The Misfits" (1961). She also felt betrayed by him because she found a notebook in which he wrote that he never loved anyone other than his daughter.

She co-starred with Clark Gable and Montgomery Clift in "The Misfits" (1961), and like Clift she was an emotional wreck dependent upon drugs and alcohol. Gable died two months after completing the film and his death affected her very much.

Marilyn and Miller divorced in 1961 amid rumors that she was having an affair with President John F. Kennedy. It has been said that she wanted Kennedy to divorce his wife Jackie after his first term in office and marry her, but instead he stopped seeing her, a rejection which to her was devastating.

Jackie Kennedy knew about her husband's affair with Marilyn, but they knew Jackie hated California, so they were safe to be together there. Kennedy and Marilyn stayed at his friend actor Peter Lawford's house or he would drive her to Bing Crosby's house in

Palm Springs if Kennedy was there and whether Crosby was at home or away somewhere. If Kennedy had more urgent need of Marilyn, Lawford would fly with her on Air Force One to be with Kennedy in a hotel in Manhattan. Jackie once noticed blonde hairs in the presidential bed in the White House, so she knew that Marilyn spent at least one night there. Marilyn phoned Jackie about JFK's plan to marry her, and Jackie replied that she was welcome to the job if she was up to living in a goldfish bowl.

When JFK decided Marilyn was a security risk for him with the FBI, he asked his younger brother Robert Kennedy to take her off his hands, and Bobby did this by having his own affair with her. He later also dropped her, but not before having some good times together including skinny-dipping with her at a nude beach. Marilyn was not sure, later, whether the baby she was carrying was the President's or his brother's. In either case, Lawford took her to Lake Tahoe where she had an abortion. She may not have had it willingly because she had been drinking and on drugs. After the abortion, she began each morning with Bloody Mary's and amphetamines.

She was committed to a psychiatric clinic, but DiMaggio had her released. Two months later she was found dead on August 5, 1962 in her home in Los Angeles at the age of 39. She and DiMaggio had remained friends after heir divorce and he directed her funeral. He also reportedly had white roses delivered weekly to her grave for nearly two decades after her death.

Marilyn's death was attributed to an overdose of barbiturates, but it remains uncertain if that was accidental or suicide. Some speculate that President Kennedy had her murdered, to silence her so she could not tell the media about their relationship, while others say a Mafia hit man killed her. Still others say she killed herself, one way or another, intentionally or not. It all makes for high drama, whether any of it is true or not.

Her tragic death shocked the world and she has remained as one of the most beautiful film actresses ever. *People* magazine has voted her "The Sexiest Woman of the Century."

Marilyn's sexual preference was the subject of controversy and still is today, some writers including Dan Littauer saying in 2012 that she struggled with being a lesbian and that she married to conceal her true lesbian sexuality. There has been no verifiable proof; however, since her childhood there were signals into the nature of lesbianism. She never knew her birth father, and her mother was mentally unstable. She moved between orphanages and foster homes where sometimes her male guardians sexually abused her.

Jean Negulesco, who directed Marilyn in "How to Marry a Millionaire" said, after her death, "Her whole existence was a search for identity, and her sexual identity was a complete mystery. She once told me she had never had an orgasm with a man in her entire life." This was confirmed in taped transcripts of sessions with Dr. Ralph Greenson, the psychoanalyst she saw near the end of her life.

Also in the transcripts she said she had had affairs with Joan Crawford, Marlene Dietrich, Barbara Stanwyck, Elizabeth Taylor and her acting coaches Natasha Lytess and Paula Strasberg. However, Greenson said the affairs may only have been in her mind. Marilyn also reportedly one night had seduced a 16-year-old girl from her fan club while they bonded because of shared memories of their troubled early family life since they had been in the same orphanage although not at the same time, and neither of them knew their birth fathers.

Betty Grable said she had found Marilyn's pursuit of her during "How to Marry a Millionaire" "sometimes scary." Judy Garland, who had been married to three gay men during her five husbands, also said that Marilyn pursued and propositioned her.

Biographers suggest that because of Marilyn's success and the pressure on her to be a film sex goddess, she was unable to lead a fulfilled life that would suit her sexuality. Michael Thornton wrote in the *London Daily Mail* that her heart and passion was oriented towards women. Marilyn also told her close friend, actor Ted Jordan, that she and Natasha Lytees were sleeping together, adding, "Why not? Sex is something you do with people you like. What could be wrong with a natural act?"

Her biographer Tony Jerris wrote in *Marilyn Monroe: My Little Secret,* about whether she was a full-fledged lesbian, that he didn't think so. "She was just a free spirit. She was a very open person." Marilyn Monroe's tragic death and the truth of her sexual preference went with her to her grave, but those who knew and loved her hope she now rests in peace.

On Love -- "I have feelings, too. I am still human. All I want is to be loved, for myself."

On Men -- "A man has a tendency to accept you the way you are, while most women immediately start to pick flaws and want to change you."

"The real lover is the man who can thrill you by kissing your forehead or smiling into your eyes or just staring into space."

"I don't mind living in a man's world as long as I can be a woman in it."

"Next to my husbands, and along with Marlon Brando, I think Yves Montand (*French actor married to French actress Simone Signoret*) was the most attractive man I've ever known."

"A woman can't be alone. She needs a man. A man and woman support and strengthen each other. She just can't do it by herself."

"A man is more frank and sincere with his emotions than a woman. We girls, I'm afraid, have a tendency to hide our feelings."

"In fact, my popularity seems almost entirely a masculine phenomenon."

"There is just no comparison between having a dinner date with a man and staying home playing canasta with the girls."

"A strong man doesn't have to be dominant toward a woman. He doesn't match his strength against a woman weak with love for him. He matches it against the world."

"Confidentially, the type of male I find most enjoyable for a friend is one who has enough fire and assurance to speak up for his convictions."

"It's often just enough to be with someone. I don't need to touch them. Not even talk. A feeling passes between you both. You're not alone."

"Naturally, there are times when every woman likes to be flattered, to feel she is the most important thing in someone's world. Only a man can paint this picture."

"I have noticed that men usually leave married women alone and are inclined to treat all wives with respect. This is no great credit to married women."

"If your man is a sports enthusiast, you may have to resign yourself to his spouting off in a monotone on a prize fight, football game, or pennant race."

"The truth is, I've never fooled anyone. I've let men sometimes fool themselves."

"If you can make a girl laugh, you can make her do anything."

(*About Arthur Miller while looking for a man interested in more than her body.*) "He sat and held my toe, and we just looked into each other's eyes."\

(*Miller later said about his marriage to Marilyn*): "She was a whirling light to me then… All paradox and enticing mystery, street-tough one moment, then lifted by a lyrical and poetic sensitivity that few retain past adolescence."

On Marriage -- (*In 1954 on her marriage to Joe DiMaggio after he had retired from baseball*): "Joe will always come first with me. He is the human being closest to my heart. He's the most important person in my life. Everything else is second. But he understands that my career is very important to me. I fought hard to get it. Sometimes starved."

"And the same goes for his career, with me… I'm not too interested in baseball. I've been around Joe long enough to pick up a few rules and expressions. But I wouldn't break my neck to go to a game with him. I'm not crazy about watching television, either. But Joe loves it. That's his idea of real fun, staying home and watching television, mainly western movies, baseball, and boxing. I like to read and I have to study my scripts." (*And be seen at night club and movie events, which he cared little or nothing about. Their honeymoon was in Japan but she spent part of it visiting U.S servicemen at camps in Korea. It was the start of him having to deal with her movie star celebrity that often kept them apart.*)

"Marriage is something you learn more about while you live it. Joe and I have had our quarrels. Just like other married couples. But there's a way to handle a disagreement. Every wife should know her man. When I sense there's something wrong, I ask 'What's the matter? Sorry if I did something,' If Joe doesn't answer, I don't push it. There are some men who, when they have trouble, become silent. You have to respect that., if that's your man. Later, when what was wrong is worn thin, Joe will come to me and say, 'I'm sorry.' I'll look at him and say, 'What's there to be sorry about?' You'd be surprised how nice it can be, if done this way."

(*After each failed marriage, she said she would rather be miserable on her own than in tumultuous relationships*): "It's better to be unhappy alone than unhappy with someone."

(*On her first meeting with Arthur Miller in a party in 1952*): "I know you don't think I'm very bright. I guess I'm not sometimes. But I read when I have a chance. And I'll read your plays. You know, it would be nice if, after I read them, I could talk to you about them. That would be nice. That would be wonderful. You're married and so am I, so let's just be friends"

(*Marilyn tells Miller in 1956*): "I want to marry you, Arthur. I'll be a good wife to you, too. I wasn't such a good wife, I guess, to two other men. But I didn't love them like I love you. And I'm older now. I've learned things… Do you know, I can cook? Frozen, mostly. But I'll learn Jewish cooking, from your mother. I'll learn your religion. I'll study everything about you until we're like one person... I want to be *you*, Arthur. I want to be your goodness, your strength. Oh, Arthur, can we get married soon? Right away?"

(*On the break-up of her marriage to Miller, their careers often setting them at odds with each other, he left her on November 11, 1960. He packed his suitcase in their apartment, took up his coat, and walked to the door. Looking back at her, he said, "Good-bye, Marilyn." She pleaded with him to stop so they could talk things out, as they had before, but he looked back at her and said, "Good-bye, Marilyn." She pleaded...* "Arthur... Arthur... Please don't go. You know I can't stand being alone. You... know... *that*." *He left and that was the end of their marriage.*

The Inner Woman -- "I am good, but not an angel. I do sin, but I am not the devil. I am just a small girl in a big world trying to find someone to love."

"I'm selfish, impatient and a little insecure. I make mistakes, I am out of control and at times hard to handle. But if you can't handle me at my worst, then you sure as hell don't deserve me at my best."

"I am not a victim of emotional conflicts. I am human."

"Sometimes I feel my whole life has been one big rejection."

"One of the best things that ever happened to me is that I'm a woman. That is the way all females should feel."

"If there is only one thing in my life that I am proud of, it's that I've never been a kept woman. I kept myself. I have always taken pride in the fact that I was on my own."

"First, I'm trying to prove to myself that I'm a person. Then maybe I'll convince myself that I'm an actress."

"We should all start to live before we get too old."

"Millions of people live their entire lives without finding themselves. But it is something I must do."

"Dreaming about being an actress is more exciting than being one."

"I'm one of the world's most self-conscious people. I really have to struggle."

"I once wanted to prove myself by being a great actress. Now I want to prove that I'm a person. Then maybe I'll be a great actress."

"I'm very definitely a woman, and I enjoy it." (*And, she said*): "I dress for men. I believe your body should make your clothes look good, instead of using clothes to make the body conform to what is considered fashionable at the moment, distorted or not... Men like simplicity in clothes. A woman will think of a dress for itself, but a man will think of it in relationship to the woman who is wearing it. So do I."

"What good am I? I can't have kids. I can't cook. I've been divorced three times. Who would want me?"

"What good is it being Marilyn Monroe? Why can't I just be an ordinary woman?""

"I never wanted to be Marilyn. It just happened. Marilyn's like a veil I wear over Norma Jean."

"Respect is one of life's greatest treasures. I mean, what does it all add up to if you don't have that?"

"I want to be an artist, not a celluloid aphrodisiac."

"I wish I knew why I am so anguished."

"You know, most people really don't know me."

(*In an article she wrote in 1952*): "I think the thing I really missed most in my life was the feeling of being wanted and needed. My mother was ill and hospitalized when I needed her most. (*When Marilyn was growing up.*) The families I lived with were good to me, all right, but for the most part I definitely felt myself an outsider."

"I am alone. I am always alone no matter what."

As others saw Marilyn:

"I love Marilyn. I think she was incredibly beautiful and a very underrated actress. I am a curvy woman who is blonde, and perhaps both comfortable in our femininity, but I think that is as far as the comparison goes." – *Scarlett Johansson*

"She once got her life so balled up that the studio hired a full-time secretary maid for her. So Marilyn soon got the secretary as balled up as she was, and she ended waiting on the secretary, instead of vice-versa." – *Jane Russell*

"We were very close. Once when we were doing that picture 'How to Marry a Millionaire' (1953) together, I got a call on the set: my younger daughter had had a fall. I ran home and the one person to call was Marilyn. She did an awful lot to boost things up for movies when everything was at a low state; there'll never be anyone like her for looks, for attitude, for all of it." – *Betty Grable*

"She seemed to have a kind of unconscious glow about her physical self that was innocent, like a child. When she posed nude, it was 'Gee, I am kind of, you know, sort of dishy,' like she enjoyed it without being egotistical." – *Elizabeth Taylor*

"She's the original good time that was had by all." – *Bette Davis.*

"Marilyn was frightened, insecure. You couldn't dislike Marilyn. She had no meanness in her, no bitchery." – *Lauren Bacall.*

"When you look at Marilyn on the screen, you don't want anything bad to happen to her. You really care that she should be all right... happy." – *Natalie Wood*

Mary Tyler Moore

Three marriages and divorces, being taken for a ride by one of her husbands, and a son's tragic accidental death would have turned most women sour on life and love, but not the indomitable Mary. Her spirit to be a survivor is an inspiration in the ladies' room.

"There is a dark side. I tend not to be as optimistic as Mary Richards. I have an anger in me that I carry from my childhood experiences. I expect a lot of myself and I'm not too kind to myself."

"Sometimes you have to get to know someone really well to realize you're really strangers."

"You can't be brave if you've only had wonderful things happen to you."

"I'm an experienced woman; I've been around... well, alright, I might not've been around, but I've been... nearly."

Born in Brooklyn, New York on December 29, 1936, her father was a clerk. She had a troubled girlhood with two younger sisters because their mother became an alcoholic. The family moved to California when she was eight. After high school in 1955, she married Richard Meeker (*who she described as "the boy next door"*) when she was 17 and gave birth to her only child, a son.

Her show business career began that same year as a dancing kitchen appliance in a Hotpoint television commercial. Television roles followed and she became famous and beloved as his wife in "The Dick Van Dyke" show from 1961 to 1966. She appeared in movies, divorced Meeker in 1962, and later that year married network executive Grant Tinker. She returned to television in 1970 as television newswoman Mary Richards in "The Mary Tyler Moore Show" which became a major critical and audience success over the next seven years.

Despite her fame and fortune, Moore's personal life was often tragic. Her sister died of a drug overdose at the age 21 in 1978, and her brother of cancer. Her son accidentally shot and killed himself in 1980, which devastated her. She has not been in perfect health, diagnosed as a diabetic, has had a brain tumor removed, and had a spell with alcoholism in the mid-1970s.

She and Tinker divorced in 1981 and two years later she married her doctor, Robert Levine. She has won two Tony awards for Broadway shows and received the Screen Actors Guild Lifetime Achievement Award in 2011.

On Men and Divorce – "Having lived with a man who I put through medical school and who then, upon graduating and about to become an intern and resident, dumped me, CBS chose that over my having been divorced. They said there's nothing funny about divorce. And not only that, they'd think she was divorced from Dick Van Dyke!"

The Inner Woman -- "There are certain things about me that I will never tell to anyone because I am a very private person. But basically what you see is who I am. I'm independent, I do like to be liked, I do look for the good side of life and people. I'm positive, I'm disciplined, I like my life in order, and I'm neat as a pin. I love order and discipline. God, I sound like a Nazi, don't I?"

"Take chances, make mistakes. That's how you grow. Pain nourishes your courage. You have to fail in order to practice being brave."

"I feel about my dogs now, and all the dogs I had prior to them, the way I feel about children – they are that important to me. When I have lost a dog, I have gone into a mourning period that lasted for months."

"Having a dream is what keeps you alive."

(*On living with Type 1 diabetes*): "Diabetes is an all-too-personal time bomb which can go off today, tomorrow, next year, or ten years from now – a time bomb affecting millions like me."

"Grant once said, 'I never heard Mary complain about the diabetes during our marriage.' He meant it as praise for my ability to be strong, but I think now that that statement is evidence of what was wrong with us. We never shared our fears or showed any kind of weakness. And the fear of revealing too much was always there."

"Chronic disease, like a troublesome relative, is something you can learn to manage but never quite escape. And while each and every person who has Type 1 (*diabetes*) prays for a cure, and would give anything to stop thinking about it for just a year, a month, a week, a day even; the ironic truth is that only when you own it – accept it, embrace it, make it your own, do you start to be free of many of its emotional and physical burden."

"Couldn't you just slap my face for being so positive and optimistic?"

Rita Moreno

This multi-talented lady was lucky in love, married only once, to a doctor for 45 years until his death, and having a daughter with him. Her problem was her career, although very successful, was wrought with feeling degraded and under-used by being cast at what she wasn't in real life, a sexpot Hispanic.

"I had battled racism and sexism all my life. Now I had to battle ageism. Growing old in Hollywood is a serious defect."

"My perseverance paid off."

Born Rosita Dolores Alverio in Humacao, Puerto Rico on December 11, 1931 to a seamstress and a farmer. She and her mother moved to New York City when she was six years old and she soon began her career as a dancer. At age 11 she dubbed Spanish-language in Hollywood movies and was not yet 14 when she made her Broadway debut. She turned to films, but thought her roles were degrading, playing a sexy Hispanic. She was married only once, to Dr. Lenny Gordon, an internist and cardiologist, from 1965 until his death in 2010, and gave birth to a daughter with him.

Her big break in films came when she was cast as Anita, the Puerto Rican girlfriend of the leader of a gang called the Sharks in "West Side Story" (1961) for which she won the Academy Award as best supporting actress, the first Hispanic woman to win an Oscar. But the role was traumatic because it reminded her of her less than happy girlhood in Puerto Rico. She also won a Tony Award as best featured actress in a musical for "The Ritz" (1975), and has won two Emmys for her work on television in "The Muppet Show" and "The Rockford Files."

In 2004 President George W. Bush awarded her the Presidential Medal of Freedom. In 2010 she was awarded the American National Medal of the Arts for her services and contributions to the arts. When she stood over her star on the Hollywood Walk of Fame in 2005 she fell on top of it, weeping, and later saying. "I had been dreaming of this day since I was six!"

On Love -- "Not every woman has known great love, but I have been lucky enough to have had two." (*She did not reveal who the other was, besides her husband, but probably meant her daughter because she also has said* "Motherhood is a romance, too.*"*)

"There is a thin razor-sharp line between love and obsession."

"Can a man love too much? I'll never know."

On Men -- She was disappointed about Elvis Presley because they had for a while been lovers, but to her he was more like "a baby brother" than a "stud."

"Jack Nicholson was the most obliging of co-stars."

The Inner Woman -- "Bigger than life is not difficult for me. I *am* bigger than life."

"Rita Hayworth was my inspiration" (*In acting in films.*)

"I personally detest violence, even in make-believe."

"I'm deeply grateful for the applause, and I thrive in the spotlight." "Staying active and persevering is part and parcel of the character of a performer. You always have to be able to get up, dust yourself off, and move forward."

"I have since learned – in my seventies and eighties – the real value of women friends."

"I could do it all, but Hollywood still didn't quite know what to do with me."

Lupita Nyong'o

Success in films came unexpected and fast to this young lady of Mexican and African heritage. It has yet to be seen if happiness in her personal life is going to be as successful. We hope so.

(To young girls of color): *"I hope that my presence on your screens and in magazines may lead you, young girl, on a similar journey. That you will feel the validation for your beauty, but also get to the deeper business of feeling beautiful inside. There is no shade in that beauty."*

"What I have learned for myself is that I don't have to be anybody else; and that myself is good enough; and that when I am being true to that self, then I can avail myself to extraordinary things. You have to allow for the impossible to be possible."

Born Lupita Amondi Nyong'o in Mexico City on March 1, 1983, her father was a political science college professor there and her first name is short for Guadalupe, the city in Mexico. Her parents returned to their native Kenya when she was less than a year old and she grew up there as her father became a professor at the University of Nairobi.

She was inspired to become an actress at the age of three when she saw the film "The Color Purple" in 1985. She returned to Mexico at the age of 16 to learn Spanish, then was graduated from Hampshire

College, Amherst, Massachusetts, with a bachelor's degree in film and theatre studies in 2003.

While working as a production helper on the film "The Constant Gardener" in 2005, its star, Ralph Fiennes, encouraged her to become an actress, saying if it was something she couldn't imagine doing without. She followed his advice by getting a master's degree in acting from the Yale School of Drama in 2012 where she was called "a gifted actress."

Just before graduation she was cast as the sexually abused slave girl in "12 Years a Slave' and won the Academy Award for best supporting actress, becoming the sixth black actress to win an Oscar, the first Kenyan, and the first Mexican.

She then became a cover girl for her beauty and was named to *Harper's Bazaar's* "best dressed" list. In 2014, *People* magazine named her "The Most Beautiful Woman." She makes more movies and endorses a line of perfume and cosmetics. At this writing in 2016 she was starring in "Eclipse," a play on Broadway and preparing for a new film.

The Inner Woman -- "I grew up in a world where the majority of people were black, so that wasn't the defining quality of anyone. When you're describing someone, you don't start out with 'He's black, He's white.'"

(*Growing up as a young girl of Kenyan descent in* Mexico City) "My one prayer to God, the miracle worker, was that I would wake up lighter skinned. The morning would come and I would be so excited about seeing my new skin that I would refuse to look down at myself before I was in front of a mirror, because I wanted to see my fair face first. And every day I experienced just the same disappointment at being just as dark as I had been the day before.

"I tried to negotiate with God. I told him I would stop steeling sugar cubes at night if he gave me what I wanted. I would listen to my mother's every word and never lose my school sweater again if he just made me a little lighter. But, I guess God was unimpressed with my bargaining chips because I never woke up lighter."

"I discovered that joy is not the negation of pain, but rather acknowledging the presence of pain and feeling happiness in spite of it."

"As human beings, what makes us able to empathize with people is a connection that is not necessarily understood mentally."

(On accepting the Oscar for "12 Years a Slave," *thanking the producer of the film and her family and Yale drama coaches*): "When I look down at this golden statue, may it remind me and every little child that no matter where you're from, your dreams are valid. Thank you."

Michelle Obama

The First Lady to the President of the United States, Barack Obama, and to the county, she is a not only a fashion role model for women of all color, but as a woman of many accomplishments including earning a law degree and working as an advocate of social justice for all people. Her marriage and being mother of two daughters has been happy and fulfilling. Her future after the White House looks very bright.

"I am an example of what is possible when girls from the very beginning of their lives are loved and nurtured by people around them. I was surrounded by extraordinary women in my life who taught me about quiet strength and dignity."
"One of the lessons that I grew up with was to always stay true to yourself and never let what somebody else says distract you from your goals. And so when I hear about negative and false attacks, I really don't invest any energy in them, because I know who I am."

Born Michelle LaVaughn Robinson in Chicago, Illinois on January 17, 1954, her mother was a homemaker and her father a city water plant employee. Both of her parents traced their lineage back to Civil War slaves. Michelle and her brother Craig, a year younger than she, grew up in a second floor apartment of a house on the city's South Side that her parents rented from her great aunt who lived downstairs. She was an honor student in high school and studied sociology and African American studies at Princeton University, graduating in 1985. She became active in supporting minority issues, ran a day care center for minority children, and tutored students.

She earned a doctoral degree from Harvard Law School, then returned to Chicago to work at a law firm where she met Barack Obama. They began dating in 1989 and married three years later. Obama then became a U. S. Senator and then the first black to become President of the United States, in 2009, and she became the first African American First Lady of the United States. The Obama's have two daughters, Malian Ann, and Natasha.

During Obama's two terms as President, Michelle has been an advocate of education, organic food, education, social justice, and same-sex marriage. Her beauty and "classic and confident look" made her world-famous and she was named one of the world's most inspiring women and among the top ten of the world's best-dressed women. Many say there is a lot more to Michelle Obama than her looks and what she wears. She keeps her private life to herself, but has said many things that give some glimpses into her inner woman.

On Men -- "What I notice about men, all men, is that their order is me, my family. God is in there somewhere, but me is first."

On Love -- "My mother's love has always been a sustaining force for our family, and one of the greatest joys is seeing her integrity, her compassion, her intelligence reflected in my daughters."

On Marriage -- (*Advocating same-sex marriage*): "This is an important issue for millions of Americans, and for Barack and me, it really comes down to the values of fairness and equality we want to pass down to our girls. These are basic values that kids learn at a very young age that we want to encourage them to apply in all areas of their lives."

The Inner Woman -- "You can't make decisions based on fear and the possibility of what might happen."

"One of the lessons that I grew up with was to always stay true to yourself and never let what somebody else says distract you from your goals. And so when I hear about negative and false attacks, I really don't invest any energy in them, because I know who I am."

"Just do what works for you, because there will always be someone who thinks differently."

"We should always have three friends in our lives -- one who walks ahead who we look up to and follow; one who walks beside us, who is with us every step of our journey; and then, one who we reach back for and bring along after we've cleared the way."

"You may not always have a comfortable life and you will not always be able to solve all of the world's problems at once but don't ever underestimate the importance you can have because history has shown us that courage can be contagious and hope can take on a life of its own."

"Good relationships feel good. They feel right. They don't hurt."

"Do not bring people in your life who weigh you down, and trust your instincts. Good relationships feel good. They feel right. They don't hurt. They're not painful. That's not just with somebody you want to marry, but it's with the friends you choose. It's with the people you surround yourself with."

"My most important title is still 'mom-in-chief.' My daughters are still the heart of my heart and the center of my world."

"Women in particular need to keep an eye on their physical and mental health, because if we're scurrying to and from appointments and errands, we don't have a lot of time to take care of ourselves. We need to do a better job of putting ourselves higher on our own 'to do' list."

Merle Oberon

Cathy: "Heathcliff, make the world stop right here. Make everything stop and stand still and never move again. Make the moors never change and you and I never change."

Heathcliff: "The moors and I will never change. Don't you, Cathy."

Cathy: "I can't. I can't. No matter what I ever do or say, Heathcliff, this is me now; standing on this hill with you. This is me forever."

But Cathy's pledge of love did not last forever in "Wuthering Heights" (1939). She wanted a passionate lover but also luxury and Heathcliff could only provide the former, so she settled for the latter with another man she really did not love.

Merle Oberon was a lot like Cathy, who lived in a dream world of her own making. Born to an Indian mother in the slums of Bombay and a British father who deserted them, she invented herself so she could become a great movie star. She would not accept the alternatives… poverty or prostitution. Hollywood did not want actresses of mixed blood in the 1930's, so she said she was an aristocrat from the more exotic-sounding Tasmania, an island off the southern coast of Australia that was considered British and more acceptable.

She changed her name from O'Brien to the more romantic Oberon and said the woman traveling with her was her maid when in fact she was her mother. The subterfuge worked and Merle Oberon, the great beauty with a greater imagination, became a top film star in Hollywood in the 1930's and 1940's. In real life, such as it was real to her, she said:

"Without security, it is difficult for a woman to look or feel beautiful."

Born Estelle Merle O'Brien Thompson on February 19, 1911 in Bombay, India, of Welsh-Indian parents. She was educated in India and went to London at the age of 17 with hopes of becoming a movie star. She traveled with a wealthy young Englishman. She became a star at the Cafe de Paris and was in a relationship with a black American jazz musician called Hutch. At the same time she dated American golfing tycoon Charles Sweeney.

Merle only got small, unbilled parts for three years, then was discovered by British filmmaker Alexander Korda when he saw her in line for tea at a movie studio and was struck by her exotic beauty. Korda cast her as Anne Boleyn in "The Private Life of Henry III" (1939) opposite Charles Laughton who won the Academy Award for his stout performance. Later that year she married Korda and when he was knighted she became Lady Korda.

She made one more picture in England, "The Scarlet Pimpernel" (1934), and her co-star, fell in love with her. He was married but often unfaithful. She then went to Hollywood to try her luck there. She scored in "The Dark Angel" (1935) and was nominated for a best actress Oscar. More fine films followed until she made the film for which she is best remembered, "Wuthering Heights" (1939) opposite Laurence Olivier. Her performance as Cathy and his as Heathcliff are among the most moving and memorable in films.

After that, she made 15 films in the 1940s. She starred in "A Night in Paradise" 1946), but at first balked at her lover in the film, Turhan Bey, a Turkish actor who had made a name for himself in Maria Montez sand-and-sex films. Oberon changed her mind about Bey when he came up to her shirtless. Director Arthur Lubin said, "Merle took one look at his bulging biceps and immediately changed her mind about him." She then engaged in an affair with him, while he was in another one with Lana Turner.

While married to cinematographer Lucian Ballard in 1948, and filming "Berlin Express," she slept with her leading man, Robert Ryan. Later, she spent a night with Eddie Fisher., and there were other men in her life. She continued as a star for the next quarter century, her final film being "Interval" (1973). She retired to her home in Malibu, California where she died of a massive stroke on November 23, 1979 at the age of 68, still beautiful.

Oberon was married four times: Alexander Korda (1939-1945); Lucien Ballard (1945-1949); Bruno Pagliai (1957-1973) with whom she adopted a boy and a girl; Robert Wolders who was 25 years younger than she, married in 1975 until her death in 1979. Her face was scarred in a London car crash in 1937 and Ballard designed a small spotlight that reduced the flaws.

She didn't want anyone to know she was half Indian, so she said the dark-skinned woman who lived in her house was her maid. In truth, the woman was her mother, an Eurasian who was half Irish and half Singhalese who came from Ceylon, now Sri Lanka. Her mother gave birth to her when she became pregnant by a British tea planter when she was 14. He married her so Merle would be born legitimate, then divorced and left, but died three years later.

While a struggling young actress in London she attracted the attention of Ray Milland who was then also a young star-to-be. He said of her, "She was the most exotically beautiful creature I had even seen… I didn't take my eyes off her for the next nine months."

Merle Oberon was a very elusive person when it came to interviews or quotes, most of the time keeping her thoughts to herself, but what she said about beauty defines herself. She was not only discreet about her love life but mainly silent. Her life was an act, but she did both beautifully and left us with wonderful illusions.

The Inner Woman – "Even when I was single, I owned homes and gardens. I buy beauty when other women buy jewels. Land is security to me. I need gardens that are mine to walk on."

On Men – (on Ernst Lubitsch who directed her in "That Uncertain Feeling" 1941): "That was probably the happiest picture I ever made because Lubitsch was such a funny man, such a darling man."

Rosie O'Donnell

Twice married and divorced, Rosie later found her true sexual preference in a partnership with another woman, the Oscar-winning daughter of a famous actor. She loves being a mother of three adopted children.

"I don't think you choose whether or not you're gay."

"Part of the reason I've never said that I was gay until now was because I didn't want that adjective assigned to my name for all of eternity. You know, 'Gay Rosie O'Donnell.'"

"I'm not asking that people accept homosexuality. I'm not asking that they believe like I do that it's inborn. I'm not asking that. All I'm asking is don't let these children suffer without a family because of your bias."

"I want the same standard applied to homosexuals as is applied to heterosexuals."

Born Rosann O'Donnell in Commack, Long Island, New York on March 21, 1962, the middle of five children, her father was a spy camera engineer for the defense industry. When she was ten, her mother died. An early job was in a Sears catalog department, filling orders. She dropped out of college when she was 18 and began appearing on television shows. In 1996 she had her own syndicated television show, "The Rosie O'Donnell Show."

She was married and divorced twice, to Kelli O'Donnell (2004-2008) with whom she had four adopted children, and to Michelle Rounds (2012-2015) also an adopted daughter. She and Rounds had a nasty divorce and custody battle. In 2015 she was reportedly seen intimately dining with actress Tatum O'Neal, grown daughter of actor Ryan O'Neal. She and Tatum now live together. Tatum reportedly said she had a newfound attraction to women.

O'Donnell's signature phrase in show business is "What a cutie patootie." Her role models are Barbra Streisand and Bette Midler. She is good friends with television producer Penny Marshall, and her best friend is Madonna. Her favorite film is "The Sound of Music" (1965). She has tattoos on one of her ankles. A philanthropist, she donated $5,700,000 to Hurricane Katrina relief efforts in 2006. In 2012 she suffered a heart attack.

On Love -- "I was 29 and I really fell in love (*in 1991*), I think, for the first time. I was vulnerable in a way I didn't think I could be."

"If you fall in love with someone gay and you're the opposite gender, it's not going to work."

The Inner Woman -- "I was an abused kid."

"Radical Christianity is just as threatening as radical Islam in a country like America."

"We will never bring peace at the hands of war. As a species we have to rise above it."

"I think what children need is love, security, stability, consistency, and kindness."

"I know I'm a really good mother. I know it."

"I don't think it negates your skills as a parent if you're homosexual."

"I don't think America knows what a gay parent looks like. I am the gay parent. America has watched me parent my children on television for six years. They know what kind of parent I am."

"It takes a lot to be a foster parent."

"There are some heterosexuals that have the heterosexual behavior that is appalling sexually, that is deviant and bad and not really moral and Christ-like and Biblical. But those people are never questioned as to whether or not they're allowed to be a parent."

"Unfortunately in the gay community, oftentimes people that get the most attention are the most flamboyant and loud. And that's not to dismiss them, because drag queens and, you know, leather motorcycle women, they have their place in the gay community as well. But they're not – they don't define the gay community by any stretch of the imagination."

"My job is mostly to entertain and be funny. It's the main reason why I continue to push myself and my career to do more and more as the amount that you're able to raise for charity and to give to charity by my celebrity."

"I am sure I will cause tremendous seismic shifts in the culture again."

"I think life is easier if you're straight."

"The gray has gone away, I am living in bright Technicolor."

Bree Olson

"I send a very strong message to young girls: Don't do porn."

"There's nothing wrong with porn, but how people treat you for the rest of your life; it's not worth it."

"When I go out, I feel as if I'm wearing 'slut' across my forehead."

Born Rachel Marie Oberlin on October 7. 1986 in Houston, Texas, when she was two years old she and her parents moved to Fort Wayne, Indiana, where she now lives. Her maternal grandparents were Ukrainians who emigrated to Texas after being Nazi concentration camp survivors during World War II. As a teenager, her first job was working on an Indiana farm as a corn husker, then as a waitress at a local restaurant.

She had decided as a pre-teenager to become a porn star, and took her acting name from a high school friend named Bree and combined it with Olson, after the movies' Olsen Twins, Mary-Kate and Ashley Olsen.. After high school, she attended Indiana University off and on for three years, studying premed to become a doctor. She dropped out when she was nineteen and a half to start acting in adult films because she had been in a four-relationship until then. She said she earned between $3,000 and $4,000 a month in about 300 adult films from 2006 to 2011 before changing to mainstream films.

Bree also is critical of the pornography industry, believing it is run by "faceless men," but not of the profession itself. She describes herself as being bisexual and was in a one-month relationship with actor Charlie Sheen in 2011, sharing his home with other women as one of his live-in "goddesses."

Since leaving the adult film industry and working in mainstream films and television shows, she has found the transition has not been easy because of society's perception of former porn actresses. People who recognize her in public call her ugly, demeaning names. She has had trouble finding mainstream work and making friends. She says no one wants anything to do with her after they find out about her former life.

More quotes from Bree, from a video interview on Youtube: "Real Women, Real Stories":

"To all young women thinking about doing porn, I don't hate porn. I didn't have any bad experiences. But trust me when I tell you not to do it. When you do porn you automatically become a segregated part of society that is held to prejudice without the support of activists for your human rights. Porn isn't bad… how people will treat you for the rest of your life is."

"There's nothing wrong with porn, and nothing wrong with embracing you sexuality, but there are some things that, no matter how open-minded you are, other people never will be."

"You're just going to live a life of crap in front of you in dealing with people, companies. Employers can turn you down based on past experience or 'morality clauses.'"

"I have really gotten to the point where there are days to weeks at a time where I don't leave the house because I don't feel like facing the world. People treat me as if I am a pedophile. They don't treat me like an ex-sex worker. They treat me like I would somehow be damaging to children."

When asked how she would like to be treated: "I wish people would treat me like they would treat a married registered nurse with 2.5 kids in Indiana," she says, tearfully. "I would be so happy."

Jackie Kennedy Onassis

Few women lived a fuller life more in the public eye than the very private former First Lady who then married one of the richest men in the world. She knew her President-husband was in affairs with other women including the top film sex goddess of their time, yet she stuck with him to his tragic end. In many ways, the legendary curse of the Kennedy family enfulfed her as well. But she was another survivor, like many women famous or not.

"I don't think there are any men who are faithful to their wives."

"When Harvard men say they have graduated from Radcliffe, then we've made it."

"On a potential husband, all I ask is someone with a little imagination, but they are hard to find."

"There are two kinds of women, those who want power in the world, and those who want power in bed."

Born Jacqueline Lee Bouvier in Southampton, New York on July 18, 1929 to a Wall Street stock boker and his wife, they divorced in 1940 and her mother married Standard Oil tycoon Hugh Auchincloss Jr. in 1942 when Jackie was 13. She attended primary schools in New York City and Virginia, then was graduated from George Washington University in 1951 with a degree in French.

While working as a photographer for the *Washington-Times Herald* she met John F. Kennedy when he was a U.S. House of Representative from Massachusetts and they married in 1953. Jackie suffered a miscarriage in 1955 but two years later gave birth to a daughter, Caroline, then a son, John F. Kennedy Jr., in 1960, both by Caesarian section. A second son was born prematurely in 1963 and died two days later. She felt guilty about his death because she had been a heavy smoker, up to three packs a day, before the dangers of smoking were known.

Kennedy was elected President of the United States in 1960 and Jackie, at age 31, became one of the youngest First Ladies. She kept busy having the interior of the White House restored and became a fashion role model to women all over the world. After Kennedy was assassinated on November 22, 1963, with whom she was riding in a limousine, she removed her wedding ring and slipped it onto her dying husband's finger saying, "Now I have nothing left."

Jackie and her children moved to Europe where she met and married Greek shipping tycoon Aristotle Onassis in 1968, one of the richest men in the world. She reportedly married him because he could provide the privacy she wanted for herself and her children. Onasssis died in 1975 and Jackie agreed to an inheritance settlementr of $26 million.

She and her children then moved to New York City where she became a book editor. From the mid-1970s until her death, her companion was Maurice Tempelsman, a Belgian industrialist and diamond merchant. Jackie died in her sleep at home on May 19, 1944 of non-Hodgkin's lymphoma, a form of cancer, at the age of 64. She left her children an estate of almost $44 million.

On Men -- "I think the best thing I can do is to be a distraction. A husband lives and breathes his work all day long. If he comes home to more table thumping, how can the poor man ever relax?"

The Inner women -- "The only thing I do not want to be called is First Lady. It sounds like a saddle horse." (*Although she loved horses and rode them since she was two years old.*)

"I am a woman above everything else."

"I want to live my life, not record it."

"Someone said where do you get your opinions and I said I get all my opinions from my husband (*Kennedy*). It was really a rather terribly Victorian or Adriatic relationship, which I think is the best."

(*Terrified during the Cuban Missile Crisis, of being separated from JFK*): "I just want to be with you, and I want to die with you, and the children do, too, than live without you."

(*On Kennedy's assassination*): "He didn't even have the satisfaction of being killed for civil rights. It had to be some silly little Communist."

"The only routine with me is no routine at all."

"Whenever I was upset by something in the papers Jack always told me to be more tolerant, like a horse flicking away flies in the summer."

"One must not let oneself be overwhelmed by sadness."

"I think women should never be in politics. We're just not suited to it."

"There are many little ways to enlarge your child's world. Love of books is the best of all."

"If you bungle raising your children, I don't think whatever else you do matters very much."

On Love and Marriage -- (*On JFK*): "Now, I think that I should have known that he was magic all along. I did know it, but I should have guessed that it would be too much to grow old with. So now, he is a legend when he would have preferred to be a man."

Anna Paquin

A beautiful young Academy Award winner, Anna Paquin is another actress of today's generation who although married, came out as being bisexual, as well as giving birth to twins with her husband,, a boy and a girl.

(On her bisexuality): *"For me, it's not really an issue because I'm someone who believes being bisexual is actually a thing. It's not made up. It's not a lack of decision. It's not being greedy or numerous other ignorant things I've heard at this point."*

*"I'm proud to be a happily married bisexual mother. Marriage is about love. For a bisexual, it's not about gender. That's not the deciding factor for who they're attracted to…. (*Sexual orientation*) is a minor biographical detail."*

"My sexuality is something I'm completely comfortable with and open about. There's a lot of prejudice toward us, but the more people talk about it, the less of a big deal it will be. And that will be better for everyone."

"Acting is pretending to be someone else… I'm Anna Paquin. I'm bisexual and I give a damn!"

Born Anna Helene Paquin in Winnipeg, Manitoba, Canada on July 24, 1982, her father was a physical education teacher and her mother an English teacher. Her parents divorced when she was four years old, and she moved with her mother to New Zealand, her mother's native country.

She made a sensational film debut at the age of nine in "The Piano" in 1993 which won her an Academy Award as best supporting actress. She completed high school in Los Angeles, then studied for a year at Columbia University in New York.

She became a stage actress in New York and London from 2001 to 2004 and then starred in a television series, "True Blood" which ran seven years, ending in 2014. She married actor Stephen Moyer in 2010, having come out as bisexual months before marrying him.

They have had twins together, a son and a daughter, now three years old, and are still married at this writing in 2016.

Moyer said that for him, it was "love at first bite" when he and Pacquin were filming the vampire movie "True Blood." "We were both single at the time, and there was just this kind of spark... by day three or four – oh, this is going to sound so syrupy – but I knew I wanted to spend the rest of my life with her. It was within seconds, really, and it just became a thing." She told him she was bisexual, but it didn't matter to him. From a previous marriage, he is also the father of young teenagers, a boy and a girl.

The Inner Woman -- "I just do what feels right. I think the great thing about getting to do what I do (*acting*) is that you can try out being a different person without having to screw up your life to do it."

"You'll live a full and happy life if you pursue things you think are important and live the life you want to live."

"I think it's an amazing quality to be able to roll with the punches and not be totally ruined as a person because life's been rough for you. That's a really admirable way to go through your life."

"You find happiness where you find it."

Dorothy Parker

Probably the wittiest woman in American literature, she was a totally feminine heterosexual, but married to a bisexual man. What she says in her articles and poems in the 1930's and 1940's about men and society's shortcomings are as timely as today.

"I require three things in a man: he must be handsome, ruthless, and stupid."

"Now I know the things I know, and I do the things I do; and if you do not like me so, to hell, my love, with you!"

"It serves me right for putting all my eggs in one bastard."

Born Dorothy Rothschild in Long Branch, New Jersey on August 22, 1893 to a father of German Jewish descent and a mother of Scottish descent, her mother died when Dorothy was four years old. Her father remarried in 1900, and Dorothy hated both him and her stepmother, referring to her as their housekeeper. She accused her father of being physically abusive to her.

Although she was part Jewish, she attended a Catholic high school where she became shockingly satiric, calling the Virgin Mary's Immaculate Conception "Spontaneous Combustion," for which she was expelled. Her stepmother died in 1903 and her father ten years later when she was 20 years old.

Her unhappy youth ended and in 1917 she met and married Wall Street stockbroker Edwin Pond Parker II, but they divorced in 1928. She became a humor writer for *The New Yorker* magazine and was a founding member of the legendary Algonquin Round Table and the only woman member of the luncheon club along with playwrights Robert E. Sherwood and Charles MacArthur, comic Harpo Marx, and writers Robert Benchley, Alexander Woolcott. Parker divorced her husband in 1928 and then had affairs with MacArthur, publisher Seward Collins and others. She became pregnant with MacArthur but had an abortion and was so depressed for that decision that she attempted suicide.

She recovered and married actor Alan Campbell in 1934. He was reported to be bisexual and Parker said in public that he was "queer as a billy goat." They went to Hollywood where they signed film contracts to write screenplays in which he earned $250 a week and she $1,000 a week. She wrote the script for the 1937 film "A Star Is Born," together with Campbell and Robert Carson, and they were nominated for an Academy Award for best screenplay writing. She received a similar nomination for "Smash-Up, the Story of a Woman" in 1947.

She divorced Campbell in 1947 after having found he was having a long-standing affair with a married woman. She then remarried Parker in 1950, but in 1961 reconciled with Campbell until his suicide by drug overdose in 1963. Parker died on June 7, 1967 from a heart attack at the age of 73. She left a fortune to Dr. Martin Luther King, Jr., and after his death her estate was passed on to the NAACP, The National Association for the Advancement of Colored People.

On Men -- "Men seldom make passes at girls who wear glasses."

On Love -- "Four be the things I'd have been better without: love, curiosity, freckles, and doubt."

The Inner Woman -- (*In later years, recalling her fellow members of The Roundtable in earlier years*): "These were no giants. Think who was writing in those days – (*Ring*) Lardner, (*F. Scott*) Fitzgerald, (*William*) Faulkner, (*Ernest*) Hemingway. Those were the real giants. The Round Table was just a lot of people telling jokes and telling each other how good they were... Just a bunch of loudmouths showing off... There was no truth in anything they said. It was the terrible day of the wisecrack, so there didn't have to be any truth."

(*On Hollywood*): :"The only 'ism' Hollywood believes in is plagiarism."

(*On most people*): "Their pooled emotions wouldn't fill a teaspoon."

"You can lead a horticulture, but you can't make her think."

"Beauty is only skin deep, but ugly goes clean to the bone."

"If you have any young friends who aspire to become writers, the second greatest favor you can do them is to present them with copies of *The Elements of Style*. The first greatest, of course, is to shoot them now, while they're happy."

"I'd like to have money. And I'd like to be a good writer. These two can come together, and I hope they will, but if that's too adorable, I'd rather have money."

"I hate writing, I love having written."

"The two most beautiful words in the English language are 'check enclosed."

"There's a hell of a distance between wise-cracking and wit. Wit has truth in it; wise-cracking is simply calisthenics with words."

"The best way to keep children at home is to make the home atmosphere pleasant, and let the air out of the tires."

"I'd rather have a bottle in front of me than a frontal lobotomy."

"Money cannot buy health, but I'd settle for a diamond-studded wheelchair."

(*Witty to the end, she had this epitaph on her grave marker read*): "Excuse my dust!"

Dolly Parton

Born poor and growing up on a farm in Tennessee, she overcame poverty and other obstacles to become a major star on stage and in films and on television, partly because of poking fun at herself, most notably her extra large breasts. She only married once, more than 40 years ago, and remains happily married. She often jokes about herself and men, from experience.

"I do have large boobs. Always had them. I've pushed them up, whacked them around Why not make fun of them? I've made a fortune with them."

"I was the first woman to burn my bra – it took the fire department four days to put it out."

"My weaknesses have always been food and men – in that order."

Born Dolly Rebecca Parton in Sevierville Tennessee on January 19, 1946, her tobacco farmer father had been one of fifteen children and her mother one of ten. Dolly became one of their twelve children,

Growing up in a small one-room house on a poor farm in Locust Ridge, in the heart of Smokey mountains. They gave each other I.O.U.'s for Christmas presents.

Her singing career began at the age of 12 on Knoxville television and a year later she began recording and appearing at the Grand Ole Opry. After high school, she moved to Nashville to further her singing career. She fell in love with Carl Dean who ran an asphalt street paving business, they married in 1966, and remain married at this writing.

In 1991 she began a ten-year stretch singing on the Porter Wagoner television show, then left and rose to fame as a singer and songwriter, winning many country music awards and became known as "The Iron Butterfly" and the "Queen of Country Music." Although only five feet tall, she was endowed with large breasts and became known as much for them as for her singing. She admitted to having breast implants, increasing her measurements from 38CC to 48DD.

She made several movies and founded Dollywood, a theme park in Pigeon Forge, Tennessee. The world's first cloned mammon, Dolly the sheep, was named at her. She was unable to bear children because of an allergic reaction to birth control pills, but has reared her and Dean's siblings, and has devoted time and money to children's literacy causes. She won a lifetime achievement award in 2007 from the Academy of Country Music.

The Inner Woman -- "I'm not offended by dumb blonde jokes because I know that I'm not dumb. I also know I'm not blonde."

"I describe my look as a blend of Mother Goose, Cinderella, and the local hooker!"

"I like to buy clothes that are two sizes too small and then take them in a little."

"If you don't like the road you're walking, start paving another one."

"A bird and a fish can fall in love, but where do they make a home?"

"I'm a homebody, and I'm family-oriented. I don't get out much unless it's a special occasion. So I guess people might be surprised at just how calm I really am."

"I like a lot of makeup. I like a lot of hair. I like flashy clothes. I like to show off. That's who I am."

"If you want to see the rainbow, you gotta put up with the rain."

Princess Diana

Unhappy in marriage, she found love outside of it after taking off the wedding ring. Like the *Mona Lisa*, she was enigmatic, and herself a woman with a lot of love to give, to her husband who didn't it want it, at least not from her. She became one of the great women survivors although, sadly, not for long.

"When Charles proposed marriage, I repeatedly told him I loved him. He replied, 'Whatever love means.'"

"I know that I can give love for a minute, for half an hour; for a day, for a month, but I can give and I'm very happy to do that and I want to do that. If you find someone you love in your life, then hang on to that love."

"There were three of us in this marriage, so it was a bit crowded. I want to knock her block off."

"Being a princess isn't all it's cracked up to be."

Born Diana Frances Spencer in Park House, Sandringham, Norfolk, England to British aristocrats Francies Roche and John Spencer, then Viscount Althrop, he had wanted a son and heir, not a daughter. She grew up in a family with close ties to the royal family since her parents' home was next door to the royal family's summer residence.

Her parents divorced in 1969 when she was six years old and she said she could never forget the sight of her mother leaving with luggage, never to return. Her mother had been having an affair with another man whom she later married after her divorce from Spencer. Her father won custody of Diana and her older sister and brother because of her mother's infidelity.

Her parents' divorce remained an emotional scar in Diana as she felt abandoned and not wanted. Feelings of low self-esteem caused her to develop bulimia nervosa, an eating disorder in which she went on eating binges, then to avoid putting on extra weight she threw up.

She became Lady Diana Spencer when her father inherited the title of the 8th Earl of Spencer in 1975 when she was 14. She attended a private high school and then a finishing school in Switzerland. Diana met Prince Charles at a royal family event at Sandrigham; they began dating and became engaged in 1981. Their marriage when she was 20 in 1981 at St. Paul's Cathedral in London in the Church of England religion and the event was watched on television by almost a billion people around the world.

Charles had relationships with a number of women in his youth. His great-uncle Lord Mountbatten advised him: "A man should sow his wild oats and have as many affairs as he can before settling down, but for a wife he must choose a suitable, attractive, and sweet-charactered girl before she has met anyone else she might fall for… It is disturbing for women to have experiences if they have to remain on a pedestal after marriage."

Charles took his favorite uncle's advice and married Diana, although his heart settled on Camilla Parker whom he met at a polo match in 1970 and loved ever since. She married British Army officer Andrew Parker Bowles in 1973 with whom she had two children, and Charles married Diana eight years later, in 1981. Camilla and Bowles divorced in 1995.

Diana met the royal criteria for his bride, being titled and single and, he hoped fertile so that she could give him a son and heir, if and when he became king of England. Charles nonetheless panicked that he was rushing into a marriage with a girl he hardly knew. Diana, however, appeared to be genuinely in love with him. Both did consider calling off the wedding because each knew their relationship was deeply flawed because of his feelings for Camilla. Regarding Diana, Charles had only briefly courted her and they had been engaged for only five months and he found that she was "not the jolly country girl he had assumed" but instead was a vulnerable, complicated woman.

Diana shared Charles' doubts about marrying, later telling her biographer Andrew Morton: "I can't marry him, I can't do this, this is absolutely impossible." But she was told it was too late to back out because "Your face is (*already*) on the tea towels." A confidant said later, "She had no idea her bridegroom also had to be coaxed to the altar." Diana became loved by the public, but after her marriage, remained uncertain about Charles' love for her, since he was often seen with Camilla.

Diana gave birth to two sons, first to Prince William and then two years later to Prince Henry "Harry." Diana said that when Charles saw that he was the father of another boy, he seemed disinterested and went off to play polo after learning of Harry's birth. It reminded her that her father had not wanted her, but a son.

The so-called "fairy tale" marriage continued to go downhill as Charles kept seeing Camilla, and he and Diana separated in 1992. Four years later, at Queen Elizabeth's urging, they divorced on August 28, 1996.. She was given a generous settlement and was allowed to keep her title of "Princess of Wales," but agreed to give up the title of "Her Royal Highness" if Charles became king. This required her, officially, to curtsey to others in the royal family including Charles and even her children, to whom she had been given equal access with Charles.

Diana continued her charitable work but was still constantly followed by photographers, as she had been during her marriage. Trying to escape them, she died in an automobile crash in a Paris tunnel on August 31, 1997 at the age of 36. She was in a car with her then-boyfriend Dodi Fayed, a wealthy Saudi Arabian.

An investigation found that the driver had been under the influence of alcohol at the time of the crash. The world mourned her as being a "Princess of the People." Charles kept seeing Camilla after Diana's death and they married in 2005.

On Men -- "People think that at the end of the day a man is the only answer. Actually, a fulfilling job is better for me."

On Marriage -- "To me, marriage seems to be the biggest and most responsible step to be taken in one's life."

"It wasn't a difficult decision for me (*marriage with Charles*). It was what I wanted."

"The night before the wedding, I had a bad attack of nerves. (*She had doubts that Charles loved her and that instead he was in love with Camilla Parker-Bowles*).

"I had a very bad fit of bulimia the night before the wedding. I ate everything I could possibly find. I was sick as a parrot that night.
The next morning, I felt I was a lamb to the slaughter. I knew it, and couldn't do anything about it. Walking down the aisle, I saw Camilla sitting among the guests and knew Charles had given her a ring.
(*She wondered if the ring symbolized that in his mind, Charles was also marrying Camilla.*)

"The bulimia continued on our honeymoon and throughout the marriage. I had it for years before I met Charles, from childhood anxieties from feeling unwanted because I was born a girl instead of a boy, the trauma of my parents' divorce, and not feeling wanted or loved by my husband. The Camilla thing. I was desperate, desperate."

On Divorce -- "I think like any marriage, especially when you've had divorced parents like myself, you want to try even harder to make it work."

The Inner Woman -- "Call me Diana. Not Princess Diana."

"Everyone needs to be valued. Everyone has the potential to give something back."

"Carry out a random act of kindness, with no expectation of reward, safe in the knowledge that one day someone might do the same for you."

"Only do what your heart tells you."

"Life is just a journey."

"I have a woman's instinct and it's always a good one."

"It's not sissy to show your feeling."

"I'm absolutely petrified of the Queen (*Elizabeth II*). I shake all over when I'm in her presence. I can't look her in the eye, and just go to pieces whenever she comes into the room. She tries to be nice and put me at my ease, but I am so embarrassed when I am with her."

"I'm lucky enough in the fact that I have found my role… I love being with people. I knew what my job was. It was to go out and meet the people and love them."

"It's vital that the monarchy keeps in touch with the people. It's what I try to do."

"I resented that I was never encouraged by the royal family or anyone. I was shy inside and cried for an hour before every function. After a while, I was instructed not to make any public statements except those approved beforehand by the palace. I also was not allowed to give any private interviews to reporters. I felt isolated and began to call myself the PoW, or Prisoner of Wales."

"I don't go by the rule book. I lead from the heart, not the head. I wear my heart on my sleeve."

"Helping people in need is a good and essential part of my life, a kind of destiny."

"Hugs can do great amounts of good -- especially for children… I always feed my children love and affection. It's so important."

Queen Elizabeth II of England

Few women have ever done it better or longer, being a queen. Despite her dowdy dresses and hats to laugh at, she has retained her regal stature and status not only with the British people but worldwide. And she has done it through wars and being married just once, to the right man. It's unlikely that she is ever alone in a public ladies' room, but maybe she talks to herself there. And believe it or not, she has a sense of humor and at times uses some pretty frank language.

"This thing called love, it cries like a baby in a cradle all night. It swings, it jives, it shales all over like a jelly fish. I kinda like it."

"My husband has quite simply been my strength and stay all these years, and I owe him a debt greater than he would ever claim."

"I have to be seen to be believed."

Born Elizabeth Alexandra Mary on April 21, 1926 of Caesarian section in the London home of King George V, her paternal grandfather. Her father was Prince Albert, Duke of York, the second son of King George V, and her mother Elizabeth, Duchess of Kent. Baptized in the Anglican Church, she was named Elizabeth after her mother and Mary after her paternal grandmother, but her close family called her "Lilibet." Her only sibling, Princess Margaret, was born in 1930. The princesses were educated at home under the supervision of their mother and governesses, taught history, language, literature, and music.

Described at an early age as being sensible and well-behaved,, Elizabeth loved horses and dogs. Her father acceded to the throne upon the abdication of his brother Edward VIII in 1936 in order to marry the British divorcee Wallace Simpson. Upon her father's death in 1952 Elizabeth became Queen of the United Kingdom, Canada, Australia, and New Zealand. She married Philip, Duke of Edinburgh, with whom she had four children: Charles, Anne, Andrew, and Edward.

In 2016 she was Britain's longest-lived monarch, surpassing her great-great-grandmother Queen Victoria, and also became the longest reigning queen in world history, celebrating her Diamond Jubilee in 2012. She gets a little personal at times in her quotes and also shows a delightful sense of humor.

On Marriage -- (*Her poem to her husband*):

"Ooh, you're the best friend that I ever had
I've been with you such a long time
You're my sunshine and I want you to know
That my feelings are true
I really love you
Oh, you're my best friend."

The Inner Woman -- "We lost the American colonies because we lacked the statesmanship to know the right time and the manner of yielding what is impossible to keep."

"To all those who have suffered as a consequence of our troubled past I extend my sincere thoughts and deep sympathy. With the benefit of historical hindsight we can all see things which we would wish had been done differently, or not at all."

(*Upon becoming queen*): "I declare before you all that my whole life, whether it be long or short, shall be devoted to your service and the service of our great imperial family to which we all belong."

"I cannot lead you into battle. I do not give you laws or administer justice, but I can do something else – I can give my heart and my devotion to these old lands and to all the peoples of our brotherhood of nations."

"The world is not the most pleasant place. Eventually your parents leave you and nobody is going to go out of their way to protect you unconditionally. You need to learn to stand up for yourself and what you believe, and sometimes, pardon my language, kick some ass."

"I know of no single formula for success. But over the years I have observed that some attributes of leadership are universal and are often about finding ways of encouraging people to combine their efforts, their talents, their insights, their enthusiasm and their inspiration to work together."

"When life seems hard, the courageous do not lie down and accept defeat; instead, they are all the more determined to struggle for a better future."

"It's all to do with training: you can do a lot if you're properly trained."

"Good memories are our second chance at happiness."

"Like all the best families, we have our share of eccentricities of impetuous and wayward youngsters and of family disagreements."

(*On being criticized for her serious expression*): "I simply ache from smiling. Why are women expected to beam all the time? It's unfair. If a man looks solemn, it's automatically assumed he's a serious person, not a miserable one."

"Family does not necessarily mean blood relatives, but often a description of a community, organization, or nation."

"It has been women who have breathed gentleness and care into the hard progress of humankind."

"Let us not take ourselves too seriously. None of us has a monopoly on wisdom."

"True patriotism doesn't exclude an understanding of the patriotism of others."

"Work is the rent you pay for the room you occupy on earth."

"For Christians, as for all people of faith, reflection, meditation, and prayer helps us to renew ourselves in God's love, as we strive daily to become better people. The Christmas message shows us that this love is for everyone. There is no one beyond its reach."

"To what greater inspiration and counsel can we turn than to the imperishable truth to be found in this treasure house, the *Bible*?"

"For me, heaven is likely to be a bit of a come-down."

(*When an intruder entered her bedroom in 1982*): "I realized immediately it wasn't a servant because they don't slam doors."

"The upward course of a nation's history is due in the long run to the soundness of heart of its average men and women."

(*After being criticized for not responding faster to Princess Diana's death*): "First, I want to pay tribute to Diana myself. She was an exceptional and gifted human being. In good times and bad, she never lost her capacity to smile and laugh, nor to inspire others with her warmth and kindness. I admired and respected her – for her energy and commitment to others, and especially for her devotion to her two boys.

"I hope that tomorrow we can all, wherever we are, join in expressing our grief at Diana's loss, and gratitude for her all-too-short life. It is a chance to show to the whole world the British nation united in grief and respect."

"Grief is the price we pay for love."

(*To a photographer, each time she sits for a portrait*): "Now then, with teeth, or without?"

Ayn Rand

Few people knew the enigmatic Ayn Rand, and perhaps fewer understood the depths of her writing, but basically she believed in independent men and women.

"I swear by my life and my love of it that I will never live for the sake of another man, nor ask another man to live for mine."

"To say 'I love you,' one must know first how to say the 'I.'"

"Love is blind, they say; sex is impervious to reason and mocks the power of all philosophers. But, in fact, a person's sexual choice is

the result and sum of their fundamental convictions. Tell me what a person finds sexually attractive and I will tell you their entire philosophy of life. Show me the person they sleep with and I will tell you their value of themselves."

Born Alisa Zinov'yevna Rosenbaum in Russia on February 2, 1905, she was the eldest of three daughters born to a pharmacist and his wife, both non-observant Jews. She was bored with school and began writing novels and screenplays when she was eight. The Russian Revolution broke out in 1917 when she was 12 and she preferred Alexander Kerensky over Czar Nicholas II.

She emigrated to the United States in 1926 when she was 21 and continued writing plays and novels. She had a play produced on Broadway in 1935 and had two unsuccessful novels published before she became famous for her 1957 novel, *Atlas Shrugged*, and also *The Fountainhead* which was made into a film starring Gary Cooper, and for which she wrote the screenplay. Among her other screenplays was "Love Letters," a 1945 paranormal romance with Jennifer Jones and Joseph Cotten for which she was nominated for an Academy Award for best screenplay.

After writing *Atlas Shrugged,* she fell into a deep depression. It became her final work of fiction and she turned from being a novelist to a popular philosopher.

She was married to actor Frank O'Connor from 1928 until his death in 1979, but had an affair of several years with Nathaniel Braden who shared her philosophy which she called Objectivism and in 1958 he established an institute to promote it with lectures and books.

Some considered Objectivism to be a cult or religion as Rand took strong positions on subjects from literature and music to sexuality. She believed that reason is the only way to gain knowledge, while rejecting spiritual faith and religion. She considered political force and war to be immoral, and supported laissez-faire capitalism. That is French for "leave alone," meaning that the government leaves the people alone regarding all economic activities; a separation of economy and state.

Rand became active in anti-Communist movements in the United States, and while critics were mixed on her literary works, she was a strong influence on American conservatives.

She believed in women's rights but was opposed to abortion, the Vietnam War, and called homosexuality both "immoral" and "disgusting. Her affair with Branden ended when he began having relations with another woman, criticizing him for being dishonest and for his "irrational behavior in his private life." She was a heavy smoker, under went surgery for lung cancer, and died at her home in New York City of heart failure on March 6, 1982.

On Love, Sex, and Men -- "No matter what corruption they'e taught about the virtue of selflessness, sex is the most profoundly selfish of all acts, an act which they cannot perform for any motive but their own enjoyment – just try to think of performing it in a spirit of selfless charity! – an act which is not possible in self-abasement, only in self-exultation, only on the confidence of being desired and being worthy of desire. It is an act that forces them to stand naked in spirit, as well as in body, and accept their real ego as their standard of value. They will always be attracted to the person who reflects their deepest vision of themselves, the person whose surrender permits them to experience – or to fake – a sense of self-esteem. Love is our response to our highest values—and can be nothing else."

The Inner woman -- (*On the theme of* Atlas Shrugged): "(*It was about*) The role of the mind in man's existence – and, as a corollary, the demonstration of a new moral philosophy, the morality of rational self-interest." (*The basic tents of her philosophy of Objectivism.*)

(*On Objectivism*): "The concept of man as a heroic being, with his own happiness as the moral purpose of his life, with productive achievement as his noblest activity, and reason as his only absolute."

"The question isn't who is going to let me; it's who is going to stop me."

(*From* Atlas Shrugged*):* "Do not let your fire go out, spark by irreplaceable spark in the hopeless swamps of the not-quite, the not-yet, and the not-at-all. Do not let the hero in your soul perish in lonely frustration for the life you deserted and have never been able to reach. The world you desire can be won. It exists... it is real...it is possible... it's yours.

"If you tell a beautiful woman that she is beautiful, what have you given her? It's no more than a fact and it has cost you nothing. But if you tell an ugly woman that she is beautiful, you offer her the great homage of corrupting the concept of beauty.

"To love a woman for her virtues is meaningless. She's earned it, it's a payment, not a gift. But to love her for her vices is a real gift, unearned and undeserved. To love her for her vices is to defile all virtue for her sake – and that is a real tribute of love, because you sacrifice your conscience, your reason, your integrity and your invaluable self-esteem."

"Learn to value yourself, which remains: fight for your happiness."

"My happiness is not the means to any end. It is the end. It is its own goal. It is its own purpose."

"I regret nothing, There have been things I missed, but I ask no questions, because I have loved it (*her life*) such as it has been, even the moments of emptiness, even the unanswered – and that I loved it, that is the unanswered in my life."

Nancy Reagan

A one-man woman whose father's name was "Loyal," she was totally that to her only husband, letting both her heart and the stars rule him after he left off being a movie star and took up residence in the Oval Office of the White House for eight years. Afterward, through his illness, she continued to love and nursed him until his death. Even to those whose politics differed from her's and her husband's, she was admired for her steadfastness in giving Ronald Reagan what he wanted most – a loving wife.

"Our relationship is very special. We were very much in love and still are. When I say my life began with Ronnie, well, it's true. It did. I can't imagine life without him."

"Everything just fell into place with Ronnie and me. We completed each other."

"I knew that being his wife was the role I wanted to play."

Born Anne Frances Robbins at Sloane Hospital for Women in New York City on July 6, 1921, from her birth she was called Nancy. Her father was Kenneth Seymour Robbins, a car salesman, and her mother an actress, Edith Luckett. Her parents separated and her mother traveled to find work, leaving Nancy to be reared her first years of life with an aunt and uncle in Bethesda, Maryland. Her parents divorced when she was seven years old in 1928. She missed her mother very much during her girlhood. Her mother married Loyal Davis, a prominent neurosurgeon in 1929 and they remained married until his death in 1982. He formally adopted Nancy, giving her his last name.

The Daviess moved to Chicago and she grew up liking her stepfather very much, calling him "a man of integrity who exemplified old-fashioned values." She graduated from the Girls' Latin School of Chicago in 1939 and then from Smith College in Massachusetts in 1943 where she majored in English and drama. She then worked as a sales clerk at Marshall Field's department store in Chicago and then as a nurse's aide.

Her mother's stage acting friends, actress Zasu Pitts and actors Walter Huston and Spencer Tracy, encouraged her to become an actress and she acted in stage plays and musicals before becoming a film actress in the 1940s and 1950s, never becoming a real star despite her dark-haired beauty. During Nancy's years as an actress, she dated several actors including Robert Stack, Peter Lawford, and Clark Gable, who she called the nicest of the stars she had met. She and Ronald Reagan made one film together, ten years before their marriage, "Hellcats of the Navy," a 1942 World War II submarine adventure.

She met Reagan again in 1949 when she was a member of the Screen Actors Guild, of which he was then president. They began dating but Reagan was marriage-shy after his divorce from actress

Jane Wyman to whom he had been married from 1940 to 1948. He eventually proposed to Nancy in their favorite booth at Chasen's, a Beverly Hills restaurant.

After three years of dating, the Reagan's were married on March 4, 1952 in a small ceremony, the only guests being his best friend William Holden as best man and Holden's then-wife actress Brenda Marshall as matron of honor. Their first child, Patricia Ann Reagan, was born two months after their marriage and became as an adult an actress known as Patti Davis. Their son, Ronald Prescott Reagan, was born six years later, in 1958. He married and became a liberal news commentator on radio and television. Nancy also became stepmother to Reagan's children by Wyman, their birth daughter Maureen Reagan and adopted son Michael Reagan.

Reagan left films to enter politics and became governor of California from 1967 to 1975, then President of the United States, and Nancy was America's First Lady during his two terms in the presidency from 1981 to 1989. After his presidency they retired to a home in Bel Air, Los Angeles, and he was diagnosed with Alzheimer's disease in 1994. Nancy then spent most of her time caring for him until his death at the age of 93 in 2004.

Since then she has been active with the Reagan Library and supporting embryonic stem cell research. Upon Reagan's death in 2004, it ended what their friend actor Charlton Heston called "The greatest love affair in the history of the American Presidency." Nancy Reagan died at home in Los Angeles on March 6, 2016 of congestive heart failure at the age of 94.

On Her Marriage to Reagan -- "What can you say about a man who on Mother's Day sends flowers to his mother-on-law, with a note thanking her for making him the happiest man on the Earth?"

"My job is being 'Mrs. Ronald Reagan.'"

"For eight years, I was sleeping with the President, and if that doesn't give you special access, I don't know what does!"

(*About the 1981 assassination attempt on Reagan, she wrote in her diary*): "Nothing can happen to my Ronnie. My life would be over."

(*In a letter to her, he wrote*): "Whatever I treasure and enjoy…all would be without meaning if I didn't have you."

The Inner Woman -- (*About her childhood*): "My favorite times were when Mother had a job in New York, and Aunt Virgie (*her mother's sister*), would take me by train to stay with her."

"I think a woman gets more if she acts feminine."

"I chose to have a (*film*) career, and I enjoyed it while I had it. The movies were custard pie compared to politics."

"It is true that when you're in the White House alone, it is a lonely place. Big and lonely."

"When people say, 'You have Alzheimer's,' you have no idea what Alzheimer's is. You know it's not good. You know there's no light at the end of the tunnel. That's the only way you can go. But you really don't know anything about it. And you don't know what to expect. You have to be very careful what you say when you're looking at them over their bed. Because once in a while, they understand it."

"I have been criticized and ridiculed for turning to astrology, but after a while, I reached the point where I didn't care."

"Embryonic stem cell research has the potential to alleviate so much suffering. Surely, by working together, we can harness its life-giving potential."

"Feminism is the ability to choose what you want to do."

"I'm against abortion. On the other hand, I believe in a woman's choice. I do not believe in abortion at will. I do not believe that if a woman just wants to have an abortion, she should. I do believe if you have an abortion you are committing murder."

"I am a big believer that eventually everything comes back to you. You get back what you give out."

"Just say no to drugs!"

"To my young friends out there: Life can be great, but not when you can't see it. So, open your eyes to life; to see if in the vivid colors that God gave us as a precious gift to His children, to enjoy life to the fullest, and to make it count. Say yes to your life."

"There's a big, wonderful world out there for you. It belongs to you. It's exciting and stimulating and rewarding. Don't cheat yourselves out of this promise."

Debbie Reynolds

Three times married and divorced, her public loved her more than her husbands. She was, like one of the real-life women who did not go down with the *Titanic* sinking, portraying her in the 1964 film, "The Unsinkable Molly Brown," a survivor.

(At age 82, about why her marriages failed): *"My three husbands all left me for another woman and obviously I wasn't a very sexual lady. My husbands all repeatedly said the same thing, that I was not a very passionate woman."*

(Reynolds said she is fine with her lack of passion): *"I have never wished that I had more sex. I was never a sex queen in real life and I was never pursued by men. I was friends with Elizabeth Taylor, Ava Gardner, and Lana Turner, and they craved and loved sex and talked about it. They were very sensuous women, desiring passion. It seemed that I was more interested in raising my children, not in pursuing my husbands."*

Born Mary Frances Reynolds in El Paso, Texas on April 1, 1932, she was the second child of a carpenter for the Southern Pacific Railroad and his wife. She won a beauty contest when she was 16 impersonating vivacious Betty Hutton and began appearing in MGM movies as a sweet, innocent teenager. She became a beloved star when she was not yet 20, dancing in films for the first time, opposite Gene Kelly in "Singin' in the Rain" (1952) which catapulted her to stardom in the satire of the earl days of talking pictures which has become one of the most loved musicals in movie history. She scored with the public and critics again as "The Unsinkable Molly Brown" (1964) when she was only 31 and won a best actress Academy Award nomination for her lively performance.

Her personal life, however, was not as bright. She married singer-actor Eddie Fisher in 1955 but lost him to Elizabeth Taylor in 1959. Her second husband, shoe magnet Harry Karl (1960-1973) lost both her fortune and his through gambling. She married Richard Hamlett in 1984 but they divorced in 1996. She had a son by Fisher and a daughter, actress Carrie Fisher who became famous as Princess Leia in "Star Wars" (1977).

Debbie opened a museum in Las Vegas with her large collection of movie memorabilia including more than 3,000 famous film costumes and accessories such as Judy Garland's ruby red slippers from "The Wizard of Oz," hundreds of movie posters, and film equipment from silent films to the 1970s.

Her collection was then housed in Hollywood in 1997 but it has been financially difficult for her. She has devoted most of her time and money to the movie museum, sometimes so broke that she lived in her automobile. She has plans to reopen the museum in Hollywood near Graumam's Chinese Theater.

Reynolds is active in The Thalians, an organization for the treatment of mental health. In recent years, she has appeared in television shows including "Will and Grace." She and Elizabeth Taylor had a much-publicized falling out over losing Eddie Fisher to her, but they reconciled years later while on a cruise ship together. They then appeared together in a television movie, "These Old Broads" (2001) Reynolds is active in The Thalians, an organization for the treatment of mental health. In recent years, she has appeared in television shows including "Will and Grace."

She and Elizabeth Taylor had a much-publicized falling out over losing Eddie Fisher to her, but they reconciled years later while on a cruise ship together. They then appeared together in a television movie, "These Old Broads" (2001) written by Carrie Fisher. Reynolds has been awarded a Lifetime Achievement award from the Screen Actors Guild.

The Inner Woman -- "I stopped making movies because I didn't like taking my clothes off. Maybe it's realism, but in my opinion it's utter filth."

"Making 'Singin' in the Rain' and childbirth were the two hardest things I ever had to do in my life."

"I loved going to the movies (*while growing up*). I always had a thing for a fairy-tale ending."

(*On Carrie Fisher*): "People used to call her 'Debbie Reynolds' daughter.' Now they call me 'Princess Leia's mother!'"

(*On reconciling with Elizabeth Taylor*): "Elizabeth and I went on a cruise ship... she sent a note to me and I sent a note to her to say, 'Let's just forget about it.' She had her good side. At least once she got over her sex drive." (*In her will, Taylor left Reynolds a sapphire bracelet, necklace and earring as symbols of their renewed friendship.*)

Joan Rivers

Another woman who was unlucky in marriage, she never lost her sense of humor about men and life., even gaining fame and fortune from laughing at them and it.

"A man can sleep around, no questions asked, but if a woman makes nineteen or twenty mistakes, she's a tramp."

"I blame my mother for my poor sex life. All she told me was 'The man does it on top and the woman underneath.' For three years my husband and I slept in bunk beds."

"It's so long since I've had sex, I've forgotten who ties up who."

Born Joan Alexandra Molinsky in Brooklyn, New York City, on June 8, 1933 to a doctor and his wife, both Russian Jewish immigrants. She was a shoe buyer for Lord & Taylor department store in Manhattan before entering show business as a comedienne, first on radio and then as a stand-up comic, appearing in clubs and then on television. She won a Daytime Emmy Award in 1990 for best talk show host and was nominated for a Tony Award and a Grammy Award for best comedy recording. Rivers authored several self-help and humor books as well as an autobiography.

She had cosmetic plastic surgery many times including an eye-lift and had her nose thinned, and joked about it. She advocated plastic surgery for older women saying that if a woman can afford it, it is worth it for her self-esteem. She also had Botox and collagen injections every four months from a dermatologist. She developed the eating disorder, bulimia nervosa, and thought of committing suicide, but recovered through counseling and the support of her family.

When she was 22, she met department store heir James Bennat Sanger in August 1955, they were married in September, and the marriage was annulled after six months because he did not want to have children, but had not told her that before their wedding. She then married film and television producer Edgar Rosenberg in 1965 and had a daughter with him. The marriage lasted 22 years until he committed suicide in 1987 shortly after she said she wanted them to separate.

She had several affairs during their marriage including one night with actor Robert Mitchum in the 1960s and also had an affair with actor Gabriel Dell, the best-looking of the grown-up Bowery Boys in the films. Active in various social causes, she was a strong supporter of AIDS/HIV research, was the national spokesperson for the Cystic Fibrosis Foundation and served as an honorary member of the American Foundation for Suicide Prevention.

During minor surgery at an outpatient clinic in 2014 she stopped breathing and was put on life support. She died on September 4, 2014 of anoxic encephalopathy after a reportedly unnecessary and botched operation while in a medically-induced coma at the age of 81. Many of the greats of show business attended her funeral. Her daughter Melissa said after Joan's death, "My mother's greatest joy in life was to make people laugh. Although that is difficult to do right now, I know her final wish would be that we return to laughing soon."

On Men -- "Forty for you, sixty for me. And equal partners we will be."

"Men who look down my dress usually compliment me on my shoes."

(*Joking*): "My husband wanted to be cremated. I told him I'd scatter his ashes at Neiman Marcus (*the department store*). That way, I'd visit him every day."

On Love ((*Also joking*) -- "Before we make love, my husband takes a pain killer."

The Inner Woman -- "The first time I heard of Madonna, I thought she was a nun. Nowadays, people wonder, What has Madonna got? Has she got beauty, talent, charisma? The correct answer is: Nun of the above."

"Madonna and Sean Penn – beauty and the beast, but guess which one?"

"Liz Taylor should be grateful to me… my jokes are one the reasons she went on a diet. It was embarrassing. When I took her to Sea World and Shama the Whale jumped out of the water, she asked if it came with vegetables."

(*On childbirth*): "Knock me out with the first pain, and wake me up when the hairdresser arrives."

"I'm very competitive. And I think that's what has kept me going. I'm not gracious. The only thing that's saving me is my age. Because I don't care. I've been up, I've been down. I've been fired. I've been hired. I've been broke. What are you gonna do to me? Not like me? I don't give a damn."

"That awful, vulgar, loud woman on stage, that's not me. I wouldn't want to be her friend."

"With all the plastic surgery I've had, I'm worried that when I die, God won't recognize me!"

"I don't exercise. If God had wanted me to bend over, he would have put diamonds on the floor."

"The first time I see a jogger smiling, I'll consider it."

"My best birth control now is just to leave the lights on."

"Yesterday is history, tomorrow is a mystery, today is God's gift, that's why they call it the present."

"I enjoy life when things are happening. I don't care if it's good things or bad things. That means you're alive."

"I hate housework! You make the beds, you do the dishes and six months later you have to start all over again."

"Life goes by so fast. Enjoy it. Calm down. It's all funny. Everyone gets so upset about the wrong things."

"People say that money is not the key to happiness, but I always figured if you have enough money, you can have a key made."

"Don't follow any advice, no matter how good, until you feel as deeply in your spirit as you think in your mind that the counsel is wise."

"Never floss with a stranger."

"I'm grateful for every day I'm still alive. Everything is still working. I attribute it to eating a lot of processed foods. I think it's the preservatives that keep me going. That, and I eat as much chocolate as I can get my hands on."

"Life is very tough. If you don't laugh, it's tough."

"I have no methods; all I do is accept people as they are."

"I never dwell on what happened. You can't change it. Move forward. Don't waste your energy on being angry at something that somebody did six months ago or a year ago. It's over. Done. Move forward."

On her marriage to Rosenberg -- "My husband and I had always worked wonderfully together, I on stage and Edgar behind the scenes. Ours was the kind you rarely see in Hollywood: genuine, deep, and abiding. We loved each other and our daughter (*Melissa*), we loved the life we had built for ourselves, and the way we had seamlessly blended career and family. Like any couple, we had our fights and rough times. But we were as good a team as two people who live and work together can be."

(*On his emotional decline and death*): "I was losing everything – my best friend, the only stability in my life, the only person I totally trusted, my rock. Suddenly I realized that I drew all my strength from Edgar."

"It was only in the weeks and months after Edgar's death that I realized that every widow's experiences are as unique as the marriage she had."

"Edgar suffered greatly and changed from a secure man into a self-doubting, bitter, and depressed one. He was angry all the time and frequently turned his anger on me. His black moods lasted longer and longer, until they were no longer moods but an endless dependency. It was so painful for me to see Edgar in such misery – painful and frightening. What had happened to the man I had known and loved for so many years?

"All that summer I tried desperately to convince him to get psychiatric care, something beyond his occasional talks with a psychologist, but he ignored my pleas. Finally, I had to accept the fact that Edgar was a drowning man, and that he was taking me down with him, to the bottom of a sea of despair where I could be no good to him, to myself, or to our daughter. I was so weary of fighting him, so tired of trying to help someone who refused my outstretched hand and my support, that I simply did not know how I could continue."

"From the moment I heard about Edgar's suicide, many different emotions kept me from thinking clearly. First, I was overcome by despair. And then came the anger. At first I felt guilty about being angry, but I've since learned that it's all right and even healthy to feel anger at someone who has died, whether from suicide, sickness, or old age."

(*She wrote to her daughter in her book* From Mother to Daughter: Thoughts and Advice on Life, Love, and Marriage): "Most healing processes begin with laughter. Laughter kept your father and me going for twenty unforgettable years... until, tragically, he stopped laughing."

(*Also to her daughter*): "Whether the latter part of this cycle (*of life or marriage*) takes a loved one from you or John (*her daughter's husband*) my darling, always remember that the human heart is our strongest organ, for it is indomitable. The musicians are right: *The beat goes on*. There is life after pain, after loss, after death. And no matter how dark things become, sunny days and laughter always, always return. God will help us turn the page to begin the new chapter."

"Once they're dead, death just scrubs (*celebrities*) clean. Everybody says, 'Oh, they were wonderul.' Suddenly, Grace Kelly didn't drink."

Julia Roberts

After several engagements to other men, she got lucky in marriage the second time around. The famous "Pretty Woman" has become a role model for all women who won't quit until Cupid gets it right for them.

"You know it's love when all you want is that person to be happy, even if you're not part of their happiness."

"I believe that two people are connected at the heart, and it doesn't matter what you do, or who you are, or where you live; there are no boundaries or barriers if two people are destined to be together."

"If you love someone, you say it, right then, out loud. Otherwise, the moment just passes you by."

"True love doesn't come to you. It has to be inside you."

Born Julia Fiona Roberts on October 28, 1967 in Smyrna, Georgia, her father was a vacuum cleaner salesman and her mother a real estate agent and then a stage actress and acting coach. When she was a little girl loving animals she wanted to become a veterinarian but later studied journalism. When her brother, Eric Roberts, became an actor in Hollywood she decided to become an actress.

Her break came in the 1988 film "Mystic Pizza" and she went on to superstardom in "Pretty Woman" in 1990 and was nominated for an Academy Award as best actress. She won the best actress Oscar in 2000 for "Erin Brockovich," playing the real life whistle blower on fuel contamination. She married singer-song writer Lyle Lovett in 1993 but they divorced in 1995. She then lived with actor Niam Neeson and was briefly engaged to actor Kiefer Sutherland and later engaged to actor Dylan McDermott before marrying cinematographer Daniel Moder in 2002 and they have had three children together including twins, a boy and a girl.

Besides continuing to star in films as perhaps America's favorite film star, she has become active with UNICEF charities and visited

Besides continuing to star in films as perhaps America's favorite film star, she has become active with UNICEF charities and visited many countries to promote goodwill. She also raises money to research a cure for Rett Syndrome, a potentially fatal disease that randomly strikes girls aged 2 to 6 years. She has been named as one of the 50 Most Beautiful People in the World, is among the ten top box office stars, earning $20 million per film. She has a ranch with Moder in Taos, New Mexico and a home in New York City.

The Inner Woman -- "I'm just an ordinary person who has an extraordinary job. I get dressed up like a doll, a nice man puts lipstick on my lips, and I say words. It's deeply satisfying."

(*On never doing a nude scene*): "I just don't feel that my algebra teacher should ever know what my butt looks like."

(*On her marriage to Moder):* "We are happy as clams. I am fulfilled by my own life on an hourly basis. Every little moment is amazing if you let yourself access it. I learn that all the time from my kids; children are so filled with wonder. My youngest son woke up at 5 a.m. the other morning and said to me, 'It's a beautiful day, Mama!' What's more precious than that?"

"I believe that the way you feel about your life will eventually show up on your face."

(*On managing work, fame, and family*): "Family values. That's actually values in general. That's all there is. Fame is just a summer breeze that comes and goes. But to have a bedrock of knowing who you are, that's what it's all about."

(*On working with Meryl Streep in the 2013 film "August: Osage County"*): "I've never seen anyone work harder than she does. She doesn't just snap her fingers and be a genius. To work with Meryl Streep is a dream come true. To know her is an honor. She is such a beautiful person."

"It's my privilege and honor to cook three meals a day for my family, and it's a luxury on a level that I didn't even realize, because it can be relentless for me on some days. You have pride in how you take care of your family."

"The older you get, the more fragile you understand life to be. I think that's good motivation for getting out of bed joyfully each day."

(*She loves to shop*): "Show me a mall, and I'm happy."

"I think less is more, when it comes to kissing in the movies."

"I think that I am a deeply optimistic person."

"I am completely happy with my life. I love everything about it."

Jane Russell

The buxom brunette film sex goddess of the 1940's and 1950's even survived millionaire womanizer Howard Hughes who made her a star with the help of her cleavage. She found happiness in two marriages but the one that lasted longest and best was her third. When she learned she was unable to conceive, she adopted three children.

"I was born to be married."

"I have always believed that every girl should marry, and that marriage should come first. You're made that way. Your constitution and needs are set up that way. Of course, a girl has to take on the responsibilities of marriage to make it successful and happy. You can't say to a marriage, 'stay there until I get through working and have time for you,' nor can you be geared to thinking only of yourself."

Born Ernestine Jane Geraldine Russell on June 21, 1921 in Bemidji, Minnesota her father was a U.S. Army lieutenant and her mother an actress with a traveling stage group. After her father left the army, the family moved to California and Jane grew up there with four brothers. Jane acted in high school plays and was encouraged by her mother to enter show business. After high school graduation she worked for a doctor whose practice specialized in foot disorders.

When her father died, she helped support the family by modeling, by then becoming a buxom dark-haired beauty. Multi-millionaire aircraft tycoon, moviemaker and womanizer Howard Hughes saw her photograph on an office wall and put her in the female lead of his Billy the Kid western "The Outlaw" (1941). He didn't care that she did not know how to act, he saw a fortune in her figure and ample breasts. Advertisements of her in a low-cut, tight-fitting, off-the-shoulder blouse barely containing her breasts were plastered over billboards and printed in magazines all over the country.

Besides designing airplanes, Hughes designed a "cantilever bra" to hold in her breasts. Because of censorship problem, the highly sexed film was made in 1941 but not shown in most theaters until 1946 when it became a box office sensation. Hughes said of her stardom: "There are two good reasons why men go to see her. Those are enough." Like Dolly Parton years later, Russell capitalized on her voluptuousness, laughing all the way to the bank. Hughes kept her under a personal 7-year contract but did not put her in another film until 1946. A series of sexy dramas followed with Robert Mitchum often making torrid love to her (*on-screen only*).

She had an affair with actor John Payne in 1942, then the next year decided to marry her high school sweetheart, Bob Waterfield who was by then a football star. They adopted three children because she was unable to conceive. After their divorce in 1967. Jane and actor Roger Barrett met in Chicago, Illinois on June 15, 1968, when they were both performing in a stage show.

They were married on August 25, but three months later he died of a heart attack on November 18. Jane said later that their mutual interest in religion played a very important part in their whirlwind romance that led to their marriage. She then was married to real estate developer John Calvin Peoples from 1974 until his death of heart failure at the age of 70 in 1999. Russell founded the World Adoption International Fund that has placed 51,000 children with parents.

Her endowments are honored in Alaskan mountains as "The Jane Russell Peaks." Bob Hope said, "I introduced her to GIs at camp shows in World War II as "The two and only Jane Russell." American troops in the Korean War named two embattled hills in her honor.

Although her movie fame was largely the result of her sexy look, she was in real life a modest and religious Christian woman who held weekly *Bible* study at her home and led a wholesome life. She had macular degeneration and wore hearing aids in both ears.

A staunch pro-life activist, she was against abortion, even in cases of incest or rape. Called "The Brunette Bombshell," she died of respiratory failure on February 28, 2011 in Santa Maria, California.

On Marriage – "A man has his place – a woman hers, and they can't switch places."

"I don't necessarily believe marriage is a fifty-fifty proposition. In some situations, the wife wins; in others, the husband. I believe in the husband being the head of the family."

"Next to my mother and the wonderful faith she gave me, the most important influence on my life has been my husband, Robert Waterfield. I fell in love with him when I was 14. He was two years ahead of me in (*high*) school at Van Nuys, and had a hot rod car, a terrific reputation as an athlete, and all the girls in school chasing him. He didn't notice me at all, not till I was seventeen and he and his buddy saw me and a girlfriend at the beach one day. From then on, Robert and I saw each other almost every night for five years until we got married." (*They eloped to Las Vegas and were married there on April 24, 1943*).

(*On her marriage to Bob Waterfield*): "We laughed ourselves silly sometimes. It was black humor, like my father's... Of course, I married my father the first time." (*In a 1953 interview*): "Robert and I were not something incidental that happened along the way to each other. Our marriage is the most important thing in our lives. I was pretty fortunate in the beginning, that I didn't make a picture immediately after 'The Outlaw.' For almost three years I was with

Robert, getting my chance to be a real wife. My every thought and action was built around my marriage to assure it a good foundation."

On Sex and Sex Appeal -- (*In 1954, on sex appeal*): "I've had it for ten years. It can be overdone. It's like too much of one thing. You've got to have something else. I think a person who has nothing but sex appeal might as well drop dead... Maybe I'm just resigned to it by now. I get awfully sick of it, and those awful Jane Russell jokes. But I have to remind myself, where would I be without it? No place, probably. So I go along with it."

"Sex appeal is good, but not in bad taste. Then it's ugly."

The Inner Woman -- (*In a 1953 interview*): "I couldn't be happy alone. Since I married Robert, I have never been homesick, no matter where we are. (*When he was in the Army in World War II*), we traveled and lived away from home, California, for many months. But wherever Robert is, that's home for me."

"Yes, Howard Hughes invented a bra for me. Or, he tried to. And one of the seamless ones like they have now. He was way ahead of his time. But I never wore it in 'The Outlaw,' and he never knew. He wasn't going to take my clothes off to check if I had it on. I just told him I did."

(*In 2003*): "These days I am a teetotal, mean-spirited, ring-wing, narrow-minded conservative Christian, but not a racist."
"I have faith in people."

"People should never, ever have an abortion. Don't talk to me about it being a woman's right to choose what she does with her own body. The choice is between life and death."

(*About becoming pregnant at age 18*): "The only solution was to find a quack and get an abortion. I had a botched abortion and it was terrible. Afterwards, my own doctor said, 'What butcher did this to you?' I had to be taken to hospital. I was so ill, I nearly died. I've never known pain like it."

"I've been working a lot to get the *Bible* back in schools because I think a great deal of our loss of wisdom as a society results from the fact that a lot of children have never read the *Bible*."

(*Her mother once told her*): "You have a path from heaven and if you fall off of it, it'll be a problem, Jane." "It was always the case where no matter what way I wanted to go, the Lord wanted me to go this way."

"I want to save America. I do not want a one-world order, a one-world government, at all. I think our Founding Fathers had exactly the right idea, and we've got a great country, and let's go back to God."

George Sand

A very modern woman back in the 1800's, the famous male cross-dresser is not a frequent visitor to the ladies' room these days, but what she has to say about men and relationships is as right-on as it was back in her time.

She married once, unhappily, and afterward preferred relationships and partners, mostly with men. Her loves included the great classical pianist and composer Fredric Chopin, but it was rumored that she also slept with at least one woman. She was a liberated woman and an advocate of women's rights long before the movement of modern times.

"There is only one happiness in life, to love and be loved."

"Once my heart was captured, reason was shown the door, deliberately and with a sort of frantic joy. I accepted everything, I believed everything, without struggle, without suffering, without regret, without false shame. How can one blush for what one adores?"

Born Amantine Lucile Aurore Dupin in Paris, France on July 1, 1804, she became known by her writing pseudonym, George Sand. She came from an aristocratic family, her father Maurice Dupin whose ancestors were remotely related to French kings, while her mother was a commoner. Author of numerous books of poetry and novels and plays, she has become more famous for her romantic relationships with Polish composer and pianist Frederic Chopin.

When she was 18 she married much older Francois Dudevant in 1822, and they had a son and daughter together. She left him in 1831 and began almost five years of affairs with other men. She legally separated from Dudevant in 1835 and took her children with her. From 1837 to 1847 she had a romantic affair with Chopin.

She also had an intimate friendship with actress Marie Dorval which was rumored to be a lesbian affair. One letter Sand wrote to Dorval said she was "wanting you either in your dressing room or in your bed."

Her writing career began in an 1831 collaboration with writer Jules Sandeau in which they signed their short stories "Jules Sand." A year later she published her first novel under the pen name George Sand because it made it easier to be published and also gained her better entrance into the man's world. She shocked society by wearing men's suits and smoking tobacco in public.

Despite her aristocratic lineage, she wrote mainly as a socialist, siding with the poor and working class, and also advocated women's rights. During the 1848 French Revolution she published her own anti-monarchy newspaper in a workers' cooperative.

The Russian playwright Ivan Turgenev said of her, "What a brave man she was, and what a good woman." One of her lovers called her "The most womanly woman." She died at Nohant near Chateauroux in France on June 8, 1876 at the age of 71. Films about her include "A Song to Remember" (1945).

On Love -- "Women love always: when Earth slips from them, they take refuge in Heaven."

"The prayers of a lover are more imperious (*dominant*) than the menaces of the whole world."

"No human creature can give orders to love."

The Inner Woman -- "Work is not man's punishment. It is his reward and his strength and his pleasure."

"We cannot tear out a single page of our life, but we can throw the whole book in the fire."

"Try to keep your soul young and quivering right up to old age."

"Don't walk in front of me, I may not follow. Don't walk behind me, I may not lead."

"Guard well within yourself that treasure, kindness. Know how to give without hesitation, how to lose without regret, how to acquire without meanness."

"One changes from day to day, and… after a few years have passed one has completely altered."

"Vanity is the quicksand of reason."

"The artist's vocation is to send light into the human heart."

"The beauty that addresses itself to the eyes is only the spell of the moment; the eye of the body is not always that of the soul."

"Faith is an excitement and an enthusiasm: it is a condition of intellectual magnificence to which we must cling to as a treasure, and not squander on our way through life in the small coin of empty words, or in exact and priggish argument."

"One approaches the journey's end. But the end is a goal, not a catastrophe."

Susan Sarandon

Her parents divorced after 40 years of marriage, and her marriage only lasted 12 years, then she had two sons with a new partner, so she has a lot to share about men and marriage or not marrying.

"Making love is like hitting a baseball. You just gotta relax and concentrate."

"I think one of the reasons I haven't married Tim is that I hate that couples assumption... that once you're committed to someone, you stop treating each other as individuals. I like getting up knowing I am choosing to be with that person."

Born Susan Abigail Tomalin in New York City on October 4, 1946, she was the eldest of nine children. Her father was a television producer and advertising executive, and her mother a housewife of Sicilian ancestry, having been abandoned at the age of two and grew up in the care of nuns in an institution. Her parents divorced in 1982 after 40 years of marriage. Sarandon was a cheerleader at Edison High School in Edison, New Jersey. She attended Catholic University of America Drama School where she met actor Chris Sarandon and they married in 1967 but divorced in 1979.

After a few minor roles in films she got major recognition playing a young woman who becomes involved with a transvestite in "The Rocky Horror Picture Show" (1975), and starred with Kevin Costner in "Bull Durham" (1988). She began an affair with another actor in the latter film, Tim Robbins, from 1988 to 2009, and had two sons with him.

Nominated four times for best actress Academy Awards, she won it for "Dead Man Walking" (1995). She continues as one of the top Hollywood film stars, is active in humanitarian causes, is a UNICEF goodwill ambassador, and was chosen by *People* magazine as one of the 50 most beautiful women in the world.

On Men -- "Mel Gibson is somewhere to the right of Attila the Hun. He's beautiful, but only on the outside."

On Sexuality -- "Sexuality is something that develops and becomes stronger and stronger the older you get. If you can continue to say yes to life and to maintain generosity of spirit, you become more and more of who you are."

"The thing about breasts is that you have to choose between having a mind and having breasts. I'd be nice if you could have both. Anyway, I think my breasts have been highly overrated. You have to be careful not to be upstaged by your breasts. I've gotten curvier as I've gotten older. Directors cast the men they want to be and the women they want to have."

The Inner Woman -- "I haven't yet had any plastic surgery, but I won't knock it. I think women have the right to do anything they want to their bodies that makes them feel good about themselves... I don't like it when surgeons take a perfectly interesting woman and she ends up looking like a female impersonator with these gigantic breasts. It's just so extreme and that worries me. I think everyone is looking the same."

"I look forward to being older, when looks become less of an issue and who you are is the point."

"Children can reinvent your world for you. Despite the statistics, nothing is hopeless, nothing is futile. We can do so much to protect children with awareness, knowledge, and lots of love."

(*In 1995, on her character in "The Hunger" (1983), in which she is seduced by a woman and the stereotype men have about lesbianism*): "They (*the film's producers*) felt that I should be really drunk, so that was their way of taking away her choice in a sense, and insisted that it not be that way, that certainly, you know, you wouldn't have to get drunk to bed Catherine Deneuve.

"I don't care what your sexual history to that point had been. It was much more interesting that she went voluntarily. I don't think, for better or worse, that women are taken very seriously in this area. I think the feeling is, when two women are together, then it's probably experimental or some kind of phase and if the right guy came along, that would all change. So it's actually something that straight men can watch and not be threatened by."

"I think the concept that there's one person who's gonna make you whole… is so detrimental. I don't think it's the other person's responsibility to make you whole at all. It's the other person's responsibility to make you laugh, to give you a dance now and then, to read the newspaper and tell you about things you don't have time to read about, to introduce you to music you don't know, to tell you when you're full of shit, to fight fair, to be good in bed, to say. 'Come on, let's go have an adventure' when you've become a little bit of a stick in the mud. But it's not their job to make you whole."

"It's better to have made decisions that turned out badly and learn from them than to feel as if you had no choice and are resentful of the turns that your life takes. My life has been filled with happy accidents. The thing that's served me well is being able to change onto a different track when its presented itself."

"When you start to develop your powers of empathy and imagination, the whole world opens up to you."

Ann Sheridan

This editor's second favorite actress, after Barbara Stanwyck. Sheridan was closer to being a real flesh-and-blood movie actress than any other, always a delight to watch and listen to. Her voice usually sounded like it had a laugh in it somewhere, reflecting her up-beat approach to life.

She was married three times to movie actors, her third marriage only lasting a year until her death. I'd like to be a fly on the wall to hear her talk about her men and men in general in the ladies' room. A male fly, of course.

(*On her first two marriages*): **"With both men there was no honesty between us. And if two people living together can't be honest, then I don't want it."**

"They nicknamed me 'The Oomph Girl,' and I loathe that name. Just being known by a nickname indicates that you're not thought of as a true actress. It's just crap! If you call an actress by her looks or a reaction, then that's all she'll ever be thought of as."

"'Oomph' is what a fat man says when he leans over to tie his shoelace in a telephone booth."

Born Clara Lou Sheridan in Denton, Texas on February 21, 1915, her father was an automobile mechanic and his wife a homemaker. She grew up being a tomboy with four siblings and played basketball while attending North Texas State Teacher's College, intending to teach. One of her sisters thought Clara Lou was pretty enough to be a movie star so she sent a photograph of her in a bathing suit to a "Search for Beauty" contest for which the winner would get a Paramount Pictures screen test and a small part in a movie. Clara Lou won and was signed to a Paramount contract at the age of 19.

She went to Warner Bros. in 1936 where her name was changed to Ann Sheridan and became known as a sex symbol called "The Oomph Girl." Her best film was playing Ronald Reagan's girlfriend in "Kings Row" (1942), then became one of the studio's major stars playing modern women. As she matured and offers of film roles were fewer, she became a popular star in television shows and series.

Sheridan was married three times, her husbands all being actors: Edward Norris, from 1936 to their divorce in 1938; George Brent from 1942 to their divorce a year later; and Scott McKay, from 1966 until her death in 1967. She preferred a quiet life, but her boss Jack Warner wanted her to be seen as a party girl off-screen so her contract required her to spend evenings in night clubs at least three times a week. She is remembered as being a fine actress and one of the most beautiful actresses of the 1940s.

On Men -- "Don't forget that all men like to be thought pretty dangerous."

"Never laugh at a man when he's serious, about anything."

(*On Errol Flynn, with whom she co-starred in several westerns*): "He was one of the wild characters of the world, but he had a strange, quiet side. He camouflaged himself completely. In all the years I knew him, I never really knew what lay underneath and doubt many people did."

(*On James Cagney, another co-star*): "Cagney off the screen is exactly like Cagney on it. It was always 'Hi ya, baby,' or 'How are ya, sweetheart?' He's a great guy. To be in a picture with him was just the greatest. He didn't smoke or drink. He could get drunk on two drinks of liquor. And he never made the party scene. To be in a picture with him was just the greatest."

(*On John Garfield, also a co-star*): "John Garfield was a dear man. He was like the little guy who brought the apple for the teacher, and here I was, this hussy with fuzzy hair and the décolletage dress. (*in one of their films,* 'They Made Me a Criminal" (1939), I was supposed to kiss John, but Buz (*director Busby Berkeley*) said, 'Hold it until I say 'cut.' I just kept on kissing him. Well, of course he (*Berkeley*) wouldn't say it, and I had John around the neck and on the floor. He was absolutely red."

The Inner Woman -- "I can whistle through my fingers, bulldog a steer, light a fire with two sticks, shoot pistol with fair accuracy, set type, and teach school."

(*On Bette Davis*): "She wasn't happy about a lot of things… She was just… temperamental? Who isn't temperamental? I'm as temperamental as all get-out if I feel I have to be."

(*On Rosalind Russell*): "Roz Russell is as hard as nails. They didn't cast her in all those tailored businesswomen's parts in the Forties for nothing. She came up the hard way, and it shows. But I'm not too much of a lady to say anything nasty or repeat any rumors. I don't want to get punched in the nose!"

"Don't think you can get by on sex appeal alone."

Britney Spears

A happy marriage has eluded Britney and relationships have fallen by the wayside. But she is a happy mother of two children that is more than enough until the right man comes along, and even if he never does.

"Either the guy's going to be really intimidated **(by the girl),** *or they're going to kiss your ass. I'm just a girl wanting a guy to love me."*

"I think you know when you've met the right person."

"I believe we all have one true love, somewhere in his world I do."

Born Britney Jean Spears in McComb, Mississippi on December 2, 1981, as a little girl she loved to sing and dance and was good at gymnastics. When she was 9, she appeared off-Broadway in a show called "Ruthless" which ran two years. At age 11 she became a Mouseketeer on television in "The All New Mickey Mouse Club" in 1989.

She made her first record in 1999 and "Baby, One More Time" was a big hit, selling 13 million copies. She toured with the boy band NSYNC. More records and music videos followed in which she was often scantily dressed and she became known as the "Princess of Pop." A natural brunette. She often dies her hair blonde.

She was in an affair with actor Justin Timberlake whom she met when they were Mouseketeers, then had other boyfriends. She got "sort of" married to a childhood friend, Jason Allen Alexander, in Las Vegas in 2004, but it was annulled 55 hours later when her manager said it was just a joke but had been taken too far. She then dated a dancer, Kevin Federline, and they married in 2004. She gave birth to both a boy and girl with him, but they divorced in 2007.

People magazine named her one of the 50 most beautiful people in the world in 1999, and the following year she said that she would go to college and study to become an entertainment lawyer. She has a tattoo of a small black-winged fairy on the back of her spine. She authored two biographical books, one with her mother. Her recordings, films, and television work have made her a very rich woman, besides getting $10 million for her Pepsi-Cola commercials and from her line of perfumes.

On Men -- (*About her breakup with Justin Timberlake*): "The most painful thing I have ever experienced was that breakup. We were together so long and I had this vision. You think you're going to spend the rest of your life together. Where I come from (*rural Mississippi*), the woman is the homemaker, and that's how I was brought up... you cook for your kids."

On Love -- "With love, you should go ahead and take the risk of getting hurt... because love is an amazing feeling."

On Sex -- (*Before her marriage*): "My views on virginity have not changed. I want to wait to have sex until I'm married. I do. I want to wait, but it's hard. I just want to live my life."

"I know I'm not ugly, but I don't see myself as a sex symbol or this goddess-attractive beautiful person at all. When I'm on stage, that's my time to do my thing and go there and be, and it's fun. It's exhilarating just to be something that you're not. And, people tend to believe it. I guess I just pull it off very well."

(*When a teenager*): "Who cares if I've had sex? It's nobody's business. Trust me, I'm not going to have a press conference to announce it. If I mess up, I'm human. If have a drink or I'm with someone, I'm human. I'm no different than anyone else my age."

On Marriage -- (*About the thought of marrying England's Prince William, before his marriage*): "I'd love that. Who wouldn't want to be a princess?"

The Inner Woman -- "I've always been very comfortable being nude. I don't feel like I have anything to hide. My family, we walked around the house naked. By the time I was 13, my dad was like, 'Uh, Britney, it's time to start covering yourself up.' I'm very free like that."

"On stage, I'm the happiest person in the world."

"Just because I look sexy on the cover of *Rolling Stone* doesn't mean I'm naughty."

"I did not have implants, I just had a growth spurt."

"I find it so funny that people find me so interesting. And, I hate when they're like 'Define your image.' I don't know what my image is. I just do my thing."

"Chocolate for me is just like an orgasm."

"When I'm under stress, I do yoga."

"When I look into a mirror, I am very critical of myself. I see a goofy girl."

"I don't listen to anybody. Nobody can tell me anything. I'm stubborn. If somebody tells me not to do something, I do it. But I do listen to Madonna. I wish I could be inside her head. I like Madonna's career, and what she's done with her family."

"I'm really just a boring homebody who loves staying home with my kids, and that's where I'm happiest."

"These parents, they think I'm a role model for their kids, that their kids look at me as some sort of idol. But it's the parents' job to make sure their kids don't turn out that shallow. That's not my responsibility. I'm not responsible for your kid."

"Don't care too much 'bout what other people think. What really mattes is your own point of view."

"Never doubt yourself. Never change who you are. Don't care what people think, and just go for it."

"Bottom line: If you love yourself, it will all work out."

Barbara Stanwyck (this editor's favorite film actress.)

She played murderesses and floozies, cowgirls, lovable ladies in drawing room romantic comedies, and a mother who sacrificed everything for her daughter, always as convincingly as if she came off the screen to be with you. It may never be known if she was lesbian or bisexual, and if her marriage to movie matinee idol Robert Taylor was for mutual love or just a "lavender" arranged marriage by their movie studio. In any case, she said she loved him, then World War II came between them, they divorced, and he married another actress.

Most of her fans do not care what her sexual preference was, they loved her for being the wonderful actress she was, and for the caring and generous person she was off-screen where everyone called her "Missy."

"How can you explain love, anyway? You can't. It's one of those things that you can recognize; you know it exists, but seek the reason for, and you are up a tree."

"It's perhaps not the future I would choose. I still think it's possible to make a success of both marriage and career, even though I didn't. But it's not a bad future. And I'm not afraid of it."

"I'm a rough old broad from Brooklyn. I intend to go on acting until I'm ninety and they won't need to paste my face with make-up."

Born Ruby Catherine Stevens in Brooklyn, New York on July 16, 1907 to working-class parents. The youngest of five children, when she was four years old, her mother died when accidentally knocked off a moving trolley car by a drunken man. Two weeks later her father, a bricklayer, left in deep grief over her death, and never returned. Barbara then was put in foster homes, as many as four a year.

She dropped out of high school when she was 14 and worked in a department store wrapping packages, then in a telephone office for $14 a week. At the age of 16 she was dancing in the chorus lines of shows on Broadway and in the Ziegfeld Follies. She took a stage name of "Barbara" from a character in a play she was in, and "Stanwyck" from another actress in that play.

She moved to Hollywood in 1928 and began her movie career. Over the following decades she proved she could expertly play any character, in films ranging from laugh-out-loud romantic comedies such as "The Lady Eve" (1941) to cold-blooded murderesses to floozies and that of a socially unacceptable mother as "Stella Dallas" (1937). She said that was her favorite role, despite losing the best actress Academy Award for her touching performance.

Two of Stanwyck's films are Christmas favorites when reruns are shown on television: "Remember the Night" with Fred MacMurray" (1940) as a shoplifter who falls in love with the lawyer (Fred MacMurray) who has to prosecute her, and "Christmas in Connecticut" (1945) as a gourmet culinary columnist who cannot cook.

She was nominated for an Oscar as best actress four times but lost to others, however received an honorary Oscar in 1992 for "superlative creativity and unique contribution to the art of screen acting."

Actors and crews with whom she worked considered her wonderful to work with for her professionalism yet easy-going attitude on the set, never allowing stardom to go to her head. They lovingly called her "Babs," "Missy," or "The Queen."

While she was a chorus girl in 1928 she married one of the top comics in vaudeville, Frank Fay, from 1928 until their divorce in 1935, having adopted a boy with him. Their marriage was considered unhappy and stormy. He became an alcoholic as his career began to take a nose dive and Barbara's began to soar. Their marriage ended when he was drunk and tossed their adopted infant son into their swimming pool.

Her second husband, despite rumors that she had affairs with Marlene Dietrich and Joan Crawford, was handsome matinee-idol Robert Taylor in 1939. His possessive mother is said to have demanded that he spend his wedding night with her, rather than with his wife, but if that is true, and if he did, no one knows.

It was widely conjectured that their studios had arranged their marriage because of rumors that he was gay or bisexual and that she was a lesbian. No one knows for sure if that was why they married. During their marriage Taylor was still most girls' dream lover, while he fell in love with Lana Turner, his co-star in the gangster drama "Johnny Eager" (1941). Turner later said she was attracted to him, one of the most handsome actors in Hollywood at the time, but they never slept together. Taylor told Barbara about his thing for Lana and she left him, but they later reconciled.

World War II then came between them as he became a Navy pilot in war zones. He returned from the war more mature but had a roving eye for other younger actresses and their marriage began to fail, ending in divorce in 1952. Two years later, Taylor married sexy Italian actress Ursula Thiess and they remained married until his death in 1969.

Readers of *Modern Screen* magazine voted on their favorite actresses in 1954. Stanwyck was up there with June Allyson, Lana Turner, Susan Hayward, and Betty Grable. She gave the magazine a rare interview and said she was surprised but very pleased. The title of the interview was "What Makes Stanwyck Tick," and she said it was her love of making movies, but was typically cryptic about her personal life.

Asked about her marriage to Robert Taylor, she said he mainly married her for friendship, but she wanted more. "Bob Taylor had this 'Pretty Boy' label pasted on him," she said, "and women were just about hiding under his bed. He would come home from work some nights all worn out. But he stuck with it because he is a fine actor. But those days weren't easy" (*for him or her or their marriage*).

The interviewer pressed Stanwyck on why she and Taylor divorced after more 11 years of marriage, but she remained silent. However, a close friend said, "Certainly I know the answer, but to provide it to you or anyone else would be an inexcusable violation of privacy."

Before her marriage to Taylor, she became a great friend of actor William , , although it was never sexual. He thanked her for encouraging him to continue in his role with her in the boxing film "Golden Boy" (1939) when he felt too inexperienced, and his performance made him a star. He publicly thanked Stanwyck in 1978 when he won the Best Actor Oscar for "Stalag 17" (1953), and she nearly broke down in tears and kissed him as the audience loudly applauded. When she won her honorary Oscar in 1992 she held it up and said, "This is for you, Golden Boy." Holden had died after falling at home in 1981.

After her film career, fans knew Barbara Stanwyck for her television work including the western series "The Big Valley" (1965), the prime-time soap opera "The Colby's" (1985), and especially her Emmy-award winning performance as a sexually-frustrated wealthy senior citizen in the hit television series "The Thorn Birds" (1983).

A heavy smoker, she died of congestive heart failure in Santa Monica, California on January 20, 1990 at the age of 83, leaving behind a career of 59 years in 93 movies and many television performances. She was listed No. 11 on the list of the American Film Institute's "100 Years of the Greatest Screen Legends."

On Men -- (*On her longtime friend, actor Joel McCrea*): "I needed a good part desperately in 1937. Samuel Goldwyn was casting 'Stella Dallas.' I wanted that part like nothing I'd ever wanted, but Goldwyn wouldn't hear of it. He wanted an unknown. Then Joel went into action. We were making a B-movie together at the time, and every spare moment he spent in a one-man campaign. He wouldn't take 'No!' Finally Goldwyn broke down to say, 'Well, she can make a test, but it won't do her any good... I still want an unknown." (*She got the part and threw her arms around McCrea declaring, "I'll love you forever for this!" (She won a best actress Academy Award nomination for her performance as a mother who sacrifices herself to enable her daughter to marry the son of the rich* man she loved but gave up to another woman more of his social class. Stanwyck and McCrea, who was happily married to actress Frances Dee, remained great friends and co-starred in several films together.)

(*While dating Robert Taylor*):"He's the handsomest man I've ever laid eyes on, but he looks about eighteen. People will think I'm his mother!"

(*On her fiance Robert Taylor being four years younger than she*): " The boy's got a lot to learn and I've got a lot to teach." (*Following their divorce, she wore his wedding ring for years afterward.*)

(*On Charlton Heston*): "He has a bad memory. He still thinks he's Moses parting the Red Sea."

The Inner Woman -- (*On Loretta Young*): "They call her Attila the Nun."

"My only problem is finding a way to play my fortieth fallen female in a different way from my thirty-ninth."

(*On the gossip columnists*): "Hedda (*Hopper*) was worse than Louella (*Parsons*). She was more vindictive." (*Hopper was homophobic, although her handsome actor son William Hopper was said to be bisexual. Raymond Burr, his co-star in the "Perry Mason" television series, 1957-1966, was gay and a cross-dresser, although this editor interviewed him once for The Chicago Tribune and Burr never made a pass at him. Burr kept him waiting almost an hour for their lunch together; so there, Raymond!*)

(*On Marilyn Monroe*): "Her body has gone to her head."

"If you feel a thing strongly enough, you should have the courage of your convictions to carry it through. That's my philosophy and it's gotten me into plenty of hot water."

"During 'Double Indemnity' (1944), Fred McMurray would go to rushes (*viewings of daily completed shots*). I remember asking Fred,

'How was I?' (*Fred's response was*) 'I don't know about you, but I was wonderful!' Such a true remark. Actors only look at themselves."

"Eyes are the greatest tool in film. Mr. Capra (*director Frank Capra*) taught me that. Sure, it's nice to say very good dialogue, if you can get it. But great movie acting… watch the eyes!"

"Put me in the last fifteen minutes of a picture and I don't care what happened before. I don't even care if I was in the rest of the damned thing. I'll take it in those fifteen minutes."

"Egotism… usually just a case of mistaken nonentity."

"Career is too pompous a word. It was a job and I have always felt privileged to be paid for doing what I love doing."

"Attention embarrasses me. I don't like to be on display."

"Some kids are born with bad blood, just like horses. When a parent has done everything possible, the only solution is to save yourself."

(*She was said to have had a difficult time with the boy she and Fay adopted. He grew from a cute child into an overweight young man neither she nor Fay got along with and Barbara was estranged from him most of her life. He is said to have felt neglected because both his parents were busy with their careers.*)

"Just be truthful. And if you can fake that, you've got it made."

(*On attending a dull party*): "It was a fete worse than death."

"I want to go on until they have to shoot me."

Gloria Steinem

Look out, girls in the ladies' room, here comes Miss Liberated Woman. Somehow, it's hard to believe she is Christian Bale's mother-in-law, but she is married to his father. Isn't he still a child star? No, of course not, although she is the woman she always was.

"Women have two choices: Either she's a feminist or a masochist."

"A liberated woman is one who has sex before marriage and a job after."

"Feminism has never been about getting a job for one woman. It's about making life more fair for women everywhere. It's not about a piece of the existing pie; there are too many of us for that. It's about baking a new pie."

"A feminist is anyone who recognizes the equality and full humanity of women and men."

Born Gloria Marie Steinen in Toledo, Ohio on March 25, 1934, her father, a traveling antiques dealer, was the son of Jewish immigrants from Germany and Poland. Her mother had a nervous breakdown at the age of 34 and was confined to mental institutions. Her parents separated when she was 10 and divorced because of her mother's illness. She later said that how her mother's illness was treated by doctors and mental health practitioners was pivotal to her understanding of social injustices and inequality toward women.

She wrote a column for *New York* magazine and was a founder of *Ms. Magazine.* She became recognized as a leader of the feminist movement after publication in 1969 of her article "After Black Power, Women's Liberation." She currently travels the world as an organizer and lecturer and media spokesperson on equality issues. She was vocal in her opposition to the Vietnam War and the Gulf War in 1991 and said incursion into the Middle East to defend democracy was a government pretense in order to benefit from oil resources there, a widely held but repressed belief.

In 1992 she co-founded Choice USA, an organization supporting lobbying for women's choice regarding abortion. In recent years she has become active in campaigns for disarmament and peace between nations. She was diagnosed with breast cancer in 1986 and trigeminal neuralgia in 1994.

She had a four-year relationship with publisher Mortimer Zuckerm, and married for the first time at the age of 66 in 2000, her husband being David Bale, father of actor Christian Bale. They were married only three years, until his death of brain cancer in 2003 at the age of 62.

The Inner Woman -- (*On her having an abortion*): "It is supposed to make us a bad person. But I must say, I never felt that. I used to sit and try to figure out how old the child would be, trying to make myself feel guilty. But I never could!... But still, I didn't tell anyone. Because I knew that out there, it wasn't positive."

(*On same-sex marriage, in a futuristic Utopia*): "What will exist is a variety of alternative life-styles... (*Because of over-population*) Single women will have the right to stay single without ridicule, without the attitudes now betrayed by 'spinster' and 'bachelor.' Lesbians or homosexuals will no longer be denied legally binding marriages, complete with mutual-support agreements and inheritance rights. Paradoxically, the number of homosexuals may get smaller. With fewer over-possessive mothers and fewer fathers who hold up an impossibly cruel or perfectionist idea of manhood, boys will be less likely to be denied or reject their identity as males."

(*In 2013, on supporting transgendering*): "(*Transgender people*) are living out real, authentic lives. Those lives should be celebrated, not questioned."

"So whatever you want to do, just do it...Making a damn fool of yourself is absolutely essential."

"A woman without a man is like a fish without a bicycle."

"We are becoming the men we wanted to marry."

Martha Stewart

One of the most successful businesswomen of all time as the queen of merchandising, her name is stamped on products from bed sheets to kitchen cabinets and Christmas trees. She was married only once, then was in relationships with a top Hollywood star and also a billionaire, but has preferred to concentrate on her career to which she seems to be married.

"I was married for 30 years. Isn't that enough? I've had my share of dirty underwear on the floor."

"I believe in a man and a woman being equal. I really believe that we (women) can do anything we set our minds to."

"All the things I love is what my business is all about."

Born Martha Helen Stewart in Jersey City, New Jersey on August 3, 1941 to middle-class parents of Polish heritage. They moved to Nutley, New Jersey when she was 10 and she sometimes worked as babysitter for the children of New York Yankee baseball stars Mickey Mantle and Yogi Berra. She became a fashion model at 15 and appeared in television commercials. Her mother taught her how to cook and sew and she learned the canning process on visits to her grandparents' home in Buffalo. New York.

While at Barnard College she met Andrew Stewart who had gotten a law degree from Yale School of Law; they married in 1961 and had a daughter together. She returned to Barnard a year after their marriage and graduated with majors in history and architectural history. She and her husband moved to Westport. Connecticut where they bought and restored an 1805 farmhouse which later became the model for the television studio of her show, "Martha Stewart Living." She became successful as a television cooking show hostess, author of cook books, and merchandising.

She divorced Stewart in 1990 and then dated actor Anthony Hopkins but broke off with him after seeing "The Silence of the Lambs." She told him she was unable to avoid thinking of him in "Silence of the Lambs" (1991) as the deranged flesh-eating Hannibal Lecter, a performance that won him a best actor Academy Award but apparently turned her stomach. She also dated Charles Simonyi who became a billionaire as head of Microsoft, but the relationship broke off in 2008.

She was convicted of insider trading charges in 2004, but despite denying her guilt, she served five months in a federal correction facility at Alderson, West Virginia. It did not hurt her career and she resumed television work, authoring cook books, and product endorsements. A great lover of animals, she has Chow Chow dogs, French bulldogs, Himalayan cats, and Friesian horses, and is active in animal rights causes.

The Inner Woman -- "I was the second of six kids. I wouldn't say we were poor; we had no money. That's different."

"I'm not supposed to say it, but I was not guilty of any crime. I became a target because I was a strong and rich woman who had been very successful."

"I think baking cookies is equal to Queen Victoria running an empire. There's no difference in how seriously you take the job, how seriously you approach your life."

"I'm very inspired by nature; you could say Mother Nature. I look at things around me and get all kinds of inspiration daily."

"If you learn something new every day, you can teach something new every day."

"Without an open-minded mind, you can never be a great success. The more you adapt, the more interesting you are."

"I'm a maniacal perfectionist. I have proven that being a perfectionist can be profitable and admirable when creating content across the board in television, books, newspapers, radio, videos."

"My new motto is: When you're through changing, you're through."

Meryl Streep

The reigning queen of films, she has been happily married to a sculptor for almost 40 years and is a devoted and loving mother of four. She loves acting and wins an Academy Award just about every year or every other year, but home is really where her heart is. She and her husband rarely go to parties or restaurants so she seldom is in a public ladies' room, but if you should see her there, she might bore the panties off of you by telling how much she is in love with her husband.

"I don't know what I would do without my husband. I'd be dead, emotionally at least, if I hadn't met him. He's the greatest."

"If you've been married for a long time, you love without looking."

"I think I was wired for family. You know how they say people are wired for religion, or wired for this or that? I always knew I would like to, if I could find the right person, have a family. I can't imagine living single."

Born Mary Louise Streep in Summit, New York on June 22, 1949, jacks descent and her mother a commercial artist of English, Irish, and German ancestry. She became interested in acting while a student at Vassar and after graduation studied at the Yale School of Drama.

Her first film. "Julia" in 1977 was followed the next year by "The Deer Hunter" for which she was nominated for an Academy Award, which was to be her first of 19 nominations and three wins, as best supporting actress for "Kramer vs. Kramer" (1979) and best actress for "Sophie's Choice" (1982), and her portrayal of British Prime Minister Margaret Thatcher in "The Iron Lady" (2011).

Her other best-known films include "Out of Africa" (1985) and "The Bridges of Madison County" (1995). A perfectionist for accuracy in the roles she plays, she practiced playing the violin six hours a day for eight weeks for "Music of the Heart" (1999).

She was romantically involved with actor John Cazale for seven years until his death at the age of 42 in 1978 from bone cancer. She and sculptor Don Gummer married in 1978, have had four children together, and remain married.

Her actress mentor was film star Jean Arthur who was known for both comedy and drama. Early in Streep's career, Bette Davis told her that Streep would be her successor as the premier American film actress. The prediction has come true as Streep is now called the greatest living film actress.

As of this writing in 2016, Streep is still the most Oscar-nominated actress, with 19 nominations. Sandra Bullock said: "The Academy Awards shouldn't even nominate Meryl Streep anymore. She should just be given an award every year. There should just be the Meryl Streep category."

President Barack Obama awarded Streep the Presidential Medal of Freedom in 2014, saying "I love her. Her husband knows I love her. Michelle knows I love her. There's nothing that either of them can do about it. Meryl is truly one of America's leading ladies."

On men -- (*On Dustin Hoffman*): "He's energized and the greatest combination of the generous and the selfish that ever lived. He wants to be the greatest actor who ever was."

The Inner Woman – "There's no road map on how to raise a family: it's always an enormous negotiation. But I have a holistic need to work and to have huge ties of live in my life. I can't imagine eschewing one for the other."

"It would be nice to have a woman President. I think half the Senate should be women, half of Parliament, half the ruling mullahs. But that will never happen, darling!"

"I try to lead as ordinary a life as I can. You can't get spoiled if you do your own ironing."

"Listening is everything. Listening is the whole deal. That's what I think. And I mean that in terms of before you work, after you work, in between work with your children, with your husband, with your friends, with your mother, with your father. It's everything. And it's where you learn everything."

"One of the most important keys to acting is curiosity. I am curious to the point of being nosy. What that means is, you want to devour lives. You're eager to put on their shoes and wear their clothes and have them become a part of you. All people contain mystery, and when you act, you want to plumb that mystery until everything is known to you."

"The great gift of human beings is that we have the power of empathy." (*To understand and share another's feeling; their experiences and emotions.*)

"Motherhood has a very humanizing effect. Everything gets reduced to essentials."

"Sometimes with my children, I remember exactly how I felt as the child in this situation, not just how it feels to be me."

"Instant gratification is not soon enough."

"I think the most liberating thing I did early on (*in acting*) was to free myself from any concern with my looks as they pertained to my work."

"My family really does come first. It always did and always will."

(*Actress-comedienne Nancy Walker on Meryl Streep*): "Meryl Streep is so talented, she could do a remake of 'The Wizard of Oz' on her own. At least all the female parts. She could act and sing Dorothy, she'd do a great Auntie Em with a Kansas twang, and she could play the Wicked Witch without too much makeup… she's already got the nose for it. She could even play the men, if she chose to. The only part even she couldn't touch would be Toto (*the dog*)."

Barbra Streisand

If any woman is more talented and famous than this girl from Brooklyn, the world has yet to know about her. Singer, song writer, actress, and movie producer and director, she has become one of the wealthiest women.

Before her two marriages, she was in relationships with several famous actors, a tennis star, a network television anchorman, and even a sitting President of the United States. Her heart now belongs to her current husband, a former and present television star. She could talk a lot about men and marriage in the ladies' room, but probably would prefer to sing, even if some of the songs would be sad.

"There is nothing more important in life than love."

"Sometimes you resent the people you love and need the most. Love is so fascinating in all its forms, and I think everyone who has ever been a mother will relate to this."

"It is every woman's dream to be some man's dream woman."

Born Barbara Joan Streisand in Brooklyn, New York on April 24, 1942, her father a high school teacher and her mother secretary at the same school. She is Jewish, of Polish, Ukrainian, and Russian descent. Her mother had a fine soprano singing voice and her maternal grandfather had been a cantor.

A few months after Streisand's first birthday, her father died from an epileptic seizure at the age of 34. She went to work at an early age to help her mother and older brother financially. She earned some money by singing at weddings and summer camp and at the age of nine had a music audition at MGM records, but it was not successful.

Still wanting to become an actress, she got a walk-on part in a stage play outside New York City and worked backstage at dinner theaters. She became an usher at the theater where the stage musical *The Sound of Music* played on Broadway early in 1960. She entered a singing contest at a gay nightclub and sang two songs, winning the contest amid "thunderous applause." She shortened her first name to Barbra, just to be different, and began singing at a nightclub for $125 a week, opening for comedienne Phyllis Diller.

Her singing career began to take off under the management of Martin Erlichman who helped her get her first role in a Broadway musical, *I Can Get It for You Wholesale* (1962). She fell in love with and lived with its star, Elliott Gould. Both she and the musical were hits and her singing "stopped the show." A mezzo-soprano, she has a range of three octaves.

Long career story short, she has become one of the best-selling music artists of all time, selling more than 245 million records worldwide and has been awarded two Academy Awards, ten Grammy Awards, five Emmys, a Special Tony Award, 11 Golden Gloves, four Peabody Awards, and the Presidential Medal of Freedom. She won the Best Actress Academy Award for her first film, "Funny Girl," tying with Katharine Hepburn and for composing the best song of the year, "Evergreen," the first woman to be so honored.

Her other hit films include "The Way We Were," co-starring Robert Redford, and "A Star Is Born," a musical of the classic Hollywood story. She became the first woman to write, produce direct, and star in a major studio film, "Yentl," in 1983, and received a Golden Globe Award for best director, the only woman to win that award.

She was married twice, to Elliott Gould, from 1983 until their divorce in 1971, having a son together, and then to actor-producer-director James Brolin whom she married in 1998. He is a film and television star best known for the series "Dr. Marcus Welby" for which he won an Emmy award. Barbra has been offered several million dollars to write her autobiography, which Brolin vigorously opposes because she would "tell all" in it, about both of their alleged affairs with others.

She has said she had romances with actors Elvis Presley, Ryan O'Neal, Kris Kristofferson, Jon Voight, Richard Gere, Warren

Beatty, Don Johnson, tennis star Andre Agassi, television newsman Peter, and President Bill Clinton, and nursed a decades-long crush on Robert Redford, her co-star in "The Way We Were" (1973).

Rumors of a Streisand-Brolin divorce persist, but she denies wanting to divorce. A large settlement would be at stake because she is worth $550 million and he $145 million. She is known for her philanthropy, raising many millions of dollars and giving more millions as gifts to causes and organizations including those working on environment preservation, voter education, protection of civil liberties, women's issues, gay rights, and nuclear disarmament.

On Men -- "Why is it men are permitted to be obsessed about their work, but women are only permitted to be obsessed about men?"

"Being a woman in music was fine, but when I wanted to direct, I was poking myself in a man's world."

"Marlon Brando. The finest actor who ever lived. He was my idol when I was 13. He's done enough work to last two lifetimes. Everything I do, I think: Can Brando play this with me?"

On Marriage -- "Why does a woman work ten years to change a man's habits and then complain that he's not the man she married?"

"What is exciting is not for one person to be stronger than the other, but for two people to have met their match and yet they are equally stubborn, as obstinate, as passionate, as crazy as the other."

On Sex and Sexual Preference -- "Nobody on this Earth has the right to tell anyone that their love for another human being is morally wrong."

The Inner Woman -- (*On her childhood*): "I was kind of a wild child. I wasn't taught the niceties of life... When I wanted love from my mother, she gave me food." (*She said her mother was stressed and overworked and couldn't give her the attention she craved.*)

"I was a personality before I became a person. I am simple, complex, generous, selfish,. Unattractive, beautiful, lazy, and driven."

"I need instant gratification."

"How I wish we lived in a time when laws were not necessary to safeguard us from discrimination."

"I can take the truth; just don't lie to me."

"I like simple things. Elastic waists, so I can eat."

"I arrived in Hollywood without having my nose fixed, my teeth capped. That is very gratifying to me. My nose was part of my heritage, and if I had talent to sing and act, why wasn't that enough?"

"I have one son. Of everything I've done in my life, nothing matches the feeling of having life growing inside you."

"I just became a singer because I could never get work as an actress."

(*On her mother not wanting her to go into show business*): "My desires were strengthened by wanting to prove to my mother that I *could* be a star."

"I don't read music. Not even essentially. Not even nonessentially."

"I need instant gratification."

"I like to stay home a lot. I like to do other things, too, like decorate or build."

"I think of myself as a girl from Brooklyn."

Elizabeth Taylor

One of the most-married women in Hollywood history, she was a film star since she was a child in 1942 and remained one all her life. She was both lucky and unlucky in love, married nine times, but the real love of her life may have been her best friend, Montgomery Clift, who was gay, as were some of her other close friends including Rock Hudson and Roddy McDowell.

She also was in relationships both during and between her marriages. Elizabeth made headlines for stealing singer Eddie Fisher from his wife Debbie Reynolds, and was often on the covers of fan magazines during her two marriages to Richard Burton. It surprised everyone when her final husband was a laborer she met at a drug rehabilitation center.

"My mother says I didn't open my eyes for eight days after I was born, but when I did, the first thing I saw was an engagement ring. I was hooked."

"I don't entirely approve of some of the things I have done, or am, or have been. But I'm me. God knows, I'm me."

"Some of my best leading men have been dogs and horses."

Born Elizabeth Rosemond Taylor in Hampstead, London, England on February 27, 1932, her father was an art dealer and her mother had been a stage actress but gave it up upon her marriage. Her parents were U.S. citizens working in London at the time of her birth. When Elizabeth was seven years old, she and her mother emigrated to America when Nazi Germany began invading northern Europe in 1939. Her father settled his business in England and soon joined them in Los Angeles, California.

An astonishingly beautiful child, Elizabeth's first film was a small part in a 1942 film when she was ten years old, and then was signed to a contract with MGM Studios. Her first film there, "Lassie Come Home" (1943) got her a lot of fan attention and she became lifelong friends with the film's young star, fellow Briton Roddy McDowell, who was a homosexual. She became a star the following year for "National Velvet."

Taylor's first love may have been handsome young football star Glenn Davis whom she met when she was 17. "I want him!" she told friends. He fell in love with her and gave her a gold football to add to her charm bracelet and she is said to have added him to it. Davis only left her to serve in the Korean War, but by the time he returned, she had become bored with him and had found love elsewhere, in the arms of William Pauley, Jr., son of a wealthy businessman. Davis then married actress Terry Moore.

Taylor graduated from juvenile parts to teenage and then to mature roles when she was 19 and co-starred with Montgomery Clift in the romantic drama "A Place in the Sun" (1951) for which she was nominated for a Best Actress Academy Award. She loved Clift off-screen but he too was a homosexual so they just became great friends, like brother and sister. After several more films, she starred in "Giant" (1955) with Rock Hudson and James Dean, both of them homosexuals (1955). By then, she was considered not only a fine actress but one of the world's great beauties.

One evening at her home during the filming of "Raintree County" in 1957, Clift had been with her and some other friends when, upon driving away afterward on a dangerous curve, his car hit a tree. Elizabeth ran to his aid and saved his life by climbing into the wreckage and removing some of his teeth to keep him from choking to death. He had facial plastic surgery and was later kept alive on drugs and finished the film, although he lost his handsome face in the accident which aged him considerably overnight.

Taylor was nominated for best actress Academy Awards several times and won for her steamy role as a call girl romancing a married man in "Butterfield 8" (1960.) Three years later she starred with Rex Harrison and Richard Burton in "Cleopatra" which was one of the costliest films ever made and not a box office success. She won her second best actress Oscar for playing a shrewish wife of a college professor in "Who's Afraid of Virginia Woolf" (1966).

Taylor was married nine times, twice to actor Richard Burton, and divorced all her husbands except Michael Todd who died during their marriage. She was 18 when she married handsome and wealthy hotel heir Conrad Hilton, Jr. (1950-1951). "This is it!" she told friends, but weeks into their marriage she realized it was a mistake; she had married partly to become independent from her mother. Elizabeth and "Nicky" Hilton had little in common, he was a heavy drinker, and abusive to her. They divorced after only nine months of marriage.

She then married British actor Michael Wilding in 1952. She had met him while filming "The Conspirator" in England in 1948. He was 20 year older than Elizabeth, but she liked that and thought they could have a "calm and quiet" relationship and he likely became a father figure to her. She had two sons with him, but as her career continued upward, his declined, and while she was away on a film location he was said to have had strippers at their home. She divorced him in 1957.

Taylor then was married to "Around the World in 80 Days" theatre and film producer Michael Todd from 1957 until his death in a plane crash in 1958. They had a daughter together, and his sudden death traumatized her. Her next husband was singer-actor Eddie Fisher (1959-1964), who was a friend of Todd's and consoled her in her grief. Their affair created a scandal because he was at the time married to actress Debbie Reynolds.

Ten days after her divorce from Fisher, Taylor married her co-star in "Cleopatra," Richard Burton in 1964 but after three tumultuous years together she divorced him in 1967. She remarried him in 1975 but divorced him permanently a year later, after having one child with him. They made eleven films together and he lavished her with diamonds, furs, painting, a yacht and a jet plane. They loved each other very much but found it difficult and then impossible to live together, partly because he was a very heavy drinker.

After their divorce, Elizabeth said "After Richard, the men in my life were just there to hold the coat, to open the door. All the men in my life after Richard were really just company." Her next husband was

U.S. Senator from Virginia John Warner (1976-1982), but she found her life with him in Washington, D.C. to be boring and lonely. She became depressed, put on weight, drank, and began abusing prescription meditations. Her final husband was Larry Fortensky (1991-1996), a construction worker she met while they were both in drug and alcohol rehabilitation at the Betty Ford Center. Their marriage lasted five years. . No one knows for sure whether Richard Burton or Montgomery Clift was the true love of her life, but this editor thinks it was Clift.

She sold her Fortensky wedding pictures to a magazine for $1 million with which she started her AIDS foundation which over twelve years raised $83 million for research and cure of the disease. She also auctioned off her diamond-and-emerald engagement ring from Burton to raise more money for the foundation. Taylor retired from acting in 2003 but is remembered as one of the most beautiful of Hollywood stars. She appeared on the covers of more than 1,000 magazines around the world, on *Life* magazine a record 14 times.

She did not like to be called "Liz." She also did not like hairy men, although Montgomery Clift was a very hairy exception. She drew the line with young Mark Harmon before they would star in the television version of "Sweet Bird of Youth" (1989). She said he had a very pretty face but looked like a hairy ape, so before she would allow him to climb in bed with her naked, she had all his considerable body hair shaved off.

On Men -- (*About Montgomery Clift*): "The most gorgeous thing in the world, and easily one of the best actors. Monty was the most emotional actor I have ever worked with. And the most contagious."

(*On Michael Jackson*): "What is a genius? What is a living legend? What is a mega star? Michael Jackson, that's all. And when you think you know him, he gives you more. I think he is one of the finest people to hit this planet, and, in my estimation, he is the true King of Pop, Rock, and Soul. He is one of the most normal people I know. He is part of my heart. We would do anything for each other. I will love Michael Jackson forever."

(*On Clark Gable*): "He was the epitome of the movie star... so romantic, such bearing, such friendliness."

(*On John Wayne*): "He is as tough as an old nut and as soft as a yellow ribbon. His image had as much impact in the world as many of our Presidents have had, but Duke was a great actor, a great humanitarian, but always himself. To be a friend was a lifetime thing."

(*On Welsh-born actor Richard Burton*): "Richard came on the set (*of 'Cleopatra,' hen they first met*) and sort of sidled over to me and said, 'Has anybody ever told you that you're a very pretty girl?' I thought, 'O gevalt, the great lover, the great wit, the great Welsh intellectual and he comes out with a corny line like that!' But then I noticed his hands were shaking as if he had Saturday night palsy. He had been drinking and had the world's worst hangover."

On Marriage -- (*On her marriage to Eddie Fisher*): "Eddie and I are rising above public opinion... I'm not taking anything away from Debbie (*Reynolds*) because she never really had it."

(*On her marriage to Michael Wilding*): "I'm afraid in those last few years I gave him a rather rough time. Sort of henpecked him and probably wasn't mature enough for him. It wasn't that we had anything to fight over. We just weren't happy... We started as husband and wife, but it ended like brother and sister. (*Wilding said of her)*: "She used to look to me for the answers... come to me for advice...like a little girl."

"I don't pretend to be an ordinary housewife."

The Inner Woman -- (*On turning 53 years old*): "I think I'm finally growing up, and about time."

"I hate being called 'Liz,' because it can sound like such a hiss."

"I had a hollow leg. I could drink everyone under the table and not get drunk. My capacity was terrifying."

"Success is a great deodorant. It takes away all your past smells."

"You'll find out who your real friends are when you're involved in a scandal."

"It someone's dumb enough to offer me a million dollars to make a picture, I'm certainly not dumb enough to turn it down."

"I believe in mind over matter and doing anything you set your mind on."

"I, along with the critics, have never taken myself very seriously."

(*On Joan Rivers*): "That horrible blonde woman? I couldn't be bothered paying attention to anything she says about me."

(*On Hollywood gossip columnists Hedda Hopper and Louella Parsons*): "They were both bitches!"

"I have the emotions of a child in the body of a woman. I was rushed into womanhood for the movies. It caused me long moments of unhappiness and doubt."

"The ups and downs, the problems and stress, along with all the happiness, have given me optimism and hope because I am living proof of survival."

"I've come through things that would have felled an ox. That fills me with optimism, not just for myself, but for our particular species."

"Straight sex, gay sex, bisexual sex, use a condom whoever you are."

Shirley Temple

Life for the most famous child star in films was not always one of singing and dancing on The Good Ship Lollipop, but she weathered the storm of an unhappy first marriage with good humor and perseverance. How could any man, much less her husband, hit her?

The spunk and optimism she possessed as a child star transferred to movie theater audiences and helped America through the 1930's Great Depression. She found true love in her second marriage and social fulfillment in being a delegate to the United Nations and a U.S. ambassador.

"Long ago, I became more interested in the real world than in make-believe."

"There's nothing like real love. Nothing."

Born Shirley Jane Temple in Santa Monica, California on April 28, 1928 to a banker and his wife. A beautiful, blonde curly-haired child showing talent at an early age for singing and dancing, she got into films when she was three year old, and quickly became the top child star of the 1930s. Her mother fashioned little Shirley's hair in pin curls for each movie, and they numbered exactly 56 curls.

Audiences loved the talented, sweet little girl and she was heavily merchandised, with dolls of her (this editor had a replica of her made from a bar of soap), cut-outs, phonograph recordings of her singing, her photograph on cups. She was the top box-office actor for four years (1935-1938), beating out over Joan Crawford, Bing Crosby, Gary Cooper, and Robert Taylor.

Frequently cast as "Little Miss Fix-It," helping save marriages, President Franklin D. Roosevelt credited her uplifting spirit in films as being an inspiration for millions of Americans who were out of work and homeless to persevere during the Great Depression of the 1930s. She was awarded a special Academy Award at the age of six in 1935, a juvenile-sized Oscar for her work the previous year. Upon receiving it from actor-writer Irvin S. Cobb, she thanked him and then asked her mother, "Mommy, can I go home now?" It brought down the house and she later explained that her award was almost the last of a long evening and she was feeling sleepy and wanted to go to bed. She presented Walt Disney with his special Academy Award for "Snow White and the Seven Dwarfs" (1937) which consisted of a regular-sized Oscar for him and also seven miniature Oscars for the dwarfs.

Temple was considered to play Dorothy in "The Wizard of Oz" (1939), but her studio, 20th Century-Fox, refused to loan her out to MGM and Judy Garland got the part. Temple's best-remembered films as a child star include "Bright Eyes" in 1934 in which she sang "On the Good Ship Lollipop" which became her signature song. As a teenager, her stand-out films included "Since You Went Away" and "The Bachelor and the Bobby-Soxer" opposite Cary Grant; and as an adult "Fort Apache" and "That Hagen Girl" opposite Ronald Reagan.

She retired from the screen in 1949, then had a series on television from 1958 to 1961, and afterwards became involved in Republican politics. President Richard Nixon named her as a U.S. delegate to the United Nations, then in 1972 she became special assistant to the chairman of the President's Council on Environment. During that service she underwent a radical mastectomy.

Later, she became U.S. ambassador to Ghana and Czechoslovakia. About her ability representing America, she was called "capable and tough." Her ex-husband John Agar tried to discourage her first appointment in 1969, telling the FBI during a background check that she was "emotionally unstable" and would "over-react if she didn't get her way." Dozens of others came to her rescue, including Ronald Reagan who called her a "very courageous woman of the highest morals." Her appointments always went through and she proved she was as hard a worker in them as she had been in acting.

Temple was married twice, her first husband being actor John Agar whom she married in 1945, had one child with him, and they divorced in 1950. She was instrumental in starting his film career, getting John Ford, who had directed her in one of her early films,

"Wee Willie Winkie" (1937), to cast him as her young husband in the 1948 western, "Fort Apache." He went on to star in a series of science-fiction and horror films. Agar said Temple's mother wrecked their marriage because she interfered in their affairs too much, but he reportedly was a drinker and sometimes physically abused her.

Two weeks after her divorce from Agar, she married San Francisco businessman Charles Black and they had two children together before his death in 2005. While they had been dating, he admitted to her that he had never seen any of her films. It didn't matter to her, she had fallen in love with him on first sight when they first met in Honolulu when he was working for a shipping company there. Her daughter with Black, Lori "Lorax" Black," became the bass player for a rock band, The Melvin's.

Both Shirley MacLaine and Shirley Jones were named after Shirley Temple. A non-alcoholic cocktail, "The Shirley Temple," was named in her honor, consisting of ginger ale or 7-Up, grenadine, and orange juice, topped with a cherry and slice of lemon. It is not known if she ever drank it. She said that out of the $3 million her films generated for her studio, she only saw $45,000 in her trust fund. It was never learned what became of the rest of the money she earned from her contract.

She died in Woodside, California on February 10, 2014 of chronic obstructive pulmonary disease at the age of 85. She was named the top child film star of all time and ranked No. 18 among The American Film Institute's 50 Greatest Screen Legends.

On Marriage -- "Shirley Temple doesn't hurt Shirley Temple Black. Shirley Temple helps Shirley Black. She is thought of as a friend, which I am!"

The Inner Woman -- "I stopped believing in Santa Claus when I was six. Mother took me to see him in a department store and he asked for my autograph."

"I guess I was an early method actress. I would go to a quiet part of the sound stage with my mother. I wouldn't think of anything sad. I would make my mind a blank. In a minute. I could cry."

(*Her mother wanted her to 'sparkle' in her films*): "Any star can be devoured by human adoration, sparkle by sparkle."

(*When she was a teenager or an adult*): "One famous movie executive who shall remain nameless, exposed himself to me in his office. I said, 'I thought you were a producer, not an exhibitor.'"

"I'm not too proud of the movies I made as a grown-up except for 'That Hagen Girl,' which nobody remembers but which gave me a chance to act."

"I class myself with Rin Tin Tin (*the dog star*). People in the (*1930's*) Depression wanted (*movie stars*) to cheer them up, and they fell in love with a dog and a little girl."

(*In 2005, to the Screen Actor's Guild*): "I've been blessed with three wonderful careers – motion pictures and television; wife, mother, and grandmother; and diplomatic services. I have one piece of advice for those of you who want to receive the 'Lifetime Achievement Award.' Start early."

"When I saw work shoes I would know that that person worked. I was very worried about people with shiny, pointed shoes as a child.
I learned that I liked the working crew the most, more than the stars. I liked the guys that I worked with very, very much. It was my extended family. We had a marvelous time. I teased them a lot, too, particularly the cameramen, who had a lot of trouble with me."

(*As an adult star*): "I do get pinched a lot. Mostly it's women, my peer group, and even older than I am, and I'm old. They tend to want to touch. If I go on tour, I'll get pinched on the arm, the back, the cheeks, the chin. They say, 'You're so cute,' or 'You were so cute.' Then they hang on, and I come home black and blue. It's a hazard."

(*When an ambassador*): "I work a 17-hour day, and I'm personally responsible for 108 staff members in the embassy."

"When I was 14, I was the oldest I ever was. I'm trying to get younger ever since."

"We would have to invent the United Nations if we did not have it, which is not an original thought."

"Time is money. Wasted time means wasted money means trouble."

"Most of the people in Ghana wouldn't know me as an actress. They'd know me for my work at the United Nations."

"The U.N. acts as the world's conscience, and over 85 percent of the work that is done by the United Nations is in the social, economic, educational and cultural fields."

"Politicians are actors, too, don't you think? Usually, if you like people and you're outgoing, not a shy little thing, you can do pretty well in politics."

"I've always been bossy."

"Many people consider me an old friend."

Mother Teresa

"Intense love does not measure; it just gives."

"Spread love everywhere you go. Let no one ever come to you without leaving happier."

"I have found the paradox, that if you love until it hurts, there can be no more hurt, only more love."

"Love begins at home, and it is not how much we do, but how much love we put into that action."

Born Agnes Gonxha Bojaxhiu in Albania in 1910, at the age of 18 she entered the Orders of the Sisters of Our Lady of Loreto in Ireland. Ordained a Roman Catholic nun as Sister Teresa in 1937, she then served as principal of a Catholic high school in Calcutta, India. While there, she was moved by the presence of the sick and dying on the city's streets. She asked for and was granted permission from the Pope to begin a ministry among the sick and founded the Missionaries of Charity which over the years extended her work onto five continents.

Called by many "a living saint," she described herself as "only an instrument" of God. She was awarded the Nobel Peace Prize in 1979 and continued ministering to the poor until her health failed and she died in Calcutta in 1997. She was named a saint on September 4, 2016.

More quotes from Mother Teresa on love, poverty, abortion:

"Let us always meet each other with a smile, for the smile is the beginning of love…We shall never know all the good that a simple smile can do… Every time you smile at someone, it is an action of love, a gift to that person, a beautiful thing."

"We think sometimes that poverty is only being hungry, naked, and homeless. The poverty of being unwanted, unloved and uncared for is the greater poverty. We must start in our own homes to remedy this kind of poverty… Even the rich are hungry for love, for being cared for, for being wanted, for having someone to call their own."

"The greatest destroyer of peace is abortion, because if a mother can kill her own child, what is left for me to kill you and you to kill me? There is nothing between… It is a poverty to decide that a child must die so that you may live as you wish."

"If we pray, we will believe; If we believe, we will love; If we love, we will serve."

"Let nothing perturb you, nothing frighten you. All things pass. God does not change, Patience achieves everything."

"Be happy in the moment, that's enough. Each moment is all we need, not more… Yesterday is gone. Tomorrow has not yet come. We have only today. Let us begin."

"I know God won't give me anything I can't handle. I just wish he didn't trust me so much."

(*When receiving the Nobel Prize for peace she was asked,* "What can we do to promote world peace?" She replied, "Go home and love your family."

"Spread love everywhere you go: first of all in your own home. Give love to your children, to your wife or husband, to a next door neighbor… Let no one ever come to you without leaving better and happier. Be the living expression of God's kindness; kindness in your face, kindness in your eyes, kindness in your smile, kindness in your warm greeting."

"The success of love is in the loving; it is not in the result of loving. Of course it is natural in love to want the best for the other person, but whether it turns out that way or not does not determine the value of what we have done."

"Life is a game. Play it."

Gene Tierney

Although never considered to be a film sex goddess, she was one of the most beautiful of Hollywood actresses, her roles ranging from innocent Polynesian native beauty to heartless wives and even a calculating murderess. She was in love affairs with actors, a prince, a count, even a sitting President, and was married three times. Mental illness tried to take its toll on her but she bravely fought the battle and won.

"I was fine when it came to cheering up others; not so fine with myself."

"My departure from Hollywood was described as a walk-out. No one understood that I was cracking up."

"I existed in a world that never is… the prison of the mind."

"A flame burns brightest just before it goes out."

Born Gene Eliza Tierney in Brooklyn, New York on November 19, 1920, her father was an insurance broker and mother a gymnastics teacher. She grew up in society and attended the best schools, including a finishing school in Switzerland. Her acting career began when she was 18, in plays on Broadway. She was "discovered" at that same age when she was on a guided tour of Warner Brothers in Hollywood. Director Anatole Litvak took one look at her and said, "Young woman, you ought to be in pictures." Film producer Darryl F. Zanuck, the head of 20th Century-Fox studios, signed her to a film contract. He said she was without question the most beautiful woman in film history.

Tierney starred in many films but is best known for her performance as the beautiful victim of murder in "Laura" (1944). Her performance as a shrewish wife in "Leave Her to Heaven" (1945), earned her a best actress Academy Award nomination. She also co-starred as Tyrone Power's leading lady in several excellent films including "The Razor's Edge" (1946).

Tierney had love affairs with Tyrone Power, Prince Aly Khan, and John F. Kennedy in 1946 but he left her because of his political aspirations. She was married twice, first to dress designer Oleg Cassini (1941-1952), with whom she had two children. Cassini married Gene after Hedy Lamarr had divorced him. Tierney and Oleg Cassini met at a friend's home and felt a mutual attraction. He called himself Count Cassini, of Russian nobility. They danced and not longer afterward he proposed and on 1941 they eloped to Las Vegas and were married. He then designed most of her clothes for her films.

Shortly after her marriage to Cassini she learned that her father, whom she had idolized, was divorcing her mother to marry a family friend. She then learned that her father, whom she idolized, had spent her entire $50,000 in savings after a failed business venture. Her salary had been paid to a company he controlled. Hurt and angry, she saw him only once before his death in 1963.

Gene became pregnant by Cassini and was on a World War II USO entertainment tour when she caught German measles. She was unaware of it when she gave birth to a daughter who was born mentally retarded and when four years old had to be institutionalized. "The emptiness inside me was devastating," Tierney wrote later in an autobiography. "Daria was a sweet little girl with golden curls and soft skin. Physically, she looked just like any other four-year old. I cried for Daria and I cried for me until I didn't know where the tears came from." Daria grew into adulthood with the mind of a child and remained institutionalized until her death years later.

A year after Daria was born, Gene was approached at a party by a former woman Marine who said they had met at a USO canteen two years earlier. The woman said she had been quarantined at the time with German measles but had sneaked out to see her at the canteen. "You were my favorite actress," she said, "and I just had to see you." Stunned, Gene said nothing.

Her marriage to Cassini was reduced to just an "entanglement" by 1946 and while filming "Dragonwyck," a Gothic melodrama, she met John F. Kennedy after his return from World War II. They discovered they shared grief of having experience with the mentally ill, since one of his sisters was retarded. They became lovers, but he was a Catholic with political ambitions. "You know, Gene," he told her, "I can never marry you." She whispered, "Bye, bye, Jack," and left him.

Gene and Cassini reconciled and had a second daughter together who was healthy and later married and had healthy children. Gene's marriage to Cassini ended in divorce in 1952. The following year she sailed on an Atlantic Ocean voyage and was in a relationship with Prince Aly Khan whom Rita Hayworth had divorced earlier that year. She returned to Hollywood and resumed her film career, but by then had been experiencing mood swings ranging from periods of euphoria to high anxiety and depression.

While filming "The Left Hand of God" in 1955, her co-star Clark Gable realized she was desperately ill. She wrote in her autobiography, "As long as I was playing someone else, everything was fine. It was when I had to be myself that the problems began."

Her brother urged her to enter a sanitarium in New York City. "There, to my eternal regret, I received my first electric shock therapy." It only gave her temporary relief, and she underwent more shock therapy at a second mental institution in Connecticut.

She eventually came close to suicide, nearly leaping from a 14th floor window of her mother's Manhattan apartment. It led to her being treated at the Menninger Clinic in Topeka, Kansas. She did not get shock treatments there, and other methods including talk therapy enabled her to recover enough to live on her own again.

She got a job in a dress shop for $40 a week, and while vacationing in Aspen, Colorado, met millionaire Houston, Texas oilman W. Howard Lee. He was 70 years old and in the process of divorcing Hedy Lamarr. He and Gene, then 50, began a relationship and despite him being cautioned that her mental illness could return, they married in 1960. They had homes in Houston and Delray Beach, Florida, and Gene wrote in her autobiography, "The only time I was really happy was in my childhood, and now."

Gene and Lee had 20 happy years together until his death in 1981. She died of emphysema in Houston on November 6, 1991 at the age of 70. She had earlier said that studio bosses wanted her to speak with a lower voice, so they had her smoke cigarettes, an unfortunate demand because a voice coach could have done that without risking her life.

On Love -- "Nothing strengthens a woman's determination to be in love quite so much as being told that she cannot."

On Men -- (*On marriage to Cassini, in a 1946 interview*): "I have a system for never staying angry at my husband. There is a room next to their bedroom which we call 'The Mad Room.' If one of us gets angry with the other, the one who is angry goes into that room. Its walls are decorated with photographs of us in loving times, and there is a phonograph with our favorite records. We have never remained angry with each other for very long."

The Inner Woman -- "Jealousy is, I think, the worst of all faults because it makes a victim of both parties."

"It was the fashion of the time *(during her film career)*, and still is, to feel that all actors are neurotic, or they would not be actors."

"Throughout my career, I was to be cast as a frontier girl, an aristocrat, an Arabian, a Eurasian, a Polynesian, and a Chinese."

"Life is a little like a message in a bottle, to be carried by the winds and the tides."

"It is difficult to write about any form of mental disease, especially your own, without sounding as if you were examining a bug under glass."

"My departure from Hollywood was described as a walk-out. No one understood that I was cracking up."

"That strange conflict in the American character: we pride ourselves on being the melting pot of the world, but we insist on regarding most immigrants with suspicion."

"Wealth, beauty, and fame are transient. When those are gone, little is left except the need to be useful."

"The things we ignore often come back to us in our sleep."

"I approached everything… my job, my family, my romances, with intensity."

"I admire anyone who rids himself of an addiction."

Lily Tomlin

The funny lady was in a romantic relationship with Jane Wagner since 1971 and they married in 2013 after 42 years together. Wagner is Tomlin's comedy writer and producer.

"If love is the answer, could you rephrase the question?"

"I had a friend who was getting married. I gave her a subscription to the magazine Modern Bride. The subscription lasted longer than the marriage."

"Reality is a crutch for people who can't cope with drugs."

Born Mary Jean Tomlin in Detroit, Michigan on September 1, 1939, her father was a factory worker and her mother a nurse's aide. She was born and grew up near the end of the 1930's Great Depression when ended when America entered World War II in 1941. After graduating from Cass Technical High School in 1957, she became a pre-medical student at Wayne State University but dropped out to pursue a career in show business. She worked as a waitress in a Howard Johnson restaurant on Broadway near Times Square and her wise-cracks to customers made them laugh, so she saw herself as a possible comedienne.

She began her career as a stand-up comic in Detroit and New York City nightclubs, then made her television debut on *The Merve Griffin Show*. She may be best known for her appearances on *Rowan & Martin's Laugh In*. Audiences loved the characters she played, especially the kooky telephone operator, Ernestine, and as Edith Ann, a precocious little girl in a big rocking chair.

She was nominated for an Academy Award as best supporting actress for playing a gospel-singing mother of two deaf children in "Nashville" (1975). She has been in a romantic relationship with Jane Wagner since 1971 and after 42 years together they married in 2013. Tomlin also is best friends with Jane Fonda. Tomlin won many awards for her records and comedy work as well as two Tony Awards, one a special award in 1977 and one for her one-woman show, "The Search for Intelligent Life in the Universe" in 1986, on which she and Jane Wagner collaborated in writing.

Tomlin says about her wife: "We share feelings about people and about the world. She's able to verbalize it and I'm able to physicalize it. She writes satirically but tenderly, and she loves farce and black comedy and broad slapstick. When you put all this together and make an audience laugh and be moved, it's just glorious."

On sex and sexuality -- (*About John Travolta*): "Maybe the major thing is how sensual he is. And sexy, too. The sensitivity and the sexuality are very strong. It's as if he had every dichotomy... masculinity, femininity, refinement, crudity. You see him, you fall in love a little bit" (*Travolta repeatedly denies vehemently that he is gay, but don't bring it up because he might sue you.*)

The Inner Woman -- "There will be sex after death. We just won't be able to feel it."

"The trouble with the rat race is that even if you win, you're still a rat."

(*When asker her feelings when d came out as a lesbian*): "I felt jealous. Because I'd been around much longer, and I'm gay. I admired her, but at the same time, I thought, 'Oh, darn it! I wish that had been me. I would have liked to have left that legacy.' So I am extremely proud of her. When I say I was jealous, I was jealous in a good way. I thought it was an extraordinary moment."

"We have reason to believe that man first walked upright to free his hands for masturbation."

"The road to success is always under construction."

"Just remember: We're all in this alone."

"Instead of working for the survival of the fittest, we should be working for the survival of the wittiest – then we can all die laughing."

Lana Turner

One of Lana's first films was the Mickey Rooney teenage comedy, "Love Finds Andy Hardy" in 1938. She looked for love ever since, but never really found it, although married eight times. Like at least half a dozen other Hollywood sex goddesses, she fell in love with Tyrone Power but found that he was not romantic enough or at all. As was said by others in the ladies' room, Ty was bisexual but preferred men. Few stars were as beautiful as Lana, and few as unlucky in love.

"I liked the boys and the boys liked me."

"A gentleman is simply a patient wolf."

"There is no such thing as love."

"The truth is, sex doesn't mean that much to me now. It never did, really. It was romance I wanted, kisses and candlelight, that sort of thing. I never did dig sex very much."

"I planned on having one husband and seven children, but it turned out the other way around."

Born Julia Jean Mildred Francis Turner in Wallace, Idaho on February 8, 1920, her father was a miner and her mother a housewife, both teenagers. Her father was murdered in an all-night crap game when she was 9 years old and she and her mother moved to California for work.

Legend says Lana was discovered for the movies while having a soda at a drug store counter, but it was not true. She went from studio to studio in search of work as an actress and at the age of 17 got a small part in "They Won't Forget" in 1937. Young men fell for her when she became known as "The Sweater Girl" and appeared in "Love Finds Andy Hardy." Turner continued making films and appearing on television, and despite being a fine actress, her love life overshadowed that and she also had a battle with alcoholism.

Turner was in the headlines in 1958 when her daughter Cheryl Crane fatally stabbed Lana's boyfriend, handsome gangster Johnny Stompanato. He had been in a rage at Lana, accusing her of having an affair with British actor Sean Connery. A jury took only 20 minutes to acquit Cheryl of a murder charge because of testimony that Stompanato had been savagely beating her mother and the stabbing was to protect Lana. His death was ruled justifiable homicide.

After his death, Lana said she had not known he had been married three times, had a son, or that he was a gangster, but others said if she had known he had ties to criminals like Mickey Cohen, it would have excited her and turned her on, not off. Stompanato was, however, often very abusive to Lana. When he told her to hop, she had to hop, and when he told her to jump, she had to jump. He also threatened her with physical harm, saying "I'll mutilate you. I'll hurt you so you'll be so repulsive you'll have to hide forever." He also threatened Connery who responded by knocking him to the floor.

The publicity about Stompanato's death did not hurt Lana's career. Audiences flocked to see her next film, a remake of the 1934 classic "The Imitation of Life" (1959) in which she gave a brilliant performance. She continued as a major star in films for two more decades, then turned to television and starred in the "Falcon Crest" prime time series (1982-1983). Her favorite actresses were Kay Francis and Norma Shearer, and Linda Darnell was a close friend. A shoe-aholic, at one time Lana owned 698 pairs.

Beautiful but unlucky in love, Lana had eight husbands, twice married to actor Stephen Crane. She also was married to bandleader Artie Shaw (for seven months in 1940); Crane (from 1943 until the marriage was annulled in 1944 after she learned he was already married to another woman), and they remarried a month later but divorced permanently after about a year and a half, having her only child with him. Her next husbands, all of whom she later divorced, were wealthy womanizing playboy Henry "Bob" Topping, Jr. (1948-1952), actor Lex Barker (1953-1957) who was a handsome hunk and played "Tarzan" in several films, and she fainted during their wedding); rancher Frederick May (1960-1962); Hollywood playboy Robert P. Eaton (1965-1969); and fraudulent hypnotist Ronald Dante (1969-1972).

When being interviewed by Hollywood gossip columnist Hedda Hopper while her future husband Lex Barker was in the room, Lana got up and moved a large vase of flowers that obstructed her view of him, telling Hopper, "He's brand new and I want to look at him."

Barker said of Lana: "Lana Turner and I had some good times together. Especially before the nuptials... Lana Turner's not an outstanding actress, but a man is better off with a woman who can't lie too well. (*He didn't think she could.*) I'd be uncomfortable married to, say (*stage actress*), Katharine Cornell."

Before Tarzan, Lana had an affair with actor Fernando Lamas while they were both married to others. He later married actress Arlene Dahl and then swimmer-actress Esther Williams. Lana suffered three still-births (1949, 1951, 1956) because of having the Rf factor, a disease of the blood and immune system. Turner had become pregnant by Artie Shaw in 1940 and again by actor Tyrone Power in 1946, but had abortions both times. Turner wrote in her autobiography that she lost her virginity to lawyer Greg Bautzer in 1938 when she was 17, and their affair ended after Joan Crawford told her she was having one with him.

Lana found Bautzer to be handsome, mature, successful, and sophisticated, and they became engaged, but he didn't want to marry her or any one, preferring a playboy's life and womanizing. She was wearing Bautzer's engagement ring when she married Artie Shaw.

The man she loved above all others was Tyrone Power, but she said about their affair together, that he was not sexually passionate. "What we shared was, to me, far more important than the physical side of love." What she did not know, perhaps, was that he was bisexual and preferred men. "Tyrone never pressured me. Later, I heard rumors of a homosexual element to his nature, but I never saw it."

In her autobiography, Lana admitted that she was not the greatest lover in bed. "I wasn't frigid (*but*) if I didn't make love for weeks, I was content." She said that holding hands, cuddling and being close were more important to her than sex itself. Diagnosed with throat cancer in 1992, Lana Turner kept smoking almost until her death in Culver City, California on June 25, 1995 at the age of 75 after a long struggle with lung cancer..

On Men and Love -- (*While dating Lex Barker in 1953 when she was 31 and had known both marriage and divorce several times, she was asked about love, and replied that there is no such thing as love.*: She went on to say that she had been in affairs since a teenager and most everyone in Hollywood was playing musical beds. She was in an affair with actor Victor Mature while he was having one with Rita Hayworth, and she (*Lana*) was in love with singer-actor Tony Martin while he was in love with actress Alice Faye. The list was a lot longer than that. It led Lana to say "Nuts" when a man said he loved her.

"A successful man is one who makes more money than a wife can spend. A successful woman is one who can find such a man."

"I find men terribly exciting, and any girl who says she doesn't is an anemic old maid, a streetwalker, or a saint."

(*On Johnny Stompanato, she wrote him twelve love letters at times when they were apart, begging for his caresses and missed him terribly*): "So much that it hurts me. It is beautiful and yet it is terrible. I am yours, and I need you, MY MAN!" The letters were found by Stompanato's gangster friends after his death, were published, and made newspaper headlines all over the world.

On Marriage -- "With each marriage, I thought that that would be 'it,' In my wildest dreams I never, never thought that I would have seven husbands. If you can believe it, I thought at the time that each marriage would last forever. You see, with one bitterly painful exception (*she did not say which one, but may have meant Tyrone Power*), when I fell in love, I married."

(On her marriage to Artie Shaw): "I was not in love with him," she said later, and that the first time she let him kiss her was at their wedding when they eloped to Las Vegas and the justice presiding told her to. "After the ceremony, we went to an all-night diner for coffee. Suddenly, I realized that my mother had no idea where I was. The taxi drove us to the telegraph office, and I wrote out a message: 'Got married in Las Vegas. Call you later. Love, Lana.' Maybe it was subconscious, but I didn't mention who is was I'd married."

(On Shaw again): "Marriage meant permanence to me, but with Artie, I began to realize it was no marriage. It was hell." In a 1940 interview after their divorce, Lana said he disliked night clubs and preferred to invite his band to their home and play and drink together. He ordered her to be bartender, and bullied her for her lack of education. She also said that while they were dating he was "cavorting around" with Betty Grable who "carried torches for him in both hands" when she and Shaw eloped. His real love, she said, was his trumpet.

(On marriage to Bob Topping): She told an interviewer in 1953 that it was "probably the only really adult romantic situation" she ever had been in. She said this despite his proposing to her by dropping a diamond ring in her martini at a night club. She said he was a womanizer who was finally ready to settle down and have a home, which she wanted, too. They did not love each other wildly, passionately, but with restraint. Their marriage lasted four years.

"Lex Barker was very handsome. Just plain handsome."

The Inner Woman -- *(On Hollywood)*: "It was all beauty and it was all talent, and if you had it, they protected you."

"I always loved a challenge."

"It's said in Hollywood that you should always forgive your enemies because you never know when you'll have to work with them."

"Humor has been the balm of my life, but it's been reserved for those close to me, not part of the public Lana."

"If I don't laugh at least three times during the day, I've had a bad day. I've got to have a minimum of at least three good laughs. I wouldn't have survived without my sense of humor, and thank God I have always been able to laugh at myself."

"The thing about happiness is that it doesn't help you to grow; only unhappiness does that."

"I'm so grateful that my bed of roses was made up equally of blossoms and thorns. I've had a privileged, creative, exciting life, and I think that the parts that were less joyous were preparing me, testing me, strengthening me."

"I'm so gullible. I'm so damn gullible. And I am so sick of me being gullible."

"My life has been a series of emergencies."

"I haven't had an easy life, but I sure hasn't been a dull one. And I'm pretty proud of the way this gal has held up."

(O*n relationships, late in her life*): "Today things are different, and I think they are healthier. People fall in love and move in together, and nobody bats an eye. They get to know each other first, to see if their romance can survive the mundane things like whether or not he picks up after himself, or she leaves hair in the sink. Or that all-important question of sharing expenses, each pulling his or her own weight. Honeymoon first, and if it lasts, then marriage. I like that."

Mae West

Queen of the sexy double-meaning one-liners, Mae was another one-of-a-kind. Come up and see her sometime in the ladies' room and hear about her boyfriends and her one husband.

"It's not the man in your life that counts. It's the life in your man."

"A hard man is good to find."

"I only like two kinds of men... foreign and domestic."

Born Mary Jane West in Brooklyn, New York on August 17, 1893, her parents were both vaudevillians and her father also a prizefighter. She began her show business career as a 5-year-old child star in vaudeville. When she was 14, she was called "The Baby Vamp," a child version of a predatory woman or vampire.

She also wrote plays, arrested for one of which was called *Sex* and considered to be obscene, and spent ten days in jail in 1926 when she was 33 years old. Two years later she rocked Broadway with her play *Diamond Lil*. She became a film star sensation with "She Done Him Wrong" in 1933, based on a play she had written earlier. The film took in $2 million at the box office in its first three months and saved its studio, Paramount Pictures, from bankruptcy. It also zoomed her young co-star Cary Grant to stardom.

Her steamy films prompted the establishment of the Motion Picture Code which put limits on what could be seen or spoken in movies. She got around those limitations by writing dialogue with double entendres so it could be taken straight or suggestive.

She made one of her most famous films with W.C. Fields, "My Little Chickadee" (1940), and it was a huge hit but their only film together because they did not get along, Mae considering him to be crude.

Her famous walk, a shimmy with a hand on one hip, was accompanied by the invitation to men: "Come up and see me sometime." It became her most famous movie line, delivered to a very young Cary Grant in "She Done Him Wrong." She was often misquoted as having said to him, "Why don't you come up and see me sometime?" She left films to perform in stage shows that she wrote, but returned to movies in "Myra Breckenridge" (1970).

She was married and divorced only once, to fellow vaudeville performer Frank Wallace (1911-1942). They married when she was 17 and he 21. At their divorce trial, she said they had only lived together a few weeks. In 1913 she began an affair with Guido Deiro, an Italian-born pianist and accordionist who became a vaudeville headliner. She became pregnant by him, but had an abortion that resulted in her being unable to have more children. They traveled together on the vaudeville circuit, but never married.

Another of her boyfriends was an African-American boxing champion, William "Gorilla" Jones. He wanted to live in the same Manhattan apartment building she lived in, but its management barred blacks from living there, so she bought the building and he moved in.

During World II, U.S. Army and Navy pilots named their inflatable lifejackets after her, and they are still called "Mae West" today. She was also close to her family and when she moved into a penthouse apartment in Hollywood, after her mother's death, she provided homes, jobs, and financial support for her father, sister, and brother. She remained living in the penthouse until her death.

She always chose the handsomest young leading men for her stage shows including movie actor Michael Ames who also went under the name of Tod Andrews, but never had affairs with them. She also became famous for taking morning enemas which she said kept her skin looking like milk. She became one of Hollywood's highest-paid stars.

Cary Grant said of her: "Mae West did have an hourglass figure. She had, besides, a minute attention span… I think Mae West doesn't live in the real world. She has so many illusions, we have to be very

Cary Grant said of her: "Mae West did have an hourglass figure. She had, besides, a minute attention span... I think Mae West doesn't live in the real world. She has so many illusions, we have to be very careful what we say when we're around her now." (*She might have said the same about him.*)

When she was 61 and still performing on stage in Las Vegas, she became romantically involved with Chester Rybinski, one of the muscle-men in her show there who later changed his name to Paul Novak. He was 30 years younger than West, a wrestler and former Mr. California. They lived together and their romance lasted until her death. He said later, "I believe I was put on this Earth to take care of Mae West."

She neither drank alcohol nor smoked. She suffered from diabetes the final 15 years of her life, dying of natural causes in Hollywood on November 22, 1980 at the age of 87. She packed a lot of sex appeal but stood just 5 feet tall. The Coca-Cola bottle reportedly was inspired by her curvaceous figure. She was called "Queen of the World" and "The Statue of Libido."

On Men -- "Men are easy to get, but hard to keep."

"His mother should have thrown him away and kept the stork."

"The best way to hold a man is in your arms."

"A man can be short and dumpy and getting bald, but if he has fire, women will like him."

"A man's kiss is his signature."

"All discarded lovers should be given a second chance, but with somebody else."

"Men are my life, diamonds are my career!"

"When women go wrong, men go right after them!"

"Is that a gun in your pocket or are you just glad to see me?"

"Don't marry a man to reform him. That's what reform schools are for."

"Women like a man with a past, but they prefer a man with a present."

"Few men know how to kiss well. Fortunately, I've always had time to teach them."

"Too much of a good thing is wonderful."

"I always save one boyfriend for a rainy day... and another in case it doesn't rain."

"The man I don't like doesn't exist."

On Marriage -- (*In a 1935 interview, on her one and only marriage, to Frank Wallace*): "Marriage is wonderful! Of course, I'm just guessing, but it must be wonderful. Since the first of the year, eight different guys have called me up to tell me I married 'em. In Oshkosh or Oskaloosa, in Tulsa or Toledo. Now it's Milwaukee and points East. They've been traveling men, singing waiters, dance men, reporters, but not a single millionaire, darn it! Which makes it bigamy, and big o'me, too... It's all right to have a man around the house, but when you wake up in the morning to find a new husband with your grapefruit...

"About my husband... I'm like Will Rogers – all I know is what I read in the papers, and I've quit reading about Wallace. I never went much for the comics, anyway... Let's get this settled once and for all...I'm not married. I never have been married. Not to Frank Wallace. Not to anyone! I'm a single gal with a single-track mind, and it doesn't run to matrimony."

"Getting married is like trading in the adoration of many for the sarcasm of one."

"Marriage is a great institution. I'm not ready for an institution."

"Men are my hobby. If I ever got married, I'd have to give it up."

On Sex and Sexuality -- "Sex is emotion in motion."

"It's better to be looked over than overlooked."

On Love -- "Love conquers all things except poverty and a toothache."

"Look your best. Who said love is blind?"

"Love thy neighbor, and if he happens to be tall, debonair, and devastating, it will be that much easier."

"A woman in love can't be reasonable, or she probably wouldn't be in love."

"Love is what you make it and who you make it with."

"Love isn't an emotion or an instinct. It's an art."

"Anything worth doing is worth doing slowly."

The Inner Woman -- *(Upon arriving in Hollywood in 1932):* "I'm not a little girl from a little town making good in a big town. I'm a big girl from a big town makin' good in a little town."

"When caught between two evils, I generally pick the one I've never tried before."

"When I'm good, I'm very good. But when I'm bad, I'm better."

"I've been rich and I've been poor, and rich is better."

"I believe in censorship. After all, I've made a fortune out of it. Right now I think censorship is necessary. The things they're doing and saying in films right now just shouldn't be allowed. There's no dignity anymore and I think that's very important."

"It ain't sin if you crack a few laws now and then, just so long as you don't break any."

"Good girls go to heaven. Bad girls go everywhere else."

"I used to be Snow White, but I drifted."

"Ten men waiting for me at the door? Send one of them home, I'm tired."

"I do all my writing in bed. Everybody knows I do my best work there."

"To err is human, but it feels divine."

"I generally avoid temptation, unless I can't resist it."

"It isn't what I do, but how I do it. It isn't what I say, but how I say it, and how I look when I do it and say it."

(*On gays*): "They're crazy about me 'cause I give 'em a chance to play. My character is sexy and with humor and they like to imitate me, the things I say, the way I say 'em, the way I move. It's easier for 'em to imitate me 'cause the gestures are exaggerated, flamboyant, sexy, and that's what they want to look like, feel like. And I've stood up for 'em, and in New York I told them, 'When you're hittin' one of those guys, you're hittin' a woman, 'cause a born homosexual is a female in a male body.'"

"My advice for those gals who think they have to take their clothes off to be a star is; Baby, once you've boned, what's left to create an illusion? Let 'em wonder. I never believed in givin' 'em too much."

"Don't cry for a man who's left you. The next one may fall for your smile."

"You are never too old to become younger!... You only live once, but if you do it right, once is enough."

Ruth Westheimer

A sex advice columnist and television sex education authority called "Dr. Ruth," she didn't always take her own advice because she was married three times. She got it right the third time and her marriage to Manfred Westheimer lasted from 1961 until his death in 1997. She was the mother of a boy and a girl. Some of her advice, in or out of the ladies' room:

"Testosterone levels are highest in the morning."

"Don't criticize in the sack. Discuss constructively later."

"The time has come when women should pay for a gigolo. Why should only rich men have young, beautiful women? Rich women should have young, beautiful men."

Born Karola Ruth Siegel in Karlstadt, Germany on June 4, 1928, her Jewish parents sent her to Switzerland to escape Nazi Germany early in World War II (1939-1945), and she later believed they were sent to Auschwitz and executed. After the war, she went to Palestine and joined the Haganah to fight for a Jewish state with whom she served as a scout and sniper. She was injured in both legs by shellfire on her 20th birthday and was confined to a hospital for the rest of the war. In 1950 she studied psychiatry at the University of Paris.

She then moved to New York City and earned a master's degree in sociology from The New School and did post-graduate work in human sexuality at New York-Presbyterian Hospital. She began a career writing and talking on sex education on a New York radio show in 1980. She also wrote a sex advice column that was syndicated nationally, appeared often on "Late Night with David Letterman" on television and became a national figure in sex education.

On Men -- "The biggest concern among men is still penis size. I tell them the vagina accommodates penises of all sizes. Then I tell them to go home, and in the privacy of their own room, stand in front of a full-length mirror, bring themselves to full erection, and admire. You will never worry about penis size again because you won't be looking down on it. You'll be looking at it from straight ahead."

"It's not a competition. No penis can duplicate the vibrations of the vibrator. And no vibrator can replace a penis."

"I don't like to see teenage men wearing very tight jeans. The sight of an erection belongs in the privacy of the bedroom, living room, or kitchen floor."

"It's up to the man to not be offended when she tells him what she needs. He shouldn't say, 'I know that!' And he shouldn't say, 'The woman that I had before you had ten orgasms without her telling me anything!'"

"Boredom is the biggest problem. The same position. Same day of the week. It becomes boring when you don't bring any added flowers home."

On Love -- "Skiers make the best lovers because they don't sit in front of a television like couch potatoes. They take a risk and they wiggle their behinds. They also meet new people on the ski lift."

The Inner Woman -- "The principal concern for women is not having an orgasm. But a woman has to take responsibility for her own orgasms."

"An orgasm is just a reflex, like a sneeze."

"A lesson taught with humor is a lesson retained."

"There will never be a day when there is no such thing as prostitution. Quote me: I would like to see prostitution legalized."

"In the Jewish tradition of the *Bible* it says, 'Speak to her softly, so that she will want to engage in sexual activity.' In today's world, there's a little bit of a danger in that people don't really talk to each other. You see couples walking in the street, each one of them texting someone else. That worries me. I am worried that the next generation will not be able to have a real conversation."

"It is a catastrophe, all of this virtual being together. I think there are people who get hooked on the Internet. If they need to look at explicitly sexual material to be aroused, there is a problem."

"It's pornography for me only when it involves violence or children."

"Many people at one time or another, when they don't have a sexual relationship, masturbate. They should. But I don't want them to masturbate the whole day. Relieve the sexual tension, then go out and find a partner."

"I gave a talk in Egypt. There were 250 couples of Muslim faith. The questions I got from them, about who should initiate, about premature ejaculation, about inability to obtain or maintain an erection, about sexual satisfaction of women, were the same questions that I get here."

Serena Williams

The tennis champion has been in relationships but never married. She may be too busy on the court.

(In a 2015 interview): ***"You don't understand me. I'm just about win."***

"I've always said that I'm insatiable (about winning in tennis).

Born Serena Jameka Williams in Saginaw, Michigan on September 26, 1981, she is the youngest of five daughters. The family moved to Compton, California where Serena began playing tennis at the age of three, her parents coaching both her and her older sister Venus. After a few years, they also were coached by Rick Macci who saw star tennis potential in both sisters.

Their parents became distressed at racial slurs against the two sisters when they were pre-teenagers in tournaments. Their tennis careers are too long to write here and books have been written about them. Serena became the top women's singles champion in the world (2002) and achieved that title for the sixth time in 2013.

Serena is regarded as the greatest female tennis player of all time and became the second-highest paid female athlete in 2015, earning more than $11 million in prize money and another $13 million in product endorsements. That same year she was named Sportsperson of the Year by *Sports Illustrated* magazine. Her sister Venus also has become a tennis star and she and Serena often have played against each other in mostly friendly sister rivalries. They won the 2000 Olympics doubles competition together. Both sisters have won four gold medals in Olympics competition.

Their elder sister Yetunde Price was shot to death in Los Angeles, California in 2003, her killer convicted of voluntary manslaughter and sentenced to 15 years in prison. Serena also has a film and television career. The sisters are active in charity work in Africa and the United States and are minor owners of the Miami Dolphins football team. Neither sister has married, but both have been rumored to be in relationships, Serena with her coach, Patrick Mouratoglou.

The Inner Woman -- "I love going shopping. I'm already a shopaholic. I'm no longer in denial, and the first step to recovering is getting out of denial."

(*On dieting*): "I could lose 20 pounds and I'm still going to have these knockers, and I'm going to have this ass, and that's just the way it is."

(*After winning the 2007 Australian Open*): "You never fail if you try. You only fail if you don't try. Go out there and try whatever you are dreaming of! Everyone's dream can come true if you just stick to it and work hard."

"For all their practice, preparation and confidence, even the best competitors in every sport have a voice of doubt inside them that says they are not good enough. I am lucky that whatever fear I have inside me, my desire to win is always stronger."

(*On adversity or losing*); "I'm not used to crying. It's a little difficult. All my life I've had to fight. It's just another fight I'm going to learn how to win, that's all. I'm just going to have to keep smiling."

"I love who I am, and I encourage other people to love and embrace who they are. But it definitely wasn't easy. It took me a while."

"Since I don't look like every other girl, it takes a while to be okay with that. To be different. But different is good."

"I'm really exciting. I smile a lot, I win a lot. And I'm really sexy."

"I am not a robot. I have a heart and I bleed."

"Tennis is just a game, family is forever. Family's first, and that's what matters most. We realize that our love goes deeper than the tennis game. Tennis is my job, but it's not my life."

"I am here to play women's tennis. I'm a lady. Predominately, most of the time. I always like to play ladies."

"You can be whatever size you are, and you can be beautiful both inside and out. We're always told what's beautiful and what's not, and that's not right."

"I'm really super feminine and I'm really soft. I'm very sensitive."

"I'm a real extrovert, but when I'm around someone new, I'm super shy."

"Billie Jean King is completely my idol."

"My dad is the nicest guy you'll ever meet, and the easiest-going."

"I love my dogs. I love going to the movies. I love designing dresses and tops. I hate losing."

"Nobody likes getting their nails done more than I do."

Oprah Winfrey

One of the most popular and successful women, and a multibillionaire, she has never married. Her early life may have made her marriage-shy, growing up in poverty in Mississippi and sexually molested as a child by family members.

"If a man wants you, nothing can keep him away. If he doesn't want you, nothing can make him stay. Stop making excuses for a man and his behavior. Allow your intuition to save you from heartache."

"Stop trying to change yourself for a relationship that's not meant to be."

"Slower is better. Never live your life for a man before you find what makes you truly happy."

"Never borrow someone else's man. If he cheated with you, he'll cheat on you."

Born Orpah Gail Winfrey in Kosciusko, Mississippi on January 24, 1954 to a teenage single mother who was a housemaid, and her father a coal miner named Vernon Winfrey. However, a Mississippi farmer, Noah Robinson, claims to be her biological father. She was named "Orpah" after a biblical woman in the *Book of Ruth*, but it became mispronounced as "Oprah." Her birth parents separated and left her, so she spent her first six years living in poverty in Mississippi with her maternal grandmother, so poor that her dresses were made of potato sacks.

Her grandmother taught her to read before the age of three and took her to church where Oprah was called "The Preacher" because she could recite *Bible* verses. Her mother then reunited with her and they moved to Milwaukee, Wisconsin, with a child named Patricia who she had in her absence and who died of cocaine addiction when she was 43. Her mother then had another daughter but gave her up for adoption because she didn't have money to raise three children, then had a boy who years later died of AIDs.

When Oprah was nine years old, she was sexually molested by a cousin, an uncle, and a family friend. She ran away from home when she was 13, but a year later became pregnant with a son who was born prematurely and died shortly after birth. She became an honors student in high school, by then living in Nashville, Tennessee, and was awarded a full scholarship to Tennessee State University, a black institution, where she studied communications. Her first job as a teenager was in a local grocery store, and when she was 17 won the Miss Black Tennessee beauty contest.

A local radio station hired her to do the news during her senior year of high school and her first two years of college. She later became the station's news co-anchor and not long afterward, was on a radio talk show in Chicago. Her rise to fame began there, starring in a television talk show named after her, which was nationally syndicated from 1986 to 2011. She also started her own magazine and began appearing in films with "The Color Purple" (1985).

She has been called "The Queen of Media" and ranked as the richest African-American of the 20th century and the greatest black philanthropist in American history. Today she is America's first and only multi-billionaire and considered to be the most influential woman in the world. She holds honorary doctorate degrees from Duke and Harvard universities and in 2013 was awarded the Presidential Medal of Freedom by President Barack Obama. She never married and her living legend continues.

On Men – "You cannot change a man's behavior. Change comes from within."

"Never let a man define who you are."

"If you feel like he is stringing you along, then he probably is. Don't stay because you think 'it will get better.' You'll be mad at yourself a year later for staying when things are not better."

"Avoid men who've got a bunch of children by a bunch of different women. He didn't marry them when he got them pregnant. Why would he treat you any differently?"

"Maintain boundaries in how a guy treats you. If something bothers you, speak up."

"He is a man; nothing more, nothing less."

"A man will only treat you the way you allow him to treat you."

"All men are *not* dogs."

"You should not be the one doing all the bending. Compromise is a two-way street."

"If a relationship ends because the man was not treating as you deserve, then heck no, you can't be friends. A friend wouldn't mistreat a friend. Don't settle."

"The only person you can control in a relationship is you."

"Always have your own set of friends separate from his."

"Never let a man know everything. He will use it against you later."

"Don't ever make him feel he is more important than you are, even if he has more education or a better job."

"Do not make him into a quasi-god."

The Inner Woman -- "The more you praise and celebrate your life, the more there is in life to celebrate."

"Think like a queen. A queen is not afraid to fail. Failure is another steppingstone to greatness."

"The biggest adventure you can take is to live the life of your dreams."

"Be thankful for what you have; you'll end up having more. If you concentrate on what you don't have, you will never, ever have enough."

"What God intended for you goes far beyond anything you can imagine."

"Real integrity is doing the right thing, knowing that nobody's going to know whether you did it or not."

"Do the thing you think you cannot do. Fail at it. Try again. Do better the second time. The only people who never tumble are those who never mount the high wire. This is your moment. Own it."

"Turn your wounds into wisdom."

"Breathe. Let go. And remind yourself that this very moment is the only one you know you have for sure. Doing the best at moment puts you in the best place for the next moment."

"Biology is the least of what makes someone a mother."

"The thing you fear most has no power. Your fear of it is what has the power. Facing the truth really will set you free."

"My idea of heaven is a great big baked potato and someone to share it with."

Kate Winslet

Kate is in her third marriage and loves her husband and being a mother.

"Love, to me, God this is so difficult… To me, love is when you meet that person and you think, 'This is it, this is who I'm supposed to be with.'"

"Loving someone is setting them free, letting them go."

Born Kate Elizabeth Winslet in Reading, Berkshire, England on October 5, 1975, her parents were both stage actors. She began her show business career at the age of 11 dancing with the Honey Monster in a breakfast cereal commercial. After studying acting, she appeared on stage in small parts, then got her breakthrough at the age of 17 when she was cast as a high-strung teenager in the film

"Heavenly Creatures" (1994). Emma Thompson was impressed with her audition for a part in "Sense and Sensibility" (1995) and Winslet won the role over more than a hundred other young actresses.

Kate became a full-fledged star as Leonardo DiCaprio's love in the blockbuster film "Titanic" (1997) and both young girls and boys all over the world fell under the spell of her beauty and charm, DiCaprio also becoming an overnight heartthrob. She got $2 million dollars for her role in the film, and was nominated for an Academy Award as best actress for her performance. But her first screen kiss was not with Leonardo; it was with a young woman, Melanie Lynskey, in "Heavenly Creatures."

After "Titanic," she turned down lead roles in two period movies to change her image by playing more earthy modern roles and has become known for choosing more risky roles that stretch her acting abilities, and her fans love her for that.

As of 2016 she has been nominated for Oscars seven times, winning once, for best actress in "The Reader" (2008), playing a former concentration camp guard during World War II. She received her seventh Oscar nomination for the biopic "Steve Jobs" (2015) and continues as one of the top and most sought-after young actresses in films. When not acting in films she is known for her pranks and devotion to her two sisters Anna Winslet and Beth Winslet, and to her brother Joss.

Kate Winslet married assistant film director Jim Threapleton in 1998 and they had a daughter together, but divorced in 2001. She then married film director Sam Mendes in 2002 and had a son with him, but after seven years of marriage they divorced in 2010.

In 2012 she married Ned Rocknroll and gave birth to a son with him. Rocknroll had divorced Elizabeth Pearson, a British heiress, to marry Winslet after the breakup of her marriage to Sam Mendes. Rocknroll had changed his real name of Abel Smith to Ned Rocknroll and worked for an uncle's space venture company. He and Pearson had been married in an odd open-air pagan ceremony officiated over by a man claiming to be a druid in September 2009, but they separated after just 20 months.

Besides Winslet's acting honors, Queen Elizabeth named her a Commander of the Order of the British Empire in 2012 for her services to drama.

On Marriage -- (*On her spur-of-the-moment marriage to Sam Mendes*): "We hadn't been planning to do it, but we thought it was rather a good idea, so we just did it."

"My husband (*Ned Rocknroll*) is not a jealous person in any way."

The Inner Woman -- "I was a wayward child, very passionate and very determined. If I made up my mind to do something, there was no stopping me."

"I was reading the script (*of* "*Heavenly Creatures*") in the back of the car and I turned to my dad and yelled, 'I've *got* to get this!' And he replied, 'Then you will.' And I thought, 'Yep, that's it. I'm bloody well going to.' And that was it. I was so determined. It was something crucial to my life. I just so communicated with her, the story and their relationship. And when I found out, I just couldn't believe it. I was so happy, I cried. I remember I was working part-time at a deli at the time because I didn't have any money and was in the middle of making a sandwich when they phoned and said I'd got the job. I burst into tears and had to leave work because I couldn't control myself. It was absolutely brilliant."

"Every woman has a mother, and every woman will have an issue with that mother and things that mother did or didn't do. It just depends on how you choose to process the lessons that you learned from your own mother."

(*In 2002, about doing nude scenes in her films*): "I like exposing myself. There's not an awful lot that embarrasses me. I'm the kind of actress that absolutely believes in exposing myself."

"The things that make me happiest in the whole world are going on the occasional picnic. Either with my children or with my partner, big family gatherings, and being able to go to the grocery store. If I can get those things in, I'm doing good."

"The whole concept of 'grounding children' is utterly stupid. They just go off and rebel and don't like you. When my kids eventually come along, I don't want them to not like me. My kids are my whole world."

"I do think it's important for young women to know that magazine covers are retouched. People don't really look like that."

"I hope I'm always learning… Life is short, and it is here to be lived. There are moments to indulge and enjoy, but always know when it's time to go home and wash my knickers."

Shelley Winters

She married four times, including two of the handsomest Italian actors. She married her final husband on her death bed, believing she finally had found the man who truly loved her.

"The best way to find out about a man is to have lunch with his ex-wife."

"In Hollywood, all the marriages are happy. It's trying to live together afterwards that causes all the problems."

"After three times. I realized marriage is not for me. I love to get married, you know, but I don't like to be married. You go away on a honeymoon, you have a great time, you come home, they want to come in the house!"

Born Shirley Schrift in East St. Louis, Illinois on August 18, 1920 to a tailor's cutter and his wife. They moved to Brooklyn where she became interested in acting while in high school. In her middle teens she worked as a Woolworth's store clerk, a model, and then became a night club dancer. Also while she was in her teens, she had two abortions, the first when she was 15 years old. She made her Broadway stage debut in 1941 and changed her name to Shelley Winters. After a mild success in plays and an operetta she pursued a movie career in Hollywood.

When she and Marilyn Monroe were both looking for work in films in the late 1940s, they shared an apartment to save on expenses. Shelley later said she taught Monroe how to act sexy by tilting her head back, lowering her eyes, and keeping her mouth partly open. She also tried to teach Marilyn some culinary skills but was unsuccessful. One night Shelley had to leave their apartment for a bit and asked Marilyn to "wash the lettuce" for their dinner salad. When Shelley returned she found Marilyn standing over the sink scrubbing the lettuce leaves in soapy water.

Small parts in films led to Shelley getting a meaty role as a party girl who is straggled by legendary actor Ronald Colman in "A Double Life" (1947) for which he won the best actor Academy Award. More films followed and she played the frumpy factory girl that Montgomery Clift let drown so he could marry rich and beautiful Elizabeth Taylor in "A Place in the Sun" (1951) for which Winters received an Academy Award nomination as best supporting actress. Her film career continued while she returned periodically to the Broadway stage.

She was married four times, first to a World War II Army captain, Mack Paul Mayer, from 1942 until their divorce in 1948. She met Italian actor Vittorio Gassman and he became her second husband in 1952 and she had a daughter with him. They divorced in 1954 and she married Italian actor Anthony Franciosa in 1957, but they divorced three years later because she disapproved of his affair with Lauren Bacall after Bacall's husband Humphrey Bogart's death.

Bacall called Winters one night saying "I've been waiting for Tony for an hour. Where the hell is he?" Shelley replied aghast, "You're complaining to me because my husband is late for a date with you?" Bacall said, "If your husband doesn't respect your marriage, why should I?"

Gassman said about his marriage to Winters: "Shelley Winters has a fondness for Italian men. She married me and then Anthony Franciosa. But she doesn't like Italy enough, and to me it was more important to be at home in Italy than to be in America with her. Mamma Italia comes first."

Winters won a best supporting actress Oscar for her role in "The Diary of Anne Frank" (1959) and again for "A Patch of Blue" in 1965. As her film career waned in the 1980s she became a fixture on television talk shows, gossiping about her Hollywood years when she said she dated or had affairs with Errol Flynn, Burt Lancaster, Marlon Brando, William Holden, Sean Connery, Clark Gable and others. She had many fun evenings with handsome Broadway and film actor Farley Granger, but he was gay and always went home to his older lover, playwright and Broadway director Arthur Laurents.

Shelley's health failed in her later years and she was confined to a wheelchair, suffered a heart attack, and died in a Beverly Hills nursing home on January 14, 2006. A few hours before she died, she married her 19-year-long companion Gerry McFord on her deathbed.

On Sex and Sexuality -- "It's sad that people are so open about their sexuality. Sex is much more fun when you have to sneak around and cover it up."

"I think on-stage nudity is disgusting, shameful, and damaging to all things American. But if I were 22 with a great body, it would be artistic, tasteful, patriotic and a progressive religious experience."

On Men -- (*On actor Fredric March*): "He was able to do a very emotional scene with tears in his eyes, and pinch my fanny at the same time."

(*On actor Robert Taylor*): " He was the sweetest man to work with (*in "A House Is Not a Home," 1964*). By that I mean he was cooperative and understanding, in contrast to most leading men today who try to either elbow you out of camera range or are off in a corner somewhere practicing 'method acting.'"

(*On Marlon Brando in the Broadway stage production of "A Streetcar Named Desire" (1951)*): "There was an electrical charge and almost an animal scene he projected over the footlights that made it impossible for the audience to think or watch the other performers on the stage. All you could do was feel, the sexual
arousal was so complete. I don't think that quality can be learned, it's just there, primitive and compelling. The only time I experienced

a similar reaction was when I saw Elvis Presley perform in Las Vegas."

(*On Norman Mailer, author of the acclaimed 1948 novel of World War II, The Naked and the Dead):* "Norman's not capable of sleeping with a starlet and using her and then just saying 'That was great, kid. Goodbye.' Unlike most men in Hollywood, he's actually a feminist. He sees women as people, not just sex objects. He reveres women. He feels there's a kind of respect they must have."

On Marriage -- "I did a picture in England one winter and it was so cold I almost got married."

"I'll never forget the night I brought my Oscar home (*for "The Diary of Anne Frank"*) and Tony (*her husband Anthony Franciosa*) took one look at it and I knew my marriage was over."

"Joanne (*Woodward*) always made it her business to hold back her career while Paul Newman (*her husband*) was on the up and up (*in his career*). And that girl is one helluva talented actress (*Woodward won a Best Actress Oscar for playing a woman with multiple personalities in "The Three Faces of Eve" in 1957*). But she knew what side of her bread was buttered on and let Paul become the superstar of the family. The result? They're still happily married today." (*Woodward probably also knew that Hollywood marriages last longer if there is only one star in the family.*)

The Inner Woman -- "Jean Arthur was always my favorite actress when I was a kid. And I love Bette Davis for a very peculiar reason. Bette Davis is not afraid to stink! There are these careful actresses who look pretty, and they're never bad, but they're never great. But Bette Davis goes; she'll take chances. I love to watch her on the set. Sometimes it's awful, but sometimes it's fantastic!

Reese Witherspoon

The very talented actress and film producer was married to one of the hottest actors in films and had two children with him. After seven years together they divorced and she was then in a relationship with another hot movie hunk, but after that ended, she gave up on actors and married a talent agent. They have had a child together and are together at this writing in 2016.

"Marriage and family come before everything. You don't want to make a movie at the cost of your relationship."

"What gets me is how any women – young women – give up their power and sense of self... thinking they're going to get more out of life if they take off their clothes and objectify themselves, instead of functioning on the principle that they're smart and capable."

Born Laura Jeanne Reese Witherspoon in New Orleans, Louisiana on March 22, 1976, her father was a U.S. Army surgeon and mother a registered nurse. Her first four years were in Wiesbaden, Germany where her father was stationed. Soon afterward the family moved to Nashville, Tennessee. Reese began her career at the age of 7 by being a child model, then won a talent contest when she was 11. Three years later she made her first film, "The Man in the Moon," as a tomboy, getting excellent reviews from film critics.

After more films, she won the best actress Academy Award for her performance in "Walk the Line" (2004) as June Carter, the all-suffering wife of country singer Johnny Cash (1932-2003) who was portrayed in the film by Joaquin Phoenix. She was nominated for the same award for "Wild" (2014).

She met actor Ryan Phillippe at her 21st birthday party and they were married from 1999 to 2008 and she had a son and daughter with him. She then was in a relationship with actor Jake Gyllenhall from 2207 to 2009. She married talent agent Jim Toth in 2011, had a child with him, and they remain married at this writing in 2016.

The Inner Woman -- "The battles that we face in this business (the movies) aren't financial, but they are moral. And I certainly think that the longer you can keep your values and your morality intact, and keep your head on your shoulders about what is important at the end of the day, you can get the most out of this business and really emerge with something wonderful."

"It's not like we go to every premiere and every celebrity function and every charity auction. We really just try to maintain our privacy and never let our public persona get out of hand."

"I'm not perfect! I'm human. I make mistakes."

"Life isn't just about you. It's about family and friends and giving back."

Natalie Wood

The child star grew up to be one of the most beautiful and beloved film actresses, but her personal life was not always full of sunshine. It was more like one of her films, "Splendor in the Grass." She also was not the innocent she often portrayed on the screen. Besides her three marriages, twice to Robert Wagner, she had been in many relationships with some of the hunkiest actors in Hollywood, always searching for love but true love eluded her and it was more like the title of another of her films, "Love with the Proper Stranger."

While married to Wagner for a second time, she may have been in an affair with her co-star in her final film, but tragically drowned in what remains a mystery 35 years later.

"Almost every girl falls in love with the wrong man. I suppose it's part of growing up."

"The only time a woman really succeeds in changing a man is when he is a baby."

"I didn't know who the hell I was. I was whoever they wanted me to be."

Born Natalia Nikolaevna Zakharenko in San Francisco, California on July 20, 1938, her father was an architect and mother a ballerina, Russian-born immigrants who could hardly speak English. At the age of four, Natalie began her lifelong film career, in a World War II home front drama, "Happy Land" (1943). Her mother tried hard to get her more film roles, with hopes of her becoming a star, but Natalie's next film was when she was seven and appeared in a melodrama, "Tomorrow Is Forever" (1946). Her breakthrough film came the following year when she played a little girl who at first does not believe in Santa Claus but later changes her mind, in "Miracle on 34th Street" (1947) which has become a Christmas classic. She appeared in 18 more films up to the early 1950s.

When she was 16 she starred with James Dean in the teenage anxt film "Rebel Without a Cause" (1955) in which they both played rebellious high school students. She won her first Academy Award nomination, for best supporting actress, in that film which has become a cult classic. She starred as Maria in "West Side Story" (1961), which won multiple Oscars but she was not nominated for one. She was nominated for best actress in "Splendor in the Grass" (1981).

She was married three times, twice to actor Robert Wagner (1957 until their divorce in 1962) and again from 1972 until her death in 1981, after having had a daughter, Courtney, with him.

In between her marriages to Wagner she was engaged to Warren Beatty and they lived together in Bel Air, California and went to the Bahamas and Europe together, but never married. Instead she married British film producer and screenwriter Richard Gregson (1969-1972), with whom she had a daughter, Natasha. She continued in films and on television, her final film being "Brainstorm," but did not live to see its release in 1983.

During time off for a Thanksgiving weekend while making the film, on November 29, 1981 she and her then-husband Wagner and her co-star in the film, Christopher Walken, went on a cruise to Catalina Island, 22 miles south and southwest of Los Angeles, California.

During that night she fell off the yacht and into the ocean and drowned. Fans around the world were shocked at her death, so young at only 43, and how she died, because she had a morbid fear of water and of drowning.

Just the year before her death, she told an interviewer: "I've always been terrified, still am, of water... dark water, sea water, or you know, river water." That fear came from nearly drowning in a rampaging river scene in "Driftwood" when she was 9 years old in 1947. Her very real cries for help were mistaken for acting by her director who had the cameras continue filming while she actually fought for her life.

How and why she fell into the ocean the night of her death remains a mystery except that the yacht's captain testified at inquests that she, Wagner, and Walken had been drinking heavily, something Natalie seldom did, and Wagner angrily accused Walken of having an affair with her, which probably was true. She left the cabin where the men were arguing and went on top deck, but no one knows what happened to her then, except that her claw marks on the yacht's dinghy indicated that after falling into the ocean, she tried desperately to hold on to the lifeboat, but to no avail. She and Wagner owned the yacht which they called *Splendor*, named after her film "Splendor in the Grass."

Her favorite actresses were Bette Davis and Elizabeth Taylor but her very favorite was Vivien Leigh, and her favorite singer was Bob Dylan. She was named after movie director Sam Wood. An anorexic because of nervousness and to keep her slender figure, she would get up in the morning and take a Dexedrine tablet, then have a bowl of chicken noodle soup and some white wine for breakfast. Dexedrine is a medication for ADHD (Attention Deficit Hyperactivity Disorder), a common condition in childhood and adolescence that can last into adulthood causing hyperactivity and impulsive behavior that may well have come from her very active career as a child star, with its stresses and responsibilities.

Natalie Wood made 56 movies in her lifetime and fans continue to remember her as one of the most loved film stars. Pallbearers at her funeral were her friends Rock Hudson, Frank Sinatra, Sir Laurence

Olivier, director Elia Kazan, Gregory Peck, David Niven, and Fred Astaire.

On Men - (*On dating Elvis Presley when she was 18*): "Elvis was so square, we'd go for hot fudge sundaes. He didn't drink, he didn't swear, he didn't even smoke. (*Natalie smoked most of her life*). It was like having the date that I never had in high school."

On Marriage -- (*Before her first marriage, to Robert Wagner*): "When I get married, it will be for keeps."

The Inner Woman -- "I saw my parents as gods whose every wish must be obeyed or I would suffer the penalty of anguish and guilt."

"In so many ways I think it's a bore to be sorry you were a child actor... so many people feel sorry for you automatically. At the time, I wasn't aware of the things I missed, so why should I think of them in retrospect? Everybody misses something or other."

(*On being a child actor*): "I spent practically all my time in the company of adults. I was very withdrawn, very shy. I did what I was told and tried not to disappoint anybody. I knew I had a duty to perform, and I was trained to follow orders."

"You get tough in this business, until you get big enough to hire people to get tough for you. Then you can sit back and be a lady."

(*On Bette Davis*): "I asked Bette Davis if she'd ever wanted to meet the Queen (*of England*). She snapped at me. 'What for? I *am* a queen!' I wasn't going to argue with her."

"I felt a little funny when we were going to do the bed scene, all four of us (*with Dyan Cannon, Elliott Gould, and Robert Culp*) in 'Bob & Carol & Ted & Alice' (1969). I'm open to suggestions, I'm no prude, but four is a crowd in my book. Fortunately, Dyan Cannon was there. The thought of another woman being in there in bed helped get me through it. It's not like it sounds. It's just that I don't think I could have done it if it had been me and three men."

(*In 1980):* "Today's films are so technological that an actor becomes starved for roles that deal with human relationships."

"The times that I have done something that I didn't respond to emotionally right away, it's generally not worked out too well."

"Not even analysis, by itself, can transform you. You must still do the changing yourself."

(*Shortly before her death*): "You know what I want? I want yesterday."

Catherine Zeta-Jones

The beautiful Welsh-born actress became a sensation on Australian television when she was 22 before going to Hollywood and becoming a star. She has been married only once, to actor Michael Douglas, son of Kirk Douglas, and they have had a son and daughter together. The last woman to meet alphabetically in the ladies' room, she has some encouraging words to say about marriage.

"Yes, I was in love with my husband at first sight and still am. We have the most solid relationship."

"For marriage to be a success, every women and every man should have her own and his own bathroom. The end."

"I do think I'm lucky I met Michael. Not just Michael Douglas the actor and producer with two Oscars on the shelf, but Michael Douglas, the love of my life. I really do think it was meant to happen."

Born Catherine Jones in Swansea, Wales, United Kingdom on September 25, 1969, her mother was a housewife and her father the manager of a candy factory. She appeared in stage plays and musicals at an early age and when she was 15 she starred in a British revival of the musical "42nd Street," playing the part of a dancer who went out a nobody and came back a star. It happened to her because she had been the star's understudy but took over one night when the star took ill and Catherine kept the leading role. She added "Zeta" to her name, which had been her maternal grandmother's, because there was another Catherine Jones in show business.

She was 22 years old when she became a big hit in a British television comedy series "The Darling Buds of May" (1991) playing an eccentric man's lovely daughter. She came to America and made several films, two of which were opposite George Clooney. She met actor Michael Douglas, son of Kirk Douglas, at a film festival in Aspen, Colorado late in 1999, they married the following year, and she has given birth to both a son and daughter with him. She has been treated for a bipolar disorder and he has won a battle with cancer. They briefly separated in 2013, but then got back together and have said it strengthened their marriage.

A female stalker wrote life-threatening letters to her for about half a year, saying she was in love with Douglas and wanted her dead. It unnerved Catherine considerably, ended in the spring of 2004, and the woman was sentenced to three years in prison. Catherine won the best supporting Academy Award for the film musical "Chicago" (2002) and a Tony Award for best leading actress in a Broadway musical, in "A Little Night Music" (2010). Queen Elizabeth awarded her Commander of the Order of the British Empire in 2010 for her services to drama, and she continues in the dual role of mother and popular movie star.

On Men -- (*On what makes a man irresistible*): "Humor and that wonderful word called 'charisma.' You can't translate it. I can't nail it on the head, other than to say that I'm completely over the top about my husband."

"Words impress me. If a man can speak eloquently and beautifully to me I just melt on the floor."

On divorce -- "I find divorces repulsive. I will never get divorced, never."

On sex and sexuality -- "I like to feel sexy. I know my husband thinks I'm sexy. I think he is, too. But I don't go out half-naked with 'sex' written across my back."

The Inner Woman -- "I like women who look like women. I hate grunge. No one's more feminist than me, but you don't have to look as if you don't give a... you know. You can be smart, bright and attractive aesthetically to others, and to yourself."

"I'm more insecure than I ever let anyone know, sometimes you protect yourself with this kind of armor that people see more than they see you."

"Being happy is the real key to beauty. It shows from the inside out."

"I rub a mixture of honey and salt all over my body to moisturize and exfoliate. You wash it off and your skin is gorgeous."

"Being glamorous is about strength and confidence. It's black and white... dramatic. You have to be strong."

"I'm not the kind of person who likes to shout out my personal issues from the rooftops, but with my bipolar becoming public, I hope fellow sufferers will know it's completely controllable. I hope I can help remove any stigma attached to it, and that those who don't have it under control will seek help with all that is available to treat it."

"We recently had an extension built, to house a closet (*in their home*). It's like the Tardis (*the red telephone booth in "Doctor Who" that takes those who enter it to another world*). "I go in there and never come out."

"I'm a terrible cook. I am not allowed to go in the kitchen anymore after I almost burned down the apartment in New York."

"I'd love to do a show in Vegas with drag queens. The tackier, the better."

Short Takes, while waiting to get in The Ladies' Room:

Eva Longoria *(March 15, 1975 --)*, television actress: "I love being a woman. I love the sexiness we get to exude. But the best thing about being a woman is the power we have over men... I love me. I love being in love and having romantic dates."

Claire Danes *(April 12, 1974 --)*, actress; *(On her husband, handsome British actor Hugh Dancy):* "He's such a cutie patootie. While relationships are work, this just didn't feel like it. It's the kind of work that feels energizing rather than enervating. I find it very freeing to know that, okay, it takes constant nurturing and attention, but I can also stop looking for the *(right)* one."

Joan Fontaine (October 22, 1917-December 15, 2013), actress. "Marriage, as an institution, is as dead as the dodo bird. (*In 1978*): "The main problem in marriage is that, for a man, sex is a hunger, like eating. If a man is hungry and can't get to a fancy French restaurant, he'll go to a hot dog stand. For a woman, what's important is love and romance."

Michelle Dockery (December 15, 1981--), star of "Downton Abbey": "I do believe in one true love." (*On her career*): "Expect nothing and hope for the best is my mantra."

Clara Bow (July 29, 1905-September 27, 1965 the "It" girl of silent films and the personification of the 1920s "Flapper"): "The more I see of men, the more I like dogs."

Alfre Woodard (November 8 1952 --), actress: "I'm a mom and a wife. That's what I do in the world. That's my identity. Second, I'm an actor."

Judi Dench (December 9, 1934), British actress: (*On her long and happy marriage to British writer-actor Michael Williams from 1971 to his death in 2011, with whom she had a daughter*): "We were just happy to be in the same room together."

Uma Thurman (April 24, 1970 --), actress: "I've learned that every working mom is a superwoman."

Helen Mirren (July 26, 1945 --), British actress: "Flesh sells. People don't want to see pictures of churches. They want to see naked bodies."

Veronica Lake (November 14, 1922-July 7, 1973), *known as "The Peek-a-Boo Girl" because of her long blonde hair covering one eye):* "I wasn't a sex symbol, I was a sex zombie... You could put all the talent I had into your left eye and still not suffer from impaired vision... If I had stayed in Hollywood, I would have ended up like Alan Ladd (*her co-star in several of her best films*) and (*actress*) Gail Russell (*both suicides*), dead and buried by now." (*She left films and found happiness in being single and working as a cocktail waitress in a Manhattan bar.*)

Paulette Goddard (June 3, 1910-April 23, 1990), 1940s film actress: "The men I married, I chose because they were intellectuals -- Charlie Chaplin, Burgess Meredith (*actors*), and Erich Maria Remarque (*German author of All Quiet on the Western Front.*) They were my second, third, and fourth. I don't count my first husband -- it wasn't memorable, and he was not an intellectual." (*She was married first to wealthy Edward James when she was 15 in 1927 but divorced after five years.*)

Raquel Welch (September 5, 1940 -- ; *a major film sex symbol of the 1960s*): "The most erogenous zone is the brain. It's all happening there. Otherwise, it's just body parts... Being a sex symbol was rather like being a convict... I couldn't stand that my husband was being unfaithful. I am Raquel Welch, understand?" (*On nudity in films*) "James Coburn once said to me, 'You know what's the sexiest thing of all? A little mystery.' And he was so right about that. When you put it all out there, there's nothing left to the imagination."

Ann-Margret (April 28, 1941 --); *called a film "Sex Kitten" in the 1960s, she has matured into being a fine actress*): "I was very flattered by the 'sex-kitten' thing, because I never thought of myself as that... The critics had an image of me, and they wouldn't accept any other. I was a cartoon character. A joke." (*On Elvis Presley, her co-star in "Viva Las Vegas" 1964*): "He's an animal. Definitely an animal. A very interesting animal."

Eve Arden (April 30, 1908-November 12, 1990), *film and television actress in the 1940s and 1950s*): "I've worked with a lot of great glamour girls in movies and the theater. And I'll admit I've often thought it would be wonderful to be a femme fatale. But then I'd always come back to thinking that if they only had what I've had… a family, real love, an anchor… they would have been so much happier during all the hours when the marquees and the floodlights are dark."

Ethel Barrymore (August 15, 1897- June 18, 1959), great *stage and film actress*: "You grow up the day you have your first real laugh at yourself."

Index

abortion, 55, 57, 73, 75,79, 82, 133, 139, 143, 194, 205, 248, 277, 291, 295, 308, 309, 328, 349, 359, 364, 380
Adrian, 141
Affleck, Ben, 223
Agar, John, 164, 345, 346
Allen, Woody, 80, 87, 179
Almodovar, Pedro, 87
Ames, Michael, 364
Andrews, Julie, **8, 9**
Andrews, Tod, 364
Aniston, Jennifer, 4, **9-11**, 183
"Ann Landers" (Esther Lederer), 203-206
Ann-Margret, 393
Annis, Francesca, **12, 13**
Anthiel, George, 200, 201
Anthony, Marc, 223
Arden, Eve, 394
Arnaz, Desi, 19-21
Arthur, Jean, 141, 332, 383
Arzner, Dorothy, 84
Asher, Nils, 129
Astaire, Fred, 138, 154, 160, 165, 388
Astor, Mary, 93
Austen, Jane, **13-16**
Bacall, Lauren, **16-19**, 77, 133, 255, 381
Bale, Christian, 327
Bale, David, 328
Ball, Lucille, **19-22**, 110
Ballard. Lucian, 266
Bankhead, Talullah, **22-25**, 214
Barden, Javier, 86, 87
Bardot, Brigitte, **26-28**
Barker, Lex, 358-361
Barry, Don "Red," 82
Barrymore, Drew, 4, **29-31**, 105, 219, 226
Barrymore, Ethel, 23, 394
Barrymore, John, 23, 29, 163
Barrymore, John Drew, 29
Barthlemess, Richard, 91
Beaton, Cecil, 129
Beatty, Warren, 79, 80, 116, 217, 232-236, 244, 386
Bennett, Constance, 94
Bergman, Ingrid, **32-35**, 129, 152, 159, 162
Berle, Milton, 146
Bening, Annette, 235
Bern, Paul, 148, 151

Bernstein, Leonard, 113
Berry, Halle, 2, **36-39**
Bey, Turhan, 266
Bible, 24, 124, 288, 308, 310, 269, 370, 373,
Binoche, Juliette, **40-42**
bisexual, 2, 23, 29, 74, 106, 110, 117, 128, 137, 141, 155, 156, 163, 164, 193, 208, 215, 271, 275-277, 321, 323, 325, 343, 357, 359
Black, Charles, 346
Blanchett, Cate, 20, **42-44**
Blane, Sally, 75
Blondell, Joan, 93
Bogart, Humphrey, 16, 17-19, 32, 35, 77, 165, 222, 381
Bombeck, Erma, **44, 45**
Bono, Sonny, 65
Bow, Clara, 84, 392
Bowles, Camilla Parker, 282-284
Boyer, Charles, 199
Brando, Marlon, 215, 226, 241, 250, 336, 382,
Brent, George, 78 , 316
Brolin, James, 335
Brooks, Louise, 128
Brothers, Joyce, **46-49**
Brown, Bobby, 173-174
Brunel, Luis, 99
Brynner, Yul, 138, 222
Bullock, Sandra, **49-51**, 332
Burlinson, Tom, 190
Burnett, Carol, **52-55**
Burr, Raymond, 325
Burton, Richard, 338-342
Bush, Barbara, **55-57**
Bush, George H.W., 55
Bush, George W., 55
Bush, Jeb, 55
Bush, Laura, **57-59**
Cagney, James, 317
Calloway, Cab, 168
Cannon, Dyan, 388
Capra, Frank, 74, 326
Carey, Mariah, **59-61**
Carl, Luc, 126
Carrey, Jim, 102
Carter, Sean Cory (Jay-Z), 197
Cassini, Oleg, 188, 351-353
Castro, Fidel, 222
Chanel, Coco, **62-64**
Channing, Carol, 20, 21
Chaplin, Charles (Charlie), 34, 393

Charles, Prince, 282-284
Charrier, Jacques, 26
Cher, 4, **65-68**
Child, Julia, **68, 69**
Chopin, Fredric, 310, 311
Clift, Montgomery, 247, 338-341, 381
Clinton, Bill, 70, 336
Clinton, Hillary Rodham, **70-73**
Coburn, James, 393
Cohen, Mickey, 358
Cohn, Harry, 170
Colbert, Claudette, **74-78,** 84
Collins, Joan, **79-81**
Colman, Ronald, 214, 381
Connery, Sean, 358, 382
Conway, Tim, 52
Coogan, Jackie, 145, 146,
Cooper, Gary, 23, 33, 77, 106, 108, 187, 290, 311, 344, 382,
Cornell, Catherine, 359
Costello, Dolores, 29
Costner, Kevin, 173, 237, 313
Count Basie, 170
Coward, Noel, 77
Crane, Cheryl, 358
Crane, Stephen, 358
Crawford, Christina, 92
Crawford, Joan, 23, 52, 77, **81-86**, 92, 94, 95, 141, 214, 249, 323, 344, 359
Crawford, Robyn, 173, 174
Crosby, Bing, 187, 247, 248, 344
Cruise, Tom, 104, 190-192
Cruz, Penelope, **86-89**
Cukor, George, 77, 86, 164, 165
Culp, Robert, 388
Cummings, Robert, 141
Dahl, Arlene, 359
Damita, Lili, 77
Dancy, Hugh, 392
Danes, Claire, 392
Dandridge, Dorothy, 39
Danson, Ted, 143
D'Arcy, Alexandre, 187
Darnell, Linda, 358
Dauriac, Romain, 179
Davis, Bette, 9, 20, 25, **89-95**, 129, 159, 214, 244, 255, 317, 332, 383, 387, 388,
Davis, Patti, 294
Dean, James, 80, 339, 386
"Dear Abby" (Abigail van Buren), 205

DeGeneres, Ellen, 10, **95-99**, 155
de Havilland, Olivia, 216, 217
Dell, Gabriel, 299
DeMille, Cecil B., 74, 201
Dench, Judi, 392
Deneuve, Catherine, **99-101**, 314
Depp, Johnny, 87, 88
De Carlo, Yvonne, 228
De Costa, Mercedes, 128
de Rossi, Portia, 96
Diaz, Cameron, 3, 4, **101-106**
DiCaprio, Leonardo, 378
Dick, Bernard F., 75
Dietrich, Marlene, 77, 78, **106-109**, 239, 249, 323
Diller, Phyllis, 21, **110-114**, 335,
DiMaggio, Joe, 247, 248, 251
Disney, Walt, 23, 345
Dockery, Michelle, 392
dogs, 37, 147, 162, 257, 286, 330, 338, 373, 376, 392
Donahue, Troy, 75
Douglas, Kirk, 389
Douglas, Michael, 389
Dressler, Marie, 148
Dunaway, Faye, 93
Edward, III, 237
Edwards, Blake, 8
Ellington, Duke, 168
Emery, John, 23
Fairbanks, Douglas, 82
Fairbanks, Jr., Douglas, 23, 82
Farrell, Charles, 140
Fay, Frank, 322
Faye, Alice, 145, 360
Fayed, Dodi, 283
Ferrer, Mel, 159
Fields, W.C., 363
Fiennes, Ralph, 12, 261
Finch, Peter, 21
Fisher, Carrie, 297
Fisher, Eddie, 266, 297, 298, 338, 340, 342,
Fitzgerald, F. Scott, 203, 278
Flynn, Errol, 24, 77, 94, 317, 382
Fonda, Henry, 114, 165
Fonda, Jane, 68, **114-121**, 219, 228, 255
Fontaine, Joan, 392
Ford, John, 132, 164, 345
Fortensky, Larry, 341
Foster, Jodie, 39

Foster, Norman, 75, 76
Franciosa, Anthony, 17, 381, 383
Francis, Kay, 358
Gabin, Jean, 107
Gable, Clark, 74, 78, 83, 94, 132, 135, 148-150, 187, 188, 213, 215, 217, 226, 241, 247, 293, 342, 352, 382
Gabor, Zsa Zsa, **121-124**, 159
Gaga, Lady, **125-127**
Garbo, Greta, 34, 81, 107, **127-130**, 159
Gardner, Ava, 93, **131-137**, 152, 169, 170, 187, 296,
Garfield, John, 317
Garland, Judy, 9, 77, **137-140**, 249, 297, 345
Gassman, Vittorio, 381
gay, gay rights, 9, 57, 66, 73, 77, 78, 81, 97, 101, 108, 116, 117, 125, 129, 141, 151, 164, 190, 192-194, 187, 205, 222, 233, 237-239, 241, 244, 249, 268-270, 323, 325, 335, 336, 338, 343, 356, 368, 382
   See also: homosexual
Gaynor, Janet, **140-142**
Gere, Richard, 335
Gibson, Mel, 144, 313
Gilbert, John, 128
God, 67, 69, 93, 150, 156, 157, 176, 196, 197, 207, 211-213, 242, 243, 261, 263, 288, 296, 301, 303, 310, 349, 350, 376
Goddard, Jean-Luc, 40
Goddard, Paulette, 34, 214, 393
Goldberg, Whoopi, 39, **143-144**
Gould, Elliott, 335, 388
Grable, Betty, **145-147**, 152, 237, 249, 255, 323, 361
Granger, Farley, 382
Grant, Cary, 33, 35, 94, 108, 123, 166, 187, 188, 226, 227, 345, 363-365
Gregory, Paul, 141
Gummer, Don, 332
Gyllenhaal, Jake, 382
Hagman, Larry, 79, 141
Hargitay, Mickey, 240-242
Harlow, Jean, **147-151,** 246
Harmon, Mark, 341
Harrison, Rex, 339
Harry, Prince, 283
Hartnett, Josh, 179
Hasselhoff, David, 180
Havoc, June, 212
Hayden, Tom, 115
Haymes, Dick, 152
Hayworth, Rita, 22, 52, **151-154**, 228, 259, 352, 360,
Heche, Anne, 96, **155-157**
Hedison, Alexandra, 96
Hemingway, Ernest, 108, 133, 278

Henreid, Paul, 89
Hepburn, Audrey, 129, **157-162**
Hepburn, Katharine, 42, 63, 84, 86, 94, 129, 159, **163-167**, 214, 237, 333
Heston, Charlton, 294
Hilton, Conrad, Jr., 121, 123, 340
Hitchcock, Alfred, 23, 109, 187, 232
Hitler, Adolph, 107, 199
Hoffman, Dustin, 332
Holden, William, 157-159, 188, 294, 324, 382
Holiday, Billie, 24
Hope, Bob, 308
Hopkins, Miriam, 93
Hopper, Hedda, 93, 358
Horne, Lena, **168-172**
homosexual, 56, 77, 135, 136, 144, 145, 161, 162, 194, 204, 205, 215, 268, 269, 291, 328, 339, 359, 368; **also see: gay**
Hopkins, 93, 328
Hopper, Dennis, 79
Hopper, Hedda, 93, 325, 343, 359
Hopper, William, 325
Houston, Whitney, **172-176**
Howard, Leslie, 17, 266
Howard, Ron, 94
Hudson, Rock, 75, 108, 222, 338, 339, 387
Huston, John, 17
Hughes, Howard, 147, 164, 306, 307, 309
Hull, Verna, 75
Hunter, Jeffrey, 164
Jackson, Michael, 91, 164, 174, 341
James, Harry, 145, 146
James-Collier, Rob, 233
Jenner, Caitlyn, **176-178**
Jennings, Peter, 336
Johansson, Scarlett, **179-182**, 255
Johnson, Don, 336
Jolie, Angelina, 4, 11, **182-186**
Jones, Shirley, 346
Joplin, Janis, 244
Kardashian, Kris, 177
Kazan, Eli, 388
Kelly, Gene, 138, 297
Kelly, Grace, 113, 138, 151, **186-189**, 303
Kelly, Patsy, 24
Kennedy, John F., 108, 169, 247, 273, 351, 352
Kennedy, Joseph P., 108
Kennedy, Joseph P. Jr., 108
Kennedy, Robert, 248
Kerr, Deborah, 135

Khan, Aly, 152, 153, 351, 352
Kidman, Nicole, **190-192**
King, Billie Jean, **193-196**, 373
King. Martin Luther, Jr., 171, 237, 278
Kinney, Taylor, 126
Kinsey, Alfred, 25
Kloss, Ilana, 194
Knowles, Beyonce, **196-198**
Knox, Courtney, 10
Kopelman, Will, 29, 105
Korda, Alexander, 266, 267
Korman, Harvey, 52
Kristofferson, Kris, 335
Ladd, Alan, 226, 393
Lady Gaga, **125-127**
Lake, Veronica, 393
Lamarr, Hedy, **198-204**, 352
Lamas. Fernando, 360
Lancaster, Burt, 383
Lanchester, Elsa, 109
Landers, Ann, **204-207**
Lang, k. d., 239
Langella, Frank, 143
Latifah, Queen, **208-2011**
Laughton, Charles, 109, 216, 266
Law, Jude, 100
Lawford, Peter, 248, 294
Lawrence, Vicki, 52
Lee, Gypsy Rose, **211-213**
Lee, Spike, 36
Lee, W. Howard, 201, 354
Leigh, Vivien, 52, 77, 83, **213-219**, 388
Leisen, Mitchell, 108
lesbian, 2, 23, 74, 75, 81, 84, 93, 95, 97, 101, 106, 107, 127, 128, 140, 141,
    155, 163, 164, 174, 175, 193, 208, 245, 249, 250, 312, 315, 322, 324,
    329, 357
Leto, Jared, 102
Lindsay, Margaret, 141
Loder, John, 201
Lohan, Lindsay, **219-221**
Lollobrigida, Gina, **221-222**, 225
Lombard, Carole, 83, 237
Longoria, Eva, 392
Lopez, Jennifer, 192, **223-225**
Loren, Sophia, 221, **225-229**
Lovett, Lyle, 305
Lubitsch, Ernst, 268
Luce, Clare Boothe, **229-231**

Luce, Henry R., 229
Luft, Sidney, 139
Lynskey, Melanie, 379
MacDaniel, Hattie, 23, 215
MacLaine, Shirley, 63, 104, **232-235**, 347
MacMurray, Fred, 108, 323
Madden, Benji, 102
Madonna, 91, 109, **235-240**, 269, 301, 321
Mafia, 249
Magnani, Anna, 89
Mailer, Norman, 384
Malcolm X, 170
Mandl, Fritz, 199
Mann, William J., 77, 164
Mansfield, Jayne, **240-243**
March, Fredric, 74, 383
Markey, Gene, 201
Martin, Mary, 79, 141
Martin, Tony, 361
Martinez, Olivier, 37
Marx, Groucho, 138
Mason, James, 139
Mastroianni, Marcello, 99, 226, 227
Mature, Victor, 361
Mayer, Louis B., 132, 139, 170, 199
McCrea, Joel, 325
McDermott, Dylan, 305
McDowall, Roddy, 339, 340
McFord, Gerry, 383
McKay, Scott, 317
Mendes, Sam, 379
Meredith, Burgess, 394
Merivale, John, 216
Merrill, Gary, 90, 91
Midler, Bette, 4, **243-245**, 269
Milland, Ray, 108, 267
Miller, Arthur, 247, 251, 253
Miller, Johnny Lee, 183
Mills, John, 94
Minnelli, 134, 136
Minnelli, Vincente, 139
Mirren, Helen, 393
Mitchum, Robert, 300
Moder, Daniel, 305, 306
Monroe, Marilyn, 86, 149, 219, 220, 226, 239, **245-255**, 326, 382
Montand. Yves, 249
Montgomery, George, 200
Moore, Mary Tyler, **256-258**

Moore, Terry, 340
Moreno, Rita, **258-260**
Morton, Andrew, 284
Moyer, Stephen, 276
Murphy, Eddie, 173
Mussolini, Benito, 199
Neeson, Liam, 305
Negulesco, Jean, 249
Newley, Anthony, 60
Newman, Paul, 135, 384
Nichols, Eboni, 209
Niven, David, 389
Nixon, Richard, 346
Norris, Edward, 317
Nyong'o, Lupita, **260-262**
Obama, Barack, 70, 262, 263, 333, 376
Obama, Michelle, **262-264**
Oberon, Merle, **265-267**
O'Connor, Frank, 291
O'Donnell, Rosie, **268-270**
O'Hagan, Helen, 75, 77
Olivier, Laurence, 77, 91, 214, 266
Olson, Bree, **270-272**
Onassis, Aristotle, 273
Onassis, Jackie Kennedy, 248, **272-275**
O'Neal, Ryan, 79, 269, 336
O'Neal, Tatum, 269
O'Toole, Peter, 165
Paquin, Anna, **275, 276**
Parker, Camilla Bowles, 283-285
Parker, Dorothy, **276-279**
Parker, Steve, 232, 233
Parsons, Louella, 134, 326, 344
Parton, Dolly, **279-281**
Payne, John, 308
Peck, Gregory, 35, 133, 158, 159, 227, 389
Penn, Sean, 236, 238, 301
Peppard, George, 80
Philip, Duke of Edinburgh, 287
Phillippe, Ryan, 385
Piaf, Edith, 107
Pickford, Mary, 82
Pitt, Brad, 4, 10, 11, 182-184
Plowright, Joan, 216
Polanski, Roman, 99
Ponti, Carlo, 221, 226
Porter, Cole, 77
Power, Tyrone, 137, 138, 164, 227, 241, 351, 357, 359, 360

Preminger, Otto, 212
Presley, Elvis, 259, 335, 383, 388, 393
Pressman, Joel, 75, 76
Princess Diana, 4, 7, 120, **281-285**, 289
Elizabeth II, Queen, 9, 283, **286-289**, 379, 390
Rainier, Prince, 186-188
Rand, Ayn, **289-292**
Reagan, Nancy, 57, **292-296**
Reagan, Ronald, 230, 292-295, 316, 345
Reagan, Ronald Prescott, 294
Reed, Maxwell, 80
Reed, Rex, 135
Reeves, Keanu, 50
Redford, Robert, 116, 335, 336
Remarque, Erich Maria, 393
Reynolds, Burt, 109
Reynolds, Debbie, **296-298**, 338, 340
Reynolds, Ryan, 179, 180
Riggs, Bobby, 193
Rin Tin Tin, 347
Ritchie, Guy, 237
Rivers, Joan, **298-303,** 343
Robards, Jason, 17
Robbins, Tim, 313
Roberts, Eric, 304
Roberts, Julia, 4, **304-306**
Rocknroll, Ned, 378
Roe v. Wade, 57
Rogers, Charles "Buddy," 82
Rogers, Ginger, 165
Rogers, Will, 366
Rooney, Mickey, 132, 133, 138, 139, 357
Roosevelt, Eleanor, 169
Roosevelt, Franklin D., 344
Rose, David, 139
Rossellini, Roberto, 32-34
Rosson, Harold, 148
Rubirosa, Porfirio, 122
Russell, Gail, 393
Russell, Jane, 255, **306-310**
Russell, Rosalind, 317
Ryan, Robert, 266
same-sex marriage, 57, 205, 206, 263, 328
Sand, George, **310-312**
Sanders, George, 121, 123
Sarandon, Susan, **313-315**
Sawyer, Diane, 177,
Selznick, David O., 214

Selznick, Myron, 214,
Shaw, Artie, 358, 359, 361
Shaw, Robert, 77
Shearer, Norma, 358
Sheridan, Ann, **315-317**
Shore, Dinah, 201
Signoret, Simone, 250
Simpson, Wallace, 286
Sinatra, Frank, 17, 18, 131, 133-136, 138, 155, 187, 387
Smith, Bessie, 208
Smith, Maggie, 233
Sommer. Elke, 122
Spears, Britney, 4, 125, **318-320**
Stauffer, Teddy, 201
Stanwyck, Barbara, 212, 249, 315, **321-326**
Steele, Alfred, 82, 83
Steinem, Gloria, **327-328**
Stewart, James, 107
Stewart, Martha, **329-330**
Stiller, Mauritz, 128, 131
Stokowsky, Leopold, 128
Stompanato, Johnny, 358, 360
Stone, Sharon, 167
Stravinsky, Igor, 62
Streep, Meryl, 89, 305, **331-333**
Streisand, Barbra, 268, **334-337**
Sutherland, Kiefer, 304
Swayze, Patrick, 144
Taylor, Elizabeth, 93, 159, 249, 255, 296-298, **338-343**, 387
Taylor, Robert, 199, 321, 323, 325, 344, 382
Tempelsman, Maurice, 273
Temple, Shirley, 233, **344-348**
Teresa, Mother, 88, **348-350**
Terry, Philip, 82
Thatcher, Margaret, 331
Theroux, Justin, 10,
Thiess, Ursula, 323
Thompson, Emma, 378
Thornton, Billy Bob, 183
Threapleton, Jim, 378
Thurman, Uma, 392
Tierney, Gene, 152, 188, **350-354**
Timberlake, Justin, 318, 319
Tinker, Grant, 256
Todd, Michael, 212, 340
Tomlin, Lily, **355-356**
Tone, Franchot, 82, 83
Topping, Henry, Jr., "Bob," 358, 361

Toth, Jim, 384
Tracy, Spencer, 77, 163-165, 293
Tran, Christina, 3
Travolta, John, 356
Truffant, Francois, 99
Tucker, Forrest, 146
Tupper, James, 155
Turner, Lana, 52, 137, 266, 296, 323, **357-362**
Turner, Ted, 117
Urban, Keith, 191,
Vadim, Roger, 26, 27, 99, 115,
Valentino, Rudolph, 75, 84
Vaughn, Vince, 10
Voight, Jon, 182, 183, 335
von Sternberg, Joseph, 106
Waggoner, Lyle, 52
Wagner, Jane, 355, 356
Wagner, Robert, 241, 385, 386, 388
Walken, Christopher, 386, 387
Walker, Nancy, 333
Warner, Jack, 94, 161, 316
Warner, John, 341
Waterfield, Bob, 307, 308
Wayne, John, 164, 342
Welch, Raquel, 393
Welles, Orson, 108, 138, 152,
West, Mae, **363-368**
Westheimer, Ruth, **369-371**
Wilding, Michael, 340, 342
William, Prince, 4, 283, 319
Williams. Esther, 86, 359
Williams, Serena, **371-373**
Williams, Venus, 371
Wilson, Earl, 24
Winfrey, Oprah, **374-377**
Winslet, Kate, **377-380**
Winters, Shelley, 17, **380-383**
Winwood, Estelle, 24
Witherspoon, Reese, **384-385**
Wood, Natalie, 4, 255, **385-389**
Woodard, Alfre, 392
Woodward, Joanne, 383
Wyman, Jane, 109, 294
Wynette, Tammy, 70
Young, Loretta, 75, 325
Young, Robert, 201, 203
Zeta-Jones, Catherine, 208, **389-391**

www.ingramcontent.com/pod-product-compliance
Lightning Source LLC
Chambersburg PA
CBHW062121280526
45788CB00001B/12